NATIONAL SEPARATISM

It should be plain that separatism, generating the collective will and organization to go it alone, is more than mere nostalgia or emphasis on ethnicity. Going back and gathering with one's own kind is only part of such closing: More important is a synergy from within, a surge of collective vitality that enables the group to create, develop, and carry on with a new sense of togetherness, which is a loss for the larger group but a gain for the smaller one—when successful.

Orrin E. Klapp, 1978

NATIONAL SEPARATISM

Edited
by
COLIN H. WILLIAMS

UNIVERSITY OF BRITISH COLUMBIA PRESS
VANCOUVER AND LONDON

Published 1982 by
University of British Columbia Press

Not for sale in the United Kingdom and Europe

Canadian Cataloguing in Publication Data

Main entry under title:
National separatism

ISBN 0-7748-0151-4

1. Nationalism—Addresses, essays, lectures. 2. Autonomy—Addresses, essays, lectures. 3. Self-determination, National—Addresses, essays, lectures. I. Williams, Colin H. (Colin Haslehurst), 1950-
JC311.N37 320.5'4 C81-091314-3

ISBN 0-7748-0151-4

Printed and bound in Canada by John Deyell Company

Preface

While teaching courses in the geography of ethnic and minority relations to undergraduates at North Staffordshire Polytechnic, I became acutely aware that there was a need for a text on 'Separatism' that would both satisfy the intellectual demands of the social scientist and sustain the interest and enthusiasm of the student. I have come to appreciate that students will not be content for long with essentially topical accounts of ethnic and national problems, without a deeper understanding of the theoretical issues involved and an appreciation of a broader comparative context.

In planning the book, my objectives were to discuss the origins of national separatism in advanced industrial states, to provide case study examples of the ways in which separatism as a process has been studied by scholars from a variety of academic disciplines, and to contribute to the cross-fertilization of ideas and perspectives in the developing multi-disciplinary field of nationalism. The contributors were selected not only for their individual eminence in their own disciplines, but also because it was anticipated that they would be representative of a variety of approaches, methodologies and empirical interests found among scholars working on nationalism. This is not to suggest that the volume is itself a comprehensive inter-disciplinary text, for example, we do not have contributors who present a social psychological or an international economist's account of the impact of separatism. Nevertheless, it is our hope that the contents and approaches adopted will lead to a greater understanding of this complex and chameleon-like phenomenon.

We wish to express our gratitude to those who have read earlier drafts of the chapters and offered criticisms and suggestions that were very helpful in preparing the final version: Denis Balsom, David Cairns, John Cartwright, Peter Nicholson, Kenneth O. Morgan, Emyr Williams and Meryl E. Williams. Needless to say, they are not responsible for the use we have made of their comments.

My task, as editor, was made easier and more satisfying by the enthusiasm of the contributors whom I now warmly thank for their willingness to participate in the project. I should also like to thank Don MacIver, North Staffordshire Polytechnic, for his constant encouragement and Mrs. Jane Perks, Cartographer in the Department of Geography and Sociology, North Staffordshire Polytechnic, for preparing all the maps and diagrams from my own drafts. I am grateful to the editors of *The Welsh History Review, Tijdschrift voor Economische en Sociale Geografie* and *Cahiers de Géographie du Québec* for permission to reproduce maps and tables which first appeared in their journals.

Finally, I should like to thank Mr. John Rhys and Mr. Alun Treharne of the University of Wales Press for their advice and assistance in the preparation of the manuscript at every stage. Diolch o galon i chwi oll.

Contents

CHAPTER 1

Introduction

Colin H. Williams

The object of this volume is to examine the processes by which separatist movements in advanced industrial states have sought to achieve what has been considered to be the national purpose of independence, and the ways in which such movements have been influenced by, and have exerted an influence on, the internal policies of states and the relations of states with each other.

It has become painfully evident that minority dissatisfaction is a central problem of our age, and a dominant theme in the historic development of the uniformly organized modern state.[1] Long established national minorities in such diverse Western states as Belgium, Canada, France, Italy, Spain, the United Kingdom and the United States of America, share certain characteristics which help explain the timing of the current nationalist resurgence. First, linguistic and cultural differences in particular regions have persisted over several generations and have survived despite strong pressures toward the assimilation of the minorities in question. Secondly, new political leaders have emerged among these national minorities who seek more political power and varying degrees of autonomy. They reject the tacit historic alliances which co-opted previous generations of ethnic leaders into the central government and they challenge the legitimacy of the established state system, claiming their own moral right to national self-determination as a full and equal partner in the international political system, a nation amongst nations. Thirdly, in all cases there is evidence of long-standing economic inequality, in which, individually and collectively, members of the subject minority have received a less than proportionate share of wealth and power. Closely allied to the question of economic inequality is that of social status and minority group rights. When economic and social inequalities coincide with linguistic and/or cultural differences a system of ethnic stratification is sometimes created. Often class conflict and ethnic conflict reinforce each other to provide a dynamic impetus to change. Where such divisions correspond with territorial boundaries this force is likely to take the form of a nationalist movement, which aims at total independence from the dominant majority. The latter is perceived as both an exploiting class and as a threat to the minority's cultural heritage, which in the final analysis, can lead to a severe weakening of group identity.

In what follows it will be argued that separatism is one form of challenging the inevitability of ethnic assimilation. It is a powerful expression of group identity and of social regeneration among culturally distinct peripheral collectivities. Moreover, it is also an instrumental political programme, capable of providing new opportunities and a path for political advancement for members of a strata often hitherto excluded from political power and privilege.

In many ways separatist movements, as Smith demonstrates, provide the classical paradigm of nationalism and as such are deserving of both an historical and a comparative treatment, if we are to understand more concerning this most flexible and chameleon-like political phenomenon. An important analytic distinction exists between territorial and ethnic separatism. The former rests its case primarily on the spatial distinctiveness of the potentially independent unit. Distance, relative isolation and a perception of an unfulfilled resource potential can be powerful mobilizing influences in the development of a separatist movement, especially when allied to a regional distinctiveness which may encompass other variables such as language, religion or a common, shared history of exploitation. The history of European imperialism, for example, abounds with cases of ex-colonial territories, whom having seceeded from their Metropolitan cores, commonly trace a particular epoch in their experience when the materials of their uniqueness were moulded by geographic isolation, into a national culture, despite the many apparent similarities in the racial origin, social structure and settlement pattern existing between Metropole and colony.

The main characteristics of the process of territorial separatism have been outlined by Whebell, who defines it as an attempt by territorially defined formal or informal organizations to achieve increased autonomy.[2] It is a process which can be observed at all territorial scales and includes both economic and cultural components. The motivation for such separatism is most often linked with some attribute of the land in terms of an environmental hazard to be overcome or some developmental potential to be realized; these are considered to be inadequately provided for by the superior establishment. The separatist group thus conceives itself to be in an unsatisfactory dependent status, and this essentially economic factor may be coupled with racial, cultural and social factors as well. This dependency status may in turn arise as a result of two alternative responses of the respective political system:

1) the inability of the political unit to meet the demands and absorb the aspirations of the dependent territory, or
2) the refusal on behalf of the competing élites to provide the framework within which the development potential of the dependent territory may be fulfilled.

When either of these two conditions obtains, and when there is no other institutionalized channel of redress through which the grievances of the dependent group may be expressed, one is likely to find the potential for a separatist movement. Such movements have as their rationale the displacement of the established élite by the aspiring national élite seeking to operate within a new territorial hierarchy, which in turn both sanctions the legitimate development of the new unit and is also capable of sustaining such development. Thus inherent in territorial separatism at the national scale we have two complementary forces first, the consciousness of deprivation and unfulfilled potential, and second, the desire for independence, coupled with the perceived capability of achieving and maintaining such independence.

In contrast, ethnic separatism rests its case on the cultural distinctiveness of the community pressing for independence. Frequently, but not necessarily, they are 'renewal' movements seeking to recover the cultural identity of a formally independent unit. For nationalist leaders, imbued with the uniqueness of their destiny and contribution to the common fund of world civilization, the incorporation of their group into a multi-national state, is inherently contrary to nature and a severe impediment to the full realization of that group's developmental potential. As Smith has demonstrated,

> the watchwords of ethnic separatism are identity, authenticity and diversity . . . it seeks through separation the restoration of a degraded community to its rightful status and dignity, yet it also sees in the status of a separate political existence, the goal of that restoration and the social embodiment of that dignity.[3]

It follows, that for independence to be achieved, the primary function is to translate the goal of separate ethnic identity into a political ideology which will animate the movement for national freedom. The remarkable feature of many contemporary separatist movements in advanced industrial states is that both types of separatism, the 'territorial' and the 'ethnic' are increasingly being combined to produce 'ethno-regional' movements which seek to liberate their respective peoples firmly settled in distinct, if subservient, homelands (Figure 1).

The importance of the nationalist resurgence cannot be ignored. It is evident that most Western states are experiencing serious ethno-regional challenges. A number of differences exist in the size, resource base, cohesiveness and level of ethnic mobilization of the separatist movements treated in this volume, together with variations in their political strategies and the threats they pose to the existing state system. The major separatist movements, and the degree of institutionalization they have achieved, are summarized in outline, in Table 1.[4] As we shall seek to demonstrate, not all attempts at increasing regional autonomy are necessarily separatist in orientation. A number of factors may be identified which serve to transform regional autonomist movements into outright separatist movements, chief of which are the historical circumstances which determined the minority's incorporation into the now dominant state, the tolerance or otherwise of the state towards politicized ethnic sentiments, the skill and industriousness of the nationalist élite in mobilizing the target population, and the prevailing international climate within which nationalist appeals are made.

In the first of the two primarily theoretical chapters, Smith locates the study of separatism within the broader context of nationalism, stressing that in many ways ethnic separatism, the principal theme of this volume, provides the classical paradigm of nationalism. He reviews several recent theories of separatism including the internal colonial thesis, Marxist inspired uneven development theories and Gellner's culture chasm thesis, before turning to his own theoretical contribution, a general framework of ethnic separatism which concentrates on the growth of 'Scientific bureaucracy' and the seminal role the intelligentsia play in politicizing ethnic identity.

The four questions which Smith's analysis chooses to address, form the basic issues which most of the succeeding chapters discuss, namely:

1) What is the social background of the ethnic revival?
2) How does the politicization of the intelligentsia occur, and with what consequences for the promotion of ethnic demands?
3) What are the conditions which favour separatism as opposed to other political routes?
4) What are the conditions which influence the political

Figure 1. Selected Minority Areas in Western Europe

Table 1 **National Separatism in Comparative Perspective**

Ethnoregional Group	*Major Ethnonational Linkage(s)*	*Degree of Institutionalization*
Québécois (6.0 million in Quebec, Canada).	*Parti Québécois*—Governing party of Quebec Province since November, 1976.	High: Successive transfer of power from Ottawa to Québec City; promise of a referendum on Sovereignty-Association fulfilled in 1980.
Scots (5.2 million in Scotland, U.K.).	*Scottish National Party*—17.24 per cent of the Scottish vote in May 1979 British general election.	Medium but diminishing; despite narrow majority in Devolution referendum the promise of legislative devolution to an elected Scottish Assembly shelved by Tory government.
Welsh (2.7 million in Wales, U.K.).	*Plaid Cymru*—8.1 per cent of Welsh vote in May 1979 British general election; *Cymdeithas yr Iaith Gymraeg*, an active, non-violent interest group committed to preserving the Welsh culture.	Low; outright rejection of Labour's Devolution proposals for an elected Assembly in March 1979 referendum.
Flemish (5+ million in Flanders and bilingual Brussels in Belgium).	*Volksunie*—(Flemish People's Party) 11.3 per cent of Flemish Belgium's vote in December 1978 general election.	Extensive institutionalization in the 'regionalized' Belgian state created by the 1970 revision of the constitution, including Cul-

Francophone Belgium composed of the Walloons (3+ million in Wallonia and the nearly one million bruxellois).	*Rassemblement Wallon* party, with 9.2 per cent of Wallonia's vote in 1978, and the *Front democratique des francophones bruxellois,* with 27.98 per cent of Brussels' total vote in 1978.	tural Councils inside the Belgian parliament, advisory regional assemblies for Flanders, Wallonia and Brussels-Brabant, strong possibility of Belgium moving toward a federal structure.
Jura francophones (60,000 citizens of northernmost part of Switzerland's German-speaking canton of Bern).	*Rassemblement Jurassien,* system—participatory party now eclipsing earlier protest movements seeking a separate canton for the region's francophones.	By referenda, area separated from Bern canton, separate status as the Republic of Jura within the Swiss Confederation.
South Tyroleans (220,000+ German-speaking inhabitants in Italy's Alto Adige region).	*Sud-Tiroler Volks Partei*—30 per cent of the vote in the Trento-Bolzano region of the 1972 Italian general election.	Limited implementation of the 1969 *Pakage* designed to guarantee political and cultural autonomy of region; 1971 the creation of Autonomous region of Trentino-Alto Adige, subdivided into German province with some local autonomy.
Alsaciens (1.3 million inhabitants of France's Alsace-Lorraine region).	Several quasi-political associations with an interest group hue seeking to preserve area's dialect and language, including the *Alsacian Party of Progress.*	Virtually none; however since the Summer violence of 1975 and 1979 France has instituted a reevaluation of its regional policies *vis à vis* its ethnoregional minorities.

Ethnoregional Group	*Major Ethnonational Linkage(s)*	*Degree of Institutionalization*
Corsicans (150,000 nationals in an island population of 250,000).	*Action pour la renaissance de la Corse*, and *Union de Peuple Corse* seeking regional autonomy and independence.	Since 1975 Corsicans have gained some limited concessions e.g. right to teach Corsican in schools, a promised reopening of a university and the appointment of Corsica's first Corsican prefect since 1870; extra grant of 446 million francs in the 1978/9 budget.
Bretons (nearly 2.4 million inhabitants in the Brittany region of France).	Three banned, paramilitary, clandestine organizations, each with a limited following and commitment to regional autonomy.	Minimal, as above; however, Giscard d'Estaing's minister of education in 1975 announced a programme of state subsidies for teaching Breton in schools, more recently a Cultural Charter has allowed additional time on radio and television for Breton-medium programmes and finance for Breton societies.
Northern Ireland's (essentially) Celtic-descended 'Catholics,' (35 per cent of the regional population).	The *Provisional* wing of the *Irish Republican Army*, a clandestine terrorist organization seeking an end to British rule, and the Pro-	Non-functional. N. Ireland has possessed a regional assembly since its partition from the rest of Ireland; for most of the half cen-

	testant domination, drawing a wider, but spasmodic following among the inhabitants than either the official IRA or its political auxillaries.	tury before its suspension Stormont was dominated by a Protestant majority largely insensitive to the needs of the Catholic minority and overtly discriminatory. Efforts to re-establish civilian government since 1973 have focused on a power-sharing committee system scheme designed to replace the former cabinet-government, majority rule system with shared authority; so far, efforts to create this system have been thwarted by the Protestant community's principal linkages to the shared power concept.
Northern Ireland's (essentially) English-Scottish descended 'Protestant' majority (65 per cent of the regional population).	*United Ulster Unionist Council,* a party committed to Loyalist-Protestant cause which won 46 of the 78 seats in the regional constituent assembly elected in June 1975; several clandestine Protestant terrorist movements.	
Frisians, (The Netherlands northernmost province).	*Frisian National Party,* since 1962 demanding local autonomy for Friesland, since 1979 has one seat in council of Warkum, four seats in Doanjewerstal, two seats in Sloten and two representatives in the States.	Virtually none; essentially a catalyst for reforming measures which other parties adopt and threaten to deflate the Frisian claim to autonomy.

Ethnoregional Group	*Major Ethnonational Linkage(s)*	*Degree of Institutionalization*
Catalonians (8 million in northeastern Spain).	*Esquerra Democratica* and *Llige*—leftist and rightist-oriented parties seeking to promote regional political autonomy.	Very limited. Some cultural autonomy developed from 1976 recognition by the Government of the region's unique identity, gradualist, devolution proposals likely.
Basques (nearly 2 million in the four provinces of northern Spain and the three of southern France).	*Euzkadi 'Ta Askatasuna* (ETA-'Basque Homeland and Liberty'), an outlawed, clandestine and violent irredentist group seeking a free Basque state in a 'European Federation of Races'; PNV (Basques Nationalist Party) *Partido Nacionalists Vasco* founded in 1895 has been the traditional voice of Basque regional autonomy. *Enbata,* a Basque association of cultural and political pro-autonomy groups in Basque France, also outlawed.	Developing: after decades of neglect and persecution, and following a violent campaign of bomb attacks and political assasinations, the Spanish state has offered a form of Home Rule to the Basque country and has legalized the use of Euskera, the Basque language. It remains to be seen whether the recent measures will placate the demands of the '*polimilis*' who have always insisted on complete sovereignty.

success or failure of ethnic separatism in the contemporary world?

Smith's theoretical overview is complemented by Orridge's historical and comparative analysis of the structure of regional and ethnic loyalties in modern European states. Setting forth the structural preconditions of autonomist nationalism Orridge explains why it was that some territories in Europe and elsewhere were more susceptible to separatist demands than others. Of the many preconditions two are deemed to have been of the utmost importance, linguistic geography, a feature analyzed in the Welsh, Belgian and Québécois case studies, and secondly, a strategic frontier position, a spatial context historically which has had a profound effect on the Spanish, Irish and Scottish cases. In addition, a number of other features of the European state system and economy also structure the preconditions of separatism. Some states, such as Spain and Hungary suffered extreme external pressure which limited their scope for administrative centralization and cultural assimilation, whilst others, such as the U.K., France and the Netherlands were able to advance the process of state-building because of their military and commercial strength. Other territories, such as Scandinavia, occupied special geo-political positions in the international economy which played a crucial part in maintaining both its internal political divisions and the preconditions of autonomist nationalism. In the latter part of his chapter Orridge turns from structural preconditions to analyzing those factors which trigger these preconditions into nationalist demands, in the nineteenth and twentieth century.

Taken together, these two theoretical chapters, serve as a context for the more detailed discussion of individual case studies which follow. However, they also point to the complexity of comparative analysis, especially when undertaken from a multidisciplinary perspective, a theme we shall return to later in this introduction.

Boyce, in the first of the case studies, deals with the only successful separatist attempt covered in detail in this volume. His analysis traces the interplay of two decisive developments in the evolution of Irish nationalism, namely the birth of revolutionary nationalism, which owed much to Protestant nationalism, and the emergence of Irish Roman Catholics as a political entity. The tension between the predominantly Anglo-Irish intelligentsia and Catholic exclusiveness does much to explain the paradox of modern Irish nationalism, and gives due prominence to the importance of historical context in the shaping and development of the separatist option. As with most nationalist movements, the Irish experience has its fair share of internal conflict, ambiguity over aims and tactics and an inherent paradox given the almost irreconcilable nature of its twin sources of support, the Anglo-Irish elite and the Catholic masses. The paradox was, that Irish nationalist ideology, with its emphasis on brotherhood with Protestants, with its secular base, was a fragmenting, not a unifying set of ideas; it could not have held together the Catholic nation, which was itself composed of different social and economic groups, which was bedevilled by localism, and which needed some core of unity, some distinctive badge of nationality, to hold together.

A different paradox is identified by MacIver as the central theme of Scottish nationalism, the essence of which is that Scotland has a clearly defined territory and a strong sense of national identity, but a traditionally weak and ambiguous political nationalism. In attempting to explain the paradox the chapter assesses the experience of the Union of Scotland and England after 1707 and traces the various responses central government has made to Scottish demands for increased autonomy. That Scotland did not follow the Irish path of separation is due in large part to the ambiguity which the Union engendered. In effect, MacIver asserts that Scottish culture and political nationalism developed on two levels:

> On one level Scots were partners in a multi-national state and a great world empire. On the other they were also members of a self-contained civil society, looking backwards on the glories of an earlier state and inwards at the curiosities and idiosyncracies of their own culture. After two centuries of Union the Scottish national identity and Scottish nationalism had acquired an ambiguity of outlook and allegiance which was the effect of dual nationality.

The rise of Scottish political nationalism illustrates the internal tensions generated by the coming together of adherents from a wide spectrum of political backgrounds, manifested in an uneasy mélange of splinter and reform groups headed by disenchanted ideologues. Historically Scottish nationalism has demonstrated the full range of autonomist demands from supporters of administrative devolution right through to advocates of complete independence. More recent developments in the SNP performances are interpreted by MacIver within the theoretical frameworks elaborated in the opening chapters and his analysis concludes with a discussion of the impact which the rise of nationalism has had on the major British political parties and an assessment of the prospects of secession in the contemporary political climate.

Whilst MacIver's chapter is primarily concerned with the constitutional and party-political developments as they affect Scotland's relationship with the rest of the United Kingdom, my own scale of analysis is more limited, focusing as it does on the internal socio-spatial variations in Welsh nationalist support. I interpret separatism in this context as a rational response to fears of increasing marginality in peripheral areas in particular. Thus the erosion of community solidarity and the changing economic order threaten to destroy particular features of Welsh identity. It is no accident that the areas of greatest nationalist support are also amongst the most marginal of Welsh regions. Initially nationalist protest against structural decline and socio-economic deprivation was focused on the most tangible manifestations of group identity, namely the Welsh language and religion. This emphasis on indigenous group markers tends to serve as the basis for the closure of the status group with the result that the language, in particular, becomes politicized. In time, as the Welsh separatist movement developed it faced the problem of all such nationalisms, how was it to politicize ethnic consciousness in other regions of the national territory? The chapter traces the extent to which Plaid Cymru succeeded in this task, by adopting a spatial analysis of the socio-economic correlates of party voting in Wales, highlighting areas of nationalist gains within the broader pattern of Welsh electoral geography. The chapter concludes with a discussion of the problems facing the small-scale, minority nationalist party in impressing its philosophy on the Welsh electorate.

A quite different approach to measuring support for separatism is provided by Hamilton and Pinard in their chapter on the Quebec independence movement. Their main concern is to identify the electoral basis of Parti Québécois support by means of a number of social survey analyses. Their research confirms many of Smith's propositions concerning the social bases of ethnic separatism and points to the pivotal role of the intelligentsia in instituting the Quiet Revolution and in shaping the political programme of the Parti Québécois. Considerable diversity within the separatist ranks over questions of strategy, political solutions and more recently over the Sovereignty-Association option illustrate the difficulty of analyzing national separatism as if it were a coherent and unambiguous concept with a logical programme of action. Economic and social-psychological grievances amongst the Québécois are tempered by fears of possible economic decline accompanying separation, which remind us forcibly that the separatist option is as much an act of faith as it is of cold, calculating reason.[5] This dualism and ambiguity is a major feature of the Québécois electorate and it remains for the governing Parti Québécois to convince the populus otherwise after the defeat of the Sovereignty-Association referendum in 1980.

Whilst Quebec, since the early seventies, has witnessed a reduction in the level of violence, the Basque region, as Medhurst demonstrates, now ranks equal with Ulster as a major centre of politically inspired violence. In many ways the Basque case defies conventional explanations of nationalist resurgence. At first sight, traditional core-periphery theories, although conceptually useful in Wales, Scotland and Quebec, are less relevant here because of the Basque regions' early industrialization and its ability to maintain its good economic performance despite recent sectoral decline in heavy industry, especially ship building. Medhurst prefers to interpret contemporary Basque nationalism as the result of a complex interaction between ethnicity, industrialization and repression. State repression has been instrumental in intensifying the communal solidarity between native Basques and working-class immigrants, and has certainly increased the general level of sympathy for the separatist cause. However, communal solidarity is fragile and could fragment still further if the increased demands for outright independence exasperated the latent conflict between indigenous Basques and portions of the largely immigrant, working class community. Medhurst ends his chapter with an assessment of the likelihood of outright secession and concludes that for a variety of reasons the realistic choice in Euskadi rests between the status quo and the reassertion of the traditional form of Spanish state hegemony, a forceful reminder of the power of the established state system in determining the limits of autonomy of minority groups within its jurisdiction and control.

The final case study, Belgium, is one of the several small European democracies that succeeded in fashioning a stable, progressive régime in a society deeply divided by religious and socio-economic differences. However, several historical factors have made a cumulative contribution to the recently hightened ethnic self-identity and cleavage in Belgium. By themselves none of these historical conditions need have fostered conflict, but taken together they provide the basis for each group to form its own identity and its fears and suspicions of the other group. The Belgian state inherited two of the most important structural preconditions identified in Orridge's analysis. It straddled a geo-linguistic zone of transition between the French-speaking sphere of influence, and the original 'Dietsch' linguistic region of the Germanic culture area. It also occupied a strategic frontier position at the interface of European great power rivalry from the sixteenth century to the present.[6]

Belgium, created from enthnically diverse populations by the major powers in 1830, has moved from a unitary state toward a relatively loose federation during the past twenty years. That she has not been seriously troubled by ethnic separatism prior to the last two decades is in large part attributable to the skill and political realism of her élites in accommodating ethno-regional demands and in reforming the political system as and when necessary. Rudolph's chapter attempts to explain this lack of outright separatist challenges by concentrating on the operation of élite accommodation in meeting ethno-regional demands. His analysis provides answers to the following three questions:

1) Why did significant ethno-regional movements not develop until recently in Belgium?
2) What factors account for their sudden emergence at the heart of contemporary Belgian politics?
3) What specific factors have prevented these movements from taking a separatist direction?

In answering each of these questions Rudolph is at pains to demonstrate that against a background of inter-regional rivalry and inter-ethnic competition for scarce resources, the Belgian electorate has developed a sophisticated assessment of the costs of separation. However, whilst calls for outright separatism might be rare, this by no means implies that a strong separatist mentality is absent. Indeed a separatist mentality in which the ethno-regional communities have sought maximum control over political affairs short of secession has been very much present, and constitutes the most salient feature of political life in contemporary Belgium, which strains to the uttermost the pattern of consociational politics adopted there.

The volume concludes with a discussion of the problems posed for modern governments by the resurgence of interest in ethnic identity. It pays particular attention to the arrangements devised for managing ethnic conflict in federal and consociational polities and stresses the salience of the separatist threat to the modern polyethnic state.

It is intended that the approaches and methodologies employed in the chapters which follow will enrich the comparative and inter-disciplinary analysis of nationalism. The overriding concern has been to set the current analysis of nationalist resurgence within its proper historical context, recognizing that many contemporary movements are the inheritors of earlier political demands and autonomist traditions whose roots are often to be found in the eighteenth and nineteenth century. We are also concerned to portray something of the positive and dynamic qualities of the nationalist challenge, which reflects the surge of collective vitality, not only in the realm of politics, which is the prime focus of this volume, but also in the myriad fields of human activity in the Arts and Sciences, which often benefit from the nationalist struggle.[7] For many peoples this struggle is much more than the quest for political independence, it is the assertion of their separate existence, a claim to be heard and to contribute to the common fund of human civilization. It remains to be seen to what extent others have ears to hear their pleas.

Notes

1. See H. Seton-Watson, *Nations and States* (London, 1977) and A. D. Smith, *Nationalism in the Twentieth Century* (Oxford, 1979).
2. C. F. J. Whebell, 'A Model of Territorial Separatism', *Proceedings of the Association of American Geographers,* 5 (April 1973), pp. 295-8.
3. A. D. Smith, 'Toward a theory of ethnic separatism', *Ethnic and Racial Studies,* 2, 1 (1979), pp. 21-37.
4. I am grateful to Prof. J. Rudolph, University of Tulsa, Oklahoma, for his permission to update and extend Table 1.
5. See C. H. Williams, 'The Desire of Nations: Québécois Ethnic Separatism in Comparative Perspective', *Cahiers de Géographie du Québec,* 24, 61 (1980), pp. 47-68.
6. For the historical background to the international conflict which this zone of transition has experienced, see for example, G. Parker, *The Dutch Revolt* (London, 1979); *idem, Spain and the Netherlands* (London, 1978).
7. For examples of the relationship between the national struggle and the promotion of literature and learning, see W. A. Wilson, *Folklore and Nationalism in Modern Finland* (Bloomington, 1976); A. R. Jones and G. Thomas, (eds.), *Presenting Saunders Lewis* (Cardiff, 1973); N. Thomas, *The Welsh Extremist* (Talybont, 1973); Louis L. Snyder, *Roots of German Nationalism* (Bloomington, 1978).

CHAPTER 2

Nationalism, Ethnic Separatism and the Intelligentsia

Anthony D. Smith

Any separatist movement must, by definition, desire the *de jure* independence and sovereignty of the unit on whose behalf it operates. In that formal sense alone, therefore, separatism is a species of nationalism. For nationalism, too, has, as one of its main goals, the attainment of maximum autonomy and freedom for the chosen entity, in addition to the other fundamental goals of cohesion and individuality which it strives to attain.[1] In fact, separatisms, too, presuppose these latter goals, and especially that of 'individuality'; and in many ways, separatist movements provide the classical paradigm of nationalism.

When people today speak loosely of the separatist revival and the ethnic renaissance in postwar Europe, they tend to minimise the degree of continuity, conceptual and historical, between these latterday movements and their nineteenth-century European predecessors. But the similarities between nineteenth-century Greek, Czech or Irish nationalist movements, and the current Basque, Scots or Corsican separatisms, are greater than their differences. True, the earlier movements were often irredentist. Poles, Germans, Italians, Greeks, Rumanians, Bulgarians and Yugoslavs wanted to unite the territories into which dynastic 'accident' had divided them, and recover 'ethnic territory' i.e. territory in which members of their ethnic group formed a majority, such as Epirus, Trieste or Macedonia. But some of these movements were also separatist, for example Bulgarians and Greeks; they wanted to secede from the Ottoman empire and set up a 'nation-state' of their own, on the Anglo-French model, or perhaps an even purer variety (ethnically). Other nationalisms were more simply separatist; the Norwegians or Croats for example.[2] The fact that the Wilsonian standards of 1918, adopted by the peacemakers at Versailles, did not generally cater for ethnic purity as the criterion of separate statehood, does not mean that there were not several ethnic groups' movements which did not set their sights on sovereign statehood for their units. Hence 'separatism' is not really new. Indeed, some of the 'recent' movements are quite old: Welsh and Scottish separatisms, for example. And, if we include their cultural origins, we have to go back to the early nineteenth, and even eighteenth, centuries.[3] More generally, the secessionist aspect of nationalist movements in the nineteenth century went hand in hand with the unification drive of some movements; and there is no need to distinguish sharply the current 'neo-nationalisms', despite some differences of emphasis and background.[4]

'Secession' and 'irredentist' movements are not the only forms of nationalism. There are also movements of 'renewal'. While secession emphasizes autonomy and individuality, and irredentism cohesion and individuality, renewal movements seek cohesion through autonomy. In each case, it is their ethnic situation which determines their direction and particular emphasis. All three subtypes are varieties of 'ethnic' nationalisms.[5] The secession movement wants to extract the selected entity from the larger unit; the irredentist movement wants to unite all members of the ethnic group into a single territorial entity; while the renewal movement operates on behalf of a formally independent unit which lacks a sentiment of solidarity, which it attempts to instil, as the French and Japanese aimed to do during the Revolution and the Meiji restoration.[6]

There is no rigid distinction between these forms of nationalism. As we have seen, a movement may start out as an attempt to secede from a larger unit, secure an independent base for the main part of the ethnic group, and then proceed to 'recover' the 'unredeemed' territories and populations. Or a movement of social renewal may involve a radical break with a larger unit in which it was incorporated, as was Turkey in the heartlands of the Ottoman empire.[7]

Nor should we distinguish too sharply between movements for outright secession and those which aim for more limited autonomy, whether a cultural autonomy or home rule. Secession movements have adopted a variety of strategies to suit their purposes and the prevailing political climate. In some cases, they have been content with control over their schools and courts and press, as was the case with the Flemish. In other cases, they desire full internal control over their finances and political self-expression, but are content to remain within the framework of the wider 'nation-state', as are the Catalans in Spain.[8] In yet other cases, they opt for separation, but if the political opposition proves insurmountable, are quite ready to accept an autonomist compromise. Since it is often genuinely difficult to be sure whether a given strategy represents a sincerely held belief or is only a tactic (and this may vary within the overall 'movement'), it seems wiser not to make too sharp a distinction between autonomism and separatism.

What is important and critical is the difference between 'ethnic' and 'territorial' separatisms. In the latter case, the basis of the unit, and its leaders' sense of apartness, is geography. There may be other differences like colour, or a dialect, but the separatist movement is ultimately staking its claim in virtue of the remoteness, and territorial distinctiveness, of 'their' unit. This was the case with Iceland in its separatist bid from Norway, as well as with the old white dominions such as New Zealand, Australia and Canada, which 'grew away', as local networks took priority over international ones.[9] Island populations, in particular, though they may possess other elements of homogeneity and distinctiveness, often evolve a predominantly territorial separatism as a result of their habitual isolation and peculiar social structures, such as the Corsican 'glens'.[10] In other cases, such as the thirteen colonies or the creole-led movements of independence in Latin America after 1810, the populations of the liberated territories shared much of their culture with their rulers. Here the immensity of the overseas distance itself, at a time of slower communications, coupled with an adaptation to a new landscape, led to the evolution of new institutions and mores and this in turn to a sense of social distance and difference.[11]

Although there are 'mixed' cases where ethnic and territorial features coincide, 'ethnic' separatisms base their claims to sovereignty or autonomy on the distinctive culture of the unit in question. It is the difference between their culture and that of their rulers, and very often the ensuing cultural discrimination, which provides the wellsprings and justification for their bid for separation. In these cases, the belief also arises that 'separatism' is an end in itself, an ideal state for an ethnic community. Only through the exercise of autonomy, or preferably sovereignty, can the group realize itself; but conversely, the goal and embodiment of such 'self-realization' is separate existence. It is this kind of separatism, in which the goal of a separate ethnic identity functions as an ideology, which has gained such force in the post-War world, and which entitles us to speak of a separatist revival, harking back to the classic secession movements of the mid-nineteenth century.

In what follows, the discussion will concentrate on the ethnic type of separatism. Ethnic separatisms comprise a majority of all ethnic nationalisms, as well as of all separatisms. Separatism in turn represents the 'purest' and simplest form of nationalism. Hence a study of ethnic separatisms can throw light on other kinds of nationalist movements, providing something of a paradigm case. By tracing the rise of these ethnic separatisms, we shall in fact be able to distinguish conditions common to all forms of nationalism from those which are specific to ethnic separatisms alone. Before attempting to do so, we shall examine some recent theories of nationalism which have a special bearing on ethnic separatisms, although the latter are rarely distinguished as a sub-variety of nationalism.

'Internal Colonialism'

Most theories of ethnic separatism relate it to the general process of economic development. Perhaps the most fashionable is the 'internal colonialism' thesis. It draws its inspiration from the work of Andre Gunder Frank, Dos Santos and others on the plight of Latin American economies, and seeks to apply their insights to the situation of peripheral ethnic groups in Europe. Frank and his followers had argued that European and North American capitalist development had entailed, and been built on, the structural under-development of peripheral economic areas like Latin America, whose hinterlands had been drained of resources to further the development of local, but above all, of Western metropolitan areas. By analogy, Michael Hechter maintains that the great western nation-states like Britain and France annexed, in the course of their political expansion, not only overseas colonies but also 'internal' ones, that is, ethnic areas within their own state frontiers, such as Scotland, Wales, Corsica or Brittany.[12] Hechter's detailed study of British national development pictures British capitalism as advancing through the systematic exploitation of the material and cultural resources of its Celtic fringe, creating a sort of 'internal America' at home. The result was a clearcut cultural division of labour: 'a system of stratification where objective cultural distinctions are superimposed upon class lines'.[13]

The separate identity of these peripheral zones has persisted into the twentieth century. Economic progress was itself responsible, because it retarded the development of the Celtic periphery. By accelerating interaction between core and periphery, industrialization has only served to underline the dependance of the Celtic periphery and its accompanying cultural stratification. Now, after a temporary eclipse from about 1910 until the mid-

1960s, 'nationalism has reemerged in the Celtic periphery largely as a reaction to this failure of regional development'.[14]

The inherent virtue of this approach to the problem of ethnic separatism is obvious enough. It recognises that most modern European societies are polyethnic or 'plural', and builds on the historians' account of their expansion as 'conquest states' from medieval times.[15] But is ethnic separatism always preceded and generated by capitalist industrialization? The idea can hardly be applied to most of the nineteenth-century secession movements in Eastern Europe, or the early twentieth-century ones in the Middle East. Their separatisms arose at a time when the commodity market was small in these areas, and when large-scale factories and concentrated proletariats had hardly made their appearance. Nor is it easy to maintain that today's separatist movements among the Moros or Nagas, among the Shan or the Kurds, were precipitated by the development of 'capitalist industrialization' in the Philippines, Burma or Iraq.[16]

But, what about Western Europe, the birthplace of industrial capitalism? Clearly, here it has penetrated the remotest hinterlands and disrupted traditional ways. But must this necessarily promote discontent, and separatist discontent at that? Here Hechter would reply affirmatively, because capitalist exploitation follows ethnic cleavages, and together with the trend to cultural assimilation into the core area, must always be to the disadvantage of ethnic minorities. Once their élites have grasped the situation, separatism must become their natural refuge, since they will realize that any development in their area can only be as a dependency.

There are several difficulties with this view. To begin with, it assumes that it is always the core which exploits the periphery, and that the latter will therefore be relatively underdeveloped. But this is not always the case. In Spain, Castile and Aragon are less developed than the 'peripheral' regions of the Basque country and Catalonia. They have been politically and economically exploited by the centre in the past, yet have retained superior levels of skills and resources, constituting in fact the most industrially advanced areas.[17] Second, the thesis assumes too readily that capitalist development and exploitation must follow cultural, i.e., ethnic, lines. But this fails to do justice to the case of high development accompanied by great deprivation within an ethnic community, for example the South of Italy and the North-east of England. Third, the thesis itself cannot deal with the problem of timing; why ethnic separatisms have emerged in Britain when they did, why they fluctuated, why they reemerged in the 1960s. Hechter does hint at the basic reasons, in an *ad hoc* way, but they are not fully developed.[18]

There are other difficulties. In itself, the 'internal colonialism' thesis cannot explain either the intensity or characteristics of particular separatisms. Nor can we continue to invoke a 'capitalist industrialization' which began in the nineteenth century and had already helped to stimulate a Welsh and Scottish separatism in the late nineteenth century, in order to explain its resurgence in the 1960s. Other factors have become more important, and of these, the minority policies of governmental élites and ethnic majorities, as they have fluctuated over time, must be given priority. Finally, the thesis also fails in treating the role of culture in largely instrumental terms, thereby refusing to acknowledge its dynamic aspect.[19]

For these reasons, the claims of the 'internal colonialism' thesis must be treated with a measure of caution. It provides only a very schematic framework, and one of limited applicability for the majority of ethnic separatisms. In particular, it fails to give due weight to the cultural and political factors which, as we shall argue, provide the main determinants of the rise of ethnic separatisms.

Uneven Development

Another attempt to root separatism, and nationalism, in the process of economic development, derives from more Marxist premisses. In his recent study of ethnic nationalism in Britain, Tom Nairn ties it to the 'uneven diffusion' of industrial capitalism, as it spread outwards from its English and French heartlands around 1800.[20] Development became an instrument for imperial exploitation and domination: 'In short, there was a sort of imperialism built into "development" '. The bourgeois revolutions of the late eighteenth century imparted to the 'raw materials' of Europe's ethnic and linguistic mosaic 'a qualitatively distinct function, an altogether new dynamism for both good and evil'.[21] Progress always came to weaker, less advanced countries in the form of imposed 'fetters' of more advanced neighbours to the west or north. Hence nationalism was an inevitable outcome of uneven economic growth and the impact of the more developed countries on the less. If the bourgeoisie is nationalism's original motor, the intelligentsia are its spokesmen. They are the medium through which the dilemma of underdevelopment is refracted and perceived. But, to be politically effective, they must rouse the people, who possess their own peculiar dialects, customs and diverse peasant life. This diversity has an almost 'prehistoric' quality, an archaic 'naturalness', which appears to be primeval and instinctive. Hence,

> the true nerve of political nationalism . . . is constituted by a distinctive relationship between the intelligentsia (acting for its class) and the people.[22]

Hence, too, nationalism involves the forced mobilization of the masses, and becomes invariably romantic and populist, in an overall situation of 'relative helplessness (or "underdevelopment")'.

For Nairn, the most subjective and ideal of phenomena, namely nationalism, is an inescapable product of the 'most brutally and hopelessly material side of the history of the last two centuries'.[23] Kant was wrong: commerce is not incompatible with war. On the contrary: the power of money, as it invades the globe, only serves to renew the 'atavistic urges', and intensifies warfare, turning national barriers into the dominant principle of social organization. Progress foments a new sort of imperialism, acculturation means westernization or Americanization.[24] In response, peripheral élites mobilized their masses against such imposed 'progress', while trying to copy the institutions of that progress. And this in turn required a romantic and populist ideology to create a 'militant, inter-class community rendered strongly (if mythically) aware of its own separate identity *vis-à-vis* the outside forces of domination'.[25]

The idea that the advance of capitalism engenders social fragmentation into competing ethnic units, is not new. We find it in all the Marxist classics, from Engels and Kautsky to Lenin.[26] The notion of 'uneven development', too, Nairn has drawn from Gellner's analysis of nationalism, to which he makes several references.[27] What is perhaps new is, first, the attempt to combine these two traditions, and second, the characterization of nationalism as essentially populist in appeal. The question is, how far can these ideas and notions help us to explain the growth of ethnic separatism?

As a general scheme, it suffers from a number of difficulties. The first is historical. Late eighteenth-century nationalism arose first, not among peripheral élites reacting to capitalist penetration, but in the core countries of England, France, the United States and Germany.[28] It is these countries which initially formulated the doctrines of nationalism, in the writings of Burke and Bolingbroke, Jefferson, Rousseau, Abbe Sieyes, Herder, Moser and later Fichte.[29] In this phase, nationalism was a unifying rather than a fragmenting force (true also in Switzerland and

Italy). Second, nationalism is not always populist in flavour, nor necessarily a 'mass' phenomenon. Indeed, there are instances where nationalists are quite chary of 'mass mobilization', as in early Indian or Turkish nationalism. Even today, ethnic separatists are predominantly drawn from the educated middle classes, and do not always adopt populist-romantic policies of mass mobilization; indeed, Nairn himself distinguishes a more romantic (is this the same as populist?) Welsh nationalism from a more forward-looking, practical Scottish movement.[30] It is the communist or marxian nationalisms which appeal to the people, and that in turn is a function of the intelligentsia's sense of isolation from other strata.[31]

Third, and perhaps most serious, the notion of 'uneven development' generating imperialism and hence nationalist reaction cannot, of itself, illuminate the reasons why ethnicity is singled out as the new basis of political action, and why separatism should become the chosen route in some cases, and not in others. The mechanism of uneven development is too schematic and all-encompassing. Why must we assume that its unevenness will correspond to pre-existing cultural divisions? Or even, for that matter, to political units? Is there not implicit in Nairn's argument an assumption about the prior nationalism of the revolutionary bourgeoisies of the core areas, and hence of ethnic discrimination on their part? If so, that is a different factor, not necessarily flowing from their capitalist operations or interests. In a sense, the argument assumes what is to be explained, the prior existence of a 'nationalist world', operating with nationalist assumptions.

Basically, these problems spring from the dual omission common to the Marxist tradition, the neglect of both political and cultural factors, which converge in the pivotal role of the intelligentsia. Nairn, as we saw, acknowledges their role, but he does not assign to it the importance which it deserves, nor does he really explain it.[32] It is here that another theory, that of Ernest Gellner, is most illuminating.

'Culture Chasms'

Gellner's original essay assigned to the intelligentsia a role of leadership in national secession movements. He argued there that during modernization, culture replaces structure and creates a class of clerks or mobile intellectuals, for whom education and therefore language is all-important. But linguistic education is today the main precondition of citizenship in a modern, industrial society; hence the size of the new units, or nations, is determined by the needs of the education system. However, modernization or industrialization is very uneven in its impact. As it proceeds outwards from western Europe, it has created new inequalities, especially among uprooted peasants who flock to the city and compete for scarce jobs and facilities. Now, *if* the new arrivals to the city can be singled out by some cultural or 'biological' (colour) characteristic, then the more established workers, jealous of their privileges, will try to exclude them. If they are successful, the excluded and ethnically different workers will join up with their culturally similar intelligentsias in a bid to secede and create their own nation-state.[33]

More recently, Gellner has expanded on some aspects of this theory, with special reference to ethnic separatism. What is now of importance is the great expansion of mobility, social and geographical, which modernization and industry require. Such mobility in turn demands both a general education at the primary level, and a specialist education thereafter, education for and on the job. For both, language is essential, in its broadest sense of any medium of communication. It remains the precondition of citizenship and hence generally determines the boundaries of nations, and the range within which the clerks may operate. Language lays down the 'limits of loyalty and the concepts in terms of which effective loyalty can be felt', and nationalism is essentially 'a movement which conceives the object of human loyalty to be a fairly large anonymous unit defined by shared language and culture'.[34]

But language is not the sole determinant of nations. Other 'cultural markers' such as religion or colour, may create new sets of boundaries or nations. They may survive into the modern era and become irremoveable. Traditional societies had no difficulty with such markers. They generally accompanied the 'deep, permanent human and moral chasms', the castes, estates or millets, which made up the complex mosaic of a traditional empire. But modern societies with their need for maximum mobility cannot accommodate these culture chasms. If mobility cannot blur the cultural differences, then 'It is at these boundaries that new nationalisms are born', and the markers provide a 'basis for an irredentism, a nationalist movement on behalf of either a unit which does not exist yet, or at least on behalf of a radical redrawing of existing boundaries'. Thus:

> If the frontier (sc. of the chasm) is not marked by anything insuperable, mobility in both directions results, and the erstwhile deep difference is obscured. If, on the other hand, the old frontier is marked by irremovable markers, then *two* new nationalisms are born.[35]

If we understand by Gellner's term 'irredentism' our use of 'ethnic separatism', then we have here a theory of nationalism which accords a special place to separatisms, and one too that gives greater weight to culture itself in their genesis. One may dispute Gellner's emphasis upon language and his linguistic definition of nationalism, but in singling out the role of mobility and the clerks, the way is opened to a more satisfactory account of ethnic separatisms and of nationalism generally.[36]

At the same time, Gellner's account of culture is, in the last analysis, largely instrumental. A certain vagueness, even a mechanical quality, clings to the notion of 'cultural markers' and chasms. Gellner tends to assume they operate uniformly. But this is not the case. Colour, for example, may act as a barrier, as it has done for the Blacks in the United States or for coloured people in Britain, without necessarily leading to separatism. In the United States, incipient separatism (for example, among the Black Panthers) has largely given way to a more communalist approach among Black élites.[37] In other countries, such as Brazil, colour has been muted by other factors, though it has at times given rise to tensions in some cities.[38] Religion, too, has varied in its effects. It was, of course, an 'insuperable barrier' in the Ottoman and Tsarist empires, where Islamic treatment of Christians and Russian Christian discrimination against Muslims and Jews was a major factor in the genesis of Turkish and Russian nationalisms.[39] (In the latter case, however, we are dealing with a dominant nationality). It was also, of course, a major focus for the budding separatisms of the Balkans and Armenians,[40] and of the Tatars and Jews.[41] Religion is still an active force in Ulster, the Ogaden, and among the Moros in the Philippines. In other cases, religion has not proved such a barrier. In Germany, the division into religious blocs did not prevent the growth of a strong pan-German nationalism;[42] and in Switzerland, even in mixed cantons like the Vaud, religion, though it did create tensions during the last century, has become part of the national edifice and 'political culture'.[43]

Besides, many ethnic separatisms today designate themselves as linguistic movements pursuing goals on behalf of a language group. This is true of Wales, Brittany, Flanders, Catalonia, Euskadi and Quebec, not to mention the smaller movements among the Occitanians, Cornish, Frisians, the Gelderland, Corsica and the Jura.[44] But for Gellner, language is an integrative force, the cement of nations whose main feature is their (relatively large) scale. Here, however, we have language acting in quite a different way, to create small linguistic units with micro-educational systems setting strict limits on the mobility of the clerks. The separatists are pointing to their vernaculars to assert the value of diversity and to create chasms that often were not there, or had become muted and politically inconsequential. And they are thereby reversing Gellner's trend towards increasing scale of political units, instead of revolutionizing an unequal society from within.

Bureaucracy and the Intelligentsia

The basic trouble with all the foregoing theories of ethnic separatism and nationalism, is that they assume too close a link between nationalism and economic development. There is no doubt that 'development' and its uneven diffusion have influenced the course of nationalism, and in some cases have provided the catalyst for its eruptions. But the attempt to tie the two phenomena too closely together fails in the long run, because it cannot explain the differing intensities or specific directions of given nationalist movements, let alone their peculiar character. It is, of course, possible to invoke an absolute or relative economic development, or lack of it, to explain the *incidence* of nationalism. But one could equally invoke other factors, and the question then becomes one of ascertaining which factor or factors have proved causally more relevant for the majority of nationalisms.

Among those factors, the growth of 'scientific' bureaucracy must rank high. Bureaucratization, in association with certain other factors, provides a key for grasping some, at least, of the dimensions of separatism and nationalism, and especially those aspects which theories of uneven development or capitalist exploitation tend to overlook. In particular, they show the agreed central role of the intelligentsia in a new light, and so come closer to the inner world of ethnicity and nationalism, which so often remains closed to general socio-economic theorizing.[45] What follows here is an attempt to outline a general framework for the study of ethnic separatism, and by extension, of all ethnic nationalisms.

The framework addresses itself to four kinds of question, and envisages therefore four sets of process in overlapping 'stages'. The first question is: what is the social background of the 'ethnic revival'?, and it seeks to elicit the ethnic character of most separatisms. The second looks at the 'politicization' of the intelligentsia, in order to understand why ethnic consciousness today so often becomes political in aims and content. The third asks: what are the conditions of separatism itself, as opposed to other political routes?, and here the focus is on processes of social contraction and government policies towards ethnic elites. Finally, there is the question of the conditions of political success of ethnic separatism, especially today.

The first of these analytic 'stages' is also the most general. It really applies to all ethnic nationalisms, and the very general processes which it involves are even relevant for purely territorial nationalisms, although the order of events may differ considerably. The second stage, too, has a more general relevance. Indeed, only in the last two stages does separatism itself command full attention, as a vitally important subtype of ethnic nationalisms. Accordingly, I shall treat the earlier stages more cursorily.

The historical and sociological point of departure is the rise of what Weber called 'rational-legal' bureaucracies.[46] Unlike the patrimonial bureaucracy of a traditional society, modern bureaucracies are more impersonal, more centralized and more efficient. They are concerned increasingly with cost-effectiveness, not just implementing commands. To this end, they increasingly incorporate 'scientific' techniques and procedures into the organization of duties. Efficiency becomes an ideal, even if in practise particular bureaucracies fall far short of it. Moreover, bureaucracies become much more interventionist. Their scope of operations is vastly enhanced. They interfere more often in matters formerly outside their purview, and regulate ever larger areas of economic and social affairs.

Two important consequences flow from the changed character and scope of modern bureaucracies. The first is an insistence on territorial boundaries of administration in which the bureaucratic regulations are effective. A prerequisite of bureaucratic efficiency is clear territorial demarcation; the population which is to be taxed, conscripted and administered must be homogenized and territorially fixed. They must become 'citizens', enjoying in theory equal rights and duties before the regulations. Historically, this was one route towards the 'national state', and it was the one adopted in western Europe under absolutism.[47]

The second effect was a demand by the bureaucracy for a new type of trained personnel to run the machine. Here bureaucratization linked up historically with another convergent trend: the growth of secular thought and critical education. The breakthrough here, of course, was at the beginning of the eighteenth century, though there had been hints of it earlier among the Italian humanists and in scientific circles in England. The new type of bureaucrat was more utilitarian in outlook and more professional in approach than earlier royal administrators; and modern bureaucracies therefore tended to attract ambitious and qualified members of a new lay stratum of the 'intelligentsia', which began to emerge into prominence in the eighteenth century.[48]

This new stratum had to face considerable opposition from the Church, the aristocrats and rulers. They were also isolated from urban artisans and the large mass of the peasantry. It was this growing sense of isolation that turned some of the intelligentsia towards a study of ethnic culture and history as a means of escaping their social situation and its accompanying political impotence. Hence the rise of a new movement of 'historicism', that is, a new understanding of historical forces and an interest in origins, growth and the event that shapes communal life. This movement emerged first in Western Europe (England, France, Switzerland and Germany) in the late eighteenth century. It can be seen in the 'neoclassical' return to an archaic and heroic antiquity, particularly Sparta and Republican Rome, and in the early Romantic cult of Ossian and Shakespeare. We find it in the work of writers and artists like Rousseau, Fuseli, Bodmer, Herder, West and Girodet. Later it spread to other countries and ethnic groups, producing an historical and literary renaissance.[49]

Such a conception was both organic and evolutionary. It affirmed the centrality of culture-communities with an identity, a past and a destiny, each one of them unique, but also expressions of a law of nature, which was universal and irreversible. It also presupposed the unity of ethnic communities around this historical core, and hence avoided the class fragmentation inherent in marxist versions of historicism. Given the fact of preexisting cultural traditions, vernaculars, myths, memories and customs, it was often easier for the isolated intellectual to attach himself to his 'native' milieu in which he had, after all, been usually socialized from infancy, before contact with 'rationalist' thought and secular education had distanced him from it. Such a movement of return to 'history' (and often language and even religious traditions) was essentially subjective, even romantic, though it could also be level-headed; but it was not necessarily 'populist'. Populism was reserved for a later stage, and presupposed different conditions.[50]

What is sometimes called 'cultural nationalism' was therefore mainly a product of the social situation of an intelligentsia which secular rationalism and bureaucracy were calling into being. More specifically, it was a product of the secular intellectual in search of a new rationale for himself and his community, now that traditional religious explanations no longer sufficed.

Herein lies the first stage in what is often termed the 'ethnic revival', in which dormant and politically irrelevant ethnic ties now assume a new force and salience in society, and then in politics.[51] Of course, other factors were at work, alongside the rise of historicism and the secular intelligentsia. Most important, was the rapid urbanization which brought members of different ethnic groups into close proximity, and into competition. The ethnic character of that competition, however, presupposes a degree of preexisting historical consciousness and cultural difference, which it is the role of the historicist intellectual to bring into the open and build upon. Even where a clearcut ethnic community is lacking, or straddles political frontiers, as in sub-Saharan Africa, even here, the historicist intellectual searches for ethnic roots in African history and builds upon African race-consciousness.[52]

Assimilation and Exclusion

But, why does the new ethnic consciousness so often assume political form? Why do the new ideas about the historic nature of culture communities, put forward by some intellectuals, become the basis for political claims?

There are several reasons for the politicization of ethnic consciousness in the modern era. The most commonly noted is the effect of rapid urbanization upon ethnic saliency. Akzin, for example, argues that newly arrived members of different ethnic groups must compete for scarce posts and facilities in the expanding cities. The competition revives ancient, but latent, ethnic antagonisms; and he points to several cases of such antagonism in nineteenth-century Eastern Europe.[53] There is also the case of overt ethnic discrimination by the the empire's or colony's rulers, based on religion, language or colour. In that case, a budding ethnic consciousness turns political in character as a direct consequence of, and reaction to, ethnic categorization from outside. Clear examples of this occurred in Tsarist Russia, where the ethnic consciousness of, first, the Tatars, and then the Jews, was inflamed and politicized by bureaucratic religious discrimination.[54]

The intelligentsia, or professional classes, in the widest sense, play a special part in the process of politicizing nascent ethnic sentiment. This is because, as a result of more general processes, they are themselves among the first to turn to politics as a solution to their social problems. We already noted the unenviable social position of the intellectuals, stranded between tradition and rationalism, and isolated from other strata. With growing exposure to 'western', secular education, many professionals find themselves similarly isolated. It is only to be expected that the professionally educated should gravitate to the new bureaucratic organizations in government, the economy and the professions; the latter are mainly situated in the capital, and they often command the channels of mobility to power and privilege. Unfortunately, even where there is little discrimination by the authorities, the number of high-level bureaucratic posts, particularly in central government, tends to fall behind demand by the ambitious and qualified, who seek assimilation into the dominant institutions, and therefore culture, of the state.

In the resulting phenomenon of thwarted mobility and professional discontent is to be found an important key to political nationalism. Fewer and fewer of the educated élites from different ethnic groups are able to find positions which match their professional qualifications. The growth of scientific bureaucracies has encouraged a whole new stratum to seek élite positions, only to disppoint the hopes of most of them. Indeed, where the lower and middle levels of bureaucracy have been opened up to entry from 'subject peoples', but the top levels have been reserved for the representatives of the ruling power (imperial or colonial), this has occasioned particularly keen resentment.[55] Conversely, where professional élites from the ruled ethnic communities have reached top-level bureaucratic positions, as in some French colonies, the politicization of ethnic consciousness was much slower, and political nationalism was long-delayed.[56]

In fact, the process of politicizing the intelligentsia cuts across the distinction between ethnic and territorial nationalisms. We find it at work in nineteenth century Eastern Europe, post-1945 Western Europe, and among the territorial nationalisms of contemporary subSaharan Africa. It is a general process of bureaucratic intrusion, and assimilation and exclusion of the intelligentsia, one that is separable from the more specific movement of historicism among some intellectuals.[57]

In the case of ethnic nationalisms, however, this process has marked consequences for the ensuing shape and character of the nationalism. For when the educated professionals find themselves unable to gain admission to posts commensurate with their degrees and talents, they tend to turn away also from the metropolitan culture of the dominant ethnic group and return to their 'own' culture, the culture of the once despised subject ethnic group. Exclusion breeds 'failed assimilation', and reawakens an ethnic consciousness among the professional élites, at exactly the moment when the intellectuals are beginning to explore the historic roots of the community. Alternatively, there may be a gap of several decades between this initial historicist exploration and the rejection and reawakening of the broader intelligentsia. Only when the two processes, historicism and reawakening, are conjoined, can the ethnic revival blossom and assume full political form.

The Separatist Option

Once an ethnic community, or rather its professional élites, have become politically aware and active, once their discontent has been harnessed by organizations and political movements, a number of options present themselves. Of these, three are relevant: communalism, autonomism and separatism; and the conditions which favour one option over another are intimately bound up with the political and economic cycle.

As mentioned at the outset, it is not profitable to distinguish too sharply between movements that aim for outright secession, including a *de jure* sovereign state, and those which are content with autonomy or home rule within a unitary or federal structure. At different times, the same movement may pursue different objectives, and *force majeure* may induce tactical limitations. Similarly, with the 'communal' movements. Here we are referring to movements which aim to influence the policies and destiny of the larger 'nation-state' in which their ethnic community is incorporated. Examples would be the current Black and Puerto Rican movements in the United States. After a brief consideration of autonomist, and even separatist options, the Black and Puerto Rican movements have settled for a policy of ethnic influence within the United States structures, particularly as a result of federal policies which have tried to draw some Black élites into governmental and professional organizations.[58] The cry for 'Black Power' and Black consciousness remains in the background; but the specific goals have shifted away from the separatist pole of the continuum.

What is it that determines how far along the road towards separatism a given ethnic movement will travel? Here there are two sorts of answer: a general one and a specific. The general one tries to tackle the question of why, particularly in the highly industrialized and educated western states, there should be a resurgence of autonomist and even separatist movements. The specific examines the particular policies of governmental élites and ethnic majorities, to determine under what conditions a given movement will opt for one of the three solutions.

Let us start with the general answer, concentrating on the West. Broadly speaking, we can distinguish two phases of Western development, particularly in Europe; the first an expansionary era in which there was considerable demand for all kinds of resources and skills, and then an epoch of contraction and decline which affected opportunities for mobility adversely. The earlier phase, which reached its peak during the last century, was associated with *laissez-faire* policies and a general liberalism in matters of employment. Thus élites from ethnic groups in outlying areas like Scotland and Corsica, could play an important part in running the imperial and state machine, because of the expansion in bureaucratic openings and the need for high levels of skill. In the present century, however, the empires were dismantled and the State, the bureaucracy, that is, increasingly intervened in the economy, determining various national needs according to bureaucratic requirements which tended to favour the dominant ethnic group within the state.

Economic contraction has been accompanied, and hastened, by a dramatic political decline in the fortunes of most western states in Europe. Britain, France, Spain, Holland, Belgium and Germany have lost their colonial empires within a remarkably short space of time, and the balance of geopolitical power has shifted irrevocably to superpowers on Europe's flanks, which overshadow the continent.[59] The political cycle which began in the seventeenth century has come full circle. One important result has been a further contraction in mobility opportunities, and therefore an intensification of internal competition for high-level posts in the economy, in government and in the professions. It is hardly surprising if this sudden and dramatic contraction, coming as it does at a moment of political disillusion and questioning of the central role of the State, should tend to push intelligentsias from minority or peripheral ethnic communities farther along the road to autonomism and separatism.

In Europe, as opposed to the developing countries, it is the autonomist option that commands most assent in peripheral ethnic groups.[60] Typically, we find a fairly strong autonomist movement with which the majority of the ethnic group are in sympathy, coupled with a small but vociferous wing pursuing separatist objectives, sometimes by terroristic methods. This is the situation today in the Basque country, in Flanders, in Brittany and Corsica, and possibly in Wales.[61] In Scotland, on the other hand, the main nationalist party is committed to separation, although it appears that once again a majority of Scots prefer the more limited autonomy offered by a devolved Assembly in Edinburgh.[62] In Catalonia, too, the majority clearly want autonomy, and even the main parties concur in the general dual sentiment of being simultaneously Catalan and Spanish.[63] Perhaps we have to go to the mountains of the northern Jura to find a population which supports the separatist movement for a new Canton for the Jurassiens.[64]

One reason for this preference for autonomism is the change in social composition among the intelligentsia itself. Formerly inspired by the romanticism of scholars, artists and writers, and led by the more liberal professions, the intelligentsia is increasingly dominated by technically and vocationally oriented professions, including technicians, agronomists, social workers and economists. Such professionals are very conscious of the economic and social problems of separatism on the part of smaller communities, within a context of intense international competition, unemployment and inflation. Hence the greater attention devoted by ethnic nationalists in the West today to economic issues, which have always taken second place for idealistic nationalists.[65] Hence also the emphasis on policies of social welfare and social equity in the autonomist programmes. It may also be that such considerations deter some of the intelligentsia and other strata from opting for total separation.

At a more specific level, the decisive factor tending towards separatism is undoubtedly the policies adopted by government élites and by ethnic majorities in the many 'plural' states of the West and elsewhere. In the West, state boundaries are well-established, and there are usually constitutional outlets for the expression of grievances. Moreover, outright ethnic discrimination is rare.[66] In its place, however, there is considerable evidence of bureaucratic insensitivity, both of unnecessary interference and of neglect in the affairs of peripheral communities. This is the main plea in Patricia Mayo's analysis of the Basque, Welsh and Breton responses to central government policies.[67] In effect, this echoes the nationalist indictment of 'Jacobin' regimentation;[68] but it also points towards a failure of western democracy to cope with ethnic minority demands, and in particular a failure of political parties to give sufficient weight to the ethnic character of local needs. This is largely the result of the peculiar character of western parties, whose basis is mainly of a class character, where it is not confessional as on the Continent. At a time when rationalism and egalitarian ideals have penetrated into the remotest hinterlands, when the ethnic élites cannot secure a foothold in central areas like the Brussels and Paris regions, or the Southeast of England, and when new vocational professions are coming to the fore, the party platforms with their traditional class interests, appear to be irrelevant and diversionary for the needs of the new technical intelligentsias. If, moreover, they cannot cope with more traditional problems of unemployment and inflation, the stage is set for more radical ethnic solutions, even perhaps separatism. For in those circumstances, it becomes apparent that democracy cannot integrate the ethnic components in a plural state, and cannot supply an overarching 'political culture' to counter historicist ethnic movements.

The above theory, then, departs from previous developmental ones, in concentrating on the rise and effects of a secular intelligentsia. My theory is not a case of *economic* development, but of the rise and effects of a secular intelligentsia, and its starting-points are sociopolitical, i.e. the growth of a certain kind of bureaucracy, and cultural, i.e. the rise and impact of a new mode of knowledge, science. The mobility aspect, too, is not wholly dependent upon economic development, though obviously that is one of a number of relevant factors at work in the background. In itself, however, development is barely relevant to a theory of ethnic nationalisms or separatisms. Similarly, the contraction of empire is seen, firstly, in political and military terms, then economic and social. Finally, the trend towards separatism or autonomism is largely dependant on élite governmental policies.

'Successful' Separatisms

A final question concerns the conditions in which separatist movements can attain their political goals. This involves a rather different set of variables. All that can be indicated here, is their overwhelmingly geopolitical and international character.

On the whole, the current epoch is hostile to ethnic separatism. In the nineteenth century, Russia had a special interest in fomenting Balkan movements against the Ottoman empire.[69] Till recently, however, the succeeding Soviet governments have not sought to support *ethnic* separatisms, only anticolonial liberation struggles of a territorial character. There are signs that this may change, despite Soviet theoretical suspicion of 'tribalism' and 'petty bourgeois' nationalism.[70] If so, other powers will be drawn increasingly into the international competition for influence in areas divided by ethnic conflicts. So far, both the West and the developing countries, however, have stood by the ethnic and territorial status quo, especially in Africa and Asia, if only for fear of destabilization and 'balkanization'.[71]

The unfavourable international climate is undoubtedly the main reason for the relative lack of success of outright separatisms since 1945, and it tends to favour instead autonomist or communalist solutions. For an ethnic separatist movement to succeed in achieving sovereign statehood, it would not only need to be backed by a superpower, and preferably an important neighbour, as Bangladesh was by India; its relative size and location would have to be such as to allow it to separate without provoking a chain reaction or a threat to vital world interests. Thus, both the Kurds and the Ibo whose attempts at secession have so far failed, were located in strategic and mineral areas. In the former case, the success of the Iraqi Kurds might have provoked Kurdish risings in neighbouring countries, and superpower intervention; in the case of the Ibo, there was always the fear that a dissolution of so important a state-nation as Nigeria might be the signal for wider fragmentation.

Nor is there much chance for separatist success in the West. Here the superpowers are stalemated, while the medium powers are, in varying degrees, hostile to fissiparous tendencies, the more so where strategic or mineral areas are involved, as in Scotland or Brittany. On the other hand, the larger size and scale of some ethnic communities and movements requires a measure of recognition in a democratic society; hence the trend towards a mild form of autonomism, which will, to some extent, accommodate the demands of the educated élites, while central governments attempt to deal with the special economic problems of the areas concerned. To the extent that this is not a token accomodation, however, there is always the possibility that the provision of semi-autonomous institutions may help to form a new generation of more activist and militant ethnic separatists, with the self-confidence to run a viable small state on modern lines.

Whatever the prospects are for ethnic separatism as such, there is little likelihood of an abatement of ethnic nationalism in the near future. Modernization itself is likely to ensure that ethnic challenges to the plural state and its bureaucratic élites continue, in the East as much as in the West and the developing world. The more historicist ethnic consciousness spreads through communalist education by ethnic intelligentsias, the stronger will be the desire for self-rule.

Notes

1. For this definition, cf. A. D. Smith, 'Nationalism, A Trend Report and Bibliography', *Current Sociology*, XX1, 3 (1973), pp. 21-6: and *idem: Nationalism in the Twentieth Century* (Oxford, 1979), chapters

1-2. For a review of older definitions, cf. L. Snyder, *The Meaning of Nationalism* (New Brunswick, 1954).

2. Or the Icelanders or Slovaks or Baltic peoples. Conversely, there are several potential irredentisms today—in the Tyrol, Ireland, Rumania, Macedonia, not to mention Somalia and Kurdistan.
3. cf. Kenneth O. Morgan 'Welsh nationalism: the historical background', and H. M. Begg & J. A. Stewart, 'The nationalist movement in Scotland', both in *Journal of Contemporary History,* 6, 1 (1971). Also H. J. Hanham, *Scottish nationalism* (London, 1969).
4. For a contrary view, cf. E. Hobsbawm, 'Some reflections on "The Break-up of Britain" ', *New Left Review,* 105 (1977), pp. 3-23.
5. The 'ethnic-territorial' typology, and the subvarieties of 'ethnic' nationalisms, are elaborated in A. D. Smith, *Theories of Nationalism* (London, 1971), ch. 9.
6. On the movement for national renewal in France, cf. B. C. Shafer, 'Bourgeois nationalism in the pamphlets on the eve of the French Revolution', *Journal of Modern History,* 10 (1938), pp. 31-50; and H. Kohn, *Prelude to nation-states: The French and German experience, 1789-1815,* (Princeton, 1967). On the renewal in Meiji Japan, cf. M. Kosaka, 'The Meiji era: The forces of rebirth', *Journal of World History,* 5 (1959), pp. 621-33.
7. A thesis convincingly argued by B. Lewis, *The Emergence of Modern Turkey* (Second edition, London, 1968).
8. S. Payne, 'Catalan and Basque nationalism', *Journal of Contemporary History,* 6, 1 (1971), pp. 15-51.
9. For the use of the notion of local networks of communications, cf. the thesis of K. Deutsch, *Nationalism and Social Communication.* (Second edition, New York, 1966).
10. cf. P. A. Thrasher, *Pasquale Paoli* (London, 1970), esp. pp. 23-5.
11. On America, cf. E. L. Tuveson, *Redeemer nation: the idea of America's millennial role* (Chicago & London, 1968). Also H. Kohn, *American nationalism* (New York, 1957). On Latin America, cf. G. Masur, *Nationalism in Latin America: Diversity and unity* (New York, 1966).
12. M. Hechter, *Internal Colonialism: The Celtic Fringe in British National Development, 1536-1966* (London, 1975).
13. Ibid., p. 30.
14. Ibid., p. 265.
15. cf. C. L. Tipton (ed.), *Nationalism in the Middle Ages* (New York, 1972).
16. Except as demonstration 'from afar'. The Iraqi Kurds, being situated near the oil wells, *are* more affected by industrialism; cf. C. J. Edmonds, 'Kurdish nationalism', *Journal of Contemporary Hisotry,* 6, 1 (1971), pp. 87-107.
17. S. Payne, op.cit.
18. On Labour failures in Wales and Scotland, cf. E. Hobsbawm; op. cit., p. 16. Hechter discusses Conservative and Labour regional economic failures on pp. 302-10, in the context of new economic perceptions.

19. In the same way, the 'internal colonialism' thesis, like most stratification theories, fails to accord sufficient dynamic weight to specifically racial differences in its account of race relations today. For a balanced critique of such theories cf. P. Cohen, 'Race relations as a sociological issue', in G. Bowker & J. Carrier (eds.), *Race and Ethnic Relations* (London, 1976), esp. pp. 10-14.
20. T. Nairn, *The Break-Up of Britain: Crisis and Neo-Nationalism* (London, 1977), esp. pp. 96-8.
21. Ibid., pp. 97, 98.
22. Ibid., p. 101. Both are mobilized against an imperialist 'development'.
23. Ibid., pp. 335-6.
24. Ibid., pp. 336-8. It is a ' "tidal wave" (in Ernest Gellner's phrase) of outside interference and control'.
25. Ibid., p. 340. This part of the argument contains teleological overtones, in which nationalism becomes 'functional' for economic development.
26. Karl Kautsky laid special emphasis on this point, cf. H. B. Davis, *Nationalism and Socialism* (London, 1967).
27. In E. Gellner, *Thought and Change* (London, 1964), ch. 7.
28. Before 1800, in fact; cf. E. Hobsbawm: op. cit., p. 14, n. 12. This is fully documented in H. Kohn's classic, *The Idea of Nationalism* (New York, 1967).
29. A. Kemilainen, *Nationalism: Problems concerning the word, concept and classification* (Yvaskyla, 1964).
30. T. Nairn, 'Scotland and Wales: Notes on Nationalist Pre-history', *Planet,* 34 (1976), pp. 1-11; and the later version in *The Break-up of Britain* ch. 4.
31. cf. J. H. Kautsky (ed.), *Political Change in Underdeveloped Countries,* Introduction, and essay by R. Lowenthal, (New York, 1962).
32. Except to say that the intelligentsia function as the 'most conscious and awakened part of the middle classes', and act as the medium through which the 'dilemma of underdevelopment' becomes 'nationalism', when it is '(so to speak) refracted into a given society, perceived in a certain way, and then acted upon'. (p. 100). At the same time, Nairn clearly thinks the 'masses' are more important for nationalism, and perhaps this prevents him from elaborating a fuller sociology of the intelligentsia and its nationalism.
33. E. Gellner, *Thought and Change* op. cit., ch. 7.
34. E. Gellner, 'Scale and nation', *Philosophy of the Social Sciences,* 3 (1973), pp. 1-17.
35. Ibid., pp. 13-14.
36. For a general discussion of Gellner's theory, cf. A. D. Smith, *Theories of Nationalism* op. cit., ch. 6.
37. On Black territorialism, cf. T. Draper, *The Rediscovery of Black Nationalism* (London, 1970), chapters 7-8.
38. C. Wagley (ed.), *Race and Class in Rural Brazil* (Paris, 1952); and P. van den Berghe, *Race and Racism* (New York, 1967), pp. 69-75.

39. On Islamic and secular elements in early Ottoman and Turkish nationalism, cf. N. Berkes, *The Development of Secularism in Turkey* (Montreal, 1964). On the role of Orthodoxy in Russian nationalism, cf. E. C. Thaden, *Conservative Nationalism in 19th Century Russia* (Seattle, 1964).
40. G. Arnakis, 'The role of religion in the development of Balkan nationalism', in B. & C. Jelavich (eds.), *The Balkans in Transition* (Berkeley, 1963); L. Nalbandian, *The Armenian Revolutionary Movement: The Development of Armenian Political Parties through the 19th Century* (Berkeley, 1963).
41. A. Bennigsen & C. Lemercier-Quelquejay, *Les mouvements nationaux chez les musulmans de la Russie,* (Paris, 1960); S. Baron, *The Russian Jew under Czars and Soviets,* (New York, 1964).
42. Indeed, emotionalist and deist versions of Christianity fed German nationalism from Schleiermacher to Lagarde and Lueger, cf. H. Kohn, *The Mind of Germany* (New York, 1960), and G. Mosse, *The Crisis of German Ideology* (New York, 1964).
43. A. Siegfried, *Switzerland* (London, 1952); and T. Warburton. 'Nationalism and Language in Switzerland and Canada', in A. D. Smith (ed.), *Nationalist Movements* (London, 1976).
44. For a brief survey of some of these movements, cf. W. Petersen, 'On the subnations of Western Europe', in N. Glazer & D. P. Moynihan (eds.), *Ethnicity, Theory and Experience* (Camb. Mass., 1975).
45. Without assuming, as Nairn does, that in the subjectivity of nationalism we are confronted with something analogous to a neurosis; op. cit. p. 359.
46. For some reasons for singling out 'bureaucracy', cf. A. D. Smith, 'The diffusion of nationalism', *British Journal of Sociology,* XXIX, 2 (1978), pp. 234-48.
47. cf. J. Strayer, 'The historical experience of nation-building in Europe', in K. Deutsch & W. Foltz (eds.), *Nation-Building* (New York 1963).
48. On this stratum, cf. A. Gella, 'An Introduction to the Sociology of the Intelligentsia', and T. Huszar, 'Changes in the Concept of Intellectuals', both in A. Gella (ed.), *The Intelligentsia and the Intellectuals,* (Beverley Hills, 1976).
49. On this movement in the arts, cf. R. Rosenblum, *Transformations in Late Eighteenth-Century Art* (Princeton, 1967).
50. cf. G. Ionescu and E. Gellner (eds.), *Populism, Its Meanings and National Characteristics,* (London, 1970), especially essays by A. Stewart and P. Worsley.
51. On this 'revival', cf. the stimulating essay by D. Bell, 'Ethnicity and Social Change', in N. Glazer & D. P. Moynihan, op. cit., pp. 141-74.
52. Both Edward Blyden and Cheikh Anta Diop represent facets of this quest, cf. K. Adelaja, 'Sources in African political thought, I—Blyden and the impact of religion on the emergence of African political thought', *Presence Africaine,* 70 (1969), pp. 7-26; and

J. F. A. Ajayi, 'The place of African history and culture in the process of nation-building in Africa south of the Sahara', *Journal of Negro Education,* 30 (1960), pp. 206-13.

53. B. Akzin, *State and Nation* (London, 1964), ch. 5.
54. cf. S. Zenkovsky, *Pan-Turkism and Islam in Russia* (Camb. Mass., 1960); and L. Greenberg, *The Jews of Russia* (New Haven, 1951).
55. India provides a good example, cf. B. T. McCulley, *English Education and the origins of Indian nationalism* (Gloucester, Mass., 1966).
56. On their problems, cf. W. H. Lewis (ed.), *French-speaking Africa: the search for identity* (New York, 1965).
57. For some examples, cf. E. Kedourie (ed.), *Nationalism in Asia and Africa* (London, 1971), Introduction, esp. pp. 81-90.
58. Through 'affirmative action' programmes also; cf. D. Bell, op. cit., p. 146; and T. Parsons, 'Some theoretical considerations on the Nature and Trends of Change of Ethnicity', in N. Glazer & D. P. Moynihan (eds.), op. cit., esp. pp. 77-9. Also, in the same volume, M. Kilson, 'Blacks and Neo-Ethnicity in American Political Life', in ibid., esp. pp. 255-6, 263-4; but Kilson also emphasizes the continuing militancy of American 'neo-ethnic' movements. For a general review of the role of ethnicity today and the 'ethnic revival', cf. A. H. Halsey, 'Ethnicity: a primordial social bond?', *Ethnic and Racial Studies,* I, 1 (1978), pp. 124-8.
59. cf. G. Barraclough, *An Introduction to Contemporary History* (Harmondsworth, 1967).
60. cf. the excellent analysis of European ethnic issues by J. Krejci, 'Ethnic Problems in Europe', in S. Giner & M. S. Archer (eds.), *Contemporary Europe: Social Structures and Cultural Patterns* (London, 1978).
61. Support for separatism seems to be confined to the core Welsh-speaking areas in the upland, western half of the country: 'Thus, in general it seems that support for political separatism amongst the respondents is strongest in the areas and amongst the groups subject to the strongest Welsh cultural influence, rather than being a more widespread politically based phenomenon', C. J. Thomas & C. H. Williams, 'Language and Nationalism in Wales: a case study', *Ethnic and Racial Studies,* I, 2, (1978), pp. 235-58.
62. According to recent election results. cf. the earlier discussions in N. MacCormick (ed.), *The Scottish Debate: Essays on Scottish Nationalism* (London, 1970).
63. cf. S. Payne, op. cit., esp. on Prat de la Riba, pp. 21-2, and the regionalism of the 1960s, which has been confirmed today.
64. The Jura issue is discussed in W. Petersen, 'On the Subnations of Western Europe', in N. Glazer & D. P. Moynihan (eds.), op. cit., esp. pp. 193-5; and in K. B. Mayer, 'The Jura Problem: Ethnic Conflict in Switzerland', *Social Research,* 35 (1968), pp. 704-41.
65. Both Nairn and Hechter draw attention to this changeover to an economic perception of ethnic autonomy and consciousness from the earlier cultural perceptions.

66. Except against coloured immigrants and 'guest workers'; but on the incoherence and vagaries of policies and sentiments towards the latter, cf. S. Giner & J. Salcedo, 'Migrant workers in European social structures', in S. Giner & M. S. Archer (eds.), op. cit., pp. 94-123.
67. P. Mayo, *The Roots of Identity* (London, 1974).
68. In France, the Jacobin tradition is still prevalent, cf. C. Coulon, 'French political science and regional diversity', *Ethnic and Racial Studies* I/1, 1978, 80-99, though it is resisted by Guy Heraud's ethnopolitics, and, of course, the various autonomist movements.
69. On this, cf. M. B. Petrovich, *The Emergence of Russian PanSlavism, 1856-70.* (New York, 1956).
70. cf. the recent volumes by K. N. Brutents, *National Liberation Revolutions Today* (Moscow, 1977); and USSR Academy of Sciences; *The Evolution of Nationalism in Asia and Africa* (Moscow, 1976).
71. On these fears in Africa, cf. B. Neuberger, 'The African Concept of Balkanisation', *Journal of Modern African Studies* XIII (1976), pp. 523-9.

CHAPTER 3

Separatist and Autonomist Nationalisms: The Structure of Regional Loyalties in the Modern State

A. W. Orridge

Since the late 1960s interest in the persistence of ethnic and cultural divisions in advanced industrial societies has re-awakened. In Europe and elsewhere important separatist and autonomist nationalisms have re-emerged and in the United States ethnic identities among the descendants of immigrants have remained strong. Previous assumptions of assimilation into one national culture for each society have been severely questioned.[1] These matters should not, however, be viewed in a purely contemporary context. They are best seen as the most recent form of an issue of more general significance: the structure of regional and ethnic loyalties in modern states. Areas and groups with distinctive identities have, of course, been an age-old problem for rulers, but the advent of the idea of the culturally uniform state, or nation state, has made them of special importance for modern rulers. These loyalties often have deep historical roots, they have presented problems for almost all European states for centuries, and there are no signs that they are generally disappearing. A satisfactory approach must therefore be concerned with more than answers to questions such as: why electoral success for Scottish nationalism in the early 1970s? It must locate the structure of regional and ethnic loyalties as one of the central long-term issues faced by modern states. It is in this spirit that this essay will approach one element of this general problem by investigating the conditions under which separatist or autonomist nationalism has developed in European states over the last two centuries.

Conceptual Preliminaries

A number of preliminary points need to be established to avoid misunderstanding. First, it will be assumed that nationalism, both in general and in particular cases, is something contingent and historically recent and not, as nationalists themselves have sometimes argued, an expression of primordial identity. Local and regional loyalties are indeed historically common, but the belief that political boundaries should coincide with such identities and that they divide up the world in a mutually exclusive and exhaustive fashion is recent and very far from the realities of many parts of the world.[2]

Secondly, it should be made clear what exactly is meant by autonomist and separatist nationalism. Here I shall offer only a limited set of distinctions dealing mainly with Europe, not a full-blown classification. They are not quite identical to those used by Smith in his chapter but neither are they inconsistent with his distinctions. *State nationalism* is manifested by groups and regions close to the centre of an old and well-established state. Culture and state will have developed hand in hand over centuries and be mutually reinforcing. The population of smaller old-established states may be almost entirely composed of groups whose national identity is of this sort, such as the Netherlands, Denmark and Sweden, but in larger states they will be preponderant rather than all encompassing, as with the English in the United Kingdom. *Unification nationalism* and *irredentism* I define in the same way as Smith. They are attempts to unite culturally similar groups and territories into a larger and more powerful state. In the case of irredentism, a fragment is not politically independent and must be detached from an already existing and culturally alien state. Common culture precedes political structure in these sorts of nationalism and their political embodiments are typically a mixture of parties or movements and the state of one of the more important and politically dynamic fragments, such as Prussia or Piedmont. *Autonomist nationalism,* the main concern of this essay, has certain similarities with irredentism, for in this type also a part of a larger state rejects the state and claims to belong to a separate national group, but in this case it claims to be the core of a nationality, not a detached fragment. Like Smith, the difference between autonomist nationalism, the claim for some institutional recognition within the larger state, and separatist nationalism, the demand for complete independence, will be treated as a matter of degree. Movements can move rapidly from one to the other and for the rest of the essay the term autonomist nationalism will be used to refer to both. In this kind of nationalism common culture clearly precedes political structure and provides its basis.[3]

Each of these types is derived from the European experience of nationalism, which will be my main concern, although they are not confined to Europe. It is especially important to distinguish autonomist nationalism from perhaps the most common type of nationalism elsewhere in the world in this century, Afro-Asian anti-imperialist nationalism. Autonomist nationalism, like the other types of nationalism in Europe, is marked by the importance of the element of perceived cultural distinctiveness and internal similarity. In the case of state and unification nationalism, this interacts with the state to form the political community; in the case of irredentist and autonomist nationalisms, it provides the necessary basis for nationalist political activity. This cultural infrastructure of nationalism contrasts strongly with anti-imperialist nationalism in which the territories in question often are defined by boundaries drawn by imperial powers without reference to ethnic divisions. What has united their inhabitants has been less a sense of common belonging than a common distance from and dislike of white rule. The cultural infrastructure of nationality is frequently almost entirely absent and, as is very well known, the departure of the common enemy has often left the new state with a formidable task of creating a new sense of common allegiance.[4] Another difference follows from this.

The distance between the colonized and the colonizer in Africa and Asia was generally so great that very few colonies have failed to demand and gain political independence, whereas the development of autonomist nationalism in areas annexed by European states over the centuries has been much more varied. Some areas that were once the site of independent and powerful administrations have seemingly been absorbed completely, such as Burgundy, while others have maintained their distinctiveness, such as Brittany. To use Schermerhorn's terminology, while the Afro-Asian possessions of European powers were the result of colonization sequences, in which racially and culturally distinct groups controlled territories at a great distance from their homeland, the intra-European expansion of states proceeded more commonly by annexation sequences, in which geographically contiguous areas were acquired and cultures were hence likely to be much more similar. In Schermerhorn's view, the typical result of the former is racialism and a great gap between ruler and ruled, while the latter is more likely to produce cultural pluralism and there is a possibility of assimilation.[5]

If these distinctions are accepted, it is possible to list the cases of European autonomist nationalism: most of the Balkan states, Corsica, Czechoslovakia, especially Bohemia, Estonia, Finland, Greece, Hungary, Ireland, Latvia, Lithuania, and Norway, which have all achieved independence either permanently or temporarily, and the Basque Country, Bavaria, Brittany, Catalonia, Flanders, Scotland, the Ukraine and Wales, which remain within larger states with varying degrees of institutional recognition. Doubtless other cases could be added in which the desire for autonomy is either less widespread in the population or more limited in scope, but these are the cases about which there can be little disagreement.

Structural Preconditions: The Foundations of National Identity

We must examine now under what circumstances élites can make it plausible for part of the population of a state to believe that they are a potential independent nation.[8] First, there must be some core territory in which the group is concentrated and is sufficiently high a proportion of the total population for it to be credible for élites to claim the region as a national homeland. Here there is a great difference between autonomist and irredentist nationalism. The élites of a potential autonomist nationalism argue that the group occupies the core of a possible national state and this argument will carry little weight if a large proportion of the inhabitants of the territory in question will clearly never express attachment to the putative nation. This is surely the major reason why groups which are racially or culturally distinct but geographically dispersed, such as blacks in the United States, display little widespread enthusiasm for the idea of a territorial state for themselves.[9] But if the aim of the nationalists is to join an existing core outside the state, as with irredentism, this sort of geographic logic disappears. The group considers itself to be a fragment of a larger whole and can argue that it if were joined to the core, it and the population of the core would form a massive majority in the larger territory now including its own region. The most geographically intermingled groups can then consider themselves as part of the majority in an enlarged version of some existing state. Northern Ireland and Cyprus present all-too-obvious contemporary examples. A far greater degree of geographical distinctiveness is required by an autonomist nationalism (although this can be hazy at the edges, so to speak, see p. 52 below).

Secondly, there must be one or more characteristics that provide the basis for separateness and community in the potential nationality. I shall call these *bases of community* for they provide that cultural infrastructure which was mentioned earlier as a distinctive feature of this kind of nationalism.[10] In anti-colonial nationalisms the division between the colonized and the colonizer fulfills the same nationality-defining role, but the difference between the colonizer and the colonized is much more important than the similarities among the colonized. It is a basis for rejection rather than a reflection of an internal sense of community. European autonomist nationalisms have typically possessed far greater cultural unity than this. Even when the eventual independent state has included a number of cultural groups, as in the case of Czechoslovakia, there has been a core nationality which provided the support for autonomist nationalism and which is by some distance the largest single element in the state.[11]

As many writers have pointed out, there is no one indispensable basis of community, a variety of social differences can play this role.[12] However by no means all social differences are equally appropriate. To provide a basis for an autonomist nationalism, they must accord with the first condition and occur in a regionally concentrated form and they must also provide the sort of cultural infrastructure that makes it possible for people to conceive of themselves as a national community. Language, far and away the most frequent basis of community in Europe, and religion, important in certain cases such as Ireland, are perhaps the most appropriate—a point I shall return to a little later. But economic divisions often fail to meet both criteria, whether they be class divisions or differences between regional economies.

First, there is no European autonomist nationalism that has been distinguished from the rest of the metropolitan state in which it found itself solely by economic factors. Even in those cases in which an important role in the formation of national identity has been played by class, such as the landlord tenant conflict of nineteenth-century Ireland, or by regional economy, such as the industrial character of Catalonia, these have coincided with and reinforced other bases of community, religion in the first case, language in the second. Equally divided agrarian societies in which there was no difference of language or religion between landlord and tenant, such as, say, the ethnically Hungarian areas of nineteenth-century Hungary, did not provide a basis for peasant anti-landlord nationalism. Distinctive regional economies with no accompanying cultural differences, such as East Anglia, have developed no nationalism. Thus economic divisions act as reinforcements for characteristics such as language and religion in defining nationalities, not as substitutes for them. In part this may be because language and religion have certain features of status groups in Weber's sense. Unlike objective economic features such as class, they necessarily carry some awareness of their existence among those they characterize because they are elements of life style. In a sense they are already communities.[13] This is not to deny that nationalist élites often have to devote much effort to convert dialects into national languages and parochial loyalties into a wider sense of identity (see p. 52 below). Also, whereas linguistic and, to a lesser extent, religious loyalties can be transmuted into national identity without immense difficulty, a purely economic grouping lacks the element of cultural uniqueness that is important for self-definition as a nationality (see also the discussion on pp. 50-51 below).

Economic differences in any case do not always fit the first precondition—regional concentration. Distinctive economic regions clearly do, but classes are more recalcitrant, although here there is a major difference between industrial and agrarian class divisions. The strata of an industrial society are rarely regionally isolated or ethnically exclusive. Where there are large numbers of manual workers, there are also sizeable managerial and commercial classes and these are rarely completely ethnically or culturally distinct from the proletariat. In no European autonomist nationalism has industrial class conflict played a strong nationality-defining role. Indeed it is notable that in those cases in which autonomist nationalism has affected areas of substantial industrialization, the nationalist movement has often divided *internally* along class lines and left-wing nationalist parties have opposed right-wing nationalist parties, as with the Czech and Finnish Social Democrats and the Catalan *Esquerra.*[14] The autonomist nationalism has possessed its own middle class, if on a smaller scale than the dominant group in the state. Some types of agrarian class divisions however can occur in a fashion that enables them to serve as a supplementary basis for national identity. If one aspect of the rural class structure is a small number of landlords owning most of the land and a large rural mass of a different culture, the class division supported by a cultural factor can provide a basis for national identity for those in the agrarian sector. This occurred in nineteenth-century Ireland and in a number of areas of Central and Eastern Europe where German, Magyar or Polish landlords confronted Slav peasantries speaking a different language. This difference between industrial and agrarian class divisions is probably partly a result of the much smaller proportional size and greater apparent dispensibility of a class of landlord rentiers compared to a commercial and industrial middle class, and partly because it is much easier to preserve the ethnic distinctiveness of a landlord class in an ethnically mixed area than a commercial middle class.[15]

The latter point can again helpfully be phrased in terms of Weber's stratification concepts. Relatively immobile wealth used mainly as a source of rent creates property classes *(Bestizklassen)* which change composition only slowly and these are much more likely to become status groups of an ethnically distinct kind than commercial or acquisition classes *(Erwerbklassen)* whose position depends on the active use of skills or capital on the market. The greater mobility of a market economy makes it much more difficult to deny subordinate groups access to all positively favoured acquisition class positions.[16]

Thus economic divisions do not always occur in a regionally concentrated fashion and even when they do, they act as reinforcements for characteristics such as language and religion, not as substitutes for them. It should be stressed that I am dealing here with economic divisions solely as possible bases of community and this by no means exhausts the relationship between classes and nationalism.[17]

One further basis of community should be mentioned. If a territory retains certain elements of independent institutional life after it has been acquired by a larger state, these can also provide a basis for a later sense of national identity. Well-known examples are the Scottish legal and educational systems and the Basque *fueros,* but regionally distinctive institutions of this sort were widespread in some areas of Europe until well into the nineteenth century.[18] Institutional distinctiveness of this sort carries with it both a degree of consciousness of separate identity and some sort of organizational framework and thus is highly suitable as a basis of community.

These distinguishing characteristics may operate as substitutes for one another (with the exception of economic divisions) or coincide and reinforce one another but they are by no means equivalent in their community-forming potential. Language has been by far the most common basis of autonomist nationalisms in Europe.[19] Often it is a unique possession of the potential autonomist nationality and is a possession of 'the people' as a whole. It thus fits well the nationalist claim that their group possesses a unique and popular culture in some sense prior to any existing state and its boundaries. Religion on the other hand is rarely peculiar to one region, it is shared with others and usually carries ideas of universal applicability to all the faithful. Where religion has been apparently the main basis of community of an autonomist nationality, the religion and especially its clerical organization has usually been the vehicle through which an earlier but now reduced or disappeared cultural or political distinctiveness has been preserved as a sense of separateness, as in the case of the Irish. In this particular case, most nationalists have wanted to deny that religion defines Irishness and to emphasize culture and the revival of language. Regionally concentrated groups defined solely by religious distinctiveness, with no present or earlier cultural peculiarity, have not usually defined their position as a nationality.[20] Institutional distinctiveness is appropriate for nationalist purposes, because it also is unique to the potential nationality, but its survival capacity is lower than that of language. Linguistic differences can be reduced by assimilation over long periods,[21] but institutions can simply be abolished by rulers in a strong position or can perish in warfare or domestic turmoil. Many such institutions have disappeared in periods such as the Napoleonic Wars. Of all European autonomist nationalisms, only the Scots have distinctive institutions as perhaps their main basis of community and it is no accident that they inhabit one of the regions of Europe least disturbed by cataclysm in the last two centuries. It is thus not surprising that language is the most frequent distinguishing characteristic of European autonomist nationalisms. Finally, it hardly needs to be stressed that these bases of community are not 'givens' which of themselves create a widespread senses of common identity. Political élites and events have to work on them to produce a political consciousness of regional identity.

A third structural precondition of autonomist nationalism is to some extent a deduction from the first two. If there are sizeable groups in the territory which are closely associated with the dominant power they should either be concentrated at the top of the social hierarchy, especially in political administration or land ownership, or, if they spread further down the social structure than this, they should themselves be regionally concentrated, as with Protestants in Ulster or Germans in the Sudetenland in Bohemia. In the first case, they can then seem dispensable; in the second case, despite their numbers, there is still a substantial territory in which the autonomist nationality can feel itself to be overwhelmingly in the majority.

These structural preconditions locate those areas vulnerable to autonomist nationalism, the places where it is a possibility, not the actual cases. Also they say nothing about the circumstances or the period in which they may be converted into autonomist nationalism. These matters will be explored in the third section. Next I want to examine in which areas of Europe and for what reasons these structural preconditions were most frequently found within states at the beginning of the nineteenth century—the dawn of modern nationalism—for by no means all states were and are equally susceptible.

The Historical Origins of Autonomist Nationalism

There were in fact very few states in nineteenth-century Europe from which these preconditions were completely absent, but the areas in which they were found most frequently and in which the groups thus defined were most sizeable are, firstly, a belt running through the Low Countries and Switzerland and, secondly, a number of areas on the edges of Europe: the fringes of the Iberian peninsula and the British Isles; Scandinavia; Eastern Europe east of a line roughly corresponding to the present-day borders of Eastern Germany and Austria; and the Balkans.[22] What sorts of historical circumstances have created these preconditions? A discussion of this kind is necessarily highly speculative (although there are a number of recent precedents in the work of writers such as Anderson, Linz, Rokkan, Skocpol, Tilly and Wallerstein[23]). It is also necessary to sound an initial note of caution about some concepts widely used in the treatment of topics of this nature: nation and state-building and centre and periphery. To use these terms is to compare cases, implicitly or explicitly, with a model of a state that becomes increasingly administratively centralized and attempts, with varying degrees of success, to impose the culture of the groups most closely associated with it on outlying regions. The classic case is France. This language can carry teleological assumptions, either that state and nation building was an immanent tendency in European history, or that rulers actually intended to build modern states and nations but had greater and lesser degrees of success. The former assumption is clearly not acceptable and the latter is highly questionable, especially the nation-building part.[24] It is more accurate to argue that developments followed the rationale of the periods in which they occurred—dynastic acquisition, religious conflict, and the strengthening of administration to increase financial resources for military purposes, for example—and that some of these developments were, unintentionally, more favourable to the emergence of later autonomist nationalism than others. The ideal-type nation state can then be viewed as one possible outcome, rather than the historical norm. Furthermore, other varieties of state cannot be treated simply as modifications according to the degree of periphery integration. This is far too simple a notion to cope with the complexities of European states. Political and economic 'centres' frequently fail to coincide, as in Spain, some states lack any obvious 'centre', such as Belgium and Switzerland, and no simple model could do justice to the regional structure of Austria-Hungary.[25]

Let us then examine the range of factors that affected the development of the preconditions of autonomist nationalism.

A. Social Foundations

A first set of factors concerns the raw material with which rulers have had to work throughout modern European history. Here two matters in particular seem to have had considerable consequences.

1. Linguistic Geography. The present European situation of distinct and internally uniform national languages is no natural state of affairs. In many cases the national languages are at least as much a product of the nation state as a cause of it. It is to a large extent the presence of a political vehicle that explains why Danish, Norwegian and Swedish varieties of Norse have become separate national languages and the absence of such a vehicle which explains why the dialects of medieval England and France have been submerged in a unified national language, and not any greater degree of variation in the initial dialects. In the long and slow change from the medieval pattern of endlessly varying peasant dialects surmounted by one literary language, Latin, towards the present linguistic geography of Europe, the traces of the activities of states and political movements are writ large.[26] However, not all linguistic divisions are so malleable. It is one thing to impose a standard French on speakers of a variety of Romance dialects, it is another to make a common language from Slavonic and Germanic dialects. Certain linguistic differences have proved very difficult to eradicate. The most important differences separate Romance, Germanic and Slavonic languages. A major fracture line runs across Europe east-west between Romance and Germanic and another north-south through central Europe between Germanic and Slavonic languages and, to continue the metaphor, other non-assimilable languages have created smaller fault zones in the Basque Country, Finland, Hungary, the Celtic fringes of the British

Isles, and Brittany. Wherever these lines have defined regionally distinct groups within larger states, the groups have preserved their linguistic distinctiveness unless they have either been physically removed, as with many German-speaking groups in Eastern Europe since the war, or they have been converted into speakers of the very different dominant language, as in much of Ireland. If these languages have survived, there has been no question of slow absorption through the erosion of dialects. In only one instance have these barriers been crossed—modern English—and this occurred long before systematic efforts were made to connect languages and states. These are not, of course, the *only* linguistic divisions which have provided a basis of community for autonomist nationalisms, rather they are the only ones which seem to operate relatively independently of political factors. Of states which have not lain across many of these lines, some have achieved a high degree of linguistic uniformity, such as France, and some have not, such as Spain. But none of the states severely fragmented by them, such as Austria-Hungary, Switzerland and Belgium, have even seriously attempted linguistic uniformity.[27]

2. *Frontier Position.* From early medieval times Europe was extending its culture, institutions and population to the south in the Iberian peninsula and along its eastern edges generally.[28] The location of a territory on these frontiers seems to have had major consequences for the later development of autonomist nationalism. These frontier areas tended to bequeath certain difficult features to the states that emerged along them. They were areas of conquest not merely in the sense of dynastic acquisition but also of considerable population movement so that there was a marked intermingling of ethnically distinct groups, a much-noted feature of Eastern Europe and in this case the population movement continued until well into the eighteenth century.[29] Also the nobilities of the most powerful political units in these areas—Germans, Magyars and Poles in Eastern Europe—often found themselves in the position of an ethnically distinct noble stratum above peasantries speaking a different language. Here there was little possibility of the kind of slow assimilation of master and peasant culture that occurred in longer settled areas, such as England, and, as I argued earlier, this is a class situation that is especially conducive to later autonomist nationalism. In a number of cases it persisted until well into the nineteenth century.[30] Outside these frontier areas, ethnically distinct landlord strata were rare.

These two factors account for a great many of the cases but

certain other factors have been highly influential in some instances and have reinforced the preconditions of autonomist nationalism in others.

B. The European State System and Economy

Here we examine a set of factors that relate to the period from roughly 1500 to 1800 in which the multiplicity of medieval political units was reduced to the few dozen of the nineteenth century. It is vital to consider these political structures not as isolated entities pursuing separate but similar paths, the single country approach, but to see them within the larger European context, both political and economic, for this had an enormous influence on the shape of European states.[31] The place of certain states in the European system made it difficult or unnecessary for them to pursue the kind of homogenizing policies that were important if there was to be later development in the direction of the nation state, although some of these states also had the characteristics discussed in the last section, reinforcing their difficulties.

1. Extreme External Pressure. Some areas had political structures so dominated by external pressure that few resources were left for administrative centralization and cultural assimilation. Both Spain and the Habsburg possessions in Eastern Europe were deeply affected by this sort of pressure from two directions. First, both areas were on the European frontier with Islam, a matter that had effects on state structure as well as ethnic composition. In the case of the eastern Habsburg possessions, this frontier was in Hungary and later in the Balkans; in the case of Spain it was firstly in southern Spain itself and later in the battle for control of the western Mediterranean. The struggle with the Ottoman Turks to retain or regain disputed territory was bitter and prolonged and a policy of centralization that might produce conflict with domestic allies located near to the Islamic threat was an expensive luxury. Aragonese and Hungarian privileges and institutions benefitted from this factor, the former until the end of the sixteenth century, the latter until well into the eighteenth century.[32] To some extent this danger from unreliable territories bordering on international rivals was also true within Europe, but Austria and Spain also suffered at the same time from a second sort of distracting external pressure: involvement in the widely-dispersed possessions and European ambitions of the Habsburg dynasty.

These directed the attention of rulers again and again away

from Spain and the Danubian territories towards possessions and sites of conflict in the German Empire, Italy and the Low Countries. At least partly as a consequence of this, in both cases thoroughgoing and successful attempts at administrative centralization were delayed until the eighteenth century, when prospects of European hegemony had vanished and even great power status was in doubt. Thus the Austrian and Hungarian estates retained many of their privileges until the onset of modern nationalism in the nineteenth century and in Spain the Basques retained their *fueros* until the same period and the Catalans, even after losing their estates in the early eighteenth century, retained their legal and taxation systems.[33] The regional identities that persisted until the nineteenth century were correspondingly strengthened. This pattern contrasts strongly with the administrative history of states with more compact possessions and fewer pretensions at an early stage in the process of extending governmental control, such as France and England (not however the whole of the later United Kingdom), although neither of these instances faced the cultural diversity that confronted the eastern Habsburgs.[34]

While some states thus preserved the preconditions of later autonomist nationalism through extreme pressure, others did so because of their strength.

2. The Economy and Sources of War Finance. One of the major forces promoting central control and administrative reform in states such as France, Prussia and Sweden was the need to gain adequate funds and therefore troops for the aims of rulers in a world that was militarily highly competitive and in which the cost of war was rapidly expanding.[35] States with a less pressing dependence on coercive tax-gathering machinery were also freer of this particular pressure towards a uniformity and centralization that threatened the preconditions of later autonomist nationalism.

Paradoxically, but not inconsistently, Habsburg Spain was partially released from this pressure during the late sixteenth and early seventeenth centuries because of its control of American gold and silver. This reinforced the lack of concern of the monarchy for administrative control outside Castile.[36] In a rather different way, and in a fashion that reflected more durable financial power, states with commercial and maritime strength were less dependent on internal administrative control for resources. In Britain and the Netherlands a set of mutually reinforcing factors connected to commercial success reduced the pressure for internal control. Let us take Britain as the main example. As an insular state it was less subject to invasion and hence had a smaller need for a large and costly permanent army—an oft-cited feature of British history.[37] The main permanent defence arm of a maritime state was naval. Navies were admittedly more expensive than armies on a man-for-man basis, because of their high capital costs, but the total military costs necessary to maintain Britain's status, even at the height of its eighteenth-century competition with France, and even when a continental army and subsidies to allies are added, were lower than those of France, which needed a much larger army and a navy of something like the same size.[38] As successful commercial powers, both Britain and the Netherlands were in any event more prosperous in relation to population size than more agrarian states such as France and Prussia, and could thus bear taxation with less opposition. Also the sources of much finance, whether through taxation or borrowing, were mercantile classes and commercially-oriented aristocracies which could see clearly the connection between the main item of expenditure—navies—and their trading prosperity, thus reducing their hostility to the extraction of resources. The very shape of the economy also aided the state. Much the simplest taxes to collect until quite recent times were customs and excises, and the revenues from them were both easier to gather and larger in the most advanced exchange economies.[39] Finally, and possibly most important of all, commercial success meant commercial sophistication and some have argued that the superior borrowing capacities of the British and Dutch authorities was the most significant single factor in success in the long struggle with France in the seventeenth and eighteenth centuries.[40]

There were periods when these factors were in abeyance, as in Britain under the early Stuarts, and some applied more to Britain than to the Netherlands, such as insular position, but in the long run they operated in both countries to reduce the need for coercive tax-gathering and hence to preserve provincial privileges. The provinces of the Netherlands maintained their separate status until the French Revolution.[41] Scotland and Ireland were brought closer to control from London in the early modern period not as part of a systematic subjugation of provinces for revenue purposes but when they seemed to pose a threat to security and foreign policy. Tudor policy in Ireland was motivated to a large extent by foreign, especially Spanish, intrigue with native magnates and only reluctantly went beyond what was necessary to restore security.[42] The later destruction of the

Catholic aristocracy took place because of its involvement with the losing side in the great civil struggles of seventeenth-century England, not as part of any policy of combatting regional distinctiveness. Similarly, the Union of the English and Scottish parliaments was provoked by the actual and potential interference of the Scots and their parliament with a unified foreign policy and a secure succession to the throne.[43] Once the immediate difficulties presented by Irish or Scottish autonomy had been removed, there was no pressing financial or administrative need to go further, and hence many of the preconditions of autonomist nationalism survived.[44]

Let us now turn to some factors of more limited significance in this period, which either served mainly to reinforce factors already analysed or which affected only certain regions.

3. Special Regions in the International Economy. The role of certain regions in the European economy deeply influenced their political and social institutions.

First, the 'second serfdom' of eastern Europe powerfully buttressed certain already-existing cultural divisions. In many areas east of the River Elbe, the rent-gathering landlord system, or *grundherrschaft,* of the late medieval period, with a peasantry comparatively free of the elements of personal subjection, was replaced from the sixteenth century onwards by the *gutsherrschaft,* the cultivation of the lord's much-extended demesne land by unfree or serf labour. This development occurred especially in Brandenberg-Prussia, the southern Baltic littoral, Poland, Bohemia and Hungary. The causes of this development are complex and vary from case to case, but it seems to be widely agreed that one major factor in the northern cases at least, was the demand in Western Europe for grain and the capacity to produce this grain in the basins of rivers that flowed into the Baltic, from where it could be cheaply shipped to the market. It is often argued that in a situation of chronic labour shortage the only way to meet this opportunity to grow a labour intensive product was to encroach on peasant liberties and tie the worker to the land.[45] The consequence in some ethnically mixed areas was to reinforce the pattern of ethnically distinct landowning strata that had developed in medieval times and which was conducive to the later development of autonomist nationalism, for the *gutsherrschaft* ended any possibility of the weakening of ethnic and status barriers.

Secondly, the whole of Scandinavia was affected by its place in the European economy. Sweden, Denmark and Norway possessed cultures in medieval times that were at least as closely related as those of England or France, there was a lengthy period in which they were all ruled by one monarch in the Kalmar Union, and even after the end of this arrangement, the idea of a pan-Scandinavian state occupied the minds of Danish and Swedish rulers at times.[46] Why did this unified state never occur? At certain points in the sixteenth and seventeenth centuries both Sweden and Denmark were close to its achievement.[47] At least one important reason was that such a state would have had almost complete control over the Baltic trade routes in which Western European salt, herring and manufactured goods were exchanged for grain, tar, timber and other raw materials in the great ports of the southern Baltic shore. This trade was the foundation of the prosperity of first the northern Hanse towns and later of the Netherlands, and was also of importance to English commerce. At several points in the sixteenth and seventeenth centuries these powers intervened to prevent either Denmark or Sweden swallowing the other, thus preserving Scandinavian divisions.[48] After the destruction of Swedish power by Russia early in the eighteenth century, all Scandinavian pretensions to regional dominance were over and the region was left with two states, Denmark and Sweden, each with poorly integrated dependent territories that changed hands during the Napoleonic period, Norway and Finland. Their roles in the European economy thus played a crucial part in maintaining both the political division of Scandinavia and the preconditions of autonomist nationalism in the region.

4. The Need for Control of Religion. For most European states from the sixteenth to the eighteenth centuries religious uniformity was far more important than ethnic homogeneity and great efforts were made to achieve it, or at least to gain firm control over those not professing the religion of the state, for these were always likely sources of internal dissent and targets of intrigue by foreign powers. This factor worked both for and against the survival of the preconditions of autonomist nationalism. In many places it promoted homogenization, as with the policies of conversion or expulsion directed against Huguenots in France and Moriscos (Muslims) and Jews in Spain. In other places, especially Bohemia and Ireland, a rebellious and religiously distinct provincial aristocracy provoked the controlling power to destroy it and replace it with an ethnically alien landlord class of the same religious complexion as the rulers. In Ireland the continuously troublesome Catholic aristocracy, both Gaelic and Anglo-Norman, was virtually destroyed in the seventeenth century and replaced by the Anglo-Irish Protestant Ascendancy, while in Bohemia the Protestant Czech nobility was conclusively defeated at the outset of the Thirty Years War and its place largely taken by a Germanized Catholic aristocracy of diverse origins. Here the religious division did not persist, but the *gutsherrschaft* agrarian order ensured the survival of ethnic and linguistic differences.[49]

C. International Cataclysms

As noted earlier, distinctive institutions are always vulnerable to the effects of war and this was a factor of great importance in the survival of institutional bases of community into the nineteenth century. Defeat and occupation were, for example, of great importance in the weakening and eventual demise of estates in places as different as Aragon and Prussia.[50] No single period was more important in this respect than the Napoleonic Wars. Institutional distinctiveness, especially if not reinforced by linguistic or religious divisions, and particularly in the regions closest to France, was eroded on a massive scale by the regimes set up by the French and by the decisions of the Congress of Vienna in the aftermath of the wars. In Belgium, the Netherlands, Switzerland, Northern and Central Italy and Spain, the particularist institutions of the *Ancien Régime* were swept aside wholesale and replaced at least temporarily by administration on the French pattern. The simplification of the political boundaries of Germany in this period is well known. Some institutions emerged in a modified form after the Wars, but many did not, as in Belgium, and others were greatly weakened. In areas either distant from or untouched by France, estates and regional privileges flourished more healthily, as in the Habsburg possessions and in the United Kingdom, although here the Irish Parliament was a casualty of the Wars.[51]

These factors are not equal in importance and they obviously do not include all the matters that would have to be taken into account in the detailed study of any individual case, but they do, I think, offer substantial reasons for the existence of the preconditions of autonomist nationalism in all the most important cases. This survey also makes clear that these forces did not operate equally in all states as they emerged in the nineteenth century. Some, such as France, Denmark and the Netherlands (after the secession of Belgium in 1830), were not too far distant from the ideal-type nation state; others such as the United Kingdom, Sweden and Spain consisted of a central territory whose relation to the state was of the nation state type, but also sizeable territories with the preconditions of autonomist nationalism; yet others, such as Belgium, Switzerland and the Habsburg monarchy, in a sense consisted of nothing but a collection of territories that all exhibited the preconditions of autonomist nationalism. This variation also indicates the utility of approaching this subject through the study of the place of states in a larger European context rather than through the use of models that concentrate on factors internal to each state, such as internal colonialism or core-periphery. The variation between states is as important as what they share, and generalizations about the development of the preconditions of autonomist nationalism are better obtained at the level of the state system than at the level of general models of the individual state.

The Triggering of Autonomist Nationalism in the Nineteenth and Twentieth Centuries

Let us now turn to the final concern of this chapter, the factors that trigger these preconditions into nationalist demands for political autonomy at various points in the last two centuries. The main general explanations are to be found in the theories examined in detail in Smith's chapter, such as internal colonialism and uneven development. These general accounts are usually linked to an aspect of the impact of development or modernization on a territory, in some sense of these much-abused concepts. (Also they usually attempt to explain most aspects of autonomist nationalism, including those I have called preconditions. Here I shall treat them as accounts of triggering factors alone.) It is worthwhile to add to these general accounts a number of explanations intended to deal more particularly with the contemporary 'wave' of autonomist nationalism and which therefore refer to factors operating mainly in the post-war period.[52]

One such explanation is an amendment to the various impact-of-modernization accounts which argues that the full effect of modernization has been delayed in some areas until the last thirty years and that therefore in these regions the decay of a purely parochial awareness is a relatively recent development.[53] A further range of explanations refer to the reduced significance of the larger European states since the Second World War. Some have argued that decolonization has greatly reduced the prestige of former imperial states and removed the material and psychological rewards of empire that previously went to certain potential autonomist nationalisms such as the Scots. It has also presented these regions with the example of anti-colonial nationalism.[54] Others have argued that even *within* Europe the rationale for the large state has been much reduced in an era in which military effectiveness depends on the superpowers, in which economic integration is proceeding rapidly, and in which, allegedly, control over multi-national enterprises can no longer be exercised even by larger European states. Before 1939, military protection and economic control from London or Paris may have seemed of crucial importance in Edinburgh or Nantes, but this hardly applies in the late twentieth century.[55]

Another series of explanations point to internal developments in western societies, especially bureaucratization, centralization, and the growth of the state. Three related arguments have been advanced. First, it has been suggested that the claim of interventionist governments to be able to solve the problems of regional economies have rebounded upon them when they have failed, for the aroused expectation of a political solution persisted and attached itself to other purveyors of such remedies, nationalist parties.[56] Secondly, some have argued that the growth of centralized and bureaucratic administration both in government and other spheres has produced a hostile reaction in areas excluded from its presence but suffering from its activities. In its most self-conscious forms, this argument could be connected with the more critical forms of post-industrial society theory and neo-corporatist theory.[57] Finally, and more loosely, it has been suggested that contemporary autonomist nationalism is one aspect of a more general rejection of the bureaucratic and materialist culture of the contemporary West and an espousal of 'small is beautiful'.[58]

As they stand these explanations face many empirical problems. The most general accounts suffer from obvious exceptions. Some territories which ought to display autonomist nationalism on their prescriptions have not done so. Switzerland presents this sort of difficulty for most of the theories.[59] On the other hand some territories which have produced autonomist movements have not experienced the factors in question. (Examples can be found in Smith's analysis). Also, while most autonomist nationalisms in Europe emerged before the First World War, thus roughly coinciding with the development, uneven or otherwise, which supplies the motive force of most of the general theories, other cases were delayed until well after the Second World War, long after the impact of development or modernization, such as Scotland. The more limited explanations which deal only with the recent cases necessarily meet the latter problem, but they also face exceptions. To take only the most obvious example, why has France, with the most precipitous and war-strewn descent from Empire and the most rigidly centralized of western European states, suffered less than the United Kingdom, even given the wider spread of the preconditions of autonomist nationalism in the second case?[60] The problem with all of these explanations is not that they are simply wrong; there are typically clear instances in which the factors that they refer to have been influential. The difficulty is that, once again, they are applied generally to every substantial state and do not take into account the variations produced by the place in the state system that a country occupies. We have seen that this helps to produce great differences in the occurrence of the preconditions of autonomist nationalism; it also at a later date affects the capacity of the state to manage such things as autonomist nationalism and hence the extent to which it is subject to these various factors.

First, some states have had such limited international responsibilities throughout the nineteenth and twentieth centuries that it has been possible to defuse many varieties of internal conflict, including national conflict, by procedures that emphasize consensus and the autonomy of groups above all else. Such states have also generally been small and hence have been less affected by any decline in the salience of larger states since the Second World War. I refer here to so-called consociational Europe, especially Switzerland and, to a lesser extent, Belgium.[61]

Secondly, during any particular period in the last two centuries, the states that have suffered most from autonomist nationalism have been those which were both vulnerable because they possessed its preconditions *and* weakest within the state system at that time. Thus, in the pre-1920 period, it was the Ottoman Empire in Europe, Austria-Hungary and Spain that were troubled most extensively by autonomist nationalism and these were the large states that were least effective by the standards of the time, such as military capacity, industrialization, and colonial possessions. Internal attacks on these states had more prospects of success, while membership in these states was less rewarding than in more powerful larger states. In effect, they seemed more dispensable. In accordance with the same principle, Sweden was hardly enough of a great power to claim a plausible or beneficial hegemony over Norway. Other states which also possessed the potential for autonomist nationalism but which were more successful in this period, such as the United Kingdom, were less troubled, although not untouched.[62] Similarly, in the post-Second World War period, autonomist nationalisms, insofar as they have been genuinely novel and not continuations of older but suppressed conflicts, have affected states which both possess their preconditions and are comparatively weak. The decline in the prestige of larger European states and the reaction against centralism have not hit all states equally hard, they have gained most purchase in those states which lag by the standards of the time, especially sustained economic growth, as with the United Kingdom.

It is worth noting that sudden declines in the strength of the state because of international turmoil can have a similar effect—increasing its apparent dispensability. Many of the nationalities of Austria-Hungary contemplated no more than an extensive federalism until the defeat and possible dismemberment of the state became apparent in the latter stages of the First World War. In Russia, the end of the Tsarist state and the Revolution so weakened the empire that scarcely a European or Asian possession failed to develop an autonomist nationalism, some of which were temporarily or permanently successful, such as Estonia, Finland, Latvia and Lithuania.[63] By the same token, sudden increases in the power of the state through internal changes of regime can have profound effects on the fate of autonomist nationalisms. The more or less complete disappearence of such movements in Spain between 1940 and 1960 and in the USSR since the 1920s is almost entirely the result of the willingness and ability of both states to suppress them.[64]

Thus autonomist nationalisms can be better understood if the forces that promote them are acknowledged to affect states in very different international positions and if it is recognized that these positions and the domestic strength of the state can alter, sometimes quite rapidly. For the fate of such nationalisms, the influence of war, revolution and fluctuations in the international standing of the state they confront have been at least as significant as any more general factors, and certainly as important as their own capacity to gain widespread support. Once again universal explanations and single country models alone are not enough.

Finally, let us look briefly at two major states that have not so far been dealt with yet which raise interesting questions about autonomist nationalism. The unification nationalisms of Germany and Italy welded together culturally similar fragments into great powers, but there were cultural differences between the fragments, such as strong dialects in Italy, and some preserved a range of privileges and institutions within the larger state, as with the constituent states of the Second German

Empire.[65] However, despite periods of failure for these states in the twentieth century, there has little danger of refragmentation from these distinctive regions.[66] Bavaria has come closest to this with the Bavarian People's Party in the 1920s and the Christian Social Union in the post-war period, but these bodies have or had at least as much a confessional as a regional chracter and furthermore they have claimed to represent an authentic Germanism especially found in Bavaria rather than a non-German Bavarian identity.[67] One reason for this may be that in both countries the coincidence of state formation with the onset of urbanization and industrialization meant that the newly-emerging supra-local identities of the mass of the population crystallized around the new state as the most 'progressive' political vehicle of the region in a way that could not happen in older-established states with much regional diversity.[68] Particular factors within each state may also be of importance. The most evidently distinctive region of Germany, Bavaria, has always had its character recognized under non-dictatorial regimes by various federal arrangements.[69] It has been argued that the most distinctive and depressed, Italian region, the south, has been integrated into modern Italy not through mass political alignments, but through a multitude of clientalist arrangements which have prevented the development of a wider regional consciousness.[70] It may also be, however, that the kind of factor discussed immediately above, the strength and success of the state, may again be important. The historical circumstances of the advent of the larger state were very different from those in the case of other potential autonomist nationalisms. The impact of nationalism in the nineteenth century was not on the culturally differentiated regions of a large and possibly unsuccessful state but on fragments which, even when politically dependent, had been with few exceptions demonstrably weak in international competition over several centuries. For all the problems of the new states at some points in the twentieth century, security and prosperity may in general have seemed better served within them than under any conceivable state of affairs outside them. Whatever the explanation, regional distinctiveness remains and has been managed rather than dissolved. These states therefore still preserve the potential for autonomist nationalism at some future date.

I have, of course, offered only a sketch map of a vast territory, but even as it stands it has three main advantages. First, by separating preconditions from triggering factors it is possible to have a general analysis not tied too closely to any one precipitating cause. No single factor is universally applicable and it is realistic to allow a variety of them, not all operating in the same period. Secondly, by proceeding at the level of the state system rather than at the level of the individual case it is possible to see that states vary greatly in potential for autonomist nationalisms, and also, even given this variation, in their susceptibility to such threats in any particular period. Force, successful accommodation, or political effectiveness can stave off potential autonomist nationalisms for long periods. Finally, this approach makes the subject open-ended. Wherever these preconditions exist within states, a weakening of the state can provide political entrepreneurs with an opportunity to redirect loyalties. Switzerland and West Germany are not eternally guaranteed success in the management of their regional divisions. Regional and ethnic loyalties may ebb and flow in importance but they will be an important problem for states for some time yet.

Notes

1. For discussions and rejections of the assimilationist literature see, Walker Connor, 'National-Building or Nation-Destroying?', *World Politics*, 24 (1972) pp. 317-55, and Michael Hechter, *Internal Colonialism: The Celtic Fringe in British National Development, 1536-1966* (London, 1975), chapter 2.
2. For lengthier discussions of this point see, for example, E. Gellner, *Thought and Change* (London, 1964), pp. 150-3, and E. Kedourie, *Nationalism* (London, 1961), chapter 1. For an opposing viewpoint see some of the pieces in C. Leon Tipton (ed.), *Nationalism in the Middle Ages* (New York, 1972).
3. The classification of individual instances can of course change. The most powerful independent unit of a fragmented culture group may build its own state nationalism, then provide the basis for a unification nationalism, and then involve itself in irredentist claims to the territory of other states, such as Prussia. Some groups have a choice of self-definitions, such as Flemish speakers, who could claim to be a separate Fleming nationality or an irredenta of a greater Netherlands or even of a greater Germany.
4. This point is made in many places but for an account that emphasizes the differences between European and Afro-Asian nationalism see, J. H. Kautsky (ed.), *Political Change in Underdeveloped Countries* (New York, 1962), 'Introduction', pp. 32-8. There are, as always, borderline cases such as Yugoslavia, which faces problems of cultural diversity as severe as any in Africa, and Vietnam, which possesses a culture more ancient than many in Europe, but in general the distinction holds.

5. These concepts are to be found in R. A. Schermerhorn, *Comparative Ethnic Relations* (New York, 1970), chapters 3, 4, and 6. This difference is akin to, but not identical to, Smith's distinction between geographical and ethnic separatism.
6. See, for example, the multitude of groups examined in Meic Stephens, *Linguistic Minorities in Western Europe* (Llandysul, 1976), although not all of these are potential separatisms. I should stress that I have confined this list to the European frontiers of the USSR.
7. A. W. Orridge, 'Uneven Development and Nationalism', Parts I and II, *Political Studies*, XXIX (1981), pp. 1-15.
8. I make no claims for originality in this list of basic conditions, although I believe much of the discussion to be novel. For other such lists see Pierre L. van den Berghe, 'Ethnic Pluralism in Industrial Societies: A Special Case', *Ethnicity*, 3 (1976), pp. 242-55, especially pp. 248-9, and A. D. Smith, 'The Formation of Nationalist Movements', p. 9 ff., in A. D. Smith (ed.), *Nationalist Movements* (London, 1976).
9. See T. Draper, *The Rediscovery of Black Nationalism* (London, 1971). The Jews are of course the great exception to this generalization.
10. These are referred to as similarity dis-similarity criteria in B. Akzin, *State and Nation* (London, 1964), pp. 30-1.
11. R. W. Seton-Watson, *Britain and the Dictators* (Cambridge, 1939), pp. 322-3, gives 34.7 per cent of the population of inter-war Czechoslovakia as non-Czechoslovak, and this is not counting Slovaks as a separate group. In the same period national minorities made up 25 per cent of the Rumanian and 26.4 per cent of the Latvian population.
12. See, for example, Akzin, *State and Nation*, pp. 30-1, and Smith, 'The Formation of Nationalists Movements', pp. 17-19.
13. Max Weber, *Economy and Society*, (eds. G. Roth and C. Wittich) (Berkeley, Calif., 1968), Vol. 2, ch. IX, pp. 932-8.
14. For the Finnish Social Democrats see J. H. Wuorinen, *A History of Finland* (New York, 1965), pp. 200-1; for the Czech Social Democrats see A. H. Herman, *A History of the Czechs* (London, 1975), pp. 105-9, and C. A. Macartney, *The Habsburg Empire, 1790-1918* (London, 1968), pp. 792-5; and for the Catalan *Esquerra* see G. Brennan, *The Spanish Labyrinth* (Cambridge, 1960 (1950)), pp. 65-6, 240-1, 276-7, and Juan J. Linz, 'The Party System of Spain', p. 297, in S. M. Lipset and S. Rokkan, (eds.), *Party Systems and Voter Alignments* (New York, 1967).
15. Some sociologists of agrarian political movements in general have noted that a combination of rentier landlords and small family holdings makes for explosive rural politics even in the absence of ethnic divisions. See Theda Skocpol, *States and Revolutions* (Cambridge, 1979), p. 116 and Chapter 3 generally, and A. Stinchcombe, 'Agricultural Enterprise and Rural Class Relations', *American Journal of Sociology*, 67 (1961), pp. 165-76, especially pp. 169-72.
16. Weber, *Economy and Society*, Vol. 1, ch. 4., pp. 302-4.

17. Most obviously, even when nationality and class do not coincide, the potential autonomist nationality may have less than a 'fair' share of jobs of high status in its 'own' territory, a situation that fuelled German-Czech and Swedish-Finnish conflicts in nineteenth-century Bohemia and Finland. Here, however, class does not define nationality, it provides an issue around which national conflict can develop. For discussions of other aspects of class and nationalism see Gellner, *Thought and Change*, pp. 164-71; Hugh Seton-Watson, *Nations and States* (London, 1977), ch. 11; M. Hroch, *Die Vorkämpfer der nationalen Bewegung bei den kleinen Völkern Europas*, Acta Universitatis Carolinae, Philosophica et Historica, Monographica, XXIV, 1968; E. J. Hobsbawm, *The Age of Revolution* (London, 1962), pp. 167 ff.; and V. Kiernan, 'Nationalist Movements and Social Classes', in Smith, *Nationalist Movements*.
18. An account of Scottish nationalism which places much emphasis on these institutions is C. Harvie, *Scotland and Nationalism* (London, 1977), see especially pp. 16-17, 66 ff. A description of the Basque *fueros* is in Maximiano Garcia Venero, *Historia del nacionalismo Vasco* (Madrid, 1968), pp. 71-95.
19. A recent analysis of all European nationalities—autonomist and otherwise—which examines the distinctive features of nationality shows language to be easily the most common. J. Krejci, 'Ethnic Problems in Europe' in S. Giner and M. Scotford Archer (eds.), *Contemporary Europe: Social Structures and Cultural Patterns* (London, 1978), especially pp. 130-6.
20. An example might be the Catholic Dutch who, although fairly widely distributed, reach concentrations of around 90 per cent of the population in the provinces of North Brabant and Limburg. See A. Lijphart, *The Politics of Accommodation: Pluralism and Democracy in the Netherlands* (Berkeley, 1968), pp. 16-19. It should be added that when religion and nationality do coincide, as in the Irish case, a particularly fervent tone can be imparted to the national conflict. This is the burden of Patrick O'Farrell, *Ireland's English Question* (New York, 1971).
21. Although surprisingly small groups have displayed the capacity to preserve their languages, especially when they are very distinct from the dominant language in the environment. See below pp. 52-53.
22. Some may feel that widespread institutional and cultural differences were also present in the two great unification nationalisms of the mid-nineteenth century, Germany and Italy. However the fact that nationalism promoted fusion rather than disintegration makes these cases rather different. They are briefly discussed at the end of the chapter on pp. 63-5.
23. These are comparative historical accounts of the state, revolution and international economy. P. Anderson, *The Lineages of the Absolutist State* (London, 1974); Juan J. Linz, 'Early State Building and Late Peripheral Nationalism against the State: The Case of Spain', in S. Eisenstadt and S. Rokkan (eds.), *Building States and Nations* Vol. 2, (Beverley Hills, 1973); Theda Skocpol, *States and Revolutions*

(Cambridge, 1979); Charles Tilly (ed.), *The Formation of National States in Western Europe* (Princeton, 1975), both generally and for Stein Rokkan's, 'Dimensions of State Formation and Nation-Building: A Possible Paradigm for Research on Variations with Europe'; and Immanuel Wallerstein, *The Modern World-System* (New York, 1974).

24. See, for example, the comments of J. P. Cooper in the 'General Introduction' to *The New Cambridge Modern History, Vol. IV, The Decline of Spain and the Thirty Years War* (Cambridge, 1970), pp. 2-4.
25. N. J. G. Pounds and S. S. Ball, 'Core Areas and the Development of the European State System', *Annals of the Association of American Geographers*, 54 (1964), pp. 24-40, is a thorough-going geographical version of this model; E. Shils, 'Centre and Periphery' in *The Logic of Personal Knowledge: Essays Presented to Michael Polanyi* (London, 1961), is more concerned with cultural than spatial distance.
26. For fuller discussions of this interaction between the political and the linguistic see E. Haugen, 'Dialect, Language, Nation', *American Anthropologist*, 68 (1966), pp. 922-35, or Joshua A. Fishman, 'The Impact of Nationalism on Language and Language Planning', Part Two of Fishman's *Language and Nationalism* (Rowley, Mass., 1973).
27. It is difficult to find linguistic literature that discusses degrees of difference between geographically adjacent languages. One such treatment is S. Rundle, *Language as a Social and Political Factor in Europe* (London, 1945), pp. 39-40 and Map 1 on p. 43, which is consistent with the argument in the text. More purely descriptive accounts of European languages are L. Dominion, *Frontiers of Language and Nationality in Europe* (London, 1917), and A. M. Chadwick, *The Nationalities of Europe* (Cambridge, 1945), chapter I to IV.
28. And also to a more limited extent towards the west, into Wales and Ireland; see Williams, C. H. chapter 6 below.
29. See, for examples, C. Macartney, *National States and National Minorities* (London, 1934), chapters I and II. German speakers were settling in Hungary, in the wake of the retreat of the Ottoman Empire, until well into the eighteenth century. This is brought out well in the map on p. 286 of *The Penguin Atlas of World History*. Vol. 1, (Harmondsworth, 1974).
30. In Latvia, Lithuania, Estonia, Ruthenia, Bohemia and Ireland, for example, although in the last two cases the situation developed in the religious conflicts of the seventeenth century, see below pp. 25-6. Something of the same sort occurred in southern Spain as a Christian aristocracy occupied lands with a Muslim peasantry. However the dispersal and later expulsion of the Moriscos, as the Muslims were called, brought this situation to an end. See J. H. Elliott, *Imperial Spain, 1469-1716* (Harmondsworth, 1970), pp. 305-8.
31. Many of the works cited in footnote 23 above consciously adopt this approach, especially Wallerstein and Skocpol, but it is not new.

Most Marxists would claim that theories of imperialism are explicitly cast at this level and the German historian Otto Hintze advocated the approach over seventy years ago. See 'The Formation of States and Constitutional Development: A Study in History and Politics', in F. Gilbert (ed.), *The Historical Essays of Otto Hintze* (New York, 1975).

32. See, for Spain, Elliott, *Imperial Spain*, pp. 235-42, for the continued Muslim threat until at least the 1570s; for the eastern Habsburgs, V-L. Tapié, *The Rise and Fall of the Habsburg Monarchy* (London, 1971), p. 59, for the general position of the Hungarians, and pp. 85-6, 142-5, 146-9, 159-61, for the various Hungarian revolts and Ottoman attacks of the sixteenth and seventeenth centuries.
33. Large-scale administrative reform did not seriously begin in the Habsburg monarchy until the 1740s and even then it left many provincial privileges untouched. The role of interconnected European and Turkisn pressures in preventing this at an earlier date, and the consequent preservation of provincial autonomy, is discussed in W. H. McNeill, *Europe's Steppe Frontier* (Chicago, 1964), pp. 58 ff., 68-75, 94-105. Olivares' attempt to bring the rest of the Iberian peninsula under the same sort of control as the kingdom of Castile in the years leading up to 1640 collapsed under the strain of manifold external involvements and led to the revolt of the Catalans and the loss of Portugal (see Elliott, *Imperial Spain*, pp. 378-80 and ch. 9). Again, it was not until the eighteenth century that serious administrative reform began. For the position of the provinces after the defeat of the Catalan revolt of 1705-14 and the accession of the Bourbons see W. N. Hargreaves-Mawdsley, *Eighteenth-Century Spain, 1700-1788* (London, 1979), pp. 6-13.
34. Others have advanced similar arguments for the Spanish case. See Linz, 'Early State Building and Late Peripheral Nationalisms', pp. 39-49, Anderson, *Lineages of the Absolutist State*, ch. 3.
35. The classic discussion of the increasing scale of warfare in the early modern period is M. Roberts, *The Military Revolution, 1560-1660,* Inaugural Lecture, Queens University, Belfast, 1956, which is assessed and substantially confirmed in G. Parker, 'The Military Revolution, 1560-1660, A Myth?', in Parker, *Spain and the Netherlands, 1559-1659* (London, 1979) pp. 86-103. The links between government and the cost of war are analysed in Sir George Clark, *The Seventeenth Century* (London, Second edition, 1947), pp. 41-7 and 98-102, and S. E. Finer, 'State- and Nation-Building in Europe: The Role of the Military', in Tilly, *The Formation of National States in Western Europe*. The story of the rise of absolutist states in France and Prussia has been told many times. A useful discussion of the development of government in most of the major European states in the seventeenth and eighteenth centuries, with a full bibliography, is E. N. Williams, *The Ancien Régime in Europe* (Harmondsworth, 1972); chapters 5 to 8 describe the French state and 14 to 16 the Prussian state.
36. The role of American precious metals in the fortunes of the Span-

ish Habsburgs is described in Elliott, *Imperial Spain*, pp. 268-70, 285-7, 290-2, 321-3.

37. This is a point made in many places. Perhaps the classic source is Hintze, 'The Formation of States and Constitutional Development', p. 174. The Dutch did have some equivalent in their capacity to breach the dikes and flood the country against an invading army, as they did for example against the French in 1672. But this was a self-destructive measure hardly to be compared to the Channel and the North Sea.
38. The best comparative analysis of war finance in the early modern period known to me is P. G. M. Dickson and John Sperling, 'War Finance, 1689-1714' in J. S. Bromley (ed.), *The New Cambridge Modern History, Vol. VI, The Rise of Great Britain and Russia, 1688-1715/25* (Cambridge, 1970). Despite all the difficulties of poor statistics and exchange rates, it is clear that Britain's costs as France's major opponent were far lower than those of France, and that naval expenditure was a much higher proportion of British costs. A discussion of the comparative costs of armies and navies is Clark, *The Seventeenth Century*, pp. 117-21.
39. The greater proportional prosperity of the commercial and maritime powers is mentioned in many places. See, for example, P. M. Kennedy, *The Rise of British Naval Mastery* (Harmondsworth, 1976), pp. 64-7, 70-3, 87-8. The greater ease of collection of taxes on exchanges compared with taxes on income and wealth until quite recent periods, and the greater yield from the former in trading communities is analysed in G. Ardant, 'Financial Policy and the Economic Infrastructure of Modern States and Nations', in Tilly (ed.), *The Formation of National States in Western Europe*, especially pp. 176-80, 193, 196, 199, 202-4, and 207.
40. This is another frequently-made point. See P. G. M. Dickson, *The Financial Revolution in England, A Study in the Development of Public Credit, 1688-1756* (London, 1976), ch. 1. A comparative view is provided by G. Parker, 'The Emergence of Modern Finance in Europe, 1500-1730', in *The Fontana Economic History of Europe, Vol. 2, The Sixteenth and Seventeenth Centuries*, Carlo M. Cipolla (ed.), (London, 1974), especially pp. 560-82.
41. However it seems clear that military competitiveness was damaged by the maintenance of provincial privileges from the end of the seventeenth century onwards. See Kennedy, *The Rise of British Naval Mastery*, pp. 51-2, for example.
42. A discussion of Tudor policy that emphasizes these points is ch. 1 of J. C. Beckett, *The Making of Modern Ireland*, (London, 1966).
43. There is a large and growing literature on the Union and considerable dispute, particularly over the role of political bribery. However all seem agreed about motivations on the English side, which is what concerns this essay: the danger to foreign policy presented by independent Scottish ventures such as the Darien Company and the threat that the Scottish Parliament might refuse to accept the

Hanoverian succession. A useful discussion with a bibilography is T. C. Smout, 'The Road to Union', in G. Holmes (ed.), *Britain After the Glorious Revolution, 1689-1714* (London, 1969).

44. One further factor should perhaps be added. In both cases there was one unit, England and Holland, very much larger than the others, which could be depended upon to provide the bulk of the resources.
45. For discussions of the origins of the *gutsherrschaft* in these regions see F. L. Carsten, *The Origins of Prussia* (London, 1954), ch. XI; V-L. Tapié, *The Rise and Fall of the Habsburg Monarchy*, pp. 71-7; and M. Malowist, 'The Economic and Social Development of the Baltic Countries from the Fifteenth to the Seventeenth Centuries', *Economic History Review*, Second Series, 12 (1959), pp. 177-89. It should be stressed that grain was by no means the whole story, especially away from the Baltic river basins.
46. In the sixteenth century some Danish rulers had strong hopes for re-erecting the Union of the two countries, such as Frederick II in the 1560s (see M. Roberts, *The Early Vasas, A History of Sweden, 1523-1611* (Cambridge, 1968), pp. 210-18), while in the Northern War of 1655-60, Charles X of Sweden certainly contemplated the destruction of Denmark (see M. Roberts, *The Swedish Imperial Experience, 1560-1718* (Cambridge, 1979), pp. 7-8).
47. Denmark, for example, in the War of Kalmar in 1611 (see G. Parker, *Europe in Crisis, 1589-1648* (London, 1979, pp. 101-4), and Sweden, for example, in 1657-8, when Copenhagen was beseiged (see D. H. Pennington, *Seventeenth-Century Europe* (London, 1970), p. 355).
48. The intervention of Lübeck, at that time the leading northern Hanse city, was instrumental in the breaking of the Kalmar Union (see Roberts, *The Early Vasas*, pp. 11-23), and it was the activities of the Dutch in particular that ended the War of Kalmar (see Parker, *Europe in Crisis*, pp. 103-4) and the Northern War of 1655-1660 (see J. Stoye, *Europe Unfolding, 1648-1688* (London, 1969), pp. 152-5) without the destruction of either of the Scandinavian powers. For the Baltic trade and its importance see Kristof Glamann, 'European Trade, 1500-1750', in *The Fontana Economic History of Europe, The Sixteenth and Seventeenth Centuries*, especially pp. 441-3 and 455-67. It is also worth noting the Sweden, the most potent Scandinavian power of the seventeenth century, was often more interested in control of the southern Baltic shoreline, with its grain-production and trading cities, than in unified control of Jutland and the Scandinavian peninsula, although an eminent British student of this region has recently argued tht this was a reflection of military strategy rather than pursuit of economic gain. See M. Roberts, *The Swedish Imperial Experience*, ch. 1.
49. Tapié, *The Rise and Fall of the Habsburg Monarchy*, pp. 92-7, gives an account of the diverse origins of this nobility.
50. The Catalan revolt in the War of the Spanish Succession led to the

destruction of the various estates of Aragon and the Swedish occupations of Brandenburg-Prussia during the Thirty Years' War much weakened the Estates' powers of resistance to the Hohenzollern dynasty. See Carsten, *The Origins of Prussia*, (chapters XIII and XIV.

51. For brief discussions of these changes see E. J. Hobsbawm, *The Age of Revolution*, pp. 113-16 and D. Thomson, *Europe Since Napoleon* (Harmondsworth, 1966), pp. 91-8.
52. It is often assumed that all contemporary autonomist nationalisms are recent developments and hence part of a current 'wave' of such nationalisms. In fact both of the major Spanish cases, the Basques and the Catalans, were active in the early twentieth century but were suppressed by Franco. They are thus of the same 'vintage' as the classic nineteenth-century examples.
53. For this argument see Walker Connor, 'Ethno-nationalism in the First World: The Present in Historical Perspective', in Milton J. Esman (ed.), *Ethnic Conflict in the Western World* (Ithaca, N.Y., 1977), pp. 27-30; Anthony D. Smith, *Nationalism in the Twentieth Century* (Oxford, 1979), pp. 161-2.
54. For example, see Milton J. Esman, 'Scottish Nationalism, North Sea Oil, and the British Response', in Esman (ed.), *Ethnic Conflict in the Western World*, p. 260.
55. This argument has been advanced in Tom Nairn, *The Break-Up* of Britain (London, 1977), pp. 178-9; E. J. Hobsbawn, 'Reflections on *The Break-Up of Britain*', *New Left Review*, 105, (1977), pp. 3-23, especially pp. 5-7. and A. H. Birch, 'Minority Nationalist Movements and Theories of Political Integration', *World Politics,* 30 (1978), pp. 325-44, especially pp. 334-6.
56. See Harvie, *Scotland and Nationalism*, p. 164, and Arend Lijphart, 'Political Theories and the Explanation of Ethnic Conflict', in Esman (ed.), *Ethnic Conflict in the Western World*, pp. 58-9.
57. Milton J. Esman, 'Perspectives on Ethnic Conflict in Industrialized Societies', in Esman (ed.), *Ethnic Conflict in the Western World* offers this explanation, as does Cynthia H. Enloe, *Ethnic Conflict and Political Development* (Boston, 1973), pp. 273-4. Alain Touraine, *The Post-Industrial Society* (London, 1974), p. 37, mentions ethnic minorities and declining regions among the groups disadvantaged by the 'post-industrial' society.
58. Patricia Elton Mayo, *The Roots of Identity* (Harmondsworth, 1974), argues this case in moderate terms, Michael Zwerin, *A Case for the Balkanization of Practically Everyone* (London, 1976), does so in rather less measured terms. These are not, of course, the only explanations. For another, see the attempt to account for the resurgence of ethnic identity in general by the decline of the affect or warmth associated with class identity in, Daniel Bell, 'Ethnicity and Social Change', in Nathan Glazer and Daniel P. Moynihan, (eds.), *Ethnicity: Theory and Experience* (Cambridge, Mass., 1975), pp. 167-9.

59. For the sake of accuracy one should mention the *Sounderbund* of seven Catholic cantons which was defeated in a short civil war in 1847 and the contemporary dispute over the French speaking Jura. However, for a country as linguistically, religiously, and institutionally diverse as Switzerland, the prevailing impression is of success in managing potential separatism. For the *Sounderbund* see Hans Kohn, *Nationalism and Liberty, The Swiss Example* (London, 1956), chapters 12 and 15; for the Jura problem see William Petersen, 'On the Subnations of Western Europe', in Glazer and Moynihan (eds.), *Ethnicity: Theory and Experience*, pp. 193-5.
60. I do not forget Britanny, Corsica, Provence and the French Basques, but only the first two have produced autonomism on a serious scale and the areas and proportion of the population affected are less than is the case in the United Kingdom.
61. Consociational democracies are those that solve the problems of potentially deep communal divisions by allowing the various communities to live separate lives as far as possible while their élites settle the most vexed problems by negotiations in which caution and progress through unanimous agreement are key features. The creator and foremost champion of the concept is Arend Lijphart, and his most extensive treatment of the subject, containing full references to other defenders and critics, is *Democracy in Plural Societies* (New Haven, 1977).
62. Ireland is the obvious counter-example, but it did not share in the nineteenth-century achievements of Britain.
63. See Richard Pipes, *The Formation of the Soviet Union, Nationalism and Communism* (Cambridge, Mass., 1964; Revised edition).
64. There can be no doubt about the suppression of Basque and Catalan nationalism after the Spanish Civil War, see Juan J. Linz, 'Opposition to and under an Authoritarian Régime: The Case of Spain', in R. A. Dahl (ed.), *Regimes and Oppositions* (New Haven, 1973), pp. 240-52. However it has sometimes been argued that the quiescence of Soviet nationalities owes something to that state's elaborate nationalities policy, as in Alfred Cobban, *The Nation State and National Self-Determination* (London, 1969; Second edition), ch. XII, especially pp. 216-18. Useful recent surveys are E. Allworth (ed.), *Soviet Nationality Problems* (New York, 1971), and J. R. Azrael (ed.), *Soviet Nationality Policies and Practices* (New York, 1978). However, whatever the contemporary position, it can scarcely be denied that the nationalist movements of the 1917 to 1923 period were put down by force, as is clearly documented in Pipes, *The Formation of the Soviet Union*.
65. Italian unification proceeded through straightforward annexation by Piedmont and imposition of that state's constitution so that few regional institutions survived, see G. Procacci, *A History of the Italian People* (Harmondsworth, 1973), pp. 324-5. German unification on the other hand left the constituent states with many institutions and rights, including a king and a diplomatic service in the case of

Bavaria, see B. E. Howard, *The German Empire* (London, 1906), pp. 26-7 and ch. XII.

66. One should not forget the brief separatist movement in Sicily after the Second World War (Procacci, *A History of the Italian People*, p. 448) or the problems of the French-speaking Val d'Aosta and German-speaking South Tyrol or the rash of tiny regionalist parties in the early years of both the Weimar Republic and post-war West Germany see S. L. Fisher, *The Minor Parties of the Federal Republic of Germany* (The Hague, 1974), pp. 69-76. But none of these amounts to a serious attempt at refragmentation on the part of one of the major constituents of the states created in the nineteenth century.
67. A brief account in English of the Bavarian People's Party is G. Pridham, *Hitler's Rise to Power, The Nazi Movement in Bavaria, 1923-33* (St. Albans, 1973), pp. 64-70. A recent German treatment is Klaus Schohoven, *Die Bayerische Volkspartei, 1924-32* (Düsseldorf, 1972).
68. Linz, 'Early State Building and Late Peripheral Nationalism', p. 102, offers this explanation.
69. Brief discussions of modern German federalism are R. Hiscocks, *Democracy in West Germany* (London, 1957), ch. VII and Peter H. Merkl, Germany, *Yesterday and Tomorrow* (New York, 1965), pp. 214-22).
70. Luigi Graziano, 'Centre-Perphery Relations and the Italian Crisis: The Problem of Clientalism', in S. Tarrow et al. (eds.), *Territorial Politics in Industrial Nations* (New York, 1978), especially pp. 297-313.

CHAPTER 4

Separatism and the Irish Nationalist Tradition

D. G. Boyce

'Ireland's historic claim is for Separation. Ireland has authorized no man to abate that claim'.[1] Here, with his characteristically rhetorical flourish, Patrick Pearse expounded one of the most pervasive and lasting of the many myths surrounding Irish nationalism: that 'the Irish who opposed the landing of the English in 1169 were Separatists'; that 'the twelve generations of the Irish nation . . . who maintained a winning fight against English domination in Ireland were Separatist generations'; that 'up to 1691, Ireland was Separatist'; and that separatism was 'the national position'.[2] Pearse's judgement was not only historically dubious; it conveniently overlooked the fact that he himself regarded the 1912 home rule bill, which offered a limited form of devolution to Ireland, as a satisfactory settlement, providing that England kept faith, and gave effect to its promises.[3] But to Pearse, and to many who followed him, any Irish nationalist who was not a separatist, like Henry Grattan, Daniel O'Connell, or John Redmond, was not really a nationalist in Irish political terms; and he cited as proof of this contention the repudiation of the non-separatists by succeeding generations of Irishmen: Wolfe Tone, Young Ireland, the Fenians, and in his own day the Irish Volunteers, were 'the forces that maintained the continuity of the chain of the Separatist tradition' that had never once snapped through the centuries.[4]

Pearse was a firm admirer of the Ulster Volunteers who had been founded in 1912 to resist the imposition of the home rule bill on Ireland; as he put it, the Orangeman with a rifle was a much less ridiculous figure than the nationalist without a rifle; and he hoped that negotiations might be opened up with the Ulster Volunteers on the basis that 'you are erecting a provisional government of Ulster—make it a provisional government of Ireland and we will recognize and obey it'.[5] Physical force Unionism gave Pearse a sense of common ground with the

Orangemen; but his reading of Irish history had much in common with them as well. For Pearse, like the Unionists, believed that Irish nationalism, if it were to be considered nationalist at all, was at bottom separatist, hostile to Britain and to the British empire. Hence Pearse's admiration for Charles Stewart Parnell, 'less a political thinker than an embodied conviction; a flame that seared, a sword that stabbed', a nationalist leader who struck at the English with such weapons as were available, and whose 'instinct was a Separatist instinct'. To Parnell home rule was not a 'final settlement between the two nations', but a way to achieve the 'greater thing'.[6] To Pearse and to the Unionists there could be no half way house between union and separation; Irish nationalism could not be reconciled with the essential unity of the United Kingdom; and the Gladstonian tradition of reconciling 'local patriotism' with 'imperial patriotism'[7] was a chimera.

Pearse's reading of Irish history was tendentious; but his myth of the eternal separatist struggle, like many historical myths, contained certain grains of truth. It was straining credulity to maintain that a nationally united Ireland had existed from the arrival of the Gaels, for Ireland, with its conglomeration of independent kingships, its local rivalries and patriotisms, its lack of a national heartland, its topographical fragmentation easily drew the comment that 'the Irish are a byword for their prolonged failure to create an effective united Irish state'.[8] This patch-work quilt of Irish political institutions, the dynastic sub-kingdoms, the network of local supremacies were, however, altering by the twelfth century, and the High-Kingship of Ireland, while still too weak to resist external threat or the resurgence of localism in Ireland itself, was becoming the focus of political life.[9] But more significant was the saga literature of Ireland which grew from this series of dynastic struggles. One of the most famous 'cycles of the kings' was a biography of Brian Boru, written in the twelfth century in support of the pretensions of his descendants, the O'Brian kings of Ireland, and entitled 'The war of the Gaedhil (Gael) with the Gall (foreigner).' In it Irish history was depicted—not for the last time—as a struggle against foreigners (in this case the Norsemen) which reached a triumphal climax with the rise of the royal house of Dal Cas and the career of Brian.[10]

Poetic literature of this kind might be taken as evidence of separatist tendencies; and certainly the Gaels had a strong sense of race and of pride in Gaelic culture, a sense of pride and race which all Gaelic princes possessed, no matter how much they allied with the foreigner when it suited their political purposes.

Such alliances were not, of course, regarded in any sense as unpatriotic; but the poets and their patrons found it useful at least to portray them in a particular light: the battle of Clontarf in 1014, which was part of the revolt of the men of Leinster against the dominance of Brian Boru, aided and abetted by their Norse allies, was subsequently elevated into a heroic saga of a sovereign of Ireland who led the forces of the nation to victory over the foreigners.[11] It was this ability to combine patriotic literature with political self-seeking that enabled the Gaels to preserve their principles while sacrificing them for their local and particularist aims. And this was all the more important after the coming of the Normans in 1169, for, gradually but steadily, the Gaels had to adjust themselves to the realization that English power had come to Ireland to stay. There was no simple process of 'Irish' resistance to the English, lasting unbroken from 1169 to 1921; there never were two sides in Ireland whose history can be reduced to such simple proportions. But the Normans were the forerunners of the English colony in Ireland, and the presence of that colony was to have a profound impact on the nature of national identity in Ireland, and on the expression of the political rights of the country.

Now that Ireland was no longer an isolated land, contact with the foreigner gave a strength and meaning to the cultural and linguistic unity of the Gaels. The lordship of Ireland in theory covered the whole country; but in fact Ireland was governed under two systems, that of the native kings and that of feudal law in Norman-occupied territory. This division between 'native' and 'colonist', between the 'foreigners of Ireland' and the Gaels, dominated the course of Irish history and has not altogether been eradicated even today. It was never a rigid division, for at different times, and in different parts of the country, it seemed on the point of disappearing or of becoming politically meaningless. Nor was it a racial one, for intermarriage between 'settler' and 'native', and the adoption of each other's ways, made Irish society more complex than the division would suggest. But it survived and outlived local peculiarities, the lack of political unity among the Irish, and their failure to see far beyond their own regions. The Irish experience of post-twelfth century colonization paralleled that of Wales: in both cases the settler/native dichotomy came to correspond to identifiable national groups, Welsh and English, Irish and English, and, in seventeenth-century Ireland, Irish, Old English and New English.

The English presence in Ireland, like that in Wales, was not merely a military one; it was accompanied by administrative, governmental and legal innovations which were to shape the country's development and give it a new focus, replacing the high-kingship, around which Irish political ambitions could gather. By the end of the thirteenth century the English kings had given Ireland what she had never possessed before: a parliament. It was far from representative of the whole people of Ireland, and much of its legislation was anti-Gaelic; but the Norman, or, as it may now be called, the Anglo-Irish-colony soon began to make the English government realize that its position of dependence on England did not mean that its loyalty could be taken for granted. Rifts between the 'English of England' and the 'English of Ireland' occurred in 1341, 1376 and 1460; and on each occasion the Irish parliament asserted the 'rights of Ireland', claiming in 1460 that 'the land of Ireland is and at all times has been corporate of itself by the ancient laws and customs used in the same, freed of the burden of any special law of the realm of England, save only for such laws as by the lords spiritual and temporal and the commons of the said land shall have been in great council or parliament there held admitted, accepted, affirmed and proclaimed'.[12] Such claims were historically invalid; but the Anglo-Irish assertion of political rights and claims was important, in that it gave some institutional framework to the idea of a unitary Irish state, and, more important, set Irish political thinking firmly in the non-separatist framework. The Gaels still maintained their tradition of racial distinctiveness, and their myth of the native Irish fighting to throw off the foreign oppressor; but even they knew better than to try a final round with the English government, and they were always anxious to seek accommodation with the crown before they had recourse to arms. In so far as there was a separatist idea, it might indeed be said, as Pearse said, that it was to be found in Gaelic Ireland. But Gaelic separatist rebellions before the seventeenth century were essentially acts of last extremity, moved by a despairing recognition that no other arrangement or compromise with the English crown was possible. And Anglo-Irish rebellions were anything but separatist in intention; indeed, for the Anglo-Irish to seek to throw off English rule was to seek their own destruction; and nowhere is the lack of separatist intention more evident than in the rebellions of the Tudor and Stuart period.

After 1500 both the Gaelic Irish and the Anglo-Irish were faced with a new and alarming series of developments in English policy towards Ireland. First the increasing and more systematic attention paid to Irish affairs by the English government; and secondly the policy of plantation, attempted in Mary and Elizabeth's reign, and more successfully in the reign of James I. It was English reform schemes, and particularly those of Thomas Cromwell in the 1530s, that proved what has been called the 'first major rebellion in Ireland in the modern period',[13] the rebellion of the Anglo-Irish noble Kildare family in 1533-4; and it was the plantation policy, with all its dire implications for the colonists and natives alike, that, in 1598 and 1641, provoked armed revolt in Ulster that engulfed all Ireland in general civil war.

Nationalist historiography has cited these rebellions as early examples of the national spirit that maintained resistance to English rule right up to the twentieth century; but the motives of the rebels were far from those attributed to them by later generations. For these rebels—the Kildare family and Hugh O'Neill in the sixteenth century, the Native Irish and the Old English in the seventeenth—were anxious to come to terms with the English crown, and, indeed, to demonstrate that, given their just demands, they would prove good and loyal subjects to that crown. The Kildares were anxious not to lose their political and administrative primacy in Ireland, held under the authority of crown government. And their rebellion was a way of demonstrating that the crown could not rule Ireland without their assistance: that exclusion from government meant political chaos in Ireland.[14] The Gaelic chieftain Hugh O'Neill only rose in revolt when English government policy seemed to threaten his personal position in Ulster, and strained his earlier loyalty to breaking point.[15] Similarly, the Native Irish and Old English rebels of 1641, particularly the Old English, were anxious to make terms with the crown to secure their titles to their lands and prevent further encroachment on their titles by the English government and the new settlers. The Old English were rebels, paradoxically, in order to demonstrate their loyalty to the crown, but not to the English Parliament.[16] Even the Native Irish sought that the king should 'maintain that just prerogative which might encounter and remove' the danger to their land, lives and religion.[17]

The mention of religion introduces one of the major factors in the making of modern Irish nationalism; but it is important to emphasize that, until the mid-seventeenth century, religion was not the unifying force that it became shortly afterwards, and has remained ever since. The Old English were Catholics, and they were well aware that the Elizabethan conquest was a Protestant one, and a danger to them; and the Kildare rebellion of 1534 was encouraged by a 'pro papal' lobby, and given a religious dimension by that lobby. But the Old English and Native Irish were distinctive groups, and the Old English sought to maintain and emphasize that distinction, remaining aloof from Irish Catholic and English Protestant alike. Even when they joined the Native Irish in rebellion in 1641, the Old English sought to maintain their separate identity and interests. Indeed, shortly before the outbreak of the rebellion, the Old English had combined in the Irish Parliament with representatives of the New English to attack Strafford, the Lord Deputy of Ireland, and to assert the right of the king's Irish subjects 'to be governed only by the common laws of England and statutes of force in this kingdom, in the same manner and forme, as his Majesty's subjects of the Kingdom of England.'[18]

The most important factor in creating a single Catholic nation in the seventeenth century was the attitude and policy of the English government and people. The fine but deep distinctions between the Native Irish and the Old English were not appreciated by their opponents. Papists—whatever their racial origin—were regarded as disloyal, as at best 'half-subjects' of the crown. Thus Edmund Spenser, writing in the years 1595-96, constructed a dialogue between Ireneus and Eudoxus, in which Ireneus referred to the 'chiefest abuses' in Ireland which were 'grown from the English' some of whom, 'are now much more barbarous and licentious than the very wild Irish'. The Old English needed 'a sharper reformation than the Irish; for they are more stubborn and disobedient to law and government than the Irish be'.[19] Sir John Davies, whose *Discovery of the true causes why Ireland was never entirely subdued* was published in 1612, likewise referred disparagingly the the 'degenerate' Old English who 'became metamorphosed like Nebuchadnezzar, who, after he had the face of a man, had the heart of a beast'.[21] In 1598 the Old English remained stedfast to the crown; but the spectacle of Native Irish and Old English combining in rebellion in 1641 only served to confirm New English and Protestant prejudice that birds of a feather flew together. It was not the Old English, nor even the Native Irish, that destroyed the Catholic Anglo-Irish tradition, with its attempt to reconcile the Pope's spiritual primacy with their loyal duty to uphold the political authority of the English crown, but the English settlers and parliament. This fusion of two races in one Catholic nation, which would have appeared—to say the least—unlikely in the sixteenth century, was now given reality, and by the end of the seventeenth century was complete.[21] Thus William King, writing in 1691 to justify

Protestant rebellion against the Catholic King James, readily identified the 'Popish Irish interest in Ireland' and cited a letter from one Catholic bishop to another, written in 1689, which identified two parties in Ireland 'to wit, the Protestant. Newcomers and Usurpers' and 'the Catholics of Ireland'.[22] This schematic diagram was still an oversimplification, for there was by no means an identity of interest between the Presbyterians of Ulster and the Anglo-Irish members of the episcopal church; but it was accurate enough in time of political crisis in the seventeenth century. And the fusion of 'Catholic' and 'Irish' was so complete that later Irish nationalists could lament the fall of the Geraldines in the 1530s, or the Old English rebels in 1650 at the hands of Oliver Cromwell, without acknowledging that they were lamenting, not the collapse of 'Irish', but rather of Old English racial identity and power in Ireland.

It was this sense of Catholic/Irish identity that was the major factor—from the seventeenth century to the twentieth—in preventing the political assimilation of Ireland to England. Before the 1641 rebellion there were elements working towards such an assimilation: the growing prosperity of Ireland after 1603, the benefits of peace; and after the crushing of rebellion by Cromwell there was a golden opportunity to eradicate religious differences, a line of action that had earlier been proposed by Edmond Spenser who wanted 'some discreet ministers of their (the Irish) own countrymen' to be sent over, and who contrasted the zeal of the 'Popish priests' with that of the ministers of the Gospel, who could not be 'drawn forth from their warm nests to look out into God's harvest'. Protestant evangelism and education, the introduction of English customs, language and dress, the establishment of English law, could, after the Cromwellian conquest, all be pressed forward, and a drive made against Catholic worship. But this faltered during the Interregnum; too few preachers were sent; the Catholic church responded vigorously, and had earlier published devotional works in Irish; and the number of converts, although not inconsiderable, was insufficient and transient.[23] Ireland, like the Netherlands, retained its peculiar religion despite the policies of the head of state. Moreover, Englishmen were obsessed with the idea of the collective guilt of the Irish for the atrocities of the 1641 rebellion, and used Catholicism as an 'index of guilt'.[24] Most important of all, the increasing proportion of land held by Protestants after 1650 meant that the Catholics' economic interests must clash with those of the new owners of the land; and whereas it was possible that the New English interest could stand by and watch the English government concede measures of toleration to their enemies, they certainly could not stand by and see that 'which they had gotten with their lives' filched from them 'with ayes and noes'.[25] John Keating wrote:

> We sold our estates in *England,* transported us and our families into Ireland, to purchase, improve and plant there. We acquired lands under as secure titles as Acts of Parliament . . . could make them. Our conveyances both by Deeds and matters of Record are allowed good, firm and unquestioned by any Law in force at the time of the Purchase. We have had our possession 10, 12 or 15 years, and are grown old upon them. We have clearly drawn our effects from *England* and settled here, not doubting but our posterity may be so likewise. Now old proprietors . . . would have a new law to dispossess us of our estates and improvements made as aforesaid.[26]

The gulf between Catholics and their English rulers, never very wide in the period from the Reformation to 1641, was now not only deep, but possibly unbridgeable—at least, unbridgeable as long as the new Protestant ascendancy, now firmly planted because of Cromwellian policy, held sway in Ireland.[27]

Yet, paradoxically, it was this Protestant ascendancy that gave Irish nationalism an institutional framework in the eighteenth century, and which inspired later Irish nationalists to admire its achievements—or some of them—despite the century or more of political impotence and degradation that followed the Protestant victory in 1690. The Protestant ascendancy was, of course, an Anglican one, and viewed the Presbyterians of Ulster with almost as much suspicion as it viewed the Catholics; but it had come to live and stay in Ireland, and it came to identify with the country it lived in. It was quick to assert the rights of Ireland—particularly the economic rights of Ireland—against English mercantilist policies; and, more important, it had some kind of permanent institutional body around which such patriotic ideas and idealists could rally—it had a parliament which, however venal and corrupt in the normal eighteenth century manner, nevertheless developed some sense of corporate identity, which could be touchy about its relations with the English executive in Dublin Castle, and which provided a focal point for Protestant grievance and Protestant pride.

The Anglo-Irish patriots believed that they were the genuine descendants of the original Irish nation, and however absurd that claim may seem to modern eyes, they ransacked history to establish their right to make it. When William Molyneux, M.P. for Dublin University, investigated *The Case of Ireland's being bound by Acts of Parliament in England* in 1698, he was inspired to do so by the English parliament's promise to linen manufacturers in England that it would consider passing legislation prohibiting altogether the export of woollen goods from Ireland to any foreign country; but he based on this particular case a general statement of the kingdom of Ireland's constitutional rights, tracing how Ireland became a kingdom annexed to the crown of England, denying that Ireland was ever a conquered country (and thus a country that could be said to have forfeited the right to the English parliament to exercise jurisdiction over her), and describing an 'original compact' between Henry II and the people of Ireland 'that they should enjoy the like liberties and immunities, and be governed by the same . . . laws, both civil and ecclesiastical, as the people of England'. Under the 'three first Kings of Ireland under the Norman race the laws and liberties of the people of England, were granted to the people of Ireland'. Molyneux was anxious to emphasize that the kingdom of Ireland *was* annexed to the imperial crown of England, and he acknowledged that 'we must ever own it our happiness' that this was so; yet, even so, Ireland had always enacted statutes relating to the succession 'by which it appears that Ireland, tho annexed to the Crown of England has always been looked upon to be a Kingdom compleate within itself, and to have all jurisdiction to an absolute kingdom belonging, and subordinate to no legislative authority on earth'. Like Jonathan Swift, Molyneux asserted that Ireland was not a colony; she had a right to be 'partakers of the Freedoms' contained in Magna Carta.[28]

Molyneux slid easily from asserting the rights of this ancient kingdom of Ireland to assuming that he was one of its descendants: the 'laws and liberties of England were granted above 500 years ago to the People of Ireland', he concluded,[29] clearly assuming that he and his people could be numbered amongst them. Another eighteenth-century M.P. and patriot, Sir Jonah Barrington, explained that the British settlers of the seventeenth century 'evinced a more than ordinary attachment to the place of their settlement, and vied with the Irish in an inveterate hostility to the domination of their own compatriots; and in the direct descendants of those British colonists, England has since found many of the most able, distinguished, and perservering of her political opponents'.[30] Barrington even took some pride in the attempts by seventeenth-century Catholics to resist that very monarch to whom he owed his present security: Ireland was loyal to James, but England negotiated with a foreign prince to invade their country and overthrow their monarch: 'at the head of his foreign guards, William, unequivocally an usurper, marched into the metropolis of Great Britain, seized on the throne'; but Ireland defended her legitimate monarch against 'the usurpation of a foreigner'.[31]

The arguments put forward by the eighteenth-century Protestant nationalists closely resembled those stated on behalf of the Old English by Patrick Darcy in the Irish parliament in 1641, shortly before the outbreak of the rebellion that destroyed the Old English as a social and political force.[32] As far as most Protestants were concerned, these ideas and the protestant nationalism that inspired them did not outlive the end of the Irish parliament in 1800; but they inspired a political 'revolution' in 1782-3 which resulted in the Irish parliament gaining a greater measure of legislative autonomy under the inspired leadership of Henry Grattan. Later Irish nationalists, who harboured contempt and bitterness against the Protestant Ascendancy, professed to admire 'Grattan's parliament'[33] and some, like Daniel O'Connell in the 1840s and Arthur Griffith in the 1900s worked for its restoration.

But any return of a parliament to Ireland after 1800 would mean a parliament very different in character and composition from that of the Protestant Ascendancy. And the later eighteenth century and early nineteenth century saw the finishing touches in the evolution of an Irish sense of identity, of nationality. It is this question of what constituted the Irish nation, of what indeed constituted Irishness, that was of fundamental importance in the making of modern Irish nationalism; it was the emergence of a particular kind of Irish identity that caused the vast majority of Irish Protestants to abandon any regret about the dissolution of the Irish parliament in 1800, to forget that they had ever sought to defend the rights of Ireland against England. For it was now that the Catholic nation of the seventeenth century, submerged but not destroyed in the eighteenth century, was resurrected as a concept, and given political direction.

The problem of what constituted the Irish nation, of what an Irish identity consisted, did not trouble most Irish Protestants in the first three quarters of the eighteenth century. The Irish nation and the Protestants were synonymous. Yet there was some unease, found even in the exhuberant and facile pages of Sir Jonah Barrington. Barrington admitted that the penal laws bore heavily on 'four fifths of the Irish population', though he was quick to assert that these laws damaged Protestants as well, since the Catholics could blame all their failings on their implementation. He praised the Catholics for supporting the 'revolution' of 1782. He attributed the rise of the Volunteers, an armed Protestant body which played an important part in the events of 1782-3, partly to the 'warlike propensities of the Irish people, so long restrained' yet admitted that the Dissenters (who played a prominent part in the movement) were 'a people differing in character from the aboriginal inhabitants' of Ireland.[34] Faced with these contradictions, Barrington took refuge in two myths that have since been exploited by Irish nationalists: that divisions within the people of Ireland were due to English policies of 'divide and rule', of setting Irishman against Irishman; and that in any case Irishmen of different religious and political persuasions could always be relied upon to sink their differences against the common enemy, England.[35]

The question of who the 'Irish people' were was one that the Protestants could not resolve to their satisfaction; and it was left to the brutal honesty of one of the chief supporters of the union with Britain, Lord Clare (who had been a patriot in the palmy days of 1782) to state the fundamental and insoluble dilemma of the eighteenth century Protestant nationalist: 'When we speak of the People of Ireland', he said,

> it is a melancholy truth that we do not speak of the great body of the people. This is a subject on which it is extremely painful to me to be obliged to speak, but it is necessary to speak out. The ancient nobility and gentry of this Kingdom have been hardly treated: that Act by which most of us hold our estates was an act of violence . . . that gentlemen may know the extent of this summary confiscation, I will tell them that every acre in this country which pays quit rent to the Crown is held by title derived under the Act of Settlement, passed immediately after the Restoration. Gentlemen upon the opposite-bench should consider how far it may be prudent to pursue the successive claims of dignified and unequivocal independence made for Ireland by the right honourable gentlemen.[36]

The Protestant dilemma was made more cruel in the last decades of the eighteenth century by the vexed question of franchise and parliamentary reform. To admit Catholics and also Dissenters to political power could well mean the destruction of the ascendancy, as Clare feared; and this fear was rendered acute by the active efforts of many presbyterians in the north of Ireland to combine Catholic and Dissenter in a revolutionary movement, centred on the Volunteers, and aiming at the overthrow of the Ascendancy, but not, at first, the separation of England and Ireland. The French Revolution first introduced the idea of a republic into the Irish nationalist vocabulary; but the apostle of Irish republicanism Theobald Wolfe Tone admitted that the fathers of protestant nationalism, Jonathan Swift and William Molyneux, had anticipated his 'great discovery', that 'the influence of England was the radical vice of our Government'. Tone, of course, moved much further along the continuum of Irish nationalism than Swift or Molyneux, for, inspired by the French revolution, he resolved to 'break the connection with England, the never-failing source of all our political evils';[37] and to accomplish this he sought to make the object of the United Irishmen 'to unite the whole people of Ireland, to abolish the memory of all past dissensions, and to substitute the common name of Irishman in place of the denominations of Protestant, Catholic, dissenter'.[38] This is, of course one of the most oft quoted phrases in the Irish nationalist breviary; but what is not so often quoted is Tone's next comment: that 'the protestants I despaired of from the outset for obvious reasons . . . it was not to be supposed that they would ever concur in measures the certain tendency of which must be to lessen their influence as a party, how much soever the nation might gain'. And his description of the 'Catholics, who are the Irish, properly so called',[39] was another implicitly damaging admission.

Tone, however, was a shrewd observer of the 'Irish, properly so called', in one sense, though less shrewd in another. They were, he stated, 'trained from their infancy in an heriditary hatred and abhorrence of the English name, which conveys to them no ideas but those of blood, and pillage and persecution . . . strong in numbers and in misery, which makes men bold'.[40] It was this peasant misery that gave fuel to the United Irish ideas of revolution, and caused them to seek an alliance with the already existing Catholic Defencer organization, a secret society aimed at protecting the Irish Catholic peasant against his enemy, the Protestant Orangemen. Such peasant societies had existed before the 1790s, and indeed were endemic in eighteenth-century Ireland; and their aims were by no means political let alone nationalistic. But in the atmosphere of secterian tension and economic hardship in the late eighteenth century, coupled with the wave of Catholic disappointment over franchise reform in 1795, they were material for revolution, as Tone perceived.[41]

But what sort of material and for what sort of revolution? What would the aims of the 'Irish, properly so called' be? Any rising of the 'Irish' would hardly be a rising of people attached to the ideas of the French enlightenment, even though it might have a veneer of continental republicanism. Indeed, it might properly be said that the rebellion was two separate rebellions: that of the presbyterians of the North, inspired by a genuine enthusiasm for ideas of democracy, liberty and reform; and that of the Catholics in Armagh, and also in Wexford, who had not only their traditional grievances to think of, but also the tender attentions of the troops with which the government flooded the country from 1796. The dual character of the '98 rebellion is epitomized in an incident at Ballycarry, near Carrickfergus, Co. Antrim, when the local regiment of Presbyterian rebels had as its adjutant one Larry Dempsey, a deserter from the 24th Dragoons. Dempsey, waving his rusty sword, declared in his Munster Brogue, 'by J...s, boys, we'll pay the rascals this day for the Battle of the Boyne'—a *lapsus linguae* which, not surprisingly, was the cause of an animated debate among the rank and file.[42]

The sectarian violence and bitterness of the '98 rebellion spelt the beginning of the end of the Protestant Irish parliament, which was induced to abolish itself two years later;[43] it also fatally weakened, though it did not totally destroy, Protestant nationalist feeling, which surfaced even in the debates on the union, and was to reappear in the century that followed. But it could not obliterate the eighteenth-century contribution to the nationalist idea; the Protestants who had heard Henry Grattan declare that Ireland was now a nation, and who had rejoiced in the constitution of 1782, whatever the contradictions and weaknesses of their position, had given constitutional expression to the idea of Ireland as a national entity, as a country with a nation and a legislature, and possessing a sense of corporate identity. When nineteenth-century nationalist leaders came to formulate their demands, they always took as their starting point—and many of them as their finishing point—a restoration of Grattan's parliament. The precise powers of that parliament, its limited role in national life, its clumsy and difficult relationship with England were forgotten, and the legislature itself became a symbol of Ireland's 'lost nationhood'. Even the more radical and ambitious nationalists of the Young Ireland persuasion thought essentially in terms of a restoration rather than a new creation; restore Ireland's parliament, and she would be 'a nation once again'. Hence Irish nationalism offered little in the way of abstract theorizing about nationalism; for it was based on a curious mixture of historical grievances on the one hand, and an ambition to restore the parliament that, it was held, had inflicted many of these grievances on the nation in the first place.

It was this demand for a restoration of Ireland's parliament that inspired the first successful mass movement in Irish nationalist politics under the union. Daniel O'Connell feared the consequences of separation of Great Britain and Ireland which must come if Roman Catholics did not enjoy the benefits of the union;[44] and his repeal campaigns of the 1830s and 1840s were attempts to restore 'Ireland' to the 'Irish',[45] to dismantle the Protestant ascendancy and redistribute its political and social power to the majority. The fact that he would have been satisfied with Grattan's parliament did not, however, make him any less a nationalist; he simply believed that if the Roman Catholics, and especially the middle classes, the businessmen, the lawyers, were allowed to exercise the rights that their majority status entitled them to, then separation was unnecessary, and probably harmful. O'Connell gave to Irish nationalism its overwhelming, integrative character, its identification of the Irish nation with the Catholic people; he placed himself at the head of a movement that promised a utopia, a new Ireland for the old nation; and he enlisted the Roman Catholic clergy as his assistants.[46] It was this that alarmed many Protestants, and especially the Young Irelanders, who feared that O'Connell might replace a Protestant ascendancy with a Catholic one; but to the majority it made no sense to try to relegate sectarian issues, for this presupposed that equality between Catholics and Protestants existed, whereas Irish nationalism under the union was fuelled by the belief that no such equality was to be enjoyed as long as England refused self-government. To set aside sectarian issues implied that the 'common name of Irishman' applied in real social, economic, and, perhaps most important of all, psychological terms.[47] 'They're gone, they're gone, those Penal Days', ran Thomas Davis's verse, 'All creeds are equal in our land'.[48] But some creeds were more equal than others in early nineteenth century Ireland; and to most repealers in the 1840s the struggle for Grattan's parliament was one to achieve for Irish Catholics their proper place for themselves and their religion in Ireland.

The great famine of 1847-8 destroyed the repeal movement as it did the desperate attempt by the Young Irelanders to save Ireland by rebellion; and Irish politics fell back to their localized condition.[49] But when nationalist politics were revived—or revived in part and over a small part of the country—in the 1850s, they bore a new note of bitterness and were, for the first time since Tone, overtly separatist. The Fenian Brotherhood was dedicated to the establishment of a separate, but not necessarily a republican, Ireland by force of arms; constitutional means were to the Fenians degrading and demoralizing.[50] Their conspiratorial methods earned them the hostility of the Roman Catholic hierarchy, and they never managed to establish themselves as a broad based nationalist movement. But they helped make Anglo-Irish relations once more the focal point of Irish politics after the localism of the post-famine years; and they revealed that nationalist sentiment could be aroused by persistent and skilful propaganda. As the bishop of Cloyne remarked, the people were Fenians, not because they wanted to give up their faith, but because they hated the Fenian's enemy, England, the enemy of their country, their creed and their pope.[51]

Fenianism was, on its own terms, a complete failure: it did not break down sectarian barriers; it did not arouse the nation to rebellion; it did not defeat England in the field when it chanced its strength in 1867. But it was not a failure in Irish nationalist terms as a whole; and Fenianism's place in the complicated pattern of Irish nationalism that developed between 1858 and 1878 cannot be understood if nationalism is placed within a rigid, compartmentalized structure of 'constitutional' and 'revolutionary' modes, of 'separatist' and 'non-separatist' traditions. The Fenians worked hard to arouse nationalist, and anti-British sentiment for armed revolt; instead they found themselves creating, not armed rebels, but unarmed, yet highly committed, voters. In Tipperary in November 1869 a Fenian prisoner, O'Donovan Rossa, defeated a Catholic Liberal, Heron, by 1131 votes to 1028. The poll was low; but the nature of the turnout was significant, for it saw comfortable farmers at last lining up in the nationalist cause.[52] And not all local priests were hostile to the candidature of a Fenian. The reverend John Hacket made an 'exciting speech off the altar before he concluded mass' at Lisvernane, declaring that Rossa was

> compelled to eat his food like a dog for no crime, that the prisoners might have comitted an error, but they committted no crime, that it was the duty of every man to lose the last drop of blood for his country. . . The priests did not side with the people on the last occasion (i.e. the 1867 rebellion), and they were right, because there was no chance of success . . .'

He then compared O'Connell to Rossa 'in delivering the people from bondage, and W. E. Gladstone to Joshua, and prayed that W. E. Gladstone the leader of the people, like Joshua of the Israelites would lead them to liberty'.[53] It was an unlikely comparison, and one of which O'Connell and Rossa alike would have disapproved; but it pointed the way to the reconciliation of constitutional and physical force nationalism, and to the subsuming of the separatist and non-separatist traditions that lasted until the fall of Parnell in 1891.

The temptation to become involved in constitutional politics was increased after the foundation of the Home Government Association by Isaac Butt in 1870, which soon revealed that its aim of limited self-government was not unattractive to the bulk of the nationalist voters. As far as some Fenians were concerned, home government was nearer the mark than Gladstonian liberalism which had dominated Irish politics in 1868. Butt's cultivation of the extreme men was made easier by his record in the amnesty association which campaigned for the release of Fenian prisoners; and at a meeting in May 1870 in Dublin, to inaugurate the home government association, two members of the supreme council of the Irish Republican Brotherhood promised that they would not obstruct his path.[54] It was a modest beginning, but one that within a short time would see IRB men sitting as home rulers in the British parliament.

The declared aims of the Home Government Association were an extension of the Protestant nationalism first given coherence by Molyneux in the late seventeenth century. Its founder, Isaac Butt, was convinced that Ireland could only be well governed by a real union of hearts and minds, or by a properly functioning representative institution which would not separate Ireland from England, but bind them together in mutual harmony. A true union or an Irish federal parliament were part and parcel of the same desirable end, the well-being of Ireland and the United Kingdom.[55] But the general election of 1874 revealed that home rule could mean different things to different people. It could mean an attack on the Irish landlords, the enemies of the farming classes;[56] it could mean Roman Catholic denominational education;[57] above all, it could mean a 'protest . . . against the Saxon laws of England . . . a protest of Ireland for the Irish and the Irish for Ireland'.[58] The policy of home rule could act as a rallying point for those whose motive was hostility to British rule in Ireland, as well as those, like Butt himself, who saw in it a means of opening a new and hopeful era in Anglo-Irish relations. Home rule could be identified with the same national struggle as Fenianism; it was not merely a modest proposal for rearranging the government of the United Kingdom; and it was this essentially nationalistic aspiration that gave it life in the Irish countryside, especially when, under Charles Stewart Parnell, it became totally identified with the cry of 'the land for the people'.

Parnell's success was based, partly on his political skills, but also on significant changes in Irish society in the middle of the nineteenth century. The great famine accelerated the already existing process of emigration from Ireland, and increased the proportion of emigrants who came from the poorer sections of the community. In particular, the proportion of landless labourers dropped from some 16.1 per cent of the total population in 1841 to 9.1 per cent by 1881; the landless men were a decreasingly important factor in the development of a political movement based upon people who got their livelihood from the land; and the tension between labourers and farmers, which was an aspect of agrarian violence before the famine, became less commonplace, as the surviving labourers found their hardship alleviated since their services were more in demand.[59] Now a solid party base could be built up on the farming classes, although the farmers were themselves by no means a homogenous group, ranging from the rich men of County Cork to the small and poorer men of the west. Moreover, the towns in Ireland were closely linked to the rural economy, with their prosperity depending on the country.[60] And these social developments coincided with changes in the Irish electoral law which enabled the farmer to play an important role in politics in the last quarter of the century. The Irish Franchise Act of 1850 provided for the settlement of the franchise upon the occupation of property to the poor law valuation of £12 in the counties and £8 in the boroughs. Within three year 88.7 per cent of the electorate was registered on the new franchise; the poorer sections of the electorate was excluded; and this uniformly chosen electorate provided the kind of political base that O'Connell had never enjoyed. This electorate was not the half-starved rabble depicted by *Punch;* after 1850 rents lagged behind increases in the value of agricultural output, allowing tenants to become more prosperous; and since they possessed the means to exert political influence, they could use these means to maintain that prosperity in the face of bad times.[61]

The agricultural depression of 1879 checked this prosperity, and raised the spectre of an unacceptable period of hardship for the tenant farmers; and the important thing was that the prospect of economic hardship was unacceptable: no longer were the Irish farmers willing to accept economic setback as a necessary part of their lives.[62] Agrarian radicals and Fenians combined to launch the Land League to replace the existing landlord system with one 'in accord with the social rights and interests of our people'.[63] Parnell, who had made his name in parliament with his militant and at times violent speeches, was eventually persuaded to accept the leadership of the Irish National Land

League; and, slowly and imperfectly, Parnellism, that strange and uneasy alliance of agrarian, constitutional, and physical-force nationalism, was constructed.

Pearse classed Parnell as a separatist; but his rousing nationalist language disguised the essential moderation of his aim, which was the restoration of Grattan's Parliament (whose working, however, he seems to have only imperfectly understood).[64] Nevertheless, Parnell gathered to him the support of advanced nationalists, not only in Ireland, but in Great Britain and America, where the Irish emigrants formed a reserve of financial and moral support for his movement. And he did so because home rule stood, not for an exercise in limited self-government, not for a rational combination of Irish with imperial patriotism, but for passionate political ideology. It stood for the land for the people, (the people meaning the tenant farmers), the undoing not only of the union but of the conquest, for the destruction of the 'Vile garrison', the landlords.[65] It stood for another round in 'the great racial conflict, born in blood and suffering'. It was part of the 'unbroken struggle for nationhood' which was begun in 1169.[66] It was the entering into the promised land of the children of Israel.[67] And, whatever the professed moderation of the home rulers in the British parliament, their movement was based, in Ireland and in the Irish communities in Great Britain and America, on hatred of England, on the kind of sentiments that Fenianism had sought to arouse in the 1860s. When Parnell declared that no man had the right to set bounds to the march of a nation, he choose his words carefully; to clarify home rule, to present it as anything less than the historic struggle of the Irish nation, would have been to forfeit the support of many of his followers. William Redmond in Fermoy emphasized that 'there was nôt a single man from Parnell down to himself who did not hate the government of England with all the intensity and fervour of his heart'. Westminster was an 'alien assembly', full of Saxons, a foreign parliament, and one that the home rulers only attended out of necessity.[68] Thus, while Parnell was not a separatist, the movement that he led was indeed separatist, separatist in its sentiments, separatist, not in its claims, but in its aspirations.[69]

The difference between a claim and an aspiration is not a mere semantic quibble. Home rulers, when they were offered devolution of power by Gladstone in 1886, professed their satisfaction with what was promised to them. Had theirs been a separatist claim, they would have rejected home rule with scorn. But since theirs was a separatist *aspiration,* they could, like Michael

Collins and Arthur Griffith in 1921, accept less than full independence because their acceptance opened the way to freedom, it gave freedom to achieve freedom. Parnell assured the British people that the home rule bill could provide a final settlement; perhaps it was as far as he himself wanted to go; but his was essentially a tactical maneuvre, dictated by the circumstances in which Irish nationalists were placed. Since they regarded the use of force as impracticable (but not unethical), they must take what they could get under the British political system; and it made sense to reassure parliament that devolution meant no more than devolution. But in Ireland devolution meant the Catholic nation (or at least the tenant farming classes of that nation) coming into its own, winning Ireland for the Irish, liberating her from the Saxon, and from the Protestant oppressor.

Irish nationalist organization after the fall of Parnell in 1891 lost the cohesion and strength that his leadership had given it; the physical force nationalists no longer regarded the home rulers as appropriate fellow-travellers, and the party's splits and quarrels discredited and weakened the formidable machine that he had constructed. But Irish nationalism, as distinct from Irish political organization, was not weakened, nor did it show any sign of dying out under the new constructive Unionist policy of killing home rule with kindness. Had home rule been merely a desire for good government, or for a modest rearrangement of the administration of the United Kingdom, then indeed the internecine battles of the parliamentarians, the hopeless plotting of the Irish Republican Brotherhood, even the rise of the cultural nationalism of the 1880s and 1890s, might not have saved Irish nationalism from suffering the fate of Welsh nationalism. It might have become a demand for equal treatment within the United Kingdom;[70] it might have, in its cultural mode, become a pressure group, seeking to preserve the Irish language, the Irish way of life, but still within the political context of the United Kingdom. Political nationalism might have become political reformism; cultural nationalism might have remained exclusively cultural. And James Connolly's disciples would, perhaps, have discovered that their theoretician's separatism was as unlikely of realization as his socialism.

But Irish nationalism was never simply reformist or devolutionist. It was fundamentally a demand for the right of the old nation, of the majority, to rule in Ireland, a demand frustrated not only by the English majority in the British Isles, but by the Protestant minority in Ireland, who still sought to maintain their ascendancy by the device of the Union with Britain. The centenary celebrations of the 1798 rebellion, and of the rising of Robert Emmet in 1803, revealed the emotional appeal of Irish nationalist sentiment, the response that could be elicited by songs and stories of the 'boys of Wexford', of the battle of Vinegar Hill, of Emmet's speech from the dock, of the place of his execution in Dublin, where his blood ran in the streets.[71] Even John Dillon, that most constitutional of nationalists, declared that Wolfe Tone should not only be read but emulated; his writings were a 'precious inheritance to the Irish people and one which if studied and acted upon, will, in my judgement, be the best guide to the patriot's part'.[72]

This line of argument might seem to be contradicted by the history of Ireland during the last phase of the Union; for between 1912 and 1914 home rule was greeted by the reunited Irish Parliamentary party as a final and genuine reconciliation between the British and Irish people; and after 1916 separatism revived, placing the home rulers even further back along the continuum of Irish nationalism that stretched from administrative tinkering to a sovereign Irish republic. But Redmondism was not the same political phenomenon as Parnellism; nor can it be totally identified with Irish nationalism. Home rule in the Ireland of 1910 was still regarded as a step along the road to freedom, as part of the nationalist aspiration, a 'national right', an 'historical legal title'.[73] If, as T. P. O'Connor remarked wittily, devolution was the Latin for home rule,[74] then home rule was the Irish for independence. But Redmond saw other opportunities, other directions in which Irish nationalism might proceed. Now that home rule seemed destined to reach the statute book, it might be possible to forge a genuine union of hearts between Great Britain and Ireland, to create a concept of nationalism that, as Redmond put it, would turn Ireland into a 'happy and prosperous country, with a united, loyal and contented people'.[75]

But the idea of the union of hearts would have required long years of patient re-educating of nationalist Ireland; it would have needed a determined assault on the kind of ideas that the home rulers themselves had expressed in the 1798 celebrations; above all, it would have required a conversion of the Irish unionists, and especially the Ulster unionists, who were as opposed to home rule in 1912 as they had been in 1886. The example of the Ulster Volunteers was emulated in the south of Ireland, and, to the delight of the separatists, the Irish Volunteers were founded to defend the rights of Ireland. Redmond managed to assert his authority over the Irish Volunteers; but the dangers involved in drilling and arming were revealed when, following a confrontation with a party of Volunteers carrying rifles which had been landed at Howth, some Scottish soldiers fired on a crowd of civilians who had been jeering at them and hurling stones and bottles. Thirteen people were wounded and one subsequently died; and the union of hearts seemed about to perish in a fusillade fired by British soldiers.

It was saved, and then given a new and dynamic, but short-lived phase, by the European war of 1914. The war made national unity in the British Isles an essential political goal; and Redmond was able to seize the chance to convince the Liberal government that it must stop prevaricating and place the home rule bill on the statute book. And, now that Ireland 'enjoyed' home rule, now that Ireland and England were fighting in a common cause, and sharing the same experiences, Redmond moved beyond his earlier cautious advice to the British to withdraw their forces from Ireland, leaving the defence of her shores to the Irish and Ulster Volunteers,[76] to a firm and unequivocal commitment of support for Irish recruitment in the British army. Irishmen had always served in the British army, but that did not stop nationalists denouncing it as an oppressive and terrorising force, the murder machine that crushed the Boers, and would crush the Irish if they tried to emulate the Boers. But now Irishmen should go to 'wherever the firing line extends';[77] for Irish military gallantry, Redmond maintained, was essential to verify and substantiate Ireland's claim to nationhood. Like Patrick Pearse, Redmond believed that 'no people can be said to have rightly proved their nationhood and their power to maintain it until they have demonstrated their military powers; and though Irish blood has reddened the earth of every continent, never until now have we as a people set a national army in the field. . . . It is heroic deeds entering into their traditions that give life to nations—that is the recompense of those who die to perform them'.[78]

The idea of a blood sacrifice for Ireland, however, was one that might be realized on other fields than Flanders; and the mystical concept of a union of hearts, enriched by the red wine of the battlefields, was between 1916 and 1918 supplanted by the idea of 'ourselves alone', of the 'right rose tree' watered by 'our own red blood'.[79] The Easter Rising of 1916 at first appeared to vindicate and strengthen Redmond's ideal, for the unpopularity of the rebels, the feeling that they had stabbed Ireland in the back, was widespread. But the executions which followed the surrender of the rebels ensured that, as the home ruler Stephen Gwynn put it, 'Nothing would have prevented the halo of martyrdom from attaching itself to those who died by the law for the sake of Irish freedom; the tradition was too deeply ingrained in Irish history'.[80] This is not surprising; it was after all, a tradition that the parliamentarians had themselves been nourishing since the 1880s, and which they had maintained in the 1798 celebrations and in the annual pilgrimages to the memorials dedicated to the Manchester martyrs, three Fenians executed in 1869 for their part in shooting a policeman.[81]

Redmond's hope of a union of hearts was further damaged by the two sets of people it was intended to embrace. Some British Unionists responded to his emotional appeal for a new start in Anglo-Irish relations;[82] but British official hostility to nationalist Ireland was shown in a series of snubs and slights offered to nationalist requests that southern Irish troops be grouped in a special 'Irish brigade'; and the threat to impose conscription on Ireland smacked further of the English determination to 'drive Ireland'.[83] A union of hearts could not have been based merely on a new constitution for Ireland; it could only succeed if it grew out of a genuine respect for and understanding of the different political traditions of the British Isles, an understanding that might be forged in the common sufferings of the trenches, but one that was unlikely to survive the political atmosphere outside them. Sir Edward Carson caught the mood of many southern, and all northern Unionists when he affirmed that 'we are not going to abate one jot or title of our opposition to home rule, and when you come back from serving your country, you will be just as determined as you will find us at home'.[84]

John Redmond's inability to make home rule a reality, to establish some kind of government in Ireland, was fatal to his cause. Redmond claimed that Irishmen were sacrificing themselves for freedom; but freedom was as far away as ever in 1918, and the whole concept of home rule, with its emotional symbolism, its association with Irish dignity, freedom, and nationhood, was now seen to be a trick, a fraud, almost an insult to the nation. Home rule had stood for independence, and a nation once again; but from 1912, and especially from 1914, its image had been transformed; and now it stood for devolution and a wider British patriotism. This might not have proved unsuccessful in the short term (though its eventual triumph was always doubtful) if all had gone well during the war; but the rising and the conscription crisis had drained home rule of its mystique, and the party suffered losses at by-elections in 1917 and 1918, and then a complete defeat in the general election of December

1918, because it could no longer claim that it stood for the onward march of a nation: 'we would get all that we required and all that would be good for us', one home ruler declared.[85] The new voice of nationalist Ireland, Sinn Féin, captured the ideology of home rule, affirming that it stood in the Parnellite tradition,[86] demanding, not necessarily a republic, but Irish 'freedom'.[87] This is hardly to be wondered at; for the Sinn Féin party had to capture the support of the same kind of people who had formed the backbone of the Home rule movement: the shopkeepers, employers, local priests, clerk and officials, above all, the staunchly conservative but staunchly nationalist tenant farmers.[88] The loyal speeches of Redmond were replaced by the anti-British sentiments of 1917 and 1918; but this represented a return to the older tradition of nationalism, not a radical departure from it. And just as home rule had stood for an undefined independence, so the 'republic' which the Sinn Féin party pledged itself to win before allowing the people to decide what form of government they wanted, stood in the popular mind for 'independence'. In short, 'republic' was now the Irish for independence, just as home rule had been between 1886 and 1912.

The difficulties experienced by Sinn Féin after its election victory of 1918 arose from the fact that it failed to distinguish the separatist claim from the separatist aspiration. The development of the military wing of the independence movement, and the armed struggle with Britain, created martyrs for the cause of the republic; however, it was clear to anyone possessed of political reality that no British government was prepared to concede separation of any kind to Ireland. But the conflict with the crown forces, its heroic deeds, its fasts, hunger strikes, deaths in prison, 'on the hillside or in quicklime',[89] all gave the republic a mystical quality, and created the belief among many that Irishmen could live under 'no other law'.[90] And the oath which was administered to the Sinn Féin deputies in Dáil Éireann in August 1919, obliging its recipients to 'support and defend the Irish Republic', placed Irish nationalism ever more tightly into the strait-jacket of republicanism.[91] From now on nationalism and republicanism became almost synonymous; and anyone who accepted less than republicanism was a traitor to his country.

Fortunately for Ireland there were men, like Griffith and Michael Collins, who could distinguish between a claim and an aspiration. When they accepted dominion status after prolonged negotiations with the British government in 1921, the Irish leaders recognized that there was, as Collins put it 'a path to freedom'. This brought them into conflict with those like Eamon de

Valera who maintained that the republic had been established in 1916, ratified in 1919 and therefore already existed: there could be no paths leading anywhere except away from the republic.[92] Hence Ireland after 1921 came into the category of an 'unsatisfied nationalism';[93] unsatisfied partly because the 1921 agreement in the end confirmed the partition of Ireland made in the 1920 government of Ireland Act, but mainly because in the eyes of many the treaty and the grant of dominion status[94] did not do the fundamental thing: like Pearse, they believed that Ireland's historic claim was for separation and Ireland had authorized no man to abate that claim. Yet in 1921 Irishmen had accepted less than the republic and complete separation, and had acquiesed in the refusal of Ireland's claim. Not even the declaration of the republican status of Ireland in 1949 could compensate for the fact that the mystical republic of 1916 had been subverted by its enemies, and a false, illegitimate pseudo-republic substituted.

The years of the Irish struggle between 1916 and 1922 were therefore highly formative ones in the Irish nationalist tradition; their drama, self-sacrifice, and heroism resulted in the compression of hundreds of years of constitutional and political development into a mythical notion that, as Pearse put it, Ireland's separatist claim existed from the twelth century onwards. In fact, the separatist ideal was a comparatively recent one, perceptible perhaps in the Gaelic rebellions of the Tudor period, but only assuming firm and coherent expression with the conversion of Wolfe Tone and the United Irishmen to the fashionable ideas of French republicanism. The revival of separatism under the Fenians, and the rise of Parnellism in the 1880's, meant that the tone of Anglo-Irish relations was, to coin the phrase used by one critic of the *Nation* newspaper, 'Wolfe Tone';[95] for Parnellism was sustained by the dictum that Irish freedom was a developing and living force, one that could find temporary rest under home rule, and, if the Irish people so desired, move on to greater things. Thus the separatist ideal could be reconciled with the world of politics, and Tone's hope of breaking the connection with England could be regarded as an evolutionary, not a revolutionary, process.

It is possible, if unlikely, that John Redmond's union of hearts ideal might have diverted Irish nationalism into the wider imperial patriotism that Gladstone sought to evoke in 1886. It is possible, but less likely, that devolution of government would have provided, not a starting point, but the final boundary to the march of a nation; even Parnell, in the British context, said as much. But the separatist ideal was given new strength and inspiration by the Ulster revolt against home rule in 1912-14, by the 1916 rising and the executions which followed it, and by the conscription crisis of 1918. Patrick Pearse distorted Irish history when he claimed that the Irish separatist tradition had existed since the coming of the English; but he was right to identify the Orangeman with a rifle as the most heartening sight for Irish separtists in his generation. And his long list of illustrious contributors to the separtist ideal might reasonably have included the name of Sir Edward Carson, along with those of Tone, Thomas Davis, James Fintan Lalor and John Mitchel.

Notes

1. Patrick Pearse, *Political Writings and Speeches* (1918; Dublin, 1966 edition), p. 231.
2. Ibid., pp. 232, 233, 234, 238.
3. Ruth Dudley Edwards, *Patrick Pearse: The Triumph of Failure* (London, 1977), p. 155.
4. Pearse, op. cit., pp. 237-9.
5. Ibid., pp. 185-7.
6. Ibid., pp. 241-4.
7. A. C. Hepburn, *The Conflict of Nationality in Modern Ireland* (London, 1980), pp. 48-50.
8. E. Estyn Evans, *The Personality of Ireland* (Cambridge, 1973), p. 68.
9. D. O Corrain, 'Nationality and kingship in pre-Norman Ireland', in T. W. Moody (ed.), *Nationality and the Pursuit of National Independence* (Belfast, 1978), pp. 1-35; *idem*., *Ireland before the Normans* (Dublin, 1972), ch. 2, and pp. 96-7, 120-31.
10. D. O Corrain, *Ireland before the Normans*, p. 78; J. Otway-Ruthven, *A History of Medieval Ireland* (London, 1968), pp. 24-5.
11. D. O Corrain, op. cit., pp. 130-1.
12. E. Curtis, *A History of Medieval Ireland from 1086 to 1513* (London, 1978), pp. 321-3.
13. B. Bradshaw, 'Cromwellian reform and the origins of the Kildare rebellion, 1533-4' in *T.R.H.S.*, 5th series, 27 (1977), p. 22.
14. Ibid., pp. 86-93.
15. J. C. Beckett, *A Short History of Ireland* (London, 1961), pp. 62-7.
16. P. J. Corish, 'The origins of Catholic nationalism', in *A history of Irish catholicism*, Vol. III, fascicle 8 (Dublin, 1968), pp. 31-40; Aiden Clarke, *The Old English in Ireland, 1625-42* (London, 1960), *passim*.
17. Ibid., p. 222.
18. H. Kearney, *Stratford in Ireland, 1633-41* (Manchester, 1959), pp. 145-9.
19. Henry Morley (ed.), *Ireland under Elizabeth and James I described by Edmund Spenser, by Sir John Davies and by Fynes Moryson* (London, 1890), pp. 101, 192.

20. Ibid., pp. 297-8.
21. Clarke, op. cit., ch. xii; Corish, op. cit., pp. 56-63.
22. William King, *The State of the Protestants of Ireland under the late King Jame's Government* (Dublin, 1730), pp. 61, 81.
23. T. C. Barnard, *Cromwellian Ireland: English Government and Reform in Ireland, 1649-1660* (London, 1975), chapters i, v.
24. Ibid., p. 297.
25. J. C. Beckett, *The Making of Modern Ireland, 1603-1923* (London, 1966), p. 120.
26. King, op. cit., pp. 99-100.
27. As King put it, 'there was no medium, but that we or they must be undone' (op. cit., p. 256).
28. W. Molyneux, *The Case of Ireland's Being Bound* (1698) *passim*, esp. pp. 38, 55, 56, 123. For a covenient summary of early eighteenth-century Irish political ideas see C. Robbins, *The Eighteenth-Century Commonwealthman* (Harvard, 1959), ch. v.
29. Molyneux, op. cit., p. 169.
30. Sir Jonah Barrington, *Rise and Fall of the Irish Nation* (Dublin, 1853), p. 121.
31. Ibid., pp. 129-30.
32. *An argument delivered by Patrick Darcy, Esquire; by the express order of the House of Commons in the parliament of Ireland 9th June 1641* (Dublin, 1764).
33. For a recent example of this bi-focal attitude see Sean O'Sullivan 'A Similarity in our Cases', *Eire/Ireland*, xii, 4 (1977), pp. 6-24, and esp. pp. 15-16.
34. Barrington, op. cit., pp. 6, 15, 59, 61-2, 167.
35. Ibid., pp. 51, 73, 116.
36. S. Gwynn, *Henry Grattan and his times* (London, 1939), p. 228.
37. P. Mac Aonghusa and L. O Reagain, *The best of Tone* (Cork, 1972), pp. 28, 46; J. C. Beckett, *The Anglo-Irish Tradition* (London, 1976), p. 58.
38. P. Mac Aonghusa and L. O Reagain, op. cit., p. 46.
39. Ibid., p. 108.
40. Ibid., p. 110.
41. Marianne Elliott, 'The origins and transformation of early Irish Republicanism', *International Review of Social History* XXIII, 3 (1978), pp. 405-28. I am grateful to Dr. Elliott for allowing me to read this paper before publication.
42. D. H. Akenson and W. H. Crawford, *Local Poets and Social History: James Orr Bard of Ballycarry* (Belfast, Public Record Office of Northern Ireland, 1977), p. 41.
43. R. B. MacDowell, *Irish Public Opinion, 1750-1800* (London, 1944), ch. xiii.
44. M. R. O'Connell, *The Correspondence of Daniel O'Connell*, Vol. III (Dublin, 1974), p. 345; W. E. H. Lecky, *Leaders of Public Opinion in Ireland, Vol. II, Daniel O'Connell* (London, 1912), p. 164.

45. R. Dudley Edwards, *Daniel O'Connell and his World* (London, 1975), p. 43; see also O'Connell's speech at Trim (*Pilot*, 22 March 1843).
46. As Lecky put it, his aim was 'to make the priests the rulers of the country, and himself the rulers of the priests' (*Leaders of Public Opinion*, p. 19); see also G. O Tuathaigh, *Ireland Before the Famine, 1798-1848* (Dublin, 1972), pp. 57-9.
47. Jacqueline R. Hill, 'Nationalism and the Catholic church in the 1840s: views of Dublin repealers', in *Irish Historical Studies*, XIX, 76 (1975), pp. 371-95.
48. O. Dudley Edwards (ed.), *Celtic Nationalism* (London, 1968), p. 137.
49. K. T. Hoppen, 'Landlords, society and electoral politics in mid-nineteenth century Ireland', in *Past and Present*, 75 (1977), pp. 62-93.
50. J. O'Leary, *Recollections of Fenians and Fenianism* (Dublin, 1968), p. 27; R. V. Comerford, *Charles J. Kickham, 1828-82: a study in Irish Nationalism and Literature* (Dublin, 1979), p. 185; T. W. Moody (ed.), *The Fenian Movement* (Cork, 1968), p. 105.
51. P. J. Corish, 'Cardinal Cullen and the National Association of Ireland', in *Reportorium Novum*, III, i (1962), p. 17.
52. J. Lee, *The Modernization of Irish Society 1848-1918* (Dublin, 1972), pp. 18-19.
53. State Paper Office of Ireland, 'F' papers, Constabulary report, 10 Oct. 1869, 4869R.
54. Comerford, op. cit., pp. 119-25; D. Thornley, *Isaac Butt and Home Rule* (London, 1964), pp. 68, 71-3, 88-9.
55. See his argument in *The Famine in the Land* (Dublin, 1847), esp. p. 55; Thornley, op. cit., pp. 97-102.
56. *Flag of Ireland*, 3 Jan., 10 Jan., 7 Feb., 1874; *Waterford News*, 6 Feb., 1874.
57. *Waterford News* 6 Feb., 1874; *Leinster Reporter*, 12 Feb., 1874.
58. *Waterford News*, 6 Feb., 1874; see also the home rule ballads in G. D. Zimmerman, *Irish Political Street Ballads and Rebel Songs, 1798-1900 (Geneva, 1966), pp. 60-1.*
59. *K. T. Hoppen, op. cit.,* pp. 62-93; *O. MacDonagh,* 'Irish famine emigration to the United States' in *Perspectives in American History*, X (Harvard, 1976), pp. 358-9.
60. Lee, op. cit., pp. 97-9; S. Clark, 'The social composition of the land league', in *Irish Historical Studies*, 68, (1971), pp. 447-69, and ibid., 'The political mobilization of Irish farmers', in *Canadian Review of Sociology and Anthropology*, vol 12 (4:part 2) (1975), pp. 483-97.
61. K. T. Hoppen, 'Politics, the law and the Irish electorate, 1832-1850', in *English Historical Review* 92 (1977), pp. 774-6; W. E. Vaughan, 'Landlord and tenant relations in Ireland between the great famine and the land war, 1850-1878', in L. M. Cullen and T. C. Smout (eds.), *Comparative Aspects of Scotish and Irish Economic and Social History, 1600-1900* (Edinburgh, 1977), pp. 216-26.

62. P. Bew, *Land and the National Question in Ireland, 1858-1882* (Dublin, 1978), pp. 8-14, 30-2, 56-8; J. Pomfret, *The Struggle for Land in Ireland 1800-1923* (New York, 1969), pp. 101-3; J. S. Donnelly, *The Land and the People of Nineteenth-century Cork* (Dublin, 1973), pp. 6-7, 148-9, 251-6.
63. M. Davitt, *The Fall of Feudalism in Ireland* (Dublin, 1970), pp. 160-3.
64. F. S. L. Lyons, *Charles Stewart Parnell* (London, 1977), pp. 348 ff.
65. *United Ireland*, 26 Sept., 28 Nov., 19 Dec., 1885.
66. *Cork Daily Herald*, 24 Nov., 1885; *Wexford People*, 3 April, 1880.
67. *Westmeath Independent*, 10 July, 1886.
68. *United Ireland*, 13 June, 1885; see also 14 Nov., 1885 when he declared that one of the qualities required of a Parnellite M.P. was 'that he should hate with all his heart British rule in Ireland'. See also speech of John Dillon *(Connaught People*, 31 Oct., 1885), and William O'Brien's reference to Westminster as 'that foreign parliament' (*United Ireland* 21 Feb., 1885).
69. For a discussion of the crucial difference between a claim and an aspiration see Conor Cruise O'Brien, quoted in Hepburn, op. cit., pp. 205-6.
70. K. O. Morgan 'Welsh nationalism: the historical background' in *Journal of Contemporary History*, 6, (1971), pp. 153-72.
71. W. O'Brien, *Who Fears to Speak of '98* (Dublin, 1898); *United Ireland*, 13 Jan., 1898; *Freeman's Journal*, 19 and 21 Sept., 1903; 'Robert Emmet in poetry', National Library of Ireland, IR 92 E 43, Vol. I.
72. *United Ireland*, 20 Aug., 1898.
73. S. Gwynn, *The Case for Home Rule* (preface by John Redmond) (Dublin, 1911) pp. viii, 5.
74. M. Macdonagh, *The life of William O'Brien* (London, 1928), p. 170.
75. D. Gwynn, *Life of John Redmond* (London, 1932), pp. 52, 55, 202.: D. Fitzpatrick, *Politics and Irish life, 1913-1921* (Dublin, 1977), pp. 92-3.
76. F. X. Martin, *The Irish Volunteers, 1913-1915* (Dublin, 1963), pp. 146-8.
77. F. S. L. Lyons, *Ireland Since the Famine* (London, 1973), pp. 328-9.
78. M. MacDonagh, *The Irish at the Front* (London, 1916), pp. 1-14.
79. W. B. Yeats, 'The Rose Tree' in *Collected Poems* (London, 1973), p. 206.
80. S. Gwynn, *John Redmond's Last Years* (London, 1919), pp. 228-9.
81. The cult of the Manchester Martyrs, which died out after the 1916 rising, needs analysis; the National Library of Ireland has volumes of newspaper cuttings which provide some of the material for this.
82. For example Walter Long; see Gwynn, *John Redmond's Last Years* (London, 1919), p. 216.
83. Ibid., p. 212.
84. Ibid., p. 147.
85. Willie Redmond, *Munster Express*, 14 Dec., 1918.
86. See e.g. *Sligo Champion*, 30 Nov., 1918 (Mr. Osborne); *Wexford Peo-*

ple, 4 Dec., 1918 (Dr. Ryan); *Galway Vindicator*, 7 Dec., 1918 (Revd M. Hayes); *Waterford News*, 22 Nov., 1918 (Mr. Kenny).

87. See P. S. O'Hegarty, *The Victory of Sinn Féin* (Dublin, 1924) p. 2; 'Adhesion to Sinn Féin in 1918 no more committed Ireland to consider nothing but independence than adhesion to Parnell in 1885 committed Ireland to consider nothing but Home Rule'.
88. Fitzpatrick, op. cit., pp. 233, 267; D. W. Miller, *Church, State and Nation in Ireland, 1891-1921* (Dublin, 1973), p. 391.
89. Roger McHugh, 'The rising', in R. O'Driscoll (ed.), *Theatre and Nationalism in Twentieth-century Ireland* (London, 1971), p. 105.
90. F. O'Donoghue, *No Other Law* (Dublin, 1954), a biography of Liam Lynch, catches this mood perfectly.
91. Kevin B. Nowlan, 'Dail Éireann and the army: unity and division, 1919-1921', in T. Desmond Williams (ed.), *The Irish Struggle, 1916-1926* (London, 1966), p. 71.
92. E. Curtis and R. B. MacDowell, *Irish Historical Documents, 1172-1922* (London, 1977 edition), p. 328.
93. H. Seaton-Watson, 'Unsatisfied nationalisms', in *Journal of Contemporary History*, 6 (1971), pp. 3-14.
94. Ireland was given the 'same constitutional status in the community of nations known as the British Empire as the Dominion of Canada, the Commonwealth of Australia, the Dominion of New Zealand, and the Union of South Africa', subject to certain safeguards for British and imperial defence (Hepburn, op. cit., pp. 118-21).
95. J. C. Beckett, *The Making of Modern Ireland, 1603-1923* (London, 1966), p. 334.

CHAPTER 5

The Paradox of Nationalism in Scotland

D. N. MacIver

Introduction

In the House of Commons in April 1967, the Prime Minister, Harold Wilson, with the massive Labour victory of 1966 behind him, declared that his government had no plans for legislative devolution to Scotland.[1] In November of the same year, after the unexpected victory of the Scottish National Party at the Hamilton by-election, devolution was actually considered as a practical possibility by some Labour ministers. Within ten years the Labour party was struggling, not only to protect its position as the dominant party in Scottish politics, but also to gain acceptance for its own plans for legislative devolution. Moreover, preparations were actually being made to accommodate a Scottish Assembly in Edinburgh. The idea of a Scottish parliament, or indeed of the complete separation of Scotland from the United Kingdom, was no longer regarded with the same impatience and hilarity which greeted Russell Johnson's private members bill to establish a separate parliament for Scotland in 1966.[2]

This transformation of the mood and temper of Scottish politics and of attitudes to Scotland's political position in the United Kingdom was a direct result of the emergence of Scottish nationalism as an electoral force whose success threatened the major parties and whose demands challenged the established order of the British state. The dramatic and remarkable career of the SNP during the decade or so after the Hamilton election drew attention to a dimension of British political life which, even in Scotland, had long been overlooked or possibly taken for granted. The new light which this cast on British politics led to a fundamental reassessment of the hitherto orthodox view of the United Kingdom as a homogeneous political society. The idea of homogeneity rested on two general assumptions. The first was that the political, administrative, cultural and communications systems of the United Kingdom were entirely London centred, exposing the whole country to the assimilative effects of a metropolitan culture. The second assumption was that the only major cleavage in British society was class, the effects of which were more or less uniform throughout the country and compared to which other cleavages were relatively insignificant. The emergence of nationalism and the SNP together with the success of Plaid Cymru and the outbreak of communal strife in Northern Ireland appeared to challenge these assumptions. Some political scientists even rushed to redefine the United Kingdom as a multi-national state.[3] There was at least, however, a new awareness that the United Kingdom was perhaps a more diverse and polycentric society than had been hitherto supposed and that nationalism represented an important and unsuspected cleavage possibly cutting across class.

Nationalism may be said to develop and consolidate amongst a people when its members feel that what they have in common *vis-à-vis* outsiders is more important than their differences. The sentiment becomes politically significant when the people make special demands on the strength of it or demand to govern themselves as opposed to being governed or sharing government with others. National separatism can be regarded as a political programme whose objective is to achieve self-government for an ethnically defined population within a given territory on terms likely to lead to the recognition of the resulting entity as an independent national state. The minimum conditions for a successful separation on these lines are a clearly defined territory, a well-established sense of community and national identity and a substantial degree of civil autonomy. On the face of it these conditions are reasonably well satisfied in the Scottish case. On the other hand, while the professed aims of the SNP are self-government and independence for Scotland, there have been persistent doubts whether political support for the SNP is an expression of regional protest and discontent or a genuine demand for self-government. These doubts are to some extent legitimate because Scottish nationalism presents a curious paradox, the essence of which is that Scotland has a clearly defined territory and a strong sense of national identity, but a traditionally weak and ambiguous political nationalism. This paradox can only be fully understood in terms of the total Scottish experience including the significance of historic statehood, attitudes to the union with England and the unique national culture and outlook which this experience has produced. The object of this chapter is first to provide an outline of these general aspects of the question, followed by a brief discussion of modern political nationalism and finally an appreciation of the prospect of secession and the problems associated with it.

The Residue of Statehood

The origins of the Scottish state date back to the early middle ages, about the same period as those of England and France.[4] In fact Scotland first emerged as a unified kingdom in the ninth century when MacAlpine united the Gaelic kingdom of Dalriada (roughly the territory of modern Argyll) with the ancient Pictish kingdoms to the north and east. Strathclyde, Lothian and the eastern lowlands were gradually secured to the emergent Scottish crown by the absorption of the Britons and the defeat and expulsion of the Northumbrians. During the early mediaeval period the territory of Scotland was constantly in dispute with Norway to the north and England to the south. These disputes were resolved by the late thirteenth century when the last Norwegian invasion was repulsed and the border with England, which at times had reached as far south as Yorkshire, was stabilized. Since then the territorial limits of Scotland have remained virtually unchanged.

It is not surprising that the most constant and immediate factor in Scotland's development, shaping the condition of its domestic politics as much as its external affairs, was its relations with England. In this the aftermath of the Norman conquest is of particular significance. Shortly before the conquest Malcolm III, with some English aid, came to the Scottish throne after a bloody series of interdynastic struggles and assassinations. In succeeding years he secured his position with the assistance of Anglo-Norman mercenaries, to whom he gave extensive concessions of lands and titles in Scotland, and sometimes of the English crown itself.[5] Malcolm's marriage to the English princess Margaret marked the beginning of a substantial expansion of Anglo-Norman influence in Scotland. Margaret, in association with the anglophone elements in Scottish society, worked assiduously to anglicize Scottish institutions including the court, the law, the church and the system of land tenure. The net effect was to weaken the hitherto dominant influence of Picto-Gaelic culture, symbolized in the transfer of the royal seat and the centre of government from the celtic south-central Highlands to Edinburgh in the anglophone eastern lowlands. The process of anglicization went furthest in the Lowlands where conditions were more receptive but it was also significant along the north-east littoral as far as Moray and Inverness. It had scarcely any effect in the central and western Highlands where Celtic forms of social organization continued to predominate for several centuries. The result, however, was that a major cultural and socio-political cleavage was entrenched in Scottish society while the country was still engaged in relations of constant tension and frequent conflict with England.

Conflict with England became critical in the late thirteenth century when Scotland faced one of its recurrent crises in the royal succession, brought about by the untimely death of the young heiress to the throne. Edward I of England intervened with the intention of uniting the two kingdoms by a union of crowns, if possible, and by force of arms, if not. The response in Scotland, which eventually involved all sectors and levels of Scottish society, demonstrated that whatever the cultural effects of anglicization, it had not weakened the desire for political independence. Although the English invaded and suppressed opposition, a resistance movement developed which, after a prolonged campaign of guerilla warfare, devastation and siege, faced and defeated the occupying forces in open battle. Thus Scotland was re-established as an independent kingdom and recognized as such throughout Europe.

This was a crucial episode in Scottish history and its popular heroes are celebrated in Scots folklore to this day. Perhaps the most remarkable feature of these so-called Wars of Independence was the scale and scope of popular mobilization and the quality of rhetoric deployed by the Scottish protagonists, which featured a highly developed sense of national consciousness and possibly one of the earliest expressions of nationalism in Western Europe. The most famous document of the period is the Declaration of Arbroath in which the nobility and clergy of Scotland declared that they would not subject '(their) kingdom' to 'the King of the English or to the English people'. The Declaration concluded: 'It is not for glory, riches, or honours that we fight: it is for liberty alone, the liberty which no good man relinquishes but with his life.'[6]

During the centuries following the Wars of Independence, while relations with England remained tense, the Scottish State had a turbulent internal history. The task of state-building and the development of central institutions proved even more difficult in Scotland than in England. The powers of local chieftains and the residual strength of ancient cultural and regional loyalties persisted longer in Scotland. Some of the Scottish magnates possessed independent resources of territorial power and support which for the most part were denied even to the greatest barons in England. For much of the time the authority of the crown, in any case weakened at critical times by minority successions, was of little effect in the highland and border peripheries. Especially in the wild country of the central and western Highlands the central power was remote and frequently disregarded by the clan chiefs. The greatest of these, the Lord of the Isles, chief of clan Donald, could mobilize a formidable army and a great fleet and claimed the sovereign right to treat independently with the powers of Europe. Although the Lord of the Isles was eventually reduced and disinherited, the pacification and integration of the Highlands was a task which the Scottish crown never fully accomplished before the Union. Thus the problem of the Highlands continued into the modern period, perpetuating the ancient division of Scottish society to the extent indeed that Scotland has been described as comprising two nations rather than one.[7]

While the Scottish past has been an important factor in shaping the condition of modern Scotland it is equally important as political myth. This is not to suggest that it is simply legend or falsehood. The myth is a product of Scottish history, incorporating certain values and a set of beliefs about the Scottish experience which shapes the affective and cognitive perceptions of that experience as well as perceptions and evaluations of contemporary politics. For example one component of the Scottish myth is the myth of the 'lost parliament', combining an idealized conception of Scottish democracy with a protest at the supposed denial of Scottish rights in the Union, which has been effectively exploited from time to time to create a sense of political deprivation.

A more general example of the myth is provided by a recent partisan account of Scottish nationalism. 'The campaign for self-government by the nation in the northern part of the island of Britain has been continuous', wrote the author 'in one form or another, since A.D. 80, when the Roman attempt at conquest . . . met with a concerted resistance.'[8] While the extravagant rhetoric and historical falsehood of this statement may be discounted, it nevertheless presents a vivid example of the use of the myth in the nationalist interpretation of the past. The myth confirms the validity of the national experience, provides nationalists with a certain confidence in their nationhood and facilitates the dissemination and expression of nationalist ideas. An important aspect of this is that, while Scotland was divided for most of its history, the myth propagates the idea of a united Scotland and a common Scottish heritage. In making this transformation the romanticization of the Highlands and the adoption of Highland symbols such as clan, tartan and bagpipes as universally Scottish is of crucial importance. The effect is to affirm a unique Scottish identity with a shared experience and a common culture and tradition. Although contemporary Scottish nationalism is neither romantic nor traditionalist, the myth of the Scottish past has been effectively employed for the mobilization of nationalist sentiment. In this respect the myth has an important function. Since Scottish society remained divided at the time of the Union, much of the social and political integration of Scotland as well as the development of a modern industrial society occurred within the Union. As the resulting outlook and culture is as much British as Scottish, the myth provides a necessary link to a specifically Scottish experience on the basis of which the claims of the nationalists can be more easily legitimized.

While Scotland historically has been a divided society, one segment of which has had some affinity with English culture, the separate Scottish experience has not only produced a unique national culture and way of life, but also created the social institutions to maintain and transmit it. Edinburgh remains clearly a national capital and a focus of national life. The education system, the mass media, the law, the church and some commercial institutions such as the banks exist in a Scottish framework and are mainly controlled and operated from within Scotland. Although Scotland and England today share something like a common language and the same modern culture, there is a Scots language which is the vehicle of a rich folk culture of story, song and dance. Moreover, there is a distinctive Scots high culture that finds expression in several areas of Scottish life from architecture to the universities and a vigorous popular culture expressed in the singular style of which both Scots and non-Scots are immediately aware. Finally there is the old Gaelic culture, now restricted to the periphery of the west Highlands and Islands but with a somewhat greater importance in Scottish life than this territorial limitation would suggest.

In many respects the nature of Scottish culture is clearly reflected in Scottish literature.[9] This is not just English literature written by Scots, although there is that too, but a literature distinctively Scottish, rooted in Scottish life and custom, much of it written in the Scots language on both vernacular and universal themes. It ranges from the heroic poetry of the mediaeval ballad makers, through the romantic novels of Scott and the 'Scots renaissance' poetry of MacDiarmid to the regional novels of Gibbon, Gunn and Hogg. The link between culture and nation, between culture and political nationalism is strong in much of Scottish literature both before and after the union. Constant through most of it in fact is the enduring idea of Scotland as a nation, conscious of itself and its traditions, sometimes confident and proud of the Scottish national experience, sometimes anxious but never in doubt about its validity.

The most notable legacy of Scotland's historic independence however, is a unique civic culture resting on the traditional pillars of church, education and law.[10] The Church of Scotland is presbyterian, organized in a structure of assemblies in which laymen and clerics sit together, culminating in the annual General Assembly. Perhaps because the reformation in Scotland was as much a social revolution as an ecclesiastical one, the Church of Scotland has always been closely involved in society and played a leading role in national life. Indeed the most distinctive feature of the church is the wide recognition of its civil as well as its religious role so that it not only does, but is expected to, deliberate and pronounce on the social and political issues of the day. At various times in the historic past the Church has been more influential and possibly more representative of Scottish opinion than the parliament and, since the Union, even in relatively recent times it has been recognized to some extent as a surrogate parliament.

An early demonstration of the Church's concern with social issues was given by its interest in education. Soon after the reformation the Church committed itself to establishing a school in every parish. Thus in both its structure and philosophy Scottish education owes much to its early association with the Church. The characteristic features of Scottish education have been its emphasis on general education, equality of opportunity and a highly qualified teaching staff. While Scottish education has of course, not failed to modernize, these features of the traditional system remain evident. Today education in Scotland is administered by the Scottish Education Department, but it remains an entirely Scottish system, made and administered by Scots. Given the well-established significance of education in political socialization, it seems likely that this continuing autonomy is an important factor in the preservation and transmission of a distinctively Scottish civic culture.

Perhaps the most distinctive Scottish civil institution is the Scots law and the Court of Session and subordinate courts which administer it. The Scots law is more like continental than English law, although it combines features and qualities of both. The existence of a different law and legal system in Scotland has had two important consequences. The first is the development of a separate Scottish legal fraternity, centred on the Faculty of Advocates, which has always exercised considerable influence on Scottish politics and administration as well as a corporate and professional interest in maintaining a separate Scottish legal system. The second is the need to adapt all legislation and administration to the requirements of Scots law thus creating the conditions for the development of a separate Scottish administrative system.

The experience of Scotland as an independent state is significant both as historical fact and political myth. In the first place it is the experience of statehood which has created the conditions in contemporary Scotland favourable to the resumption of independence. It has also bestowed the legacy of a unique history and tradition and a distinctive civic culture which enhances the credibility of modern separatist aspirations. Moreover, the tangible residue of statehood in the border, the Scottish crown and regalia, the persistence of Edinburgh as a national capital, the literature and popular heroes of independent Scotland and their monuments, the survival of Scots law and civic institutions provide inspiration and focus for the national sentiment through which nationalist claims are legitimized. Finally, the myth of independent Scotland infuses contemporary nationalism, provides much of its emotional dynamism and sustains the matrix of culture and tradition which facilitates its expression. Indeed the myth is possibly more important than the historical fact because it is the myth that sustains nationalism and gives political significance to the history.

The Experience of the Union

After centuries of conflict and mutual suspicion, Scotland and England moved towards a full constitutional and political union in the early eighteenth century.[11] In one sense the circumstances were not propitious as Anglo-Scottish relations were as bad as they had ever been since the Union of Crowns which followed on the failure of the English royal line in 1603. On the other hand, in the aftermath of civil war and revolution both countries were deeply divided on social and ideological lines which made it easier for contending parties in each country to find allies and sympathizers in the other, thus to some extent blurring the purely national implications of the Union question at élite levels.

After a false start in 1702 negotiations were resumed in 1704 against a background of rising tension between the two countries, with the Scots threatening to dissolve the Union of the Crowns. The negotiations were protracted but a draft treaty of union was eventually agreed and presented to the Scots parliament in October 1706. It met substantial opposition and was bitterly contested until the last sitting of the Union debates in March 1707.[12] Outside it was dismissed as at best an élite bargain, and at worst a corrupt one, which has been a large part of the case against it ever since. 'The Union', said one nineteenth-century writer, 'was brought about by chicanery and corruption on the part of statesmen working through traitorous and venal tools of whom too many were to be found.'[13] The Union in fact was not especially popular in either country and in Scotland it provoked rioting in the streets of Edinburgh and almost every town from Inverness to the borders. Six years later an attempt to repeal the Treaty of Union was only narrowly defeated in the House of Lords.

The motives for the Union were indeed a mixture of the self-interest of statesmen and the complex issues of statecraft. Union, however, did offer both countries a solution to certain long-standing strategic and political problems. England was able to secure her strategic backdoor to hostile invasion, while Scotland overcame some of her disadvantages in the competition for colonial and international trade. Each country gained the recognition of the other for its respective presbyterian and anglican religious establishment while at the same time settling the question of the protestant succession. Finally, mercantile and commercial interests in both countries hoped to gain substantially from more peaceful and stable economic conditions.

Although these advantages of union were recognized in Scotland, most Scots would have preferred a less incorporate constitutional arrangement than was actually agreed. There were in fact three principal views of the union in Scotland which may still be recognized as representing the distribution of Scottish attitudes to the union today. First there was the assimilationist view in which the union was regarded primarily as a means of advancing Anglo-Scottish integration. While this view has sometimes been tempered by a certain pride in the Scottish heritage it has always been characterized by a British as opposed to a Scottish orientation to the union. Second, was the nationalistic view in which the union was rejected as a bad bargain, possibly damaging to Scottish interests. Subscribers to this view in modern times have typically attributed the economic and social ills of

Scotland to the original imperfections and subsequent failures of the Union. Both the assimilationists and the nationalist views have usually represented minorities of Scottish opinion. The third and predominant view is a practical one in which the union is regarded as a partnership though not in all respects an equal partnership. In this view the union has been considered worthy of support provided that Scottish interests were recognized and respected, the autonomy of Scottish civil and cultural life was not threatened and the disadvantages of the arrangement did not outweigh the advantages. Similarly discontent and complaints about the union have characteristically been formulated in an appeal to this conception of partnership and in terms of the supposed failures of the union in respect of Scottish interests and Scottish rights.

During the first two hundred years Scotland appeared to prosper and expand within the union. The country experienced a mercantile, industrial and technological revolution which created vast new wealth and opportunities. Merchants, who before the union were denied access to markets in England and the colonies, reaped immense gains from foreign trade especially with America and the Caribbean. This helped to generate the capital to expand trade and shipping, and finance the industrialization of the Scottish economy. Industries such as iron, steel, ship-building and all forms of heavy engineering were established and during the nineteenth century Scotland accounted for a disproportionate share of UK industrial production. The new commercial middle class swelled its numbers and its wealth, while tens of thousands of migrants settled in the rapidly growing towns of the central Lowlands. The Scottish education system produced a literate and book-learnt population with six times as many people attending university as in England in the late eighteenth century and ten times as many in secondary education. Scotland became in many respects an over-achieving society. Those who could not or chose not to join the new meritocracy found ample opportunities in a world-wide empire. Thus through the long years of British industrial and imperial expansion the Anglo-Scottish partnership appeared to work satisfactorily from the Scottish point of view.

Although Parliament was the only major Scottish institution which ceased to exist as a result of the union, Scotland at the same time lost her political independence. To a large extent, however, many of the attitudes characteristic of independence persisted. Scots made a cognitive identification with the new British state but continued to give effective support to the idea of a Scottish nation and a Scottish national identity. This was reflected in the persistent refusal to regard questions of specifically Scottish interest in United Kingdom terms as in the case of the small bank notes bill of 1825-26. Indeed it is doubtful if nationalism ever entirely disappeared from the Scottish outlook though it became in some respects increasingly less salient during the century and a half after the union. During that period there were significant changes in Scottish society whose effects were apparently assimilative. By the late eighteenth century the traditional Scottish élites had assimilated substantially to their English counterparts. The new commercial and professional élite produced by the expansion of the Scottish economy, while not welcoming assimilation, found the union served their interests well. The mass of the population included the new urban proletariat, was more concerned with the movement for the extension of social and political rights, especially the campaign for franchise reform. In eighteenth-century Scotland the distribution of the vote was even more distorted than in England; electoral corruption and jobbery were commonplace. The campaign for the reform of the system, while directed against the Scottish ruling élite, was closely linked to the campaign in England and to that extent integrationist. Indeed, given the exclusive position of the Scottish elite, a measure of integration with their English counterparts was a necessary strategy for the Scottish reformers. Groups like the United Scotsmen and the Society of the Friends of the People accepted this and made alliances with English radicals, but there was also a significant strand of nationalism in their rhetoric. Thus, while political integration was a feature of Anglo-Scottish development within the union, a peculiarly Scottish outlook on politics persisted.

Within the union Scotland continued to be governed primarily by Scots and the intervention of central government remained slight until well into the nineteenth century. Local administration was performed by the traditional Scottish institutions of local government which remained substantially intact particularly in the burghs. At first a Scottish Secretary was responsible for the coordination of central government in Scotland, assisted and advised by the Lord Advocate. In 1746, after the Jacobite rebellion, the office of Secretary was abolished and the exercise of central government authority in Scotland reverted to the Lord Advocate working with a Scottish manager who distributed patronage and acted as political broker for Scottish interests and ambitions. This régime persisted until 1828 when, on the refusal of Melville to serve in the Canning ministry, the brokerage role of the manager disappeared, and Scottish affairs became the responsibility of the Home Secretary. The baneful effects of this change became only slowly apparent. During the ensuing period the activity of the state increased considerably and direct intervention became more frequent. While local government continued to be important, there was a considerable penetration of Scottish jurisdiction by central government, a proliferation of centrally based *ad hoc* agencies and some assimilation of Scottish administrative agencies to their English counterparts. Such arrangements were out of line with the expectations of the union. The perceived threat to the autonomy of Scottish domestic government alerted the professions, the burghs and the growing business community in Scotland to a possible threat to their own interests. There was a demand for the restoration of Scottish government and administration to more clearly Scottish control which, from the 1850s onwards sustained a growing movement for Scottish Home Rule. In response to these demands the office of Secretary of State for Scotland was restored in 1884 and steadily increased its jurisdiction during the following century. In 1939 the administrative departments of the Scottish Office moved to Edinburgh and have since assumed responsibility for most of the domestic activities of government in Scotland, including central planning and economic development. In anticipation of devolution in the middle and late 1970s, some further minor functions were devolved, including the creation of a number of additional Scottish managerial and regulatory agencies.

During the middle and later nineteenth century, the belief that the Scottish character of Scottish government was being eroded produced a new measure of discontent with the union amongst a number of different groups.[14] First there were those, mainly business and professional men, who found the London government remote, anglo-centric and in the absence of a Scottish minister, inaccessible. Their typical reaction was the practical agitation which eventually led to the formation of the Scottish Office. Then there were those, mainly literary and cultural romantics, who, jealous of Scottish rights and resentful of the progress of anglicization, sought redress of perceived grievances and redefinition of the working terms and nomenclature of the union which would restore and uphold the honour of Scotland. The complaints and activities associated with this point of view have continued to influence the tone and expression of Scottish nationalism even in the modern period. The third group were the radicals, a small band at first, who later came to dominate the agitation for home rule. The connection between radicalism and home rule in Scottish politics developed with the rise of the radical reform movement and the growth of Liberal organization in Scotland in the late nineteenth century. Its most important expression was the Scottish Home Rule Association, founded in 1886, which operated as a political and parliamentary pressure group mainly within the Liberal party until the First World War. Finally there were the nationalists whose objective was to regain at least a measure of Scottish political independence. Nationalists varied considerably in their political affiliation as well as in the intensity and direction of their demands but, until the mid-twentieth century there were few amongst them who would not have been satisfied by a separate Scottish parliament with limited powers within the union.

During the years before the First World War the impulse for home rule in Scotland came mainly from two kinds of sources. There was first a diffuse, but rather élite, movement in Scotland inspired by a genuine if restrained nationalism which sought home rule mainly to resist the encroachment of central government on the autonomy of government in Scotland. The other source was the proposal for functional and limited legislative devolution which emanated from the political establishment, motivated by a desire to improve the efficiency of government institutions and a fear that the United Kingdom might disintegrate under the stress of peripheral nationalism. This was the approach which infused the Home Rule All Round movement which drew support from a variety of groups including Fabians and Imperialists as well as Liberals. The actual proposals for home rule ranged from full self-government on federal principles to a scheme by which Scottish members of parliament would sit from time to time in Scotland as a special committee on Scottish business. Most of the proponents of home rule at this time held a preference for an all party approach to the problem, but the practicability of this was severely weakened by the growth of Conservative opposition to the whole idea.

At first Gladstone's conversion to home rule for Ireland gave the Scottish movement considerable impetus and political encouragement. In fact, however, the interminable argument over the Irish question may have proved an actual hindrance to the Scottish claims. Gladstone and successive prime ministers gave priority to Ireland so that serious consideration of the Scottish case was constantly postponed. Moreover the militant and latterly violent methods of the Irish nationalists consolidated unionist opinion against home rule and created an unpleasant dilemma for the advocates of home rule in Scotland. While they were not achieving their objectives by parliamentary means they felt that public opinion in Scotland would not support a more militant course, even if they were willing, which most of them were not, to adopt such a course themselves. Scottish Home Rule thus remained a low priority for British governments, although a few concessions were made, such as the establishment of the Scottish Grand Committee in 1895. The supporters of home rule continued to pin their hopes on the Liberal party. Given the strong position of the party before the First World War and its dominant position in Scotland it was perhaps not unreasonable to assume that it was the most likely means of achieving home rule. After years of political pressure, principally from the SHRA, a bill providing for Scottish Home Rule was introduced and reached its second reading in 1913. The experience of the First World War, however, brought about a remarkable change. The salience of home rule as an issue in Scottish politics dramatically diminished. It was not simply that the demand for home rule dissipated. Considerable support for home rule remained and may in fact have increased in some sections of Scottish society during the war. What was different was that most of the powerful interests who had given momentum to the cause in the decades before the war now withdrew their support, while the decline of the Scottish economy in the post-war years diverted political attention to more urgent economic and social issues. Moreover, the rapid disappearance of the Liberal party as a major force in British politics deprived home rule of its main political advocate. The mantle of Liberalism in this as in certain other respects, was supposed to have passed to the Labour party through the ILP and its roots in the Scottish radical tradition. Nationalist sentiment together with an affirmation of home rule waxed strong in the Labour party in Scotland for a few years after the war until the mid-1920s. After this it declined as Labour was seduced by the lure of Westminster politics and turned increasingly to policies whose tendency was towards the concentration and centralization rather than the devolution of government power. Faced with this apparent desertion of their cause by the major parties the advocates of home rule either weakened or turned increasingly to the nationalist point of view which meant an intensification, and in some cases, a change in the nature of their demands.

The demand for home rule before the First World War should not be too readily interpreted as the expression of a nationalist much less of a separatist movement. There was virtually no demand for a separate state and little effort to create a nationalist mass movement. Few Scots doubted Scotland's nationhood which most of them actually believed to be widely acknowledged. Moreover, the union itself was rarely questioned. It was always felt, however, that there were specifically Scottish interests within the union which could only be protected by preserving the autonomy of Scottish institutions and this meant, if necessary, resisting the subversion of these institutions by the encroachment of central government. Much of the home rule agitation was intended to conserve what Scots understood as the spirit of the union and to assure its effectiveness. The object was to protect Scottish interests and to ensure the satisfactory working of the union partnership rather than to wreck it.

Although it has not always been expressed in overtly nationalist activities, it is doubtful that nationalism has ever ceased to be an important feature of the Scottish culture. The effect of the union on Scottish nationalism, however, was to develop and deepen a certain ambiguity in its outlook. The union itself gained a conditional legitimacy amongst élites and masses. A clear political allegiance, albeit with a peculiarly Scottish content, developed towards the British state while Scottish national pride took considerable satisfaction from Scotland's role in the development of the empire. At the same time Scotland persisted as a separate civil society within the United Kingdom, able to mobilize the resources and institutions of that society in defence of its perceived domestic interests. Moreover, the Scottish sense of nationality and cultural identity was more closely bound up with these civil institutions and their links to Scottish tradition and culture, parochial and inward-looking as it sometimes was, than with the British connection. The union sustained both, the one by its guarantee of Scottish civil institutions, the other by the exigencies of constitutional partnership and the propensity to political integration. Thus Scottish culture and nationalism developed on two levels. On one level Scots were partners in a multi-national state and a great world empire. On the other they were members of a self-contained civil society, looking backwards on the glories of an earlier state and inwards at the curiosities and idosyncracies of their own culture.[15] After two centuries of union the Scottish national identity and Scottish nationalism had acquired an ambiguity of outlook and allegiance which was the effect of dual nationality.

Despite the loss of political independence the persistence and vitality of Scottish civil institutions and the resilience of Scottish traditions protected Scottish society from structural and cultural assimilation. As the role of government in society became more extensive, a link between Scottish civil society and the British state was created by the political parties. The enfranchisement and political mobilization of the Scottish masses during the nineteenth and twentieth centuries had a generally integrative effect which provided cultural and behavioural supports for these links. Voters were recruited and socialized into United Kingdom political parties and, on most issues, Scottish voters appeared to behave in much the same way as voters in the rest of the United Kingdom. The parties themselves had a vested interest in maintaining the strength of their Scottish presence. This was particularly true of the Liberal and Labour parties who would rarely have gained power at Westminster without their Scottish seats. By sensitivity to Scottish opinion, recognition of the legitimacy of Scottish demands, adaptation of government programmes and occasional modification of the structure of government itself the parties were able to manage the stress created by different and separate Scottish interests. Scottish civil society was frequently capable of acting with formidable cohesiveness and internal unity to support these interests. The Scottish office and the Scottish departments, especially after the Second World War, provided a source of institutional pressure on the central government which ensured that Scottish interests and the Scottish point of view did not go by default.[16] Scottish MPs learned to use this system to their advantage, concentrating mainly on Scottish issues, articulating specifically Scottish demands through central institutions such as the parties, and seeking to gain special material benefits for Scotland from the policies of central governments.[17] Thus in the aggregation of interests and the making of key decisions the major parties, at grassroots and in government, were principal agents, satisficing if not optimizing Scottish demands. This system continued to work satisfactorily so long as Scottish demands did not challenge the system or the régime itself and so long as these demands could be satisfied by output-oriented solutions. During the late 1960s and the 1970s, however, conditions developed in Scotland which brought the whole system into crisis.

The Rise of Political Nationalism

The rise of modern political nationalism in Scotland was largely a direct consequence of the failure of the home rule movement in the years after the First World War. The strategy of the home rule movement was to persuade MPs and the major parties of the necessity and justice of home rule in Scotland.

After the war, however, the decline of the Liberal party and the lack of interest in the other parties meant that this strategy lost much of its credibility. At the same time, partly as an effect of the war itself and the influence of post-war conditions and partly because of an indigenous cultural renaissance, nationalism became a more prominent feature of Scottish life in the 1920s, than it was before the war. Before long home rulers and nationalists made common cause in a new political party committed to Scottish national independence. The activity of the new party contributed significantly to the politicization of national sentiment and to the gradual emergence of self-government as a mass political issue over the next fifty years. Moreover, while the concern of the early nationalist movement was mainly with cultural matters the new party developed the political and economic arguments as an increasingly important part of the nationalist case over the following decades.

In September 1918 the Scottish Home Rule Association was reconstituted with the object of working for Scottish self-government. Its case was that Scottish interests were neglected, if not actually harmed by the unionist régime. It published a newsletter, conducted public meetings, lobbyed MPs, put pressure on ministers, briefed local and parliamentary candidates and civic organizations, organized three national conventions and drafted two home rule bills. The Association found this disheartening work and was disappointed in the response. After the failure of Buchanan's and Barr's bills the leaders came to the conclusion that the cause of Scottish self-government could only be effectively promoted by means of a separate nationalist political party contesting elections and seeking support on the basis of its own programme. After some talking around the project the Association was disbanded and with elements of the SNL and SNM formed the National Party of Scotland.

The SNL was a very different organization from the SHRA. The League was at once more fundamentalist and more romantic in outlook, more literary and more radical in tone and clearly more influenced by the Irish experience and by Irish connections. Its roots were in the Highland Land League, Gaelic revivalism and a traditional sort of cultural nationalism. Much of its work was conducted through Gaelic and Highland organizations, expecially those based in London and Glasgow. The Scottish National Movement, based in Edinburgh was a much smaller and less significant organization whose object was to promote Scottish cultural revival and national independence. In the formation of the National Party of Scotland an essential mediating role was performed by John McCormick, who had already formed a Scottish National Association while an undergraduate at Glasgow University. Although he was not a member of any of the contributing organizations, McCormick became secretary of the party and remained one of the most able and most colourful leaders of the nationalist movement for the next thirty years.

The new party was committed to complete independence for Scotland and recognition of Scotland's status as a mother nation of the Empire which also implied close cooperation with England on foreign affairs and defence. The argument was that Scottish independence would also benefit England by putting the relationship between the two countries on a clear and equal footing. In pursuit of these objectives the NPS repudiated any cooperation with other parties on the grounds that they were in one way or another committed to the union. The new nationalism which the NPS incorporated and expressed was deeply rooted in the myths, traditions and structures of Scottish society, from which it drew considerable emotional energy. It also recognized, however, that Scotland was an advanced industrial society and sought to modernize the Scottish economy and ensure the development of a prosperous self-governing society on the broad base of Scotland's natural, industrial and human resources. The party was centred on Glasgow, where most of its leading members lived, but branches were established in all the principal towns of Scotland. The electoral performance of the party, while not entirely disastrous, was not very impressive. Between 1929 and 1933, it contested fifteen by-elections, in which the candidate managed to save his deposit in only seven.[18] In 1934 it merged with the Scottish Party to form the Scottish National Party.

The Scottish Party was formed in 1932 with the ostensible aim of achieving self-government for Scotland within the Empire. Unlike the NPS, whose members were mostly members or ex-members of the Labour movement, the ILP and other radical organizations, the Scottish Party consisted mainly of Conservatives and Liberals. It was a small, élite group, well-experienced in public life and politics, whose strategy was to infiltrate and pressurize other parties, although this did not exclude the possibility of putting forward its own candidates. The two parties were brought together mainly because of the desire of some of the NPS leaders, especially McCormick to harness the prestige and supposed political competence of the Scottish Party leaders to their own cause.

The conditions in which the merger was effected had significant consequences for the development of nationalist politics in Scotland. At first the new party placed less emphasis on recruitment, cadre development and organization than the old NPS which probably had deleterious effects, at least in the short term, on the electoral performance of the successor party. The most grievous point, however, was that, by the terms of the agreement, the National Party policy of full independence was toned down to something more like self-government. This precipitated a major row which split the NPS and left the nationalist movement a legacy of internal strife, which clung to it for more than twenty years. Although some of the most active and vigorous members of the NPS who objected to the terms of the merger were expelled before the merger was effected, others remained to snipe and fight another day.

The Scottish National Party therefore came into a troubled inheritance from the early nationalist movement in which the fissiparous tendencies in the movement were compounded by the bitterness of a disputed union. Coming from a variety of political backgrounds and disparate positions on the question of Scotland's political future, the nationalists coexisted uneasily and the party was riven with cleavages throughout its early years. Disputes on matters of principle, ideology and expediency were commonplace and led frequently to splits, defections and regroupings. On the central question of Scottish self-government there were four basic positions within the party. First there were the home rulers who sought some form of devolution including those who regarded home rule as a stepping stone to full independence. Then there were the federalists, whose object was a form of domestic autonomy, believing that complete independence was impracticable. These two positions were held on principle and on grounds of political expediency, i.e. having regard to what Scottish public opinion would support and what the Westminster parliament would concede. There was a considerable distance between these 'moderate' positions and the third, more nationalist position of self-government with dominion status under the crown. The fourth and most uncompromising nationalist position of full independence with complete separation was supported, before the Second World War at least, only by a tough-minded minority. These divergent conceptions of the ends and aims of nationalist activity were complicated by recurrent disagreements about subordinate questions such as cooperation with other parties, dual memberships and the economic and social policies appropriate to a nationalist programme. While these various divisions inhibited the unity and cohesion of the party during the 1930s, the main cleavage was between gradualists and home rulers on the one hand and separatist nationalists on the other. The view of most thoroughgoing nationalists was that limited home rule, discriminatory output benefits and minor legislative concessions were not an adequate response to Scottish demands. They believed that more could only be achieved by winning and holding seats at parliamentary elections even though they were chastened from time to time by the disappointing electoral performance of the party. What brought the dispute between the two factions to a head was their different responses to the onset of the Second World War. While the moderates in the party declared their loyalty and pledged their support for the government, the nationalists contested the right of the British government to embroil the people and the interests of Scotland in the war. When the party split on this issue in 1942, it was the hard-line nationalists who won the day and took control. In the short term the split did not impair the electoral performance of the party which actually improved during the last years of the war. In the long term the effect was to create a more united party which was a stronger instrument for the promotion of the nationalist cause.

The split of 1942 was a critical event in the development of political nationalism. After the split the moderates formed a series of organizations starting with the Scottish Union, followed by the Scottish Convention and then the Scottish Covenant Association. All these organizations represented a reversion to the earlier home rule style of pressure group politics. The characteristic activity of these groups was propaganda, publicity and various exercises in participation, such as the Scottish National Assembly of 1947 and a number of opinion surveys, designed to mobilize opinion and bring pressure on the political parties and the government to recognize Scottish home rule as a policy priority. For some time in the early 1950s the Covenant actually eclipsed the SNP in its membership and the scale of its activity. Despite its undoubted popular success, however, the covenant failed to secure any significant concession on home rule. This outcome left the SNP with the moral advantage on the question of strategy, confirmed its view that the moderate approach to the self-government question was bound to be unproductive and enabled it to commit the nationalist movement to the single course of challenging the major parties at the polls. This task was considerably eased by the groundwork done by the Covenant Association, while the eventual demise of the Association in 1956 eliminated a serious rival for public support. It is not clear that the SNP benefited immediately from these developments but by the early 1960s the party was on the threshold of an unprecedented and probably unexpected expansion and electoral success. The by-elections at Bridgetown in 1961 and West Lothian in 1962 presaged a new era for the SNP and nationalist politics in Scotland.

The contemporary SNP developed after the second world war following the split of 1942 and McIntyre's short lived success at the Motherwell by-election in 1945. Shortly after the war the party published a new policy document calling for 'the restoration of Scottish national sovereignty', which set out its commitment to independence for Scotland. Throughout the 1940s and 1950s, the halcyon years of post-war consensus politics, however, the electoral performance of the SNP was very discouraging. During the late 1950s and early 1960s, there was a major effort to recruit new members, establish new branches and create a central organization with a full-time staff, beginning with one organizer in 1961. These efforts to develop an effective organization together with a better coordinated and more energetic approach to elections were followed by some improvement in electoral performance. In the 1964 general election the SNP contested fifteen constituencies and lost twelve deposits to win 2.4 per cent of the vote. In 1966 this share increased to 5.0 per cent with twenty-three candidates and only ten lost deposits.[19] The advance continued during the early years of the second Wilson government with a satisfactory result at the Pollock by-election and the break-through victory at Hamilton in 1967, followed by a good showing at the Scottish local elections in 1968. In 1969 this encouraging trend went into decline culminating in a dismal performance in the local elections in 1971. In the general election of 1970 the SNP put up sixty-five candidates and again more than doubled its share of the vote. With forty-three lost deposits, however, this was an expensive gain, especially since the party's parliamentary position remained essentially unchanged. A more heartening outcome was that by taking the Western Isles from Labour and compensating for the loss of Hamilton, the SNP demonstrated that it could win seats at general elections without the special advantages that were supposed to accrue to minor parties at by-elections.

The decline in the fortunes of the SNP at the turn of the decade misled many observers to dismiss it as a spent force. The organization which the party had built up during the 1960s, however, gave it the coherence and confidence to persist through the lean years and to concentrate on the development of policy for the future. The real breakthrough for the SNP came in the early 1970s, starting with an upsurge in the opinion polls in the latter months of 1971. The discovery of commercial reserves of oil in the North Sea with its encouraging implications for the Scottish economy, boosted the morale and ambitions of the SNP. With the slogan, 'It's Scotland's Oil', the nationalists exploited the energy issue to the fullest advantage. This apparent concern for a specifically Scottish interest, together with growing discontent with the central government and the major parties, undoubtedly contributed to the swelling support for the SNP which was demonstrated in the Govan by-election victory of 1973 and the near victory at Dundee East the same year. In these favourable conditions the SNP won seven seats at the February 1974 general election and came close to doubling its share of the vote for the fourth time in succession. In the October election it maintained the momentum. It contested every Scottish constituency, won eleven seats, came second in forty-two others, lost no deposits and left the major parties in confusion. Moreover, it was winning support from all sections and classes of Scottish society, particularly amongst the younger age groups. As the second party in Scottish politics with 30 per cent of the vote and more united than perhaps ever in its history, the SNP had never been so sure of itself or so confident of the future.

A sober assessment of this performance, however, suggested that the SNP still had a considerable distance to go with a number of serious obstacles still in its path. In the 1960s the major SNP advance was in the east central Lowlands mainly at the expense of the Conservative vote in safe Labour seats.[20] Unfortunately little of this early promise was fulfilled. Of the seats threatened by the SNP in the 1960s only two (Clackmannan and East Stirling and Perth and East Perthshire) were taken in 1974. Indeed most of the parliamentary gains of 1974 were in rural seats on the western periphery (Galloway, Argyll, Western Isles) and the North East (Moray and Nairn, Banff, Aberdeenshire East, Angus South). This dependence on rural constituencies pointed to a more serious problem. With the exceptions of the by-election gains at Hamilton and Govan, both lost at the ensuing general election, and the more solid gain of Dundee East, the SNP had never been able to establish a significant presence in the major cities. This was particularly noticeable in Glasgow, where the working class Labour vote and especially the Catholic Labour vote remained remarkably steady.[21] All in all the SNP looked more than ever the party of anti-centralist protest and small town and rural populism which Hanham described in the 1960s.[22] As for the future, despite the SNP's 30 per cent of the vote and the diminished share of the major parties, caution was advised by the fact that the latter appeared to be in retreat across the length and breadth of the United Kingdom in 1974. In the years after the 1974 election, the SNP, according to opinion poll evidence retained and even increased its support which came through strongly in the local elections of 1977. When the major parties did eventually recover their position, however, they did so at the expense of the SNP. In 1978-79 the SNP experienced a major decline. At the 1979 general election it managed to hold only two parliamentary seats and less than two thirds of its 1974 share of the vote. The SNP campaign in 1979 was unusually subdued and, for the first time in more than a decade, found itself almost totally eclipsed by the campaigns of the major parties, which focussed on the predominant economic issues of inflation, employment and the cost of living.[23]

Interpretations

Despite these reservations and uncertainties, however, the success of the SNP in the mid 1970s made a very considerable impact which sent politicians, journalists and academics in search of an explanation for the apparently sudden upsurge of nationalism in Scottish politics. A number of explanations were offered in terms of the impact of immediate factors such as North Sea oil, Britain's entry to the EEC and the debate on devolution. Although some of these, especially the North Sea oil explanation, gained a considerable currency for a time in popular opinion, they were for the most part found to be weakly supported by empirical evidence. While the North Sea oil issue was a highly salient part of the nationalist campaign, its effect on the growth of support for the SNP was probably marginal and indirect. Neither is there any clear evidence that the European issue contributed significantly to the growth of the SNP, even though 70 per cent of a 1974 opinion survey agreed with the SNP view that Scotland should have independent representation in the community. As for the devolution debate, the evidence is rather more complex. The demand for self-government has been constantly at a fairly high level in Scottish public opinion over many years and independent of support for the SNP, although the latter has probably drawn more from those who favour self-government than from those who do not. The substantial increase in SNP support between the general elections of 1974 was undoubtedly attributable in large measure to the SNP's successful exploitation of the gap between the government's devolution proposals and the demands and expectations of the electorate.[24]

While some hypotheses are thus capable of empirical verification, there is another range of possible explanations, some derived from complex theories, others based on more straightforward and familiar ideas which are more difficult to assess. According to one such explanation the rise of nationalism may be understood in terms of the recent British experience of decolonization, retreat from empire and decline in world power. The argument here is that the retreat from empire revealed maladjustments and problems in the metropolitan society which in Scotland have been expressed through nationalism and rejection of the union. Scotland has been historically an exporter of practical, administrative and leadership talent which has found ample opportunity in the empire. In post-imperial times, so the argument goes, these opportunities have been denied and unsatisfied Scots have turned to the nationalist movement and the prospect of an independent Scotland as a vehicle for their frustrated ambitions. One problem with this argument is that it does not take adequate account of earlier movements demanding self-government which were active during the high noon of empire in the late nineteenth and early twentieth centuries. Moreover, Scotland in the mid-twentieth century continues to be a surplus producer and net exporter of highly qualified manpower. Emigration to other parts of the English speaking world continued during the 1960s and 1970s, at a very high level even by historical standards.

A rather more complex explanation is derived from the theory of internal colonialism. Internal colonialism is a term used to describe a situation in which a dominant ethnic, socioeconomic or regional population exploits a subordinate population in a less developed region within the state boundary. It has thus been argued that Scottish nationalism should be interpreted as the response of a subject society to internal colonial exploitation.[25] Whatever the merits of the theory of internal colonialism, few, if any, of the conditions of the theory apply to the position of Scotland within the United Kingdom. Indeed a serious misreading of Scottish history is required to maintain that they do. Scotland can scarcely be described as politically and militarily oppressed within the union. Language has not been a problem and certainly not a basis of discrimination. The autonomy of Scottish civil society, and the independent position within it of Scots law, church and education, has not been consciously threatened. As for the Scottish economy, the structure of production and employment is very similar, indeed almost identical to that of the United Kingdom as a whole. During the late nineteenth and early twentieth centuries average wages and production were actually higher in Scotland than the rest of the United Kingdom. The persistent weakness of the Scottish economy since the First World War is due mainly to the decline of heavy industry which may be more satisfactorily accounted for in terms other than those of internal colonialism.

The chronic weakness of the Scottish economy in recent decades has been associated with the idea of deprivation to support the argument that the SNP vote is a political expression by Scots of a sense of deprivation relative to the rest of the United Kingdom and of England in particular. Unemployment figures certainly show that Scotland has been persistently depressed economically even during periods of cyclical expansion and prosperity for the United Kingdom as a whole. On certain other socio-economic indicators, however, Scotland while worse off than the South East and possibly the Midlands, has been normally better off than other regions of the United Kingdom. Moreover, it is not clear that economic deprivation is a significant correlate of SNP voting. Although only 22 per cent of Scots in an opinion survey thought of Scotland as 'well off financially' compared to other parts of Britain, a lower proportion than for any other region but the North,[26] there is little evidence that this feeling contributed directly to support for the SNP.

In the late 1960s and early 1970s after the first SNP electoral break-through, it was commonplace to interpret support for the SNP as protest or displacement voting, i.e. a vote against the major parties on account of their failures in government rather than a positive vote for the SNP. This interpretation received a considerable impetus from the spectacular successes of the Liberal party in England in 1974, when it was suggested that the rise of the SNP could be understood as part of more widespread British phenomenon. According to this argument the successes of the Liberal party and the SNP were the result of disenchantment with the major parties' performance in government and a decline in the class basis of partisanship, leading to a withdrawal of voter support from the major parties. While this interpretation of the SNP vote may not be entirely implausible, there are also sound reasons why it cannot be considered wholly satisfactory. In the first place the movement of disaffected voters to an explicitly nationalist party is itself significant, especially amongst an electorate with a strong sense of separate national identity.

Secondly, while a large proportion of defectors from the major parties undoubtedly delivered their vote to the SNP, it would also appear that SNP voting, correlated strongly with support for self-government, the major policy offered by the SNP. This would suggest that, in a large proportion of cases at least, support for the SNP represented rather more than mere protest voting. Thirdly, the protest vote theory was an attempt to explain the SNP within the conventional framework of British politics and this may have obscured some features unique to the Scottish situation. The scale of SNP support, reaching 30 per cent of the vote at a general election and more in subsequent opinion polls, took it beyond the normally understood dimensions of a protest vote. A shift of allegiance on this scale could, and in fact very briefly did, alter not only the balance but the structure of politics in Scotland. It was even suggested that the Scottish political system was undergoing a fundamental realignment;[27] it seemed at least likely that the SNP had exploited a major cleavage which had previously been politically dormant.

The burden of the deprivation and protest explanations may be subsumed in a hypothesis derived from the theory of centre-periphery politics.[28] The basic proposition of this theory applicable here is that one of the major cleavages in British politics is between the centre (i.e. London, the Home Counties, the South East and possibly the Midlands) and the periphery. The centre seeks to extend its control and authority together with the values and procedures of a central government culture over the whole country. The periphery does not conform to the norms and expectations of the centre, believes that its interests are neglected and that its economic and social grievances are due to the indifference and failures of central government. This produces a conflict between two identities and two political attitudes, one centralist, the other anti-centralist. The centralist attitude has been historically expressed by the Conservative party, the party of the governing class and the centre. Those who do not embrace the values of the governing class and centralism have tended to gravitate towards the Labour party. This explains why the Conservative party is strong in the territory of the centre and why the Labour party has been able to aggregate and express the interests of the periphery. Scotland is part of the periphery which also includes the North and North West of England, Northern Ireland, Wales and the South West. Scotland, however, has an indigenous national culture and the mobilization of this has enabled the SNP to challenge and possibly even displace the Labour party as the political voice of the periphery in Scotland. The rise of the SNP, therefore, is to be understood as a localized expression of periphery discontent.

The centre-periphery explanation has much to commend it, not least its plausibility, but it does also have a number of serious shortcomings. In the first place it almost certainly overstates the success of the SNP and for that reason alone may be regarded with caution. Secondly, it is not clear what caused the shift of support to the SNP and the supposed displacement of the Labour party as the political voice of the periphery in Scotland. It has been suggested that an increase in Scottish consciousness and a heightening of Scottish identity amongst the Scottish electorate contributed to an increase in support for the SNP.[29] The problem with this, however, is that Scottish consciousness and Scottish identity have always been high in Scotland. Indeed, it is not easy to see how they could be substantially increased or, even if they were, why this should result directly in an increase of support for the SNP. Alternatively it is argued that the Labour party being itself ideologically committed to centralizing policies, is vulnerable to the consequences, as perceived on the periphery, of central government failure. Thus the SNP, with improved organization and energetic campaigning was able to exploit the growing discontent amongst the Scottish electorate with the performance of central government.[30] The difficulty with this is that, although Labour did lose ground to the SNP, the Labour vote was relatively stable in the face of the SNP attack and even at the peak of SNP success Labour remained the largest electoral party in Scotland. Moreover, discontent with the performance of central government as expressed in the withdrawal of support from the major parties was not confined to the periphery as some Liberal advances in the territory of the centre demonstrate.

The shortcomings of the explanations so far considered may be attributed to one or more of three general faults. The first is the effort to explain Scottish nationalism in terms of general theories which do not easily fit the historical and empirical evidence. While it is conceded that there are universal elements in nationalism and that nationalism, like other social phenomena, is capable of explanation in general terms, it must also be emphasised that nationalism is uniquely an expression of the civil and cultural traditions and the economic and political experience of the society in which it develops. Secondly, most explanations seek to interpret Scottish nationalism within a framework, conventional or otherwise, of British politics with a consequent tendency to overlook or obscure the peculiarly Scottish factors in the situation. Thirdly, there is a tendency to equate Scottish nationalism with the Scottish National Party and its demands which may produce an oversimplified view of the nature of nationalism in Scotland. Nationalism has always been immanent in Scottish society; Scottish culture and civil institutions are thoroughly infused with it. To this extent, however, Scottish nationalism is satisfied and secure. The autonomy and identity of Scottish civil society have never been seriously threatened from outside and are taken for granted within a Scottish culture which gives them very considerable support. The demand for political self-determination and self-government, however, raises a different order of questions and can only be fully understood with reference to the British dimension of Scottish political life.

It is therefore suggested that political nationalism in Scotland may be most satisfactorily understood as an artefact of the total Scottish experience and especially of Scottish perceptions and evaluations of the union. The union was never intended to merge the whole identity of Scotland. When the treaty was negotiated even those most eager to have it had to be convinced that Scottish interests, including the autonomy of Scottish civil institutions would be safeguarded. The union thus encompassed the Scottish parliament and the Scottish state, but not Scottish civil society or Scottish nationhood. While the treaty affirmed Scotland's incorporation into the new state of Great Britain, it also symbolized her past independence and guaranteed her continuing autonomy as a civil society. The union, therefore, was never, as in Ireland and Wales, a symbol of conquest and cultural domination but rather an agreement concluded between independent and legally equal parties. This fact has been of great importance in conditioning Scottish attitudes to the union. It has ensured that affective and cognitive orientations are rooted in the twin ideas, conceptually distinct but practically intertwined, of Scotland, its traditions, civil institutions and national identity, on the one hand, and the United Kingdom of Great Britain as a social-economic community and legitimate political régime on the other. It has meant that Scots have been conscious of belonging to a separate civil society and distinct culture within the union. It has also meant that Scots have typically perceived the union as a partnership in which there are tangible Scottish interests to be upheld. The formal constitutional position alone, of course, would scarcely support this view. The first, and indeed the only effective support for this conception of the union is the ability of Scotland to function as a civil society and mobilize its resources of autonomy, national identity and nationhood to prevent encroachment and advance Scottish claims. Thus Scottish institutions such as the law, local government and other public bodies, industrial and commercial interests, various civic groups and even the church join with and support Scottish MPs and the Scottish Office to secure the Scottish share of the material benefits of union. The United Kingdom authorities, including parliament itself, acknowledge that Scotland operates as a civil society in this way by their continued recognition of the special place within the unitary state of Scottish law and public administration.

In the twentieth century the state has had more influence on the framework of economic and social life than the civil institutions of church, law and local government which were so carefully protected in the treaty of union. The Scottish Secretary and the Scottish Office were meant to provide a Scottish presence and advance Scottish interests in the councils of the state. Since the Second World War, however, and especially in the 1960s, the system has faced a widening credibility gap. It has not been very visible or accessible to democratic control and in a centrally managed economy there were limits to the extent to which the Scottish Office could develop separate policies for Scotland. This fostered suspicion of London-based government and nourished a range of traditional Scottish grievances. It also served to promote the case for self-government, not on the grounds of English domination but of restoring the effectiveness of the union partnership. The significance of the SNP is that it mobilized these sentiments and by linking them to the strong and widespread sense of national identity and Scottish economic aspirations created a powerful political mixture. In doing so, however, the SNP did not mobilize all sections of Scottish society evenly. It was least successful in the cities and traditional industrial areas where economic expectations were depressed. It was most successful in the rural areas and small towns on the periphery and amongst the younger white collar and skilled workers in the suburbs and new towns, all areas where the influence of the traditional class politics of the cities and industrial towns was rather tenuous.

The articulation of Scottish society in relation to the union includes two dimensions, national identity and attitudes to the union, which also describe the dynamics of Scottish political nationalism. These are represented in the diagram (Figure 1). Most Scots declare a Scottish rather than a British nationality. Most also make a qualified acceptance of the union, a majority of opinion favouring some measure of self-government. This suggests that the typical outlook of most Scots on the union is represented by the inner lower region of the top right-hand quadrant. A shift of attitude towards rejection of the union or/and a more militant nationalism would result in a movement upwards and outwards towards separatism. On the other hand a move towards unionism in the diagonally opposite quadrant would be the effect of a shift to a British national identity and more unqualified acceptance of the union. The diagram illustrates the paradox of Scottish nationalism, a strong national identity associated with a weak and ambiguous political nationalism.

This central paradox of Scottish nationalism was amply demonstrated in the 1960s and the 1970s. Time and again opinion surveys showed that while devolution and independence usually came low on a list of voters' priorities, the response to a specific question on the desirability of self-government was in a majority of cases affirmative. This pattern of response had a number of consequences. First, it frustrated the nationalists by

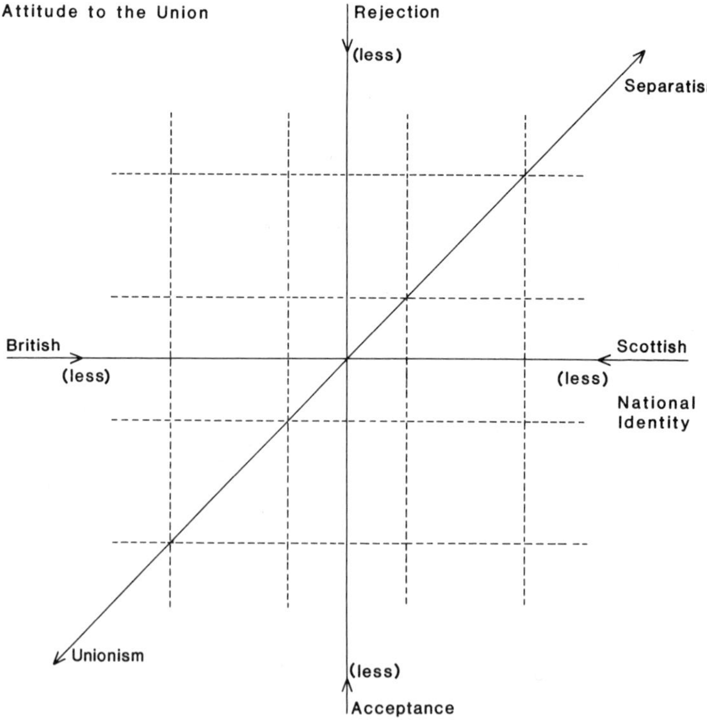

Figure 1. Attitude to the Union, National Identity

showing that although Scottish national identity was strong it was not strong enough politically to support a separatist movement. Second, it provided a justification for the major parties to respond to Scottish nationalism with marginal output concessions. Third, it provided a useful weapon to successive Secretaries of State for Scotland who could strengthen their case in cabinet by emphasizing the need to placate nationalist sentiment. Only when the nationalist issue became central in electoral politics did politicians, political commentators and indeed the SNP itself come to believe that the politics of region was being replaced by the politics of national revival and separatism. In the 1970s this is what many of them actually thought was happening.

The Prospect of Secession

Scottish political demands have been traditionally output rather than régime oriented, directed to winning specific policy benefits from the system rather than changing the system itself. Although there was fairly widespread approval for some measure of self-government, this was not a major priority for most of the electorate and the attention of policy makers was focused firmly on the problem of economic and regional policy. During the late 1960s there appeared to be a shift from output to régime oriented demands expressed in a new and growing support for self-government. The established political parties were not well-adapted to express such radical nationalist demands and their unwillingness to concede any significant measure of régime modification enabled the SNP to further exploit the self government issue in the 1970s. The Hamilton by-election marked the beginning of a period in which the self-government issue increasingly overshadowed other issues in Scottish politics and eventually dominated the legislative agenda of the United Kingdom parliament.

The success of the SNP took British political leaders and unionist politicians by surprise. They were surprised as much by the energy and suddenness with which the SNP broke through the established framework of politics as by the fact that it broke through at all. Their first reaction seemed to proceed from the assumption that the whole mood and direction of Scottish politics was changing. For the first time in over two hundred years the prospect of Scottish secession from the union loomed over the horizon of British politics and conditioned the response of unionist politicians. It conditioned their response to the claims and rhetoric of the SNP and their approach to constitutional change. The latter was calculated as much to undermine the position of the SNP as to reform the system of government in Scotland.

One of the earliest responses to the SNP was the Royal Commission on the Constitution (the Kilbrandon Commission) which was established in 1968 and reported in 1973. The majority report recommended the establishment of a Scottish legislative assembly elected by proportional representation with a jurisdiction equivalent to the existing scope of the Scottish Office and the Scottish Committees of the House of Commons. The implementation of this proposal would be accompanied by the abolition of the Scottish Office and the reduction of the number of Scottish MPs. A minority report favoured a non-legislative assembly with powers of administrative scrutiny and a less comprehensive jurisdiction, while a further memorandum of dissent proposed a system of executive devolution uniformly throughout the regions of the United Kingdom. The report made a considerable impact in Scotland and set the terms of the ensuing debate on devolution which dominated Scottish politics for the remaining years of the decade. Within the terms of this debate there were three alternative possibilities for the political future of Scotland, the maintenance of the status quo, independence and some form of devolution. In general terms the status quo was the course favoured by establishment interests in Scotland who were on balance satisfied with the existing situation while independence was the policy of the hardline nationalists. Devolution was a middle position devised to meet the approval of constitutional reformers, satisfy Scottish public opinion and disarm the SNP.

There were, however, a number of serious problems associated with each of these alternatives. The objection to the status quo was that the complaints about the lack of democratic control of Scottish Office administration in Scotland and the remoteness of central government from the Scottish people would remain. Moreover, the credibility of the SNP might be further increased, perhaps ultimately resulting in the secession of Scotland from the United Kingdom, an outcome which all British political leaders were concerned to prevent. The only comfort to unionists in this situation was that the problems associated with independence or 'separatism' (the term used in the Kilbrandon report) appeared even greater. These included the constitutional difficulties of unscrambling the union, the question of the diplomatic and trading relations of an independent Scotland with England

and whether the Scots actually wanted independence. The heart of the problem, however, was the economic viability of an independent Scotland. The nationalist case that Scotland was disadvantaged economically in the union and would actually benefit from independence appeared to impress SNP supporters but made little impact on official or independent expert opinion.[31] The Kilbrandon report did not consider the economic question to be a major obstacle to independence but took the view that Scotland would then be poorer than it would be in the union. During the 1970s, however, two developments transformed the debate. First, British entry to the EEC was presented as resolving the problem of the relations between England and Scotland. Second, the discovery of North Sea oil was assumed to provide not only the resources to regenerate the Scottish economy but also the basis for previously unimagined wealth and prosperity. For some time the unionist case against independence was in disarray, but, as the dust settled, a number of new questions emerged, not least of which was whether an independent Scotland would actually be able to sustain a claim to the oil reserves in international law.[32]

In the mid-1970s it came to be widely believed that the status quo was not an option. What most feared, and separatists perhaps hoped, was that independence could somehow come to be regarded as a serious option by default. One consequence of this was that, after the publication of the Kilbrandon report, it became very difficult to ignore or obscure the issue of devolution, as to a large extent had happened before. Thus devolution became the most widely canvassed of the possible alternative futures for the Scottish polity. Devolution, however, as the debate on the Kilbrandon report showed, could mean a range of different things. At one end of the range it meant a Scottish parliament with full legislative powers and a defined jurisdiction on almost federal lines. At the other end it meant a non-legislative assembly representing Scottish opinions with token powers of advice and scrutiny. As the government, the political parties and the various interests manoeuvred and positioned themselves on these questions, the public debate on self-government gathered momentum. During the early 1970s, the movement for some measure of self-government for Scotland grew noticeably stronger, one tangible expression being the so-called Scottish Assembly, representative of all sectors of Scottish society, which met for the first time in 1972. While such events undoubtedly added to the credibility of the SNP as well as to the force of popular demand, not all opinion could be described as moving in the same direction as the SNP or, indeed, in favour of devolution. As the nationalist surge swelled after 1973, the major political parties and the unionist interests took stock of their own positions and prepared to resist the SNP.

The forces of resistance presented a broad front against the SNP but they did not make a common cause or even a similar assessment of the situation. Most of the major sectional interests declared themselves on balance opposed to devolution even though their points of view in most cases appeared to lack both conviction and vigour. Amongst the political parties the Liberals, having been long committed to home rule for Scotland, should have been well-equipped to take advantage of the new movement of opinion. The commitment to home rule, however, did not have very high priority in the party's programme. Moreover, there was a contradiction between the Scottish Liberal Party's policy of federalism and the English Liberals' scheme for devolved regional assemblies, which may have reduced its credibility. On a number of occasions the possibility of cooperation between the Liberals and the SNP was mooted. The idea was rejected by the latter in 1964. After the 1970 election Donald Stewart, leader of the SNP, expressed a willingness to discuss cooperation on the grounds that 'the self-government issue was too important for scoring party points',[33] but nothing came of it. By the mid-1970s, the Liberals were in a weak position. Their share of the vote, which remained in single figures, was concentrated in a few constituencies, while their advocacy of federalism gained little support and was perhaps not widely understood. They were not in a very strong position, therefore, to resist the SNP.

The Conservative party, historically the party of the union in Scotland, had been a sharply declining force in Scottish politics since 1959. Although this decline was a source of considerable concern to Scottish Conservatives even before the Hamilton by-election, they appear to have been simply bewildered by the rise of the SNP. Under the Heath leadership, however, the party acknowledged the justice of some nationalist claims and recognized that some measure of devolution was both necessary and desirable. The Douglas-Home report (1970), commissioned by the party, rejected separatism and federalism in favour of limited legislative devolution. The report was adopted as party policy in 1970 and the manifesto of October 1974 included a proposal for a Scottish assembly. This was the high-water mark of Conservative commitment to devolution. The commitment was never whole-hearted and in 1976 under a new leadership it was announced that the commitment of the previous leadership was 'inoperative' and that any proposals likely to lead to separation must be rejected. This was a remarkable change of policy which suggested that the Conservative party was drawing a firm and close line against any significant measure of constitutional change.

The Labour party, whose policies since the Second World War at least had sought social and regional equalization through central government programmes, was in practice as much committed to the union as the Conservative party.[34] It was, if anything, more alarmed by the sudden breakthrough of the SNP in 1974. In the tapestry of the Labour party's political tradition, however, there were more threads from which to weave a response. Before and immediately after the First World War, the Labour party in Scotland had been closely associated with the home rule movement and home rule had featured from time to time in Labour election manifestos.[35] By renewing and updating this commitment to home rule, it was argued, the Labour party could meet the nationalists on their own ground with a reasonable chance of winning. This was the theoretical basis for the Labour party's new role as the principal agent of active resistance to the SNP.

The nationalist question, however, divided the Labour Party deeply. Apart from those who hoped it would just go away, there were two views. One view was that, however the nationalist phenomenon might be understood, it did not reflect a real desire for separation and the response should therefore be calculated in terms of a proper consideration of Scottish interests and the correct mix of centrally managed policies, i.e. a continuation of Labour's traditional policy of differential centralism and pork barrel politics. The second view was that some measure of home rule would have to be introduced not only to meet the demands of Scottish opinion but also to satisfy the requirements of open and efficient democratic government. The official position of the party before Kilbrandon was broadly in tune with the first view. The results of the 1974 elections, the subsequent shift of opinion amongst Scottish Labour MPs, continued expressions of support for devolution in Scotland itself (including the resolutions of constituency Labour parties) and the rising fear of the national leadership that Labour's position in Scotland might be seriously undermined were the main reasons for the official conversion to the second view. The Labour party in Scotland, however, persisted in its commitment to the traditional view and was only persuaded to change by direct intervention from headquarters. This left a small number of members, notably Tam Dalyell,[36] to oppose devolution, while another small group seceded to form the Scottish Labour Party to campaign for a more radical measure of self-government.[37]

By embracing the new policy the Labour party became both the most effective challenge to the SNP and the principal instrument of constitutional reform. Although it was only the spectacular rise of the SNP and the marginal parliamentary position of the new Labour government which brought Whitehall and Westminster to recognize the need for such reform, the demand for it had been articulated for decades. The Scottish political public had long felt remote from the centre of decision and there had long been a majority of Scottish opinion in favour of self-government. The specific complaints underlying these sentiments were that the powers of the Scottish Office were exercised ultimately by a central government which controlled revenue and expenditure and geared economic policy to British rather than Scottish priorities. The Secretary of State was himself bound by cabinet decisions and was bound to implement them even if he considered them harmful to Scottish interests. The responsibilities of the Scottish Office were so numerous and diverse that it was impossible for the small team of ministers to effectively control them or for parliament to adequately scrutinize them. Vast areas of decision were thus left permanently to civil servants and without political control, making the system profoundly undemocratic. In parliament, despite the activity of special Scottish committees, Scottish affairs were frequently at the mercy of an English majority whose qualifications to vote on Scottish business were fiercely disputed by Scottish MPs of all parties. Moreover, because of pressure on parliamentary time, Scottish members felt there was never enough time for Scottish business and were especially aggrieved about the infrequency of Scottish question time. Finally, nationalists in particular objected to the practice of adapting English legislation to Scottish requirements, a practice described by one of them as 'government by amendment'.[38] One reason that devolution was welcomed by many in Scotland was the hope it offered of putting right these defects in the existing system as well as neutralizing the appeal of separatism.

The new policy of the Labour party committed it to the establishment of a Scottish assembly with legislative but no revenue powers, while reserving control of general economic policy to the central government, which would also have an effective veto over the assembly by virtue of the requirement that the latter's enactments be ratified by the United Kingdom parliament. In developing this policy the Labour government made numerous parliamentary statements, presented two white papers in September 1974 and November 1975, a 'supplementary' paper in August 1976, and a bill in November 1976. The Scotland and Wales Bill, as it was called, was lost when a motion to restrict the committee stage was defeated in February 1977. With support for the SNP still rising, however, the policy could not be abandoned and in November 1977 the Scotland Bill was introduced. After an eventful passage it received the royal assent on 31 July 1978, subject to the extra-ordinary condition, attached to the bill by its opponents, that it could only be implemented if it was endorsed by 40 per cent of the electorate at a referendum. When the referendum was duly held on 1 March 1979, the unexpected result was that 32.5 per cent voted for its implementation, 30.4 per cent against and 37.1 per cent did not vote. Thus abstainers outnumbered both the supporters and opponents of devolution. Moreover of those who did vote, the 51.8 per cent who endorsed the provisions of the Scotland Act fell considerably short of the 40 per cent of the electorate required to implement it and the Act was accordingly repealed.[39]

The failure to gain sufficient support for devolution was attributed to a number of causes including the changed political situation in the spring of 1979 and the sharply diminished popularity and credibility of the government, the lack of cooperation amongst the advocates of devolution and the mismanagement of their campaign, the alleged lack of conviction within the Labour party as the principle advocates of devolution, the suggestion that voting against the government's proposal would provide the opportunity to devise a better scheme, anxiety that devolution, as the SNP proclaimed, was just a stepping-stone to independence and ironically, the anti-devolutionists' exploitation of the residual suspicion and hostility to the enlargement of government.

Whatever the reason for the failure, however, one thing was certain. In terms of constitutional change the failure of devolution put the debate on the Scottish self-government question back to where it started in 1974. Moreover, anti-devolutionists were well-prepared by the experience of 1974-79 to ensure that it stayed there. Politically, however, the question was irretrievably changed by the debate on devolution. In the first place the weak support for devolution in Wales and the improbability of English regional demand for devolution, served to further emphasize the uniqueness of Scotland within the union.

Secondly, the principle of devolution had been conceded and what had been offered in the past might not be easy to withhold in the future. Indeed within less than a year of the referendum the SNP were seeking to revive devolution and attempted to introduce a new self-government bill in March 1980. Although they failed on that occasion, however, circumstances could very easily arise in which there would be a renewed demand and need to revive devolution. Despite suffering a crushing defeat in the 1979 election, the SNP retained a strong base on which to rebuild its support and launch a new attack on the major parties and the Westminster system. Devolution might then be the only means by which the government of the United Kingdom could make a political defence of the union. Without it central government could be faced with a confrontation between unionism and separatism, the outcome of which could easily be an independent Scotland. The experience of the Norwegian and Irish independence movements amply demonstrates that the course and direction of such movements cannot be reliably predicted or controlled.

Scottish nationalism in the past has been muted partly because of the caution and reserve of the Scottish civil establishment which expressed it and partly because there was no political channel for the expression of overt nationalist demands such as self-government. The key to the SNP's success was its combination of traditional Scottish grievances, Scottish suspicion of London-based government, the demand for Scottish self-government and the promise of a better economic future on the strength of Scottish resources, especially North Sea oil. Its failure, which would not necessarily be repeated, was that it was unable to mobilize all sections of Scottish society. Its lasting significance is that it brought the self-government question, so long latent in Scottish politics, into the open and, by doing so, drew a response from central government which set a minimum level to future demands. Whether the issue is now a spent charge or a time-bomb remains to be seen.

Notes

1. House of Commons Debates, 745.*151*, 20 April, 1969.
2. House of Commons Debates, 737.456-9, 30 November, 1966.
3. R. Rose, *The United Kingdom as a Multi-national State* (University of Strathclyde, 1970.)
4. A. M. Duncan, *Scotland, the Making of the Kingdom* (Glasgow, 1975).

5. R. K. G. Ritchie, *The Normans in Scotland* (Edinburgh, 1954).
6. W. C. Dickinson, G. Donaldson, I. A. Milne, *A Source book of Scottish History* Vol. 1, (Edinburgh, 1952), pp. 131-5.
7. Maurice Ginsberg, *Nationalism* (London, 1958).
8. Douglas Young, 'A Sketch History of Scottish Nationalism' in Neil McCormick (ed.), *The Scottish Debate* (London, 1970).
9. See for example, D. D. Murison, 'Nationalism as expressed in Scottish Literature; in J. N. Wolfe (ed.), *Government and Nationalism in Scotland* (Edinburgh, 1969).
10. For a further account of these institutions see J. G. Kellas, *Modern Scotland* (London, 1968).
11. For an account of the union and various views see: D. Daiches, *Scotland and the Union* (London, 1977); W. Ferguson, *Scotland 1689 to the Present* (London, 1968); G. S. Pryde, *The Treaty of Union* (London, 1950); T. I. Rae, *The Union of 1707: its Impact on Scotland* (Glasgow, 1974); R. S. Rait, *The Parliaments of Scotland* (Glasgow, 1924); T. C. Smout, 'The Road to Union', in G. Holmes (ed.), *Britain After the Glorious Revolution* (London, 1969).
12. Sir David Hume, *A Diary of the Proceedings in the Parliament of Scotland May 21, 1700 to March 7, 1707* (Edinburgh 1828); J. M. Gray, *Memoirs of the Life of Sir John Clark of Penicuick 1676-1755* (Edinburgh 1892); W. C. MacKenzie, *Andrew Fletcher of Saltoun, His Life and Times* (Edinburgh, 1935).
13. W. Mitchell, *Home Rule for Scotland* (Edinburgh, 1892), pp. 6-7.
14. For an account of Scottish society and Scottish nationalism in the nineteenth and twentieth centuries, see H. Hanham, *Scottish Nationalism* (London, 1969), and C. Harvie, *Scotland and Nationalism* (London, 1977); J. Brand, *The National Movement in Scotland* (London, 1978).
15. Tom Nairn 'Old and New Scottish Nationalism' in T. Nairn, *The Breakup of Britain* (London, 1977), and C. Harvie, op. cit.
16. H. J. Hanham, 'The Development of the Scottish Office', in J. N. Wolfe (ed.), *Government and Nationalism in Scotland* (Edinburgh, 1969); J. Kellas, *The Scottish Political System* (Cambridge, 1975); M. J. Keating, 'Administrative Devolution in Practice: the Secretary of State for Scotland and the Scottish Office', *Public Administration* (1976).
17. M. J. Keating, *A test of Political Integration in the U.K.: the Scottish MPs* (University of Strathclyde, 1978).
18. F. W. S. Craig, *Minor Parties at British Parliamentary Elections* (London, 1975), pp. 89-97.
19. Ibid.
20. J. P. Cornford and J. A. Brand, 'Scottish Voting Behaviour' in J. N. Wolfe (ed.), op. cit.
21. J. A. Brand and D. McCrone, 'The SNP from Protest to Nationalism,' *New Society*, 20 November, 1975.
22. H. J. Hanham, *Scottish Nationalism* pp. 174-7.
23. Peter Hetherington, 'The 1979 General Election Campaign in Scot-

land', in H. N. Drucker (ed.), *The Scottish Government Yearbook, 1980*, (Edinburgh, 1980).
24. W. L. Miller, 'The Connection between SNP voting and the demand for Scottish self-government', *European Journal of Political Research*, 5, 1 (1977).
25. Michael Hechter, *Internal Colonialism* (Berkeley and Los Angeles, 1975). Hechter's argument has been severely criticized in E. Page, 'Michael Hechter's internal colonialism thesis: some theoretical and methodological problems', *European Journal of Political Research*, 6, 3 (1978).
26. Commission on the Constitution, *Research Paper No. 7* (London, 1973).
27. D. Jaensch, 'The Scottish Vote 1974: A realigning Party System', *Political Studies*, 24, 3 (1976).
28. S. H. Lipset and S. Rokkan (eds.), *Party Systems and Voter Alignments* (New York, 1967).
29. J. A. Brand, *The National Movement in Scotland*, op. cit.
30. I. Maclean, 'Another Part of the Periphery', unpublished paper, Political Studies Association, (1979).
31. G. McCrone, *Scotland's Future: the Economics of Nationalism* (London, 1969); D. Simpson, *Scottish Independence: An Economic Analysis* (Edinburgh, 1969); C. Smallwood and D. MacKay, 'The economics of independence', in M. G. Clarke and H. Drucker (eds.), *Our Changing Scotland* (Edinburgh, 1976); Economist Intelligence Unit, *The Economic Effects of Independence* (London, 1969).
32. J. P. Grant, 'Oil and Gas', in J. P. Grant (ed.), *Independence and Devolution* (Edinburgh, 1979); E. D. Brown, 'It's Scotland's Oil? Hypothetical Boundaries in the North Sea', *Marine Policy*, 2, 1, 1978.
33. *The Scotsman*, 14 July, 1970.
34. Barry Jones and M. J. Keating, *British Labour as a Centralizing Force* (University of Strathclyde, 1979).
35. M. J. Keating and D. Bleiman, *Labour and Scottish Nationalism* (London, 1979).
36. See Tam Dalyell, *Devolution: the end of Britain*? (London, 1977).
37. H. N. Drucker, *Breakaway: the Rise and Fall of the Scottish Labour Party* (Edinburgh, 1977).
38. *Mrs. Ewing's Black Book: Scotland v. Whitehall* (Edinburgh, SNP, no date) p. 18.
39. The progress of devolution in covered fully in the *Scottish Government Yearbook 1977-1980* (Edinburgh); See also D. Christie, 'Our Changing Democracy; *Scots Law Times*, 5 March, 1976; H. Drucker and R. MacAllister, 'Our changing Scottish Democracy', *New Edinburgh Review*, 31 (1976); L.Gunn and P. Lindley, 'Devolution origins events and issues', *Public Administration Bulletin*, 23 (1977); D. I. MacKay (ed.), *Scotland, the Framework for Change* (Edinburgh, 1979); E. Nevin, *The Economics of Devolution* (Cardiff, 1978).

CHAPTER 6

Separatism and the Mobilization of Welsh National Identity

Colin H. Williams

> There may be a Welsh nation, but there is not yet a Welsh state. Yet it may be that the limits of the achievement reflect accurately the limits of the aspiration.[1]

The Welsh have long displayed an ambivalence in their relationship with the English, and by extension, with the British state. Although far too simple a summary of Welsh attitudes, it does nevertheless appear true that, above all, Welsh leaders have been opportunists and enthusiastic participants in the British state system during times of economic and political expansion, and have turned inward, homeward during periods of economic depression and political decline. Ambivalence toward a powerful neighbour is a characteristic of most small, relatively less advanced nations. Generally the advantages of co-operation, even incorporation, outweigh the disadvantages of loss of autonomy for minorities who benefit from access to wider markets, increased standards of living and unfettered participation in the dominant political system. The interesting feature about Welsh nationalism is not its chequered progress during the twentieth century, but that it should exist at all, given a period of state-wide participation when Welsh based politicians, and those which they represent, have enjoyed a disproportionate influence in the development of the United Kingdom.[2]

Wales is an interesting case for students of national separatism because political affiliation in the United Kingdom has tended to cut across territorial divisions, thereby minimizing the significance of regional cultures in influencing mass political identification.[3] However, the nationalist resurgence in Scotland and Wales has re-emphasized the spatial dimension in British politics and has called into question the unitary nature of the state's system. This chapter differs from others in this volume because it seeks, as its main aim, to account for this spatial differentiation by adopting a political geographic perspective on the growth of Welsh nationalism.

Nationalism may be defined as a movement or programme of action based upon the desire of some members of a group capable of being recognized as a politically sovereign unit.[4] It becomes central when a minority's demand for automony represents the only perceived way in which it can defend or promote a scarce resource, whether that resource be natural or human, or a combination of both. This chapter will argue that the Welsh identity has served as just such a scarce resource: that cultural preservation becomes synonymous with the desire for political independence and nationalism becomes the vehicle by which such independence is to be achieved. If national self-government becomes the supreme political good, then no amount of intermediate bargaining or consensual compromise about possible forms of efficient or effective devolved government will suffice. It has to be complete self-government or nothing.

Historical Background

A sense of nationality can be traced back to the earliest times of Welsh literature[5], and remained a central theme in Welsh cultural and political life until the formal incorporation of Wales into the English political system in 1536-39. Unlike Scottish national development, the awareness of an identity of language and culture in Wales lacked any lasting institutional focus.[6] In Tudor times, and thereafter, the Welsh élite became increasingly assimilated into the developing English class system, initially as landed gentry, and subsequently as a comprador, bourgeoisie; separated from the peasantry (Y Werin) by their language, religious affiliation and political aspirations. It was not until the early nineteenth century that Wales re-emerged as a distinct political territory and challenged the existing trend toward complete integration of Wales with England. Kenneth Morgan has suggested that it was the growth of industrialization and the explosive rise of nonconformity which revolutionized Welsh life in the nineteenth century and provided the basis for a new national movement. In many ways these were to be paradoxical developments in modern Welsh history, and substantial controversy surrounds the impact of 'modernization' on the maintenance of Welsh national identity, as we shall see below. The net effect of the social transformation which took place in nineteenth-century Wales was to bring to the centre of the political stage a new set of actors, the heroes of the Welsh-speaking nonconformist majority. Radical nonconformity was to have a profound effect on the pattern and style of Welsh politics:

> For now the Welsh *pays réel*, the Welsh-speaking non-conformist majority, could participate directly in political life. The route to national liberation seemed to lie through the ballot box. The effect was a political revolution which, more than any other part of the United Kingdom, transformed the entire pattern of authority in Wales, and which also made Wales for the first time a significant element in the wider British scene.[7]

Origins of Modern Nationalism

The original Welsh nationalist movement may be defined as the *Cymru Fydd* movement, which began to press after 1886 for home rule along lines similar to those adopted by the Irish Home Rule Movement. It was founded, like many other Welsh cultural groups at this time, by exiles living in London and Liverpool in the mid-1880s. Alone amongst the radical groups in calling for Welsh separation from England, it promised to transform Welsh Liberalism into a united nationalist movement, under the twin banners of 'Home Rule' and 'Disestablishment'. In 1895 it merged with the North Wales Liberal Federation, but attempts to incorporate the South Wales Liberal Federation failed in January 1896 and the whole movement collapsed almost overnight. Therafter no prominent Welsh Liberal advocated national separatism, essentially because 'the entire Welsh national movement had been a campaign for national equality. It sought the recognition by the English government and by English opinion of the needs and national status of 'neglected Wales'. Why, then, should Welshmen wish to return to the impotence of isolation?'.[8]

Although the Home Rule issue floundered, disestablishment was achieved finally in 1920. Yet the Liberal triumph was short-lived, as the disestablishment episode represented the last vestige of the political influence of nineteenth-century radical, Welsh nonconformity. After the First World War socialism displaced the once dominant liberalism in a nation which was increasingly being drawn into the wider British political, economic and social system.

The current nationalist movement originated in 1925 with the establishment of *Plaid Cymru* (The Party of Wales). Its original membership was composed primarily of university lecturers, teachers and ministers of religion but also contained significant working class elements, especially slate quarry workers in industrial Gwynedd. They wanted to safeguard Welsh culture and its distinctive way of life. Two principal themes dominated the early philosophy of the movement. The first was the emphasis placed on the intimate relationship between a nation's territory and its language, a theme reminiscent of Ratzel's writings and a fundamental issue in nationalist ideology in nineteenth-century Europe.[9] The party recognized that Wales was divided both linguistically and spatially between a predominantly Welsh-speaking rural core in the north and west, and a predominantly English-speaking periphery in the south and north-east. They further reasoned that the best way of promoting national consciousness to foster greater unity between the Welsh regions was to emphasize those features which were unique to Wales. This was to include;

> . . . keeping Wales Welsh-speaking . . . by a) making the Welsh language the only official language of Wales, and thus a language required for all local authority transactions and mandatory for every official and servant of every local authority in Wales: b) making the Welsh language a medium of education in Wales from the elementary school through to the university.[10]

Such language nationalism is, of course, a common feature of minority group ideology (for example, the Québécois, Flemings, Afrikaners and Basques, have each politicized their respective tongues).[11] In such instances, therefore, language becomes both the symbol and the instrument for a group's cultural survival in an otherwise assimilatory environment. But language and the culture it represents are not necessarily identical.

The second main strand in nationalist thought was the primacy of Christianity to the social welfare of Wales. Early Plaid documents abound with arguments fusing the Christian ethic with the promotion of a national consciousness, thus producing a synthesis equating a Welsh-speaking society with a Christian one. The prominence of Catholic and Nonconformist thinkers amongst the early leaders accounts in part for the emphasis on religion. But religion also had a functional, organizational role. In time the Chapel system and its associated newspapers disseminated these beliefs through existing channels and served to legitimize nationalist ideology. The spiritual element in Plaid Cymru's mission emerges clearly in the following statement:

> Our main task is a spiritual one. It is to restore a sense of Welsh nationhood, a feeling of pride in our own people, a pride in the greatness of our heritage, a pride in the qualities and potentialities of our people and a sorrow for their afflications that stings as does a hurt to members of one's own family.[12]

Table 1

Welsh Speakers by Geographic County

	Thousands 1901 Welsh only (1)	1901 Total (2)	*Census Figures* 1911 Welsh only	1911 Total	1921 Welsh only	1921 Total	1931 Welsh only	1931 Total	1951 Welsh only	1951 Total	*Thousands* 1961 Welsh only	1961 Total	1971 Welsh only	1971 Total	*Percentages* 1901-1971 Summation of inter-censal percentage changes
Anglesey	22.8	43.6	17.4	42.7	15.1	41.5	11.2	41.0	4.6	38.4	2.8	37.1	2.6	37.1	15.7
Breconshire	4.7	23.1	3.0	22.9	2.6	21.4	1.1	20.5	0.3	16.3	0.3	14.9	0.6	11.7	62.2
Caernarvonshire	56.0	105.3	42.1	101.2	32.7	93.7	24.9	91.9	10.6	85.1	5.8	79.9	5.1	73.1	35.2
Cardiganshire	29.1	53.6	19.5	51.1	15.2	47.6	10.6	46.3	3.8	40.6	2.4	38.5	2.0	35.8	31.8
Carmarthenshire	44.9	113.9	30.7	127.2	27.1	135.5	15.7	141.1	7.3	127.3	4.0	120.9	4.5	103.8	6.6
Denbighshire	22.4	75.6	13.6	76.9	12.4	70.6	8.1	73.1	3.7	62.5	2.2	57.9	3.2	49.6	39.2
Flintshire	5.7	37.3	2.9	36.5	2.3	32.8	1.0	34.1	0.4	29.1	0.4	27.2	1.4	24.4	39.7
Glamorgan	52.5	344.9	31.7	393.7	25.5	368.9	9.1	355.4	3.5	231.7	4.1	201.1	8.7	141.0	73.4
Merioneth	23.1	42.8	15.9	39.0	12.7	35.2	9.1	35.5	3.7	30.0	2.0	27.8	2.6	24.9	50.9
Monmouthshire	2.0	35.1	1.5	35.2	1.0	26.9	0.5	25.0	0.6	14.1	0.9	14.4	0.6	9.3	108.5
Montgomeryshire	8.0	24.3	5.4	22.4	4.3	20.4	3.2	18.8	1.4	15.3	0.6	13.6	0.5	11.6	69.3
Pembrokeshire	9.8	28.3	6.5	27.4	5.0	26.2	3.3	25.5	1.4	23.2	0.8	21.8	1.0	19.5	36.0
Radnorshire	0.1	1.4	0.0	1.1	0.1	1.4	0.0	1.0	0.0	0.9	0.6	0.8	0.0	0.7	61.2
Wales	280.9	929.8	190.3	977.4	156.0	922.1	97.9	909.3	41.2	714.7	26.2	656.0	32.7	542.4	48.7

(1) Persons aged 3 and over speaking Welsh only.
(2) All persons aged 3 and over speaking Welsh.

Primary Source: Office of Population Census and Surveys.

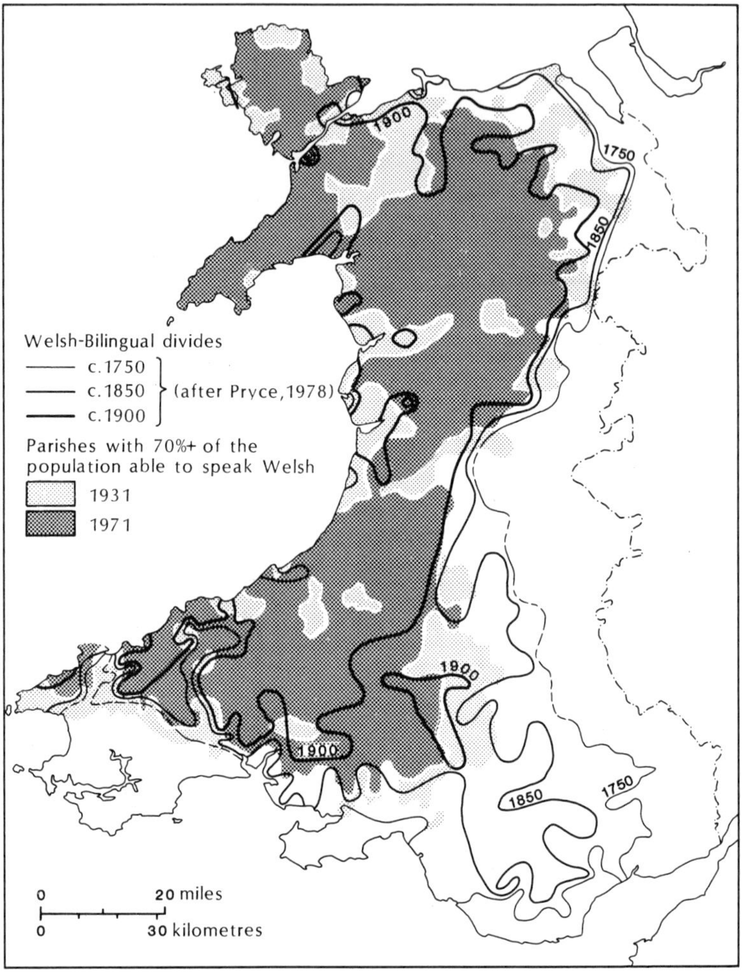

Figure 1 Retreat of the Welsh—bilingual divide c. 1750-1900 in relation to predominantly Welsh-speaking areas in 1931 and 1971

Sources: (1) D. T. Williams, 1935 and 1936; (2) W. T. R. Pryce, 1978; (3) C. H. Williams, 1978

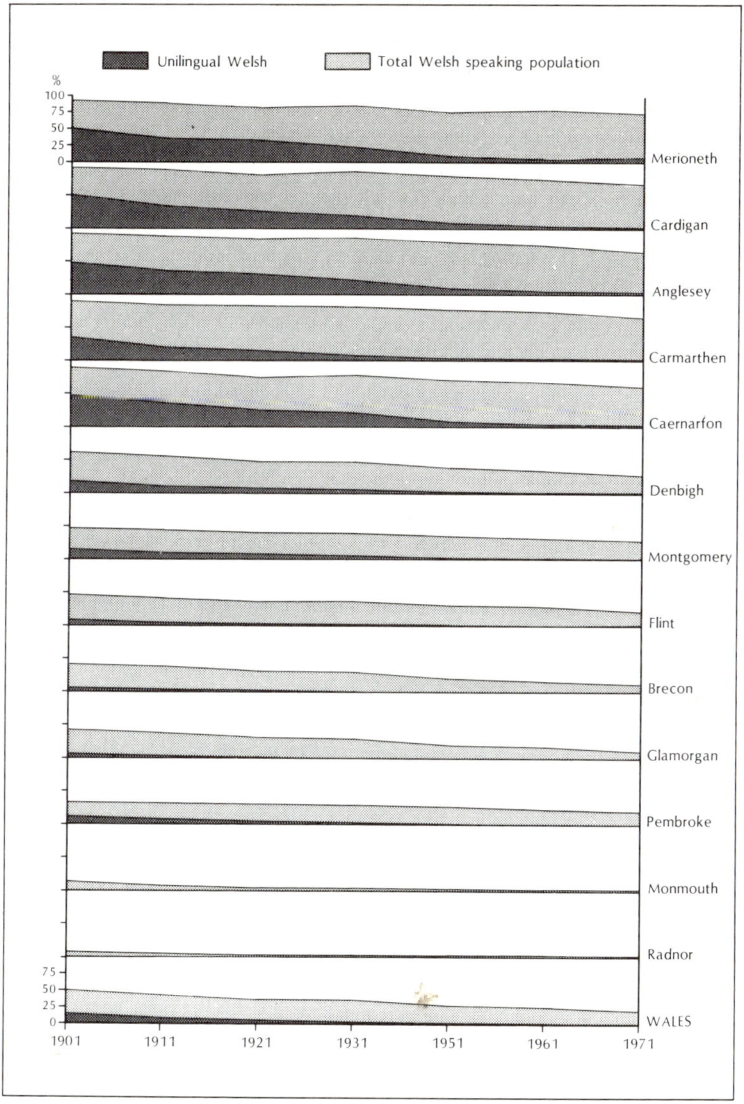

Figure 2 The decline of spoken Welsh by county, 1901-1971

Plaid Cymru from its inception was primarily a cultural nationalist pressure group formed to counteract the increased penetration of Anglicizing influences. Its leadership represented the essentially conservative values of a Nonconformist and rural Welsh society. These men viewed nationalism as the only way of preserving the heritage of a specifically Welsh past in the form of the Welsh language. This approach was articulated most forcibly by Saunders Lewis, a founding member and past president of the Welsh Nationalist Party. Lewis conceptualized the nationalist struggle as one dependent upon a prior commitment to the language issue, because he reasoned that an independent nation state was the only political solution to guarantee the continued active and political recognition must accompany any effort to encourage the language, literature and arts of a people.[13]

Logic of this type attempted to foster a sense of community politics amongst the masses, based on ties of common territory, common language and common history. It followed a pattern identified by Trent, in which élite sections attempt to portray the inequalities of social and political deprivation as community grievances rather than as individual or class-based inequalities.[14] To this end, grievance factors were identified as emanating from the unsatisfactory political relationship of Wales with England, which was producing structural strains threatening to completely destroy Welsh identity. The explicit causal relationship was acknowledged by many of the Welsh intelligentsia, including the Revd Dyfnallt Owen, who contended that 'Welsh society is fast being shattered, remembering that it is a Christian society. The new order which is being thrust upon us is a Godless civilisation. Do our Churches realise that when Welsh civilisation disappears they too will disappear.'[15] Structural strain and community grievances are important elements in nationalist development. Owen's 'new order' represented the complex interplay of a number of modernizing forces to which Wales had been subject since the mid-nineteenth century. They came to be seen as the root cause for Welsh cultural decline and consequently received much attention from these early nationalists who attributed to them the destructive characteristics which many Third World élites have identified in colonialism.[16] Seven main features may be traced in the ongoing threat of Anglicization.

Anglicization as Cultural Encroachment

Inherent in the attack on Anglicization was a fear of the cultural dominance of Anglo-Saxon precepts, tinged with an ambiguity toward the perceived effects of modernization. The most important period of Anglicization was the latter half of the nineteenth century, when South Wales in particular underwent a vast industrial expansion. This required large-scale immigrant labour, which was predominantly English in speech. There is little current agreement regarding the effects of industrialization and urbanization on Welsh language maintenance. Brinley Thomas contends that Welsh was saved by the redistribution of a growing population consequent to industrial expansion.[17] His interpretation has been supported by the work of Glanmor Williams who claims that as industrialization generated internal migration, the Welsh, unlike the Irish and Gaelic-speakers, did not have to exchange their language and homeland for industrial employment abroad. Also the rural-urban shift was capable of sustaining a new set of Welsh institutions which gave a fresh impetus to the language.[18] More recently, however, this interpretation has been challenged by research which suggests that industrialization ultimately contributed to the demise of the language and Welsh national identity, by weakening the social cohesion of traditional Welsh communities.[19]

The second factor in the process was the introduction of compulsory education subsequent to the 1870 Education Act. This, and associated educational legislation, enforced English as the sole medium of education and introduced through the formal study of the language a new awareness of English values and attitudes. Consequently the children of the Welsh masses were exposed to those influences which sought to downgrade regional cultures and identification and exalted the culture of the dominant state core and its associated value system.[20] The experience of Empire-building, understandably, made acquisition of English fluency a most instrumental motivation, and the key to participation in the developing British-dominated global economy.

Closer economic and administrative association with the rest of the United Kingdom followed the standardization of education. English became the sole official language of industry, commerce and government administration. Consequently the whole modernization process reinforced the dominance of English as the medium of advancement in an expanding economy both at home and abroad. The effects of this imitative and integrative motivation, identified by social psychologists working on attitudes to second language learning, were clearly operative in this situation, and continue to influence language choice in Wales.[21]

The result of the continued process was denigration of the value of the minority language, a status differential which over time became absorbed into the debased self-assessment of minority language speakers. This in turn leads to language particularism, whereby Welsh is compartmentalized into the two spheres of religion and literature. Elsewhere it is not fully accepted as being a functional medium of communication. Such language particularism entails obvious difficulties for a minority group, especially when the politicized élite have chosen that language as a means of nationalist identification. In such situations, the insistence on promoting a low status language as the symbol around which national unity should coalesce would appear to have a potentially disintegrative effect.

Immigration has long been a source of discontent, especially the recently increased immigration into the Welsh core of unilingual English-speakers, many of whom have purchased second homes for occasional weekend use. This 'foreign' land ownership is inflationary. The indigenous people claim that external intervention in the local property market raises the price for local purchasers to an unacceptable level. This price spiral in turn causes large scale emigration, a process identified as the fifth main factor in Anglicization.

Rural depopulation has accelerated considerably since the Depression. Large scale emigration has not only depleted the core area of its labour and resource potential, but has also been accompanied by the immigration of a predominantly old-age tier of retired persons from the industrial Midlands and north of England. This age and economic inequity is compounded by a cultural imbalance operating through language shift, as the local communities become increasingly acculturated to the immigrant speech, a process which permeates the whole socio-cultural structure of these rural areas.[22]

The sixth factor in this complex process is the fragmented nature of the Welsh transport network. Social communication theorists have stressed the importance of both physical and social communication in the development of a self-conscious nationality. In Wales, geographic isolation has provided the basis for cultural differentiation. The development of an externally derived communication system has served to reduce that isolation. The critical factors influencing the development of the transport system were defence and commerce, in that it was designed to facilitate through traffic from England to Ireland, so that the main routes run east-west along the northern and southern coasts respectively. This has had the effect of integrating South Wales economically with the Bristol region and London, and North Wales with the Lancashire conurbations of Liverpool and Manchester. Consequently Wales has a poorly developed internal road and rail system which does not contribute to its national integration.

The final element is the impact of the mass media which consistently reinforces the British dimension and the dominance of English as the accepted medium of communication. Recent developments have demonstrated how bilingual education and language planning can redress this imbalance somewhat. But given the magnitude of the task it has been concluded that without substantial assistance through formal education, or the establishment of a Welsh-medium television channel and continued subsidies to Welsh-medium publications, the language would continue to decline, even in the predominantly Welsh-speaking socio-cultural environments.[23]

Having identified Anglicization as the key threat to Welsh ethno-linguistic identity and ultimately therefore of group survival, nationalist theory is heavily imbued with cultural considerations.[24] From the very beginning the defence of the Welsh culture, and its most potent expression, the Welsh language, became a 'focus for solidarity and a motor for action'.[25] Curiously enough, the language issue-played only a minor part in the national movement before 1914. However, given the rapid pattern of decline after the first decades of the twentieth century it is fair to suggest that the language issue came to dominate Plaid Cymru's programme during the period 1925-1962.

Language as an Issue in the Promotion of Separatism

The orthodox explanation as to why language policies in multilingual states are often so acrimonious is that language conflict is peculiarly unamenable to political compromise. Language is often treated as a 'given' in many explanations of culture conflict and is assumed to be a naturally divisive issue. This is because in advanced industrial states, language to a greater extent than religion or race, is a more pervasive influence on the resultant character of the services provided by central government to ethnic minorities. Whilst it is 'possible to administer an educational programme without regard to race, religion and sex . . . it is not possible to do so without regard to language. In multilingual situations, differentiation as to language is unavoidable.'[26] In addition the competing interest groups in language conflict are also communication groups.

This model of language as a barrier to cross-cultural political co-operation might be feasible in multi-lingual polities, composed of a number of discrete unilingual regions. But it is less applicable to those cases where the ethnic minority is functionally bilingual, and to those for whom their ethnic membership does not necessarily serve as a barrier to their full participation in the political system of the state. In such circumstances it is more profitable to treat language as a variable which can be used as a grievance factor to mobilize mass support for political movements. This middle section of the chapter will demonstrate the temporal and spatial variations in the promotion of language as a political issue within the development of Welsh separatism.

Given the party's expressed aim of defending Welsh identity it concentrated its first electoral challenge in 1929 in Gwynedd, north-west Wales. Its candidate, Lewis Valentine, a young Baptist minister who reflected the close affiliation with radical nonconformity, polled only 609 votes (1.1 per cent of the total votes cast). Even though the nationalist vote doubled at each successive election, 1931 and 1935, rising to a peak of 2,534 votes, in each case the Plaid Cymru candidate lost his deposit. The party's most successful seat in pre-war years was the University of Wales constituency contested by Saunders Lewis from 1931 to 1945. The seat remained solidly Liberal until its abolition in 1950 electoral redistribution. By 1945 Plaid Cymru membership had risen to 6,050, with a reported representation of 140 branches. The war years were difficult ones for the movement as Plaid Cymru activists were bitterly attacked for their criticism of the armed struggle. Many of the members were avowed pacifists and were consequently branded as traitors for their lack of enthusiasm of the war effort. This was to have a marked influence on the future of nationalism in Wales, especially in terms of potential support and in relation to the tactics the party should adopt in pressing its claims for independence.

The initial post-war years witnessed unexpected nationalist successes in the industrial constituencies of Ogmore and Aberdare. The Ogmore election of June 1946 saw the nationalist candidate poll 30 per cent of the popular vote, cutting the Labour majority from 25,003 to only 7,947. An even more surprising result was obtained at the Aberdare by-election of December 1946, when the nationalist candidate polled 7,090 votes (20 per cent of the total) and displaced the Conservative opposition candidate who lost his deposit. Significantly Plaid Cymru's campaign in both elections was fought almost exclusively on the issue of unemployment. Language and the defence of culture did not enter into either local political debate. Nationalist flexibility on such issues was one of their major assets as a developing movement, and one which they chose to emphasize whenever local grievances could be interpreted as resulting from misrule by a government based at Westminster. But despite these localized successes the party's voting record still reflected its limited appeal, mainly in the north and west, the Welsh heartland it sought to capture.

In common with other fledgling nationalist movements, Plaid Cymru concentrated its energies on mobilizing opposition to the most tangible manifestations of English incursion. It became involved in a wide range of dissenting activities, including attempts to fire an R.A.F. bombing school on the Llŷn Peninsula in 1936. The subsequent trial of the three distinguished incendiaries was of national concern, whilst their imprisonment guaranteed increased public sympathy for the aims, if not the tactics, of language activists. Other campaigns of the period 1936-1960 included the decentralization of the BBC, attempts to resist the eviction of hill farmers to make way for War Office expansion in mid-Wales, and the campaign to gain equal status for Welsh and English which resulted in the ineffective Welsh Courts Act of 1942. These targets, and the fragmented nature of these campaigns, reflected the fact that the nationalists had little opportunity to influence through existing political channels. Public acts of disobedience were the only means open to dramatize the immediacy of what they believed to be the imminent death of the Welsh language. The Plaid Cymru experience confirms that periodic or permanent exclusion from power sharing tends to instil a deep sense of alienation amongst minorities; an alienation which, if not consumed within the political processes, can lead to demands for outright secession. Thus typically, demands for limited cultural equality, if not appeased, can lead on to demands for cultural autonomy and in turn may escalate to demands for political sovereignty.

Nevertheless, the overriding concern with cultural affairs severely limited the party's electoral base. Wales has not had a Welsh-speaking majority in this century. The difficulty for the developing nationalist movement was that by stressing cultural differences between Wales and England, it was also, by implication, emphasizing the internal cultural differentiation of language within Wales. In these circumstances nationalism was hailed as a divisive factor in Welsh politics which polarized the two speech communities and served as a vehicle for the aspirations of romantic and conservative ideologues determined to resist 'progress and social development' in Wales. In a society where class politics was dominant, the language issue was irrelevant. In common with other European societies at this time, the élite groups of industrial Wales assumed that 'issue politics' were the issues of social class. In such a perspective, shaped by the implicit Marxism of so many Western intellectuals, differences of language, religion or national background were either irrational and ought not to be taken seriously, or were a disguised attempt by the oppressor class to justify continuing oppression by deflecting conflict from the 'true' bases of social organization, the ownership of the means of production, land and capital, to a spurious 'cultural' conflict. A society, they reasoned, divided along class lines and along lines of essentially economic political issues was an acceptable society, but there was to be no room for divisions on issues that were primordial, ethnic, particularistic, and personal. Such issues and divisions were dysfunctional and irrational.

Toward the late 1950s Plaid Cymru recognized some of its strategic deficiencies and adopted a more radical approach, taking a leaf from the socialist book, but couching its arguments still in core-periphery terms, rather than social class terms.[27] Its revised manifesto attempted to address the problems of the industrial communities and advocated a massive injection of government capital to finance the redevelopment, and improve the declining infra-structure of the southern mining valleys. In large part this change of political emphasis was precipitated by the emergence of a new faction within the movement, what later analysts have termed a 'modernist' element. This development supports John Trent's observation that when social strain fragments the existing norms regulating inter-communal relations, 'a new ethnic leadership with the technical competence and ideological outlook necessary for grappling with the nation's problems must appear. Almost invariably it is formed by members of the intelligentsia who have acquired a new confidence and self-esteem.'[28] Nationalism attracted this new form of ethnic leadership because it offered an opportunity to democratize the industrial decision-making process. This was to be achieved by decentralizing power from a London-based administration, and would involve more local community-based representation on the policy-making boards of public and private concerns.

The new ethnic leadership were self-confident and technically competent, being composed of university lecturers and researchers in the applied sciences, engineering and business studies in the main. Culturally they were predominantly Anglo-Welsh, that is, unilingual English-speakers who had been raised in the industrial South East for the most part. Nationalism for them represented a force for change, a radical element which had the potential to destroy the Labour Party hegemony in South Wales. They introduced a new perspective, long missing in the traditional nationalist rhetoric, namely an economic rationale for self-government. Their argument challenged the effectiveness of British centralist policy in distributing the goods and services which citizens in the periphery had come to anticipate. They sought a restructuring of the economic and political order and argued that large-scale corporate government planning in a unitary state almost inevitably involved a neglect of the problems of the periphery. Several of the 'Modernists' had joined the party because of their disillusionment with Labour and have been described as convinced 'devolutionists' rather than fervent nationalists. However, involvement with party affairs and their subsequent socialization within nationalist social networks has led many of the ex-Labour luminaries to equate an independent, democratic, and socialist Wales with a Welsh Wales.[29] This change in the leadership composition and ideological emphasis was to have important implications for the future development of the movement, especially in relation to the priority accorded to the language issue in Plaid Cymru's electoral strategies.

The Spatial Diffusion of Nationalist Support

Smith has suggested that it is possible for the twin bases of separatism, 'ethnic' and 'territorial' to coincide, indeed many current European separatist movements rest upon territorial claims to ethnic distinctiveness.[30] One of the persistent problems facing separatist leaders is how they can best present their case to the governing élite. The question of tactics is in turn related to the ideological structure of the movement and their representativeness of the ethnic community on whose behalf sovereignty is being claimed. Traditionally students of nationalism have focussed on the social bases of separatist support, as Pinard and Hamilton do in this volume. I want to extend that traditional concern to examine the socio-spatial bases of separatist support in Wales. The most significant feature of which is that, historically, Plaid Cymru's organizational structure has long reflected its close association with Welsh-speaking areas. However, not all such areas were equally responsive to nationalist calls, the interesting research question remains; within which areas and under what circumstances does nationalism develop as a movement capable of reflecting the genuine political aspirations of a people?

The early years of campaigning (1929-55) displayed a great deal of ambiguity concerning the centrality of independence to the nationalist programme. In the initial period, 1929-45, Plaid Cymru concentrated its parliamentary challenge on four seats, Caernarfonshire, Caernarfon Boroughs, Neath and the University of Wales. Its best results were obtained in the University parliamentary contests, where Saunders Lewis gained 17.9 per cent of the votes in the 1931 general elections and Dr Gwenan Jones gained 14.4 per cent of the votes at the 1945 general election thus saving her deposit. At the July 1945 election the party fought eight seats, polling 16,447 votes, but the meagre results and financial drain caused widespread dissatisfaction amongst the leadership, especially as they had failed to increase their level of support from previously contested seats.[31] A switch of party emphasis away from the heartland constituencies to the two by-elections of Ogmore and Aberdare augered well for its challenge in the future as a protest against a Westminster-dominated government.[32]

Despite their unexpected successes in industrial South Wales the party could not capitalize on the impetus gained due to lack of human and financial resources. At the next election, February 1950, Plaid Cymru was only able to field seven candidates who together polled 17,580 votes. In Ogmore, no official Plaid candidate contested the seat, whilst in Aberdare, Wynne Samuel polled less than half the number of votes gained in 1946. A worse situation prevailed in the 1951 general election when resources permitted the fielding of only four candidates. Part of Plaid Cymru's energies had been dissipated by the recent cross-party Parliament for Wales campaign under the auspices of the non-partisan Undeb Cymru Fydd movement, which was to end in failure following the withdrawal of Liberal support in 1956. But in addition the party had incurred heavy debts from its previous partisan activities, especially the 1950 election. In between parliamentary campaigns, lack of finances and a weak organizational structure forced the movement to concentrate on highlighting specific instances of alleged misgovernment in Wales. Thus the Tryweryn episode was presented as a classic illustration of the Parliamentary tendency to overrule all-party Welsh demands that the Tryweryn valley be not drowned to provide a resevoir for Liverpool's water supply. Nationalist propaganda used such examples as a means of polarizing group interests and loyalties between an explicit Welsh, and an assimilated English, identity. Tryweryn represented the denial of Welsh culture, territory and group interests and became absorbed into the nationalist myth of Welsh suffering and powerlessness. In the short term, at least, Plaid Cymru did not benefit in terms of added political support (even in Merioneth) despite its virulent attacks on the symbols of English misrule.[33]

In the period 1955-9, Plaid Cymru witnessed increasing internal dissension over its adherence to constitutional progress toward Home Rule. The Tryweryn episode, and others of a similar nature, had revealed that Welsh MPs, of whatever persuasion, could be overruled by Westminster, even when acting in concert. Also Saunders Lewis echoed a growing doubt that the party's campaign might never be successful if it always relied on the good-will of Westminster to distribute concessions which might lead, eventually to some form of autonomy. The movement was bi-furcating. On the one hand there were those who accepted the legitimacy of the British state framework and who advocated an evolutionary, constitutional change through the pressure of the ballot box. On the other hand there were those who doubted whether such a strategy would ever prove effective and were impatient with Westminster's and the Welsh electorate's own intransigence. This split, common to many of the movements discussed in this volume, reinforces Rudolph's distinction between primarily anti-régime politics, and anti-community politics, and served to weaken the Party leadership.[34]

Despite internal conflict Plaid Cymru's performance in the 1959 general election was its best to date. Its twenty candidates polled 77,571 votes. It contested every seat within *Y Fro* and increased its share of the votes to over a fifth in both Caernarfon and Merioneth. Its average share of all votes cast in the constituencies contested was still only 10.34 per cent.[35] The introduction of the new ethnic intelligentsia influenced the choice of areas Plaid Cymru contested in this election. Outside of the Heartland base Plaid Cymru contested nine of the twenty-two seats in Glamorgan and Monmouth as compared with only four such seats in the previous election. The leadership reasoned that the decline of the Welsh-speaking portion of the population and Labour incursions into the Heartland, necessitated a counter drive amongst the potential voters of industrial South Wales who might be attracted to the nationalist movement by promises of economic reform and increased industrial democracy.

However, before Plaid Cymru could measure the effectiveness of this policy shift it was faced with the arrival of a new social movement in the form of the Welsh Language Society, established in July 1962. Many nationalists feared that the changing emphasis of the Nationalist Party would inevitably reduce the significance of the Welsh language in Plaid Cymru's programme. Others felt that Plaid Cymru's insistence on socio-political change through constitutional means was insufficient to redress the declining fortunes of the language. They began to advocate a policy of non-violent direct action, whereby language-related grievances might be publicized through acts of civil disobedience. Thus the initial aim of the Society was to have the Welsh language recognized and used as an official language equal with English in all matters of state and local authority administration in Wales. A longer term aim was to effect some kind of transformation in the Welsh psychology, to strengthen the national consciousness and 'to inject . . . a new reality into nationalism by bringing to light through the language struggle the hidden oppression in the relationship of Wales and England'. In the course of its development *Cymdeithas yr Iaith Gymraeg* was to have an important effect on the policy formulation of Plaid Cymru. Initially, however, the party's executive held an ambivalent attitude toward the Society and its deviant strategies.[36] Whilst officially condemning direct action the Party's general secretary could also acknowledge that in some circumstances recourse to direct action was justifiable, especially if it spoke on behalf of majoritarian liberties and injustices, for example:

> We criticize the activists for their lack of political judgment, but we cannot condemn them for action we considered taking ourselves. However, any widespread campaign of violent action in Wales today would be morally justifiable and politically foolish. It would alienate rather than win support. We in Plaid Cymru would have nothing to do with it . . . Violent action cannot be justified if it is a case of a minority forcing its views on the majority in Wales. But when, as in the case of Tryweryn, it is undertaken in an attempt to force the Government to respect the wishes of the people in Wales, it has ample justification.[37]

The general effect of the direct action issue was to reduce the popular appeal of nationalism.[38] At the next general election, October 1964, the party contested twenty-three out of the thirty-six Welsh constituencies. Every seat, except East Flintshire, outside of Glamorgan and Monmouth was fought. Despite contesting three more seats than in 1959 the party's total vote dropped eight thousand to 69,507 votes. Four constituencies in particular returned disappointing results, namely Anglesey, Merioneth, Llanelli and West Rhondda. The only substantial improvements

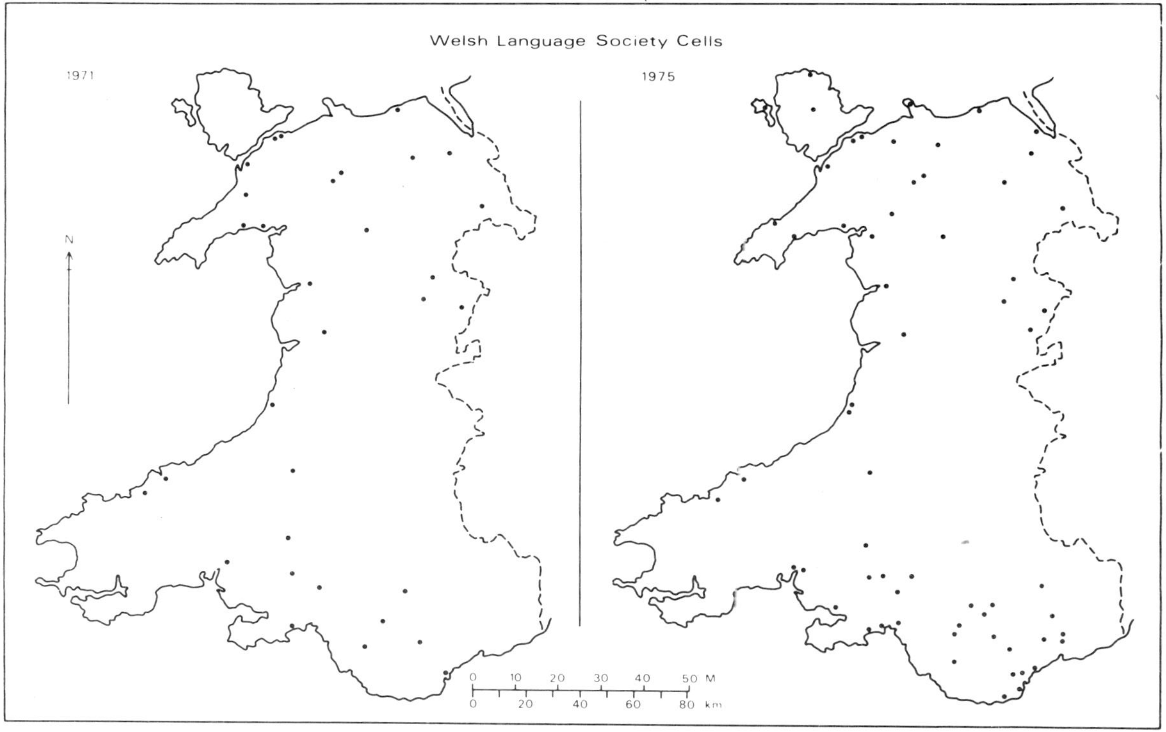

Figure 3 Welsh Language Society cells, 1971 and 1975

occurred at Caerffili, where Dr Philip Williams increased Plaid Cymru's share of the vote from 8.9 per cent to 11 per cent, and Carmarthen, where Gwynfor Evans's share of the vote rose from 5.2 per cent to 11.6 per cent of the poll. However, during the mid-sixties a number of events served to increase party morale. The first was the establishment of the Secretary of State for Wales office, which although it fell short of Nationalist demands, was a recognition of separate Welsh needs in government administration. The second was the widespread support for the Nationalist organized demonstration against the opening of the Tryweryn reservoir on 21 October 1965. The third was the publication of the Hughes-Parry Committee's report on the Welsh language, favouring Welsh being given 'equal validity' status with English in law and public administration. In the 1966 election the party contested all the north and west Wales constituencies and none in Monmouthshire. The minor gains were mainly in industrial South Wales, although in general the national picture was one of stability with Plaid polling 4.3 per cent of all votes cast. The results confirmed the mood of disillusionment with electoral politics and increased the long held suspicion that the diversity of aims and campaigns were dissipating the dynamism which the central concern with self-government should have been generating.

The Attainment of Political Maturity

The third phase in the development of Welsh nationalism could be termed the attainment of political maturity, when the party gained parliamentary representation, and was no longer a cultural-political pressure group outside the established political system. The breakthrough came when its president, Gwynfor Evans, was elected in the July 1966 Carmarthen by-election. He improved on his previous general election performance of 7,416 votes gaining a total of 16,179 votes on 14 July. The next three years saw a marked increase in party membership, branch formations and in Plaid Cymru's organizational effectiveness in electoral campaigns. A credibility gap had been breached, the electorate no longer deemed a nationalist vote as an empty protest. The growth of nationalism in Scotland served to increase the conviction of electors that an alternative existed to the traditional tripartite structure of parliamentary representation in the United Kingdom. The small nationalist movement emerged as a threat to the established Welsh Labour Party in particular, as evidenced by unexpected Nationalist gains in the March 1967 by-election at Rhondda West and at Caerffili in July 1968, both

Labour strongholds for over forty years. In the Rhondda West constituency a vigorous Plaid campaign against pit closures, economic decline and high unemployment rates succeeded in reducing the Labour share of the vote from 76.1 per cent in 1966 to only 49.0 per cent by 1967. The Nationalists increased their vote from 2,172 in the general election to 10,067 in the March by-election. A similar anti-Labour, anti-London campaign at Caerffili reduced Labour's share of the votes from 74.2 per cent in 1966 to only 45.7 per cent in July 1968. Plaid Cymru's vote increased correspondingly from 3,949 in 1966 to 14,274 in 1968. On reflection the performances were essentially 'protest votes' resembling the early post-war years, because the impetus flagged in the 1970 election, where despite contesting all the Welsh seats for the first time the party produced mixed results. Its candidates averaged 11.5 per cent of the votes, but in Carmarthen, Aberdare and Caernarfon they polled over 30 per cent, and over 20 per cent in four other seats at Anglesey, Merioneth, Caerffili and Rhondda East. However, the party lost its only Member of Parliament together with twenty-five cash deposits. Apparently its attempts to widen the appeal of nationalism and offer itself as a truly 'national' party did not succeed in mobilizing the support of significant segments of the Anglo-Welsh electorate in the industrial areas of the south and north-east.

Table 2 Wales: Votes Cast at General Elections 1959-1970

	1959	1964	1966	1970
Labour	841,447	837,022	863,693	781,941
%	56.5	57.8	60.7	51.6
Conservative	486,335	425,022	396,795	419,884
%	32.6	29.4	27.8	27.7
Liberal	78,951	106,114	89,108	103,747
%	5.3	7.3	6.3	6.9
Plaid Cymru	77,571	69,507	61,071	175,016
%	5.2	4.8	4.3	11.5
Communist	6,542	9,377	12,769	6,459
%	0.4	0.7	0.9	0.4
Others	408			29,507
%	0.0			1.9
Total electorate	1,805,684	1,805,454	1,801,872	1,960,521
% of electors voting (Wales)	82.6	80.1	79.0	77.3
% of electors voting (U.K.)	78.7	77.0	75.8	72.0

The Socio-Political Milieux of Wales

In an attempt to explain the spatial pattern of support for Plaid Cymru during this period a multi-variate analysis of the socio-economic correlates of voting in Wales was undertaken for the post-war period. This chapter reports on the results of the 1971 analysis, which employed a principal components methodology. This is a generic method of areal classification which permits the construction of grouped data units into regions which display certain similarities.[39] The justification for using a regionalization procedure rests on two convictions. First, it is of interest in its own right, as a traditional concern of spatial analysis. Second, it can describe spatial patterns of association and provide ecological contexts within which more detailed behavioural studies of the processes of ethno-linguistic change can be undertaken.[40]

Data on forty-eight variables were calculated for the 168 Local Authority units existent in Wales prior to the 1974 Local Government reorganization. The variables (Table 3) relate to the age structure, social class, residential mobility, linguistic characteristics, socio-economic attributes, household tenure and amenities, variations in the level of educational experience, voting behaviour, religiosity and cultural promotion. Thirty variables were derived from the national census of 1971 and inevitably reflect the limitations of that source. The eight voting behaviour variables were taken from the published results of the elections of 1966 and 1970, the two primary indicators of party choice closest to the census date. The other political variables selected were the incidence of Plaid Cymru branches and of the Welsh Language Society cells per 10,000 population. As with the electoral data, the party and *Cymdeithas* data was transformed from constituency units to local authority units. The final group of variables reflects the basic dimension of education and religion in Wales. Past research has shown the critical role played by religion in the maintenance of a distinct Welsh culture, whilst significant spatial variations in the distribution and strength of major religious systems have been evident throughout modern Welsh history.

Data on the four major types of religious adherence were collected from denominational handbooks and converted into appropriate indicies of denominational strength per Local Authority unit. In addition, the inclusion of Welsh-medium junior education (nursery and primary school level) together with the data on voting and religion, allows a more meaningful differentiation of Welsh regions than has hitherto been accomplished by research dependent on the census source alone.[41]

Sixty-two per cent of the estimated variance in the set of 48 variables was accounted for by seven components with eigenvalues greater than 1.5. Although the primary solution is able to summarize the greatest proportion of the variance, for purposes of precise interpretation the components may be too generally structured. Consequently a varimax rotation procedure was adopted with interesting results. The first component summarized 19.06 per cent of the data variance to form a Welsh 'ethnic' component. Three variables correlate over 0.9, namely the percentage able to speak English and Welsh (var. 26) and the percentage aged over 3 able to read and write Welsh (var. 28 + 29). These language functions are strongly associated with support for Plaid Cymru at the 1970 election, its branch organization and with non-conformist religious adherence. In addition the Welsh junior schools variable, Urdd centres and Aelwyd centres are all strongly associated on the leading components. Three modifications to an earlier Principal Component Analysis are evident and indicate, in part, how the culture complex has changed since 1961.[42] The first is the stronger loading of non-conformity in general and of Welsh non-conformity in particular by 1971, indicating a strengthening of the tie between religion and culture maintenance in the core. The second change is the relative decline in the strength of the negative Conservative loading from −0.8165 for 1959 to −0.4870 in 1970. This suggests a weakening of the party polarization evident in the 1961 analysis. Given this, an even more significant modification is the virtual eclipse of Liberal Party support by 1970. (In 1959 the Liberal variable loaded at 0.5431, by 1970 it had failed to register above the minimum threshold of 0.4). Conversely, Plaid Cymru's level of association has risen consistently from 0.7574 in 1959 to 0.831 by the 1970 election. This analysis suggests that the Nationalist Party is replacing the Liberal Party as the dominant political organization in much of rural Welsh-speaking Wales.

The spatial pattern of culture regions produced by the analysis confirms the broad division of Wales into core, domain and periphery. The Welsh core area may be described by those districts scoring over +1.0 S.D., the domain by those districts scoring between ±1.0 S.D. either side of the mean, and the periphery by those districts falling below −1.0 S.D. on Figure 4. The three leading nodes of Bala, Penllyn and Gwyrfai R.D. reflect an increase in the activity of Plaid Cymru, *Cymdeithas yr Iaith* and of

Table 3 1971 Principal Components Analysis with Varimax Rotation of 7 Components

Variables	*1*	*2*	*3*	*4*	*5*	*6*	*7*
1. Soc. Class 1	+	0.579	–	–	–	–	–
2. Soc. Class 5	–	–	+	+	+	+	+
3. Employed total	–	–	+	+	–	+	+
4. Pers < 4	–	+	+	0.817	+	–	+
5. Pers 5 – 14	–	–	–	0.761	+	+	–
6. Pers 15 – 24	–	+	+	+	+	–	0.653
7. Pers 25 – 44	–	+	+	0.805	–	–	–
8. Pers 45 – 64	+	–	+	– 0.556	–	+	–
9. Pers > 65	+	+	–	– 0.742	–	+	–
10. Owner occupied	+	+	+	–	–	–	– 0.759
11. P. rent. unfurnished	+	– 0.470	– 0.603	–	+	–	–
12. P. rent. furnished	+	+	–	–	0.507	–	+
13. Loc. Auth. housing	–	+	+	0.443	–	+	0.625
14. Basic amenities	–	0.772	–	+	+	+	+
15. Water closet	–	0.862	–	+	+	+	+
16. No bath	+	– 0.643	–	+	–	+	–
17. Car owner	+	+	– 0.531	+	+	–	–
18. Pers. p. room	–	–	+	0.744	–	–	+
19. Pop. change	–	0.702	–	0.449	+	–	–
20. Anglican	+	–	– 0.575	–	+	–	–
21. Catholic	–	0.439	+	+	–	+	–
22. Nonconformist	0.621	–	–	–	–	+	–
23. W. Nonconformist	0.765	–	–	–	–	+	–
24. Welsh 3 – 15	0.813	+	–	–	+	+	+
25. Welsh 65	0.829	+	–	–	+	–	+
26. Welsh + English	0.914	–	–	–	+	+	–
27. Int. Cens. language	–	+	–	+	–	+	–
28. Pop. read. Welsh	0.918	–	–	–	+	+	–
29. Pop. write Welsh	0.903	–	–	–	+	+	–
30. Plaid 1966	0.743	–	–	–	+	+	+

Variables	*1*	*2*	*3*	*4*	*5*	*6*	*7*
31. Liberals 1966	0.443	–	– 0.512	–	–	+	+
32. Labour 1966	–	–	0.771	+	–	–	–
33. Conservatives 1966	– 0.487	0.404	– 0.492	–	+	+	–
34. Plaid 1970	0.831	–	+	–	+	–	+
35. Liberals 1970	+	–	– 0.641	–	–	+	+
36. Labour 1970	–	–	0.797	+	–	–	–
37. Conservatives 1970	– 0.440	0.444	– 0.521	+	+	+	–
38. Urdd centres	0.603	–	–	–	–	+	–
39. Plaid branches	0.561	–	–	–	–	+	–
40. Nursery schools	+	+	–	–	+	0.599	–
41. Welsh schools	0.700	–	–	+	+	–	–
42. W.L.S. cells	+	+	–	–	–	0.587	+
43. Aelwyd branches	0.648	–	–	+	–	+	–
44. Unemployed	+	–	–	+	–	+	–
45. Female employed	–	+	+	–	–	+	+
46. Males, in agriculture	+	– 0.417	– 0.679	+	–	–	–
47. Males, unskilled	+	–	+	+	0.909	+	–
48. Males, professional	+	–	+	+	0.919	+	–
Variance	19.06	8.83	10.53	10.05	4.98	4.65	4.41
Cumulative V.	19.06	27.89	38.42	48.48	53.47	58.12	62.54
Eigen values	9.149	4.240	5.055	4.826	2.393	2.233	2.119

the Welsh-medium junior schools in these areas. However, the once solid core region of the west has become fragmented such that a bifurcated pattern is now evident, with two complimentary culture regions centered on Llŷn and Merioneth in the north, and Cardiganshire and Carmarthenshire in the south. The intervening region of north Cardiganshire and Machynlleth is not any less Welsh in terms of the proportions of Welsh-speakers. Its distinctiveness relates to the relative weakness of Welsh-medium schools and the decline of Liberal support in the area by 1970. This is an important shift in political emphasis and provides additional internal variation in the core, which has in the past been treated as a monolithic culture area. A second area which has experienced a simiar decline is Anglesey. In 1961 Anglesey was conspicuous in its deviation from the pattern that had been anticipated for predominantly Welsh-speaking areas.[42] By 1971 its position was very similar to those middle ranking portions of the core area, which suggests that the fragmentation and decline which characterized the island in 1961 was not being experienced elsewhere within the core area by 1971.

The domain also experienced a complex pattern of change in the period 1961 to 1971. Signs of an increase in cultural organization are apparent in the Ogwen, Aled, Ruthin and Hiraethog districts which reflects the establishment of more Urdd and Aelwyd branches, together with moderate increases in Nationalist support and an extension of Plaid Cymru's organizational, branch network. Other areas in the domain have experienced a decline in the maintenance of the language and culture, especially around the urban centres of Wrexham, Newtown and Llanllwchaiarn emphasizing the apparent difficulty of halting language erosion in urban areas. The southern portion of the domain is a paradox. It has suffered acute losses in terms of actual numbers of Welsh-speakers (cf. Figure 4) and yet has also witnessed increases in all the cultural activities included in the component, together with the election of a Nationalist M.P. and the expansion of Plaid Cymru's branch network. Consequently the southern domain appears to have been relatively stable during the decade, able to maintain its position *vis à vis* the core which it fringes. This stability, as recorded on Figure 4, obviously hides quite marked changes in the cultural composition of the area, and reveals one of the main deficiencies of the ecological approach. A significant decline is also evident in the coalfield district of the south. The 1961 pattern showed a broad band of 'Welshness' extending from Pontardawe to Abercarn.

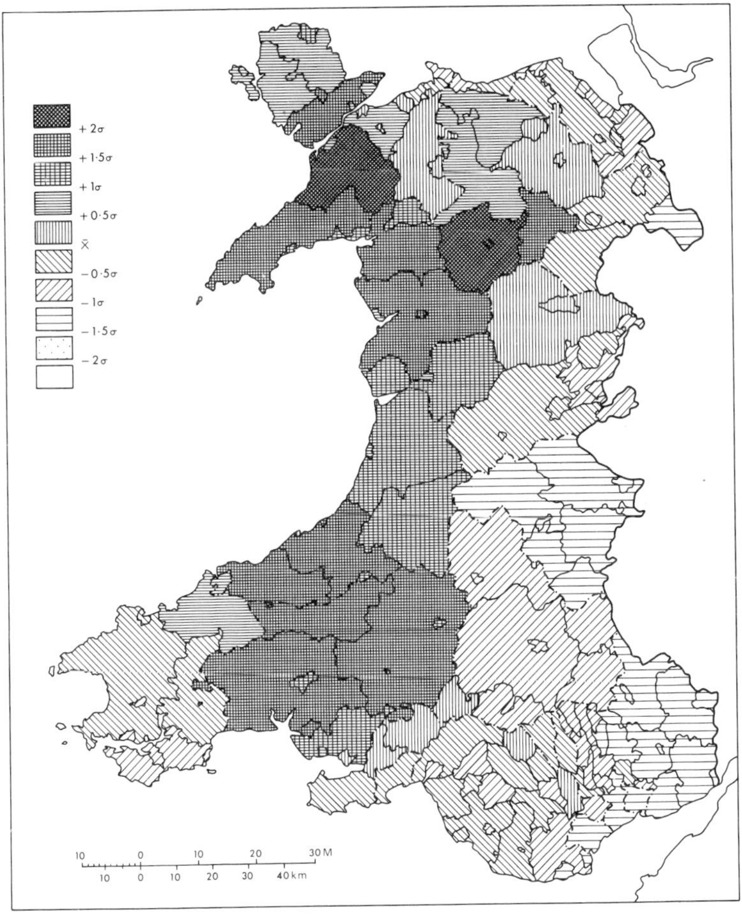

Figure 4 Principal Components Analysis, Component One 1971

By 1971 only pockets of distinctiveness remain, as at Aberdare and Caerffili, where there are strong Welsh junior schools, above average concentration of Welsh speakers and where Nationalist support is well above average for industrial South Wales.

For the rest of the country, the periphery is in the process of becoming more uniform. In part this is attributable to the less extreme negative Tory correlation, but it also relates to the general decline of a predominantly aged Welsh-speaking population which has previously inhabited the coal-rich valleys of the south. A similar uniformity characterizes most of Pembrokshire, Brecon and Radnor. However, the cultural interface of the Carmarthenshire/Brecon and Cardiganshire/Radnor border area remains a well-established feature of Welsh geography and continues to be a distinctive zone where core and periphery adjoin.

The second component distinguishes variations in housing quality along an urban-rural dimension. The highest correlations are positive and pick out an association between households having exclusive use of a water closet and all basic amenities (variables 15 and 14), males in Social Class 1 (variable 1), population change (variable 19), Conservative support (variables 33 and 37) and the distribution of Catholics in Wales (variable 21). Negative correlations associate households without a fixed bath (variable 16), the percentage of people living in rented unfurnished accommodation (variable 11) and the percentage males employed in agriculture (variable 46). This component explained 8.83 per cent of the total variance.

The good quality housing areas which have high proportions of males in Social Cass 1 and have experienced a population growth in the decade are located in two distinct Anglicized zones, the North Wales coastal belt and the south-eastern coastal suburban areas (Figure 5). These are the prosperous urban fringe areas of Cardiff and Newport in the south together with the attractive smaller urban centers of Llangefni, Menai Bridge, Bangor, Conway and the Denbighshire coastal resorts in the north. These are the traditional strongholds of Conservatism in Wales where the language is weakest and where immigration has been strongest. This explains the correlation of the Catholic distribution on this component, a reflection of the original pattern of immigration by Irish Catholics to the larger urban centres in the late nineteenth century and of subsequent coastwise Italian and Polish settlement in the twentieth century.

This component also allows us to describe a number of other significant societal features which influence party choice and the

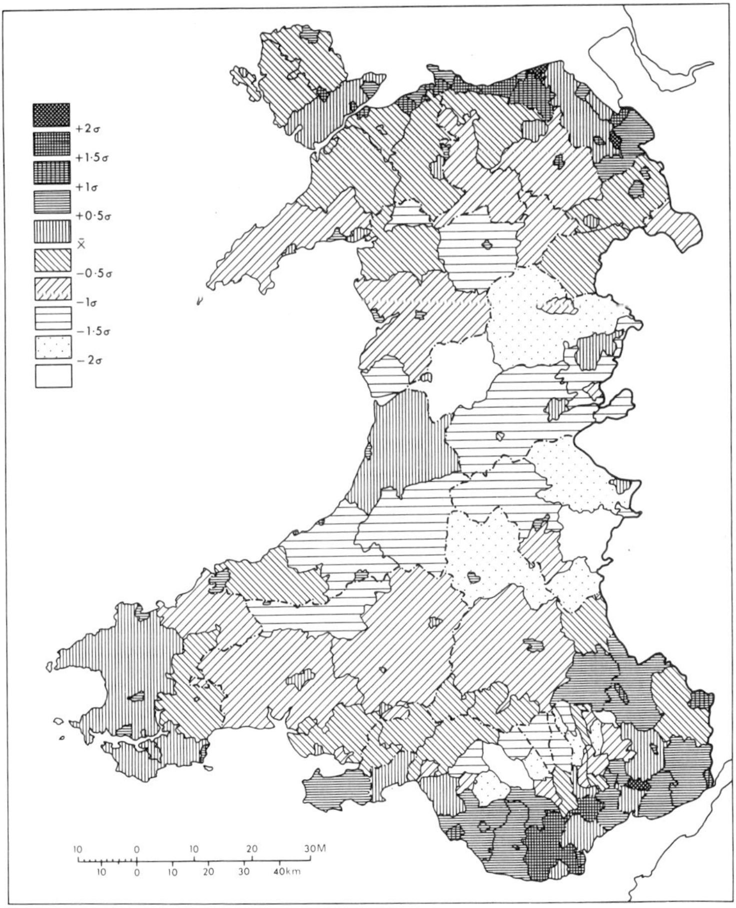

Figure 5 Principal Components Analysis, Component Two 1971

possible support for separatism. As might be expected the largest urban areas have more mixed quality housing stock, less males employed in professional classes and weaker Conservative support. They tend to form a distinct pattern comprising the ports of South Wales as at Newport, Cardiff, Barry, Port Talbot, Swansea, Burry Port and Pembroke Dock. A second category of smaller towns is evident e.g. Carmarthen, Llandeilo, Llandovery, Pwllheli, Porthmadog, Betws-y-coed, Denbigh and Deeside. In contrast to their rural hinterlands these towns did not experience large scale population outmigration and tend to represent the more healthy urban nodes in a predominantly declining rural context. However, there are signs that some rural areas have experienced growth and comparative prosperity as a result of suburbanization and urban encroachment, as happened, for example in Aberystwyth R.D., Deudraeth R.D., Gwyrfai R.D., Ogwen R.D., Nant Conwy and Aled R.D. in the north-west and Ceiriog R.D., the upper Swansea and Neath valleys and Narberth R.D. elsewhere in Wales. This pattern of suburbanization corresponds with those areas which have experienced acute language decline, 1961-1972, an association which does not bode well in a society which is becoming increasingly urban and suburban as modernization theorists in the 'sixties predicted.

A third region expresses the classic problems of rural marginality which the Nationalists have consistently claimed is a direct result of London mismanagement of the Welsh economy. The areas on Figure 5 which score below −0.5 S.D. are characterized by poor housing, high rates of outmigration, declining support for the Conservative Party, a bottom heavy class structure and high rates of males employed in agriculture. They comprise the special problem area of Mid-Wales and extend from Carmarthen R.D. in the south to Hiraethog R.D. in the north. The decline of the socio-economic infra-structure has serious effects on any attempt to maintain viable communities, and increases the fiscal burden of providing appropriate transport, educational, social and medical facilities in these sparsely populated areas.[43] The current malaise of economic marginality and cultural decline are cited by Plaid Cymru as the precussor of a wider fragmentation of Welsh society.

However, an out-moded infra-structure and sub-standard housing is by no means an essentially rural phenomena. A second major region of social deprivation exists in the central and eastern sector of the southern coalfield sector. Much of the housing stock is between seventy-five and a hundred years old and devoid of many basic amenities. Until recently, little finance, public or private, was available to upgrade the general quality of the built environment. Figure 5 reveals that urban decay is particularly acute in the Rhondda and in Blaenavon, both amongst the earliest communities to experience industrialization. The valley communities have also experienced high rates of depopulation losing primarily young families who migrate to the more prosperous coastal districts of the south and to England. There is evidence that this trend is being reversed of late as escalating land and property values in the southern commuter areas, together with local authority grants for home improvements induce more families to remain in the valley communities, travelling daily to their employment in the industrial sites north and south of the coalfield.[44]

Despite the similarity of Mid-Wales and the mining valleys in terms of their problems of depopulation and infra-structural decay, they look to different political parties and ideologies for providing a panacea to their shared problems. The third component illustrates the marked regional variation in traditional political support which has divided Wales since the First World War. The component contrasts the strong positive loading of Labour voting patterns at the 1966 and 1970 general elections (variables 32 and 36), with the negative associations of agricultural employment (variable 46), private rented unfurnished accommodation (variable 11), high rates of Anglican adherence (variable 20), above average rates of car ownership (variable 17) and support for the Conservatives and Liberals (variables 33 and 37, 31 and 35). Since 1961 a number of interesting changes in party support indicate that in general the decline of Liberal support in predominantly Welsh-speaking areas heralds an increase in the vote for Plaid Cymru, whilst in predominantly English-speaking areas a corresponding Liberal decline favours the Conservative candidates at general elections.[45]

The spatial pattern of this dimension indicates that the Labour Party's strength is still concentrated in the industrial communities of South Wales. Labour's hegemony in the coalfield district has remained despite substantial population and employment structure changes in the region, marking it out as the most distinctive socio-political region in the country. As the largest Welsh Parliamentary party Labour support is also significant in the Deeside sub-region and in the urban centres of Gwynedd, such as Holyhead, Ffestiniog, Caernarfon, Pwllheli and Barmouth, in marked contrast to other areas of the core.

Throughout this period, 1961-71, Wales in general, and the core area in particular, changed from a fairly stable pattern of

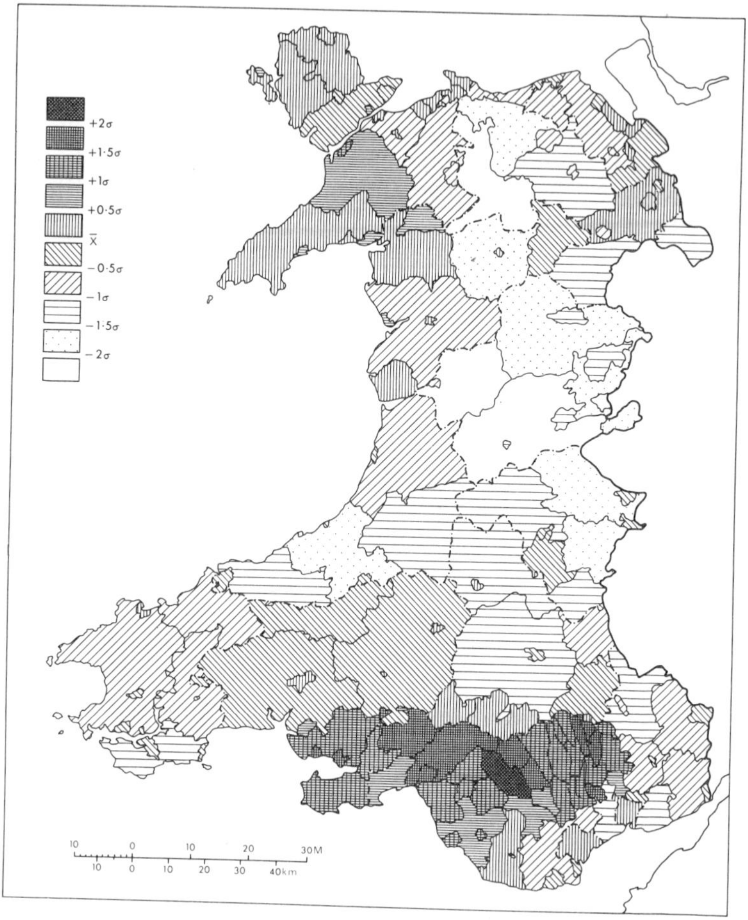

Figure 6 Principal Components Analysis, Component Three 1971

Table 4 Welsh-speaking and Nationalism by Ranked Constituency, 1961-1979

Constituency	% *W.S.P.* *1961*	% *W.N.V.* *1964-66*	% *W.N.V.* *1970*	% *W.N.V.* *1974*	% *W.N.V.* *1979*
Caernarfon	87	21.5	33.5	41.5	49.6
Carmarthen	79	14.0	30.0	39.7	32.0
Merioneth	76	14.0	24.0	38.3	40.8
Anglesey	76	6.5	22.0	20.4	20.2
Cardigan	75	9.5	20.0	13.3	14.5
Llanelli	71	7.0	17.0	12.8	7.4
Gower	59	6.5	14.0	9.1	7.1
Conway	53	7.5	11.0	10.9	8.6
Denbigh	50	7.0	11.0	9.9	9.3
Montgomery	32	8.0	12.0	8.8	8.4
Rhondda West	28	9.5	14.9	10.6	8.3*
Flint West	28	3.5	7.0	4.5	3.2
Neath	27	—	10.0	19.7	15.3
Aberdare	26	8.0	30.0	25.6	9.7
Pembroke	24	4.0	7.0	4.6	2.5
Wrexham	24	4.5	5.0	4.7	2.8
Brecon & Radnor	22	5.5	5.5	4.9	2.1
Swansea East	22	7.5	10.0	10.7	5.9
Rhondda East	21	8.0	24.0	10.6	8.3*
Merthyr	20	10.5	9.5	18.8	9.4
Aberafon	19	4.5	8.5	10.3	3.8
Ogmore	19	5.0	12.0	8.9	4.3
Swansea West	13	—	6.0	3.6	1.9
Caerffili	12	11.0	28.5	26.0	14.9
Flint East	12	2.0	4.5	2.2	1.9
Pontypridd	10	—	10.0	8.0	3.7
Ebbw Vale	7	—	6.0	6.6	6.5
Barry	7	—	7.0	3.4	2.1
Cardiff North	6	2.0	4.0	4.6	2.9
Bedwellty	5	—	10.0	7.9	6.5
Cardiff West	4	—	10.0	5.5	10.3
Cardiff S. East	4	—	5.0	2.7	1.5
Abertillery	3	—	6.5	6.0	9.9
Pontypool	3	—	5.0	4.3	2.6
Newport	2	—	4.0	1.8	0.7
Monmouth	2	—	2.5	1.5	0.9
Cardiff N.West	—	—	—	3.5	2.1

W.S.P.: Welsh-speaking population
W.N.V.: Welsh Nationalist vote
*Both Rhondda constituencies were merged into one in 1974.
Cardiff North West was a new constituency formed in 1974.
The data for 1974 is the average vote polled for the February and October general elections.

electoral competition to a more fluid and dynamic pattern. The Nationalist resurgence made its deepest impression on the Labour strongholds of the Anglicized urban areas and on rural areas north and south of the core.[46] In the middle Heartland

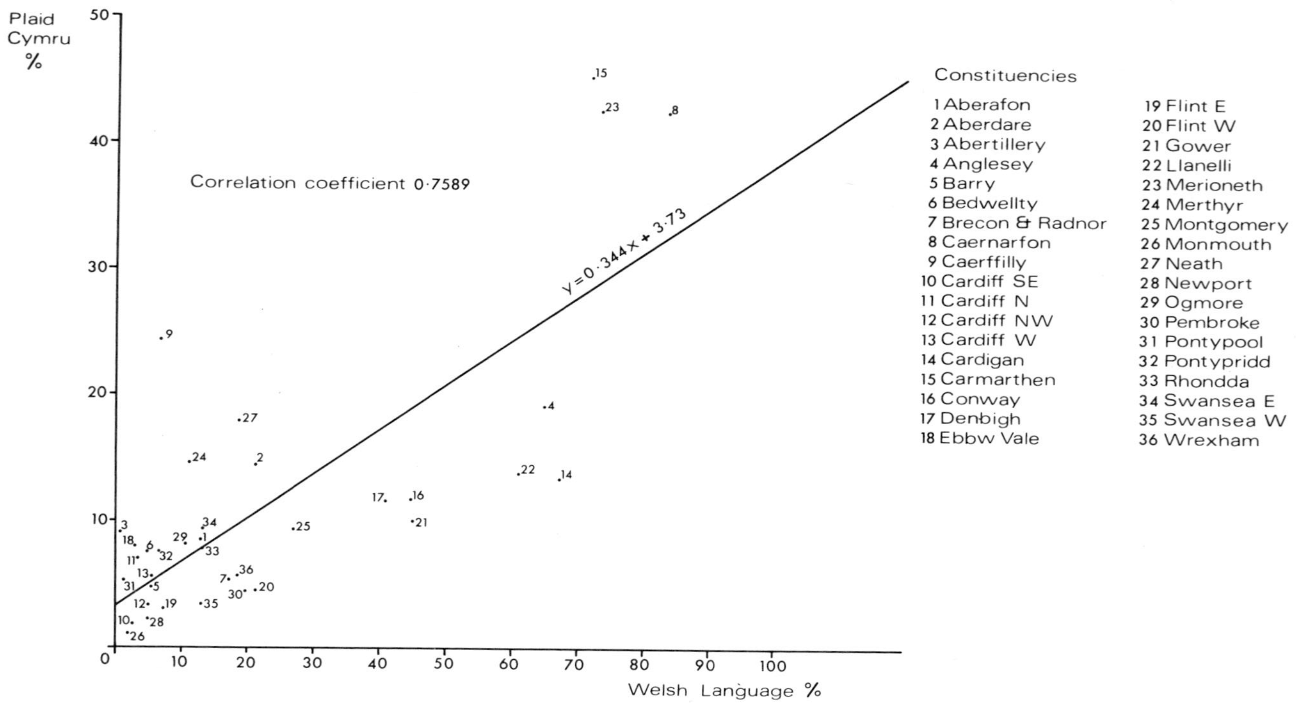

Figure 7 Plaid Cymru and language correlation, 1974, by parliamentary constituency

region it was the Liberal Party which was to suffer most as a result of increased Nationalist penetration.

It was clear that future victories for Plaid Cymru would be more likely to occur within the predominantly Welsh-speaking constituencies as demonstrated by the 1971 analysis. Given the close spatial association between nationalism and Welsh-speaking communities, elements within the movement advocated abandoning pretentions to being a 'national' party and urged the leadership to concentrate its energies on redressing the grievances of its 'natural' constituency in the rural heartland. Similar appeals to defend the interests of the core, a viewpoint dubbed the 'Fortress Wales' mentality, were expressed by other politically active pressure groups and led to demands for special planning powers to protect and conserve the traditional Welsh-speaking socio-cultural environment which was being threatened by the incursion of seasonal tourist developments, capital intensive projects related to energy production and the ever-growing demand for retirement and second homes in the core.[47] The temptation to reduce pressure on the ultimate political goal of self-government and to concentrate limited resources and manpower on representing the core at the expense of the Anglicized periphery must have been great at this time.[48] However, such short-term gains as may have been won were weighed against the larger goal and the broader consensus of the party's constituents. Many of the traditionally Welsh-speaking areas, in addition, were fragmented and foiled any suggestion of identifying extensive parts of Wales in terms of language zones for administrative, judicial and social welfare purposes. None of the core areas was by now sufficiently densely populated to justify the expenditure. Furthermore both Plaid Cymru and *Cymdeithas yr Iaith* rejected suggestions for internal administrative sub-divisions based on language predominance as they feared it would institutionalize the cultural cleavage and inevitably reduce the territorial parameters within which the separatist appeal for autonomy would be made. Moreover the Party had consistently attempted to introduce non-Welsh-speakers into its ranks after 1945, and it was this conscious attempt to diversify the linguistic base which was interpreted by *Cymdeithas yr Iaith* as a diminution of the centrality of the language issue to the nationalist cause. It was becoming more and more evident that because of the increased activity of Anglo-Welsh members, English was accepted as a working language in many branch activities and in the transactions, publicity and campaigning at national level. Whilst local cultural and social concerns continued to dominate the business of Gwynedd and Dyfed branches, in south-east Wales economic concerns, especially the problems of declining industries and rising unemployment, were the mobilizing issues. Recognizing that a change in language policy alone would not attract new supporters and improve its appeal in the Anglicized industrial areas the party committed itself to a series of wide-ranging economic and electoral reforms. These were to include demands for more community control over public enterprises, and a recommendation that a redistribution of parliamentary seats be accompanied by the introduction of an alternative or preferential franchise to provide a more equitable representation for minority political parties.[49]

In February 1974 the Nationalists wrested two seats from Labour in Caernarfon and Merioneth. The Party's president failed by only three votes to regain Carmarthen from the Labour candidate, but in the October election of the same year Gwynfor Evans did regain the seat for Plaid Cymru, and joined the other two successful Plaid candidates at Westminster.[50] Support for separatism in the industrialized areas of the south and east was slight in both 1974 elections (Figure 8). Here the appeals of community preservation and the language issue tended to alienate those amongst the 79.0 per cent non-Welsh-speakers who see separatism as, at best, irrelevant to solving socio-economic problems, and at worst, a conspiracy by an ethnic intelligentsia to force an unworkable independence on an unresponsive majority. It well represents a dilemma facing many ethnic-regional movements which are culture based, given a situation where a set of voters A', a minority within a community A are governed by community B, claim autonomy for A's against the wishes both of the majority of As and Bs.[51]

The same pattern of core area concentration was repeated for the Nationalist vote in the May 1979 general election (Figure 9). This election saw a state-wide swing to the Conservative Party, whose strength reduced the possibility of minority parties polling well. It also saw the virtual collapse of the Liberal challenge in Wales, despite the earlier Liberal upsurge in 1974 and the still remarkably high poll elsewhere throughout the U.K. in 1979. This convergence of Welsh electoral behaviour has been detailed elsewhere as a predictable response to the diminished ethno-linguistic vitality of post-war Welsh society.[52] For separatists, the election confirmed the fact that independence was still largely nurtured by those concerned with culture preservation and with community level politics, despite attempts to broaden

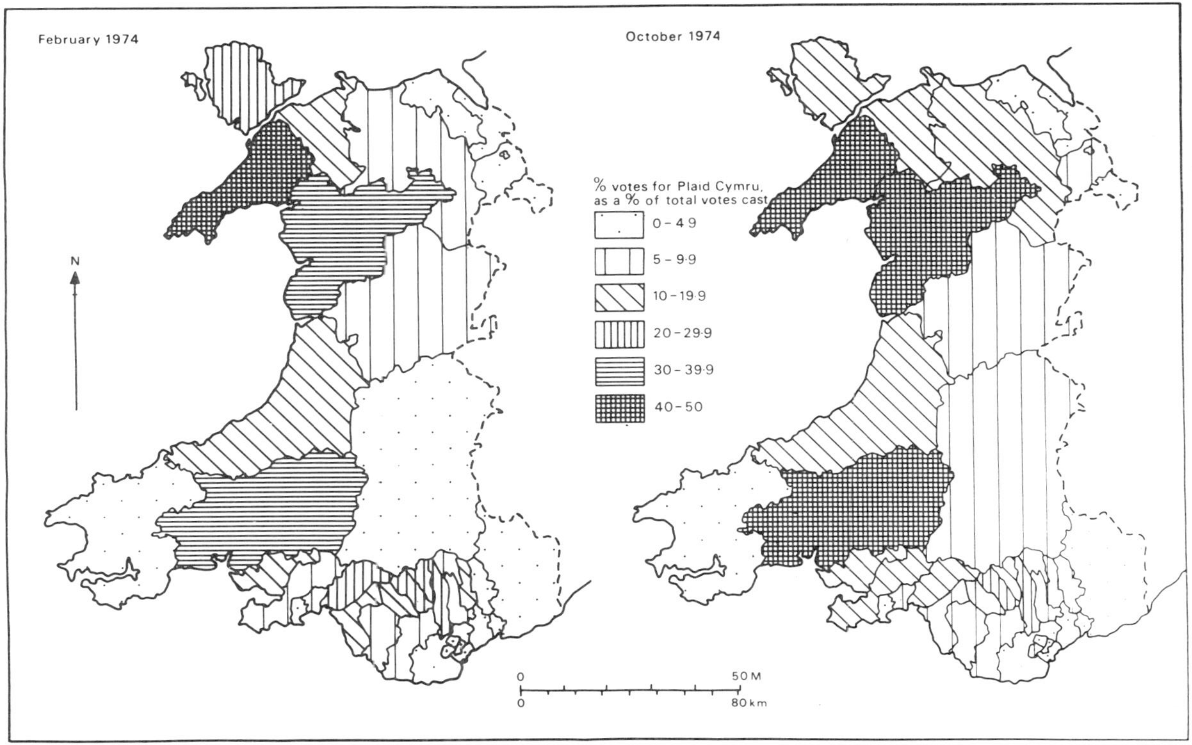

Figure 8 Percentage of votes for Plaid Cymru in February and October 1974 elections

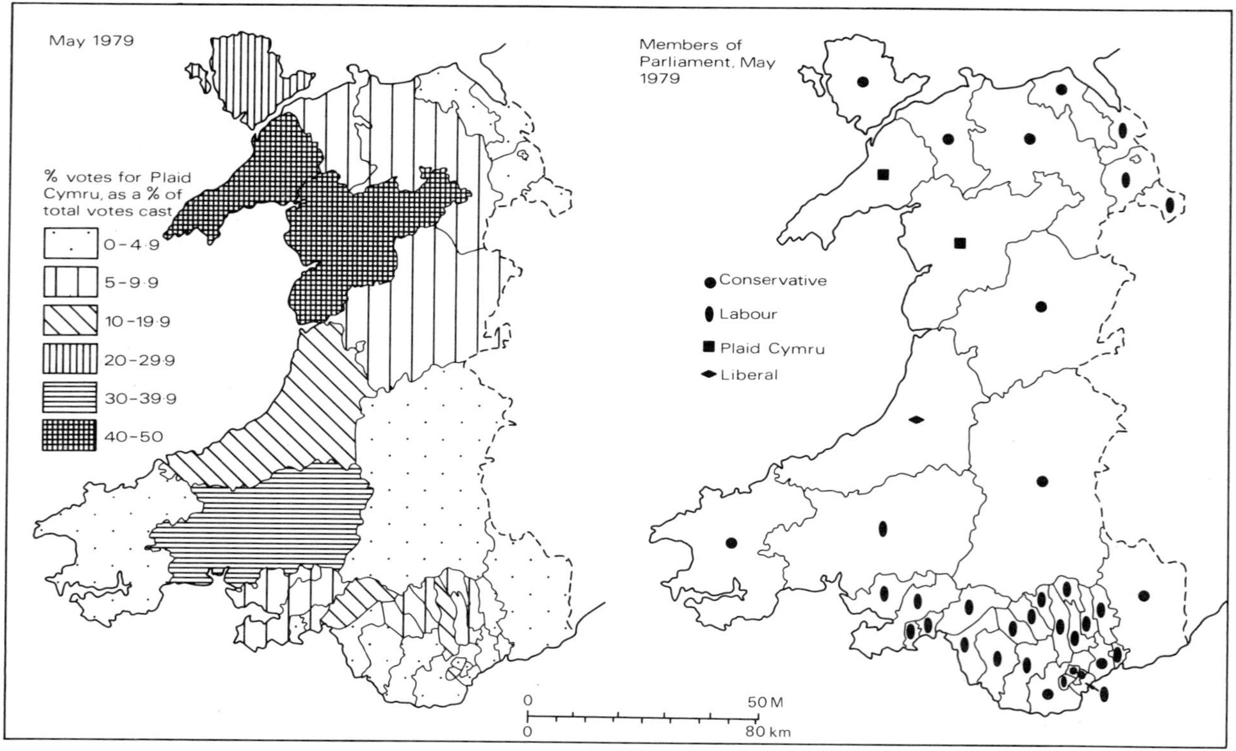

Figure 9 Percentage of votes for Plaid Cymru and Welsh Members of Parliament, May 1979 election

the territorial base to include the Anglicized areas of the industrial south.

The Devolution Referendum

Faced with government attempts to measure the popular basis for autonomy, nationalist leaders are at a disadvantage. The vote in referenda is conditioned by a consideration of the relative opportunities for improving government afforded by any new scheme, compared with the status quo and alternative, usually more radical, proposals for separation. The government which frames the devolution proposals obviously plays a seminal role. Thus in Britain, whilst the proposed Scotland Act would have given the Scottish Assembly legislative powers, no such powers were to be envisaged under the Wales Act where executive powers were to be vested in the Welsh Assembly as a consultative body.[53] The government's rationale for differentiating between Wales and Scotland in this manner was to resort to the institutional, legal and historical differences between the two countries, stressing that Wales had been integrated far longer into the Parliamentary system, under the Crown since 1536; and that sufficient guarantee for the expression of Welsh opinion was available though the thirty-six Welsh Members of Parliament and the office of the Secretary of State for Wales. Cynics might be forgiven for suggesting that the real reason for thus differentiating was the stronger support for nationalism in Scotland, and the incomparably stronger anti-devolution lobby within the Welsh Labour Movement, even though the Welsh Trades Union Congress was in principle commited to the devolution programme. The Welsh Labour plans, were framed in more moderate times than their Scottish counter-parts and without such electoral pressure were naturally more conservative—though radical compared with the prevailing Scottish Unionism.

Table 5 The Devolution Referendum Results of March 1979

County	*Total Votes*	*Yes*	*Votes %*	*No*	*Votes %*
Clwyd	145,730	31,384	21.5	114,119	78.3
Dyfed	160,359	44,849	27.9	114,947	71.6
Gwent	176,947	21,369	12.0	155,389	87.8
Gwynedd	108,834	37,363	34.3	71,157	65.3
Glamorgan Mid	232,026	46,747	20.1	184,196	79.1
Glamorgan South	166,912	21,830	13.1	144,186	86.3
Glamorgan West	159,094	29,663	18.6	128,834	80.9
Powys	53,520	9,843	18.3	43,502	81.2
All Wales	1,203,422	243,048	20.1	956,330	79.4

In addition many felt that the proposed regional assembly would be an ineffective body adding yet another layer of government to an already discredited local government system. But the principal objection to devolution in this form was economic. The extra cost of establishing a 'talking shop' would not be recouped by extra investment and increased employment. However, there is a case for arguing that it was the very lack of power to alter the socio-economic structure of the Welsh economy which led to the outright rejection of the devolution measures in the March 1st referendum. The only significant expression of support was recorded in the Liberal and Nationalist stronghold of the west (Table 5). Elsewhere the overwhelming majority voted 'No', some 79.4 per cent of the 1,203,422 who voted. Devolution supporters gained only 11.9 per cent of the votes from the 2,038,048 entitled to vote, a shortfall of the requirement of the Wales Act 1978, which insisted that at least 40 per cent of those entitled to vote should endorse the measure if it was to become statute. Supporters of regional autonomy argue that the size of the devolution opposition was a reflection of the rejection of this specific devolution measure and not of the principle of decentralization *per se*. However, it is hard to ignore the conclusion that timing is of crucial importance in political affairs such as these. Faced with rising inflation, massive unemployment and decreasing competitiveness in the international economic system, devolution was clearly a secondary issue, as far as the public were concerned, and not the pivotal question of Welsh national development as some had claimed.

The Barriers to Separatist Advance

In the course of the 1960s Plaid Cymru had attempted to broaden its appeal by formulating radical economic policies for an independent Wales. These have appealed to voters at local elections in Anglicized areas, but have not been sufficient to sustain incursions at national elections.[54] For separatism to become the central political issue as it has in Quebec, Euskadi and as it threatens so to do in Belgium, the nationalist drive has to mobilize more popular support throughout Wales. Plaid Cymru's failure to increase Welsh popular support in the late seventies, when the SNP and English Liberals were making major advances, can be interpreted from three perspectives. The Plaid Cymru challenge to British unity has been based on the call for the establishment of a culturally plural state, within which Welsh cultural autonomy would be recognized. The logic of Lewis's early political arguments was that independence was the only means by which cultural autonomy could be secured.[55] The equating of cultural preservation with independence has increasingly been challenged by those who argue that the nature of the British state has changed drastically since the early twenties. It is, they claim, now much more responsive to the needs of minority nationalities and of the constituent ethnic groups who inhabit the state. Indeed some would even argue that the conditions for cultural autonomy already exist in Wales and point to the widespread use of Welsh in education, in public broadcasting and in the deliberations of county and district authorities in some Welsh-speaking areas.[56] This dualism at the popular level is reflected within the nationalist movement itself. Its traditional supporters are the intelligensia concerned with culture preservation and with community level politics. The recent introduction of ethnically conscious bureaucrats, technologists and professionals working in the para-public sector, has infused the nationalist movement with a new concern for industrial and fiscal policy and with urban-social reforms; arguing the case for an independent Wales on *prima facie* rational and instrumental grounds as the most effective method of combining economic efficiency with democratic accountability. This duality of membership and consequent policy divergence, is a source of occasional conflict on party priorities, especially concerning the once dominant language issue.[57] This is an emotionally charged issue, producing tensions between those who see it as the essence of Welsh nationalism, and those, who whilst recognizing its symbolic importance, nevertheless seek to play down its significance because of accusations that its promotion is a threat to employment via affirmative discrimination, is a drain on the resources of education and public administration and is an anachronistic remnant of nineteenth century romantic nationalism, unlikely to attract into the nationalist ranks significant numbers of disaffected major party supporters.

A second reason for the lack of nationalist mobilization outside the core is the electoral system within which the separatist appeal is made. Third parties are traditionally disadvantaged in British general elections, but if, as is the case in Wales, there is a distinct spatial pattern of partisan support then minimum thresholds and concentration of votes can assist third parties in sparsely populated areas in returning Members of Parliament. Conversely, in industrial, populated areas minority party candidates tend to be overwhelmed by the strength of Labour majorities, and by Tory resilience in Anglicized rural areas.[58] Recent studies on electoral reform and simulation of alternative voting practices have suggested that given the spatial structure of Wales—the population distributions over which the constituency nets are laid—is such that no electoral system based on constituencies will guarantee proportional representation. Using successive alternative voting systems Johnston found that there was a considerable variation in the results, but of the four main parties the smallest variation in the possible number of seats gained was recorded by Plaid Cymru, as the following data reveals (given the original vote distribution the election outcome is particularly sensitive to the allocation of preferences). The extreme values are: Conservative 0-9; Labour 15-29; Liberal 2-10; and Plaid Cymru 4-8. In general, Conservative and Liberal performances were most volatile: Labour rarely achieved less than 20 seats, which was more than 15 per cent greater than its votes won, and Plaid Cymru usually obtained 4 to 6 seats.[59]

A third reason is that there is no necessary correlation between Welsh national identity and support for Welsh Nationalism, because other major parties are increasingly adept at presenting their case within a Welsh national context. Neither is there any *a priori* reason why one should understate the U.K. influences on voting behaviour. State-wide interests dominate the political manifestos of the majority parties, and the evidence suggest that they are particularly successful in their appeal to Welsh speakers, thus a recent study gave Plaid Cymru the support of only 17.5 per cent of Welsh speakers.[60]

Welshness is an amorphous and variable collection of cultural and social attributes, which may be expressed just as well through a Liberal or Labour vote. In Welsh polemical terms no true 'Welshman' votes Conservative (though one in five of voters in Wales do so) but many 'true' Welshmen find and agreeable home in the Liberal or Labour parties.[61] The separatists have yet to convince the electorate at large that they have a monopoly of interest on Welsh affairs, a task which has been made increasingly difficult as autonomist and devolutionist factions in other parties grow stronger and threaten to undermine much of the rationale for Plaid Cymru. In order to maintain its distinctiveness Plaid's response to this challenge has been to adopt more radical policies, thereby outflanking the Labour party in particular. The ultimate concern is still independence as a self-governing state within the Commonwealth with full membership of the United Nations and the European Economic Community. However, regional economic concerns, the question of revitalizing the economy and the accountability of Welsh industry along democratic lines are now dominant, in keeping with its political philosophy based on serving local community needs. Above all, nationalists fear that the increased centralization of the political system and the attendant burgeoning bureaucracy pose a threat to democracy and are capable of destroying the community element in Welsh life. Thus paradoxically perhaps, they advocate radical measures in order to preserve Welsh traditions and values, and prepare the ground for the 'national revival' which is the touchstone of ethnic separatism in the politically disadvantaged regions of Western Europe.

Explanations of Nationalist Resurgence

This chapter has interpreted Welsh nationalism as a reaction against territorial and ethnic encroachment, the main agent of which has been the relentless, centralizing modern state and its attendant bureaucracy. The threat to Welsh nationhood has, however, been interpreted in a number of different ways producing quite diverse explanations, the most significant of which will be examined below.

The ethnic continuity theory suggests that ethnic-regional awareness in advanced industrial states is but part of a global resurgence in ethnic identification which has come to challenge social class as an appropriate determinant of group membership and political behaviour in developed as well as less-developed polities. It is asserted that the assumptions and predictions of the modernization theorists in the 1950s and 1960s ignored the enduring salience of ethnicity, often dismissing it merely as primordialism. Specifically, such theorists have been criticized for projecting an image of human loyalties as being very malleable, such that with the developmental process, values, allegiances and self-identities would be readily transformed from the particularistic, traditional bases of social interaction, such as religion, kin and tribal ties, to the more universalistic and rational bases of interaction, interpreted primarily as social class identification. Now that such transformations have not taken place, even within the most advanced industrial states, ethnicity has re-emerged as a legitimate basis for enduring social relationships and political mobilization. Implicit in this explanation is an undocumented, but nevertheless powerful assumption, that the Third World independence movements triggered off a reverse diffusion process which fires the political aspirations of minority groups within the multi-ethnic states of the West.[62]

A second, related, explanation interprets nationalist resurgence as a 'primordial' reaction to the ever-increasing scale of social indentification and governmental decision-making. It is claimed that the development of the European Economic Community has intensified the conflict between sub-state and supra-state allegiance and interaction, and has animated a number of nationalist movements who would wish to fragment the European state system still further before contemplating any realignment in a future federated Europe. The increased bureaucratization which accompanies state modernization, whereby decision-making is further removed to remote locations, accentuates peripheral alienation. Thus the electorate come to feel less able to influence their own life style and career opportunities. As the time-honoured cultural patterns become eroded and as status begins to change, they feel the need to belong in integrated communities, not just in functional terms, but also in meaningful personal terms. Thus modernization, far from ensuring the withering away of ethnicity, actually serves to renew and to reidentify the parameters of ethnicity, whereby it becomes, not only an interest, but also an affective attachment which may redefine the meaning of the participant national state and suggest innovative social and political forms for the future. This, in essence, is Plaid Cymru's interpretation of Welsh cultural fragmentation consequent to industrialization and modernization. Whilst governments, of late, have recognized this increased alienation, little explicit recognition has been accorded the need for decentralization in political and fiscal decision-making, although some attempt has been made to answer the problem through the instrument of regional planning.[63]

The internal colonial thesis is the one which most readily incorporates a national-spatial perspective, citing uneven economic development as the key to nationalist resurgence. As applied to the United Kingdom by Hechter and others,[64] this thesis suggests that expanding nation-states incorporated not only overseas colonies but also 'internal' colonies, in other words, ethnic enclaves, within their boundaries. The result of continued economic exploitation of the ethnic periphery was a clearcut division of labour on predominantly cultural lines—'a system of stratification where objective distinctions are superimposed upon class lines'.[65] Economic progress was instrumental in delaying the development of the Celtic periphery and thus facilitated the maintenance of a distinct ethnic identity until well into the late twentieth century. By encouraging core—periphery interaction, industrialization further reinforced the dependence of the periphery, creating lower levels of prosperity, exposed and dependent economies tied to the primary sector and a consequent cultural stratification, a 'cultural division of labour'. Following spasmodic attempts to regenerate a nationalist movement from about 1918 to the mid-1960s, 'nationalism has re-emerged in the Celtic periphery largely as a reaction to this failure in regional development'.[66] Thus there is something particularly modern about the form of capitalist development which is capable of spawning reactive nationalist movements. It is not just the power of economic development which nationalist élites react to, but also the 'inevitability' of administrative centralization and cultural homogeneity which seem so characteristic of capitalist economies as expressed through the development of state education and broadcasting control.

Although there is much that is attractive about the schema, especially the imperialist-structuralist assumptions, there are difficulties concerning whether ethnic separatism is a necessary and predictable reaction to the uneven development of capitalism. Hechter would contend that because capitalist exploitation follows ethnic cleavages and promotes cultural assimilation into the core area, then industrial expansion must always be to the disadvantage of peripheral ethnic collectivities. On realizing their condition the ethnic intelligentsia must advocate separatism, if they are ever to avoid the inevitability of economic development as a perpetual dependency within the polity. Yet there are difficulties here with the type of uneven development envisaged. Spatially-uneven development is an inadequate theory of the forces dividing one nation from another. Whilst we may accept that some notion of regional inequality is present in the British case, we have no clear understanding from Hechter's theory whether or not the whole process is scale independent; whether for example, it can account for variations in Latin American development as readily as it purports so to do for Scotland, Wales or Brittany. A further assumption of the theory is that the process takes the form of a step-like difference clearly separating one region from another.[67] If this is accepted we need to know what is the requisite degree of separation involved required to produce a distinct sense of ethnic identification and also under which structural conditions the uneven-ness takes a step-like form.

A further difficulty concerns the relationship between uneven development and nationality formation. The thesis suggests, too neatly, that capitalist development and exploitation must reinforce ethnic cleavages, thereby minimizing the degree of socio-economic and structural similarity which exists between deprived regions in the core national area and the subject periphery e.g. between the industrial history of the North East of England and South Wales. If the cultural division of labour is paramount, then an alternative explanation must be found for cases of high development accompanied by great deprivation within an ethnic community. Uneven development theorists assume the existence of multiple ethnic identities and envisage uneven development as working upon them to transform them into a dominant national community coincident with the boundaries of the state. But, as Orridge has pointed out, this raises fundamental questions about the nation-defining capacities of economic differences.[68] Must uneven development then be the primary factor? Could it not be, as I argue in Wales's case, that a combination of language, religion and ancestry are the basic region-defining characteristics, at least initially, and that they, rather than economic differences, provide a more realistic basis of nationality formation? The rejoinder would be that linguistic and religious differences have long existed, but nationalism is a distinctively modern feature and it is uneven development which transforms the one into the other. Given that in a number of cases there is little to differentiate cores from peripheries it is more plausible to argue that it is development and modernization itself, and not its uneven-ness necessarily, which creates national communities, transferring loyalties from the local level to the national level in keeping with the intensification of commerce and society in an international system.[69]

Whilst the net effect of uneven development has been to erode the cohesiveness of state units, there is no necessary expectation that it will always be the core which exploits the periphery. The latter need not therefore be the disadvantaged region.[70] Also the thesis cannot adequately account for the timing of the nationalist resurgence, why it emerged during the 1960s and not at an earlier time, perhaps in the 1930s when uneven development between core and periphery in the U.K. was most acute. Some limited explanation is offered in terms of the failure of regional planning within the periphery, but this is of comparatively recent origin and cannot account for the initial establishment of nationalist parties in the United Kingdom.

Certain other weaknesses reduce the explanatory power of the thesis. Much of the significance of the internal colonial thesis seems to depend on the plausibility of its competitor, the diffusion theory. The latter has been the standard interpretation of state development in Political Science until fairly recently. It suggests that with increased core-periphery contact should come cultural standardization, regional economic equality and ultimately, political stability, as the traditional and particularistic values of the peasantry give way to the state-wide rational, performance centered and universalistic values of the citizenry. However, both the difffusion and internal colonial theory share a common preoccupation with the state as the key variable in the analysis. It is the state through its relentless bureaucratic centralism and its consequent reinforcement of the cultural division of labour, which constitutes the fundamental problem to be confronted by the Celtic periphery. Thus the deliberations of the state constitute not only the basic factor in the analysis of nationalism, but also the key to meeting its demands. Many commentators are aware that such an explanation leads one to a preoccupation with sovereignty rather than with the social basis of authority. This perpetuates the myth of government being divorced from society and produces the tendency to reify the state in historical explanation.

In the past, societal integration was founded upon force and international diplomacy, resulting in a system of state-nations, hardly dependent upon the aspirations of national minorities. In contemporary society, a form of nationalism is able to be invoked to justify both the inherent justice of the established state system (state nationalism) and it can also be used to attack the perceived inequality of subject nationalities in multi-ethnic states (ethnic nationalism). State nationalism can be readily used to satisfy the needs of a modern society for a common system of allegiance and a basis for coherence amongst a population which is increasingly spatially and socially mobile. As such it is a functional ideology in a transitional period. But as civil society becomes transformed so must the character of the state. If the state fails to satisfy the aspirations of mal-integrated minorities then a period of conflict between state nationalism and ethnic nationalism will ensue. In this context, much of the explanation for nationalist resurgence rests, not so much on the mechanics of core-periphery relations, but on the capacity of a declining state to meet the needs of territorially defined ethnic groups. Consequently political impotence or intransigence in a changing international and domestic context, rather than over-concentration of administration at Westminster, may be a better clue to peripheral discontent. Despite attempts to equalize incomes and investment between regions, government finds itself increasingly unable to control the domestic economy and social welfare of its citizenry; an inability which derives in large part from the increased scale, complexity and sensitivity of the internationalization of capital and econmic necessities. Viewed from this perspective minority nationalism in the United Kingdom might be interpreted as a politico-territorial response to a new phase in economic development; the intensification of the trend toward supra-state economies which exacerbate existing intra-state inequalities.

However, this still does not explain why nationalism is seen as the appropriate response, and why this structural problem does not spawn similar movements in the deprived regions of England. This is because the conventional theories fail to build into the equation the internal dynamics of minority ethnic groups themselves. The uneven development variable is being overworked. The drive toward ethnic assertion, and, for a minority within a minority, the promotion of separatism, is not merely a reaction to modernization, it also incorporates a growing positive concern with group self-determination.[71]

The neglect of indigenous ethno-linguistic vitality found in internal colonial accounts is a weakness also of the longer established Marxist explanations. The dominant mechanism of uneven development which Marxist theory shares is far too general to be capable of explaining why separatism, rather than co-operation or association in all its varied political forms, including co-option of the peripheral élite, is selected as the political goal; and why it is that the established cultural divisions are necessarily maintained by increased regional disparities. Also, Marxist theory suggests that in its early stages separatism will be proletarian in form, whereas Welsh nationalism has always drawn its strength from the educated middle classes and the ethnic intelligentsia. Space does not permit a more detailed treatment of the Marxist accounts[72] except to suggest that the real value of adopting such an interpretation would be in analysing a possible nationalist victory in Wales or Scotland without any subsequent diminution in the Celtic region's dependent, peripheral relations with the core. A shift from colonialism to neo-colonialism could be significant within a leading industrial state, such as the United Kingdom, as well as between that state and its overseas colonies. Here one might envisage the establishment of a successful independence movement in the periphery leading only to its reintegration into the state imperialist structure on more sophisticated, neo-colonial terms.[73] This would constitute a more 'perfect' imperialism—at least in theory—since anti-internal colonial feeling would be successfully deflected onto a comprador, bourgeois-nationalist class with all the formal trappings of independence. Overt violence and conflict would be less likely than before.

Whatever one's theoretical predeliction, it is evident that the contribution made by nationalism to Welsh politics will remain an intriguing subject for students of national separatism and provide rich material for the comparative analysis of minority group politics.

Conclusion

By comparison with many other cases treated in this volume the degree of success achieved by the Welsh Nationalist Party must appear very limited in formal, political terms. Its tally-sheet of electoral victories is meagre and it has, to date, failed to gain the transfer of power which can substantially influence and redirect the structure of Welsh economic and social life.

However, the scope and influence of the nationalist movement in Wales is far wider than the central separatist drive. Its chief impact has been to redefine social class and regional economic problems as Welsh 'national' problems. Insofar as it has mobilized Welsh national identity and brought a greater awareness of the specific needs of Welsh communities, the nationalist movement has contributed to the development of a distinctive Welsh political culture. More importantly, the nationalist case has highlighted Wales' state of dependency, and the existence of a number of dimensions of inequality which will continue to animate the minority's drive toward independent nationhood. It is evident that the majority also are determined to redefine their place and role in the United Kingdom. Thus separatism is but one of the various expressions of the search for a new design of collective equality so characteristic of contemporary Wales.

Notes

1. K. O. Morgan, 'Welsh Nationalism: The Historical Background', *Journal of Contemporary History*, 6, 1 (1971), pp. 153-72.
2. Nationalist historians will argue that those such as Lloyd George, and Labour luminaries after the First World War were not necessarily serving 'Welsh' interests at all, but were 'co-opted' by the central establishment élite. See K.O Morgan, *Rebirth of a Nation: Wales 1880-1980* (Oxford, 1981).
3. I do not mean to suggest that regional distinctiveness has not influenced the character of state-wide political parties, merely that most parties accept the legitimacy of the state, not the nation, as the defining political context. By implication also they assume the superiority of the British claim over any other allegiance i.e. Scottish or Welsh nationality.

4. The development of administrative decentralization in Wales is dealt with in J. Osmond, *Creative Conflict: The Politics of Welsh Devolution* (Llandysul, 1977); and also A. Butt Philip, *The Welsh Question: Nationalism in Welsh Politics 1945-1970*, (Cardiff, 1975). Don MacIver's chapter in this volume presents an account of the nature of central government's response to demands for home rule and independence. In contrast, the present chapter concentrates on *within-nation* differences toward separatism and the various grievances which have inspired the nationalist movement. It should be stated as the outset that the nationalist movement is far wider than mere support for Plaid Cymru would indicate. For details of the nationalist resurgence see C. H. Williams, 'Language Decline and Nationalist Resurgence in Wales', unpublished Ph.D. University of Wales (Swansea, 1978). It need hardly be said that there is no necessary relationship between support for outright independence and Plaid Cymru voting, as the thesis above reports, the Nationalist Party is able to mobilize support on a wide range of issues, some fundamental like the language and unemployment issues, others are of a short term nature, specific protest actions against central government incursion, such as the *Tân yn Llŷn* episode; see J. E. Jones, *Tros Gymru* (Swansea, 1970).
5. Kenneth O. Morgan has written, 'Bede commented on the sense of difference between the Welsh and Anglo-Saxons at the time of the coming of Augustine in 597. It provided a constant theme for Welsh poetry and prose throughout the middle ages. Giraldus Cambrensis, in his efforts to ward off the encroachment of Norman civilization upon the Welsh church in the twelfth century, gave it eloquent expression, and there were echoes of it at times in the Glyn Dŵr rising in the early fifteenth century . . . The fragmentation of Welsh political development was completed when the last independent princedoms were subjugated by Edward I in 1288'. *Journal of Contemporary History*, 6, 1 (1971), p. 154.
6. Morgan, ibid, notes that only a few distinct Welsh institutions survived the Union, such as the Courts of Great Sessions, abolished in 1830.
7. Kenneth O. Morgan, *Wales in British Politics, 1868-1922* (Cardiff, 1980) is the authoritative book on the period.
8. K. O. Morgan, op. cit. 1971, p. 166.
9. L. L. Snyder, *Roots of German Nationalism*, (Bloomington, 1978).
10. Author's translation of J. E. Jones, *Tros Gymru* (Swansea, 1970). Jones was party secretary from 1930 to 1962.
11. See, for example, W. R. Keech, 'Linguistic Diversity and Political Conflict', *Comparative Politics* (April, 1972), pp. 387-404; C. H. Williams, 'Identity through Autonomy' in A. Burnet and P. Taylor, (eds.), *Political Studies from Spatial Perspectives (London, 1981);* C. H. Williams, 'Ethnic Separatism in Western Europe', *Tijdschrift voor Economische en Sociale Geografie,* 71, 3 (1980), pp. 143-58.
12. D. M. Lloyd, *Plaid Cymru* (Cardiff, 1949). N.B. Care should be

taken not to underestimate the intial tensions between the minority Catholic element and the mainstream Free Church orientation of early Plaid Cymru members.

13. S. Lewis, *The Banned Wireless Talk* (Caernarfon, 1931).
14. J. Trent, 'The Politics of Nationalist Movements: A Reconsideration', *Canadian Review of Studies in Nationalism*, 2, 1 (1974), p. 164.
15. D. Owen, *Y Tyst*, 28 August 1941.
16. See A. D. Smith, 'Nationalism, Ethnic Separatism and the Intelligentsia', chapter 2 of this volume.
17. B. Thomas, 'Wales and the Atlantic Economy', *Scottish Journal of Political Economy*, 6 (1959), pp. 181-92.
18. 'For the first time there existed a sufficiently large Welsh-speaking urban population and a wide enough margin of prosperity to support flourishing societies and institutions'. G. Williams, 'Language, Literacy and Nationality in Wales', *History*, 56 (1971), pp. 1-16.
19. E. G. Millward, 'Industrialization did not save the Welsh language', *Welsh Nation*, (July, 1960), p. 4; P. N. Jones, 'Some aspects of immigration into the Glamorgan coalfield 1881-1911', *Transactions of the Honourable Society of Cymmrodorion* (1969), p. 93.
20. For a comparative case in the Canadian context see the complete issue of *Canadian Ethnic Studies*, 8, 1 (1976), devoted to the subject of ethnicity and education.
21. See the work of R. C. Gardner, et al. *Second Language Acquisition: A Social Psychological Approach*, Final Report to the Ontario Ministry of Education (Toronto, 1974); R. C. Gardner and W. E. Lambert, *Attitudes and Motivation in Second Language Learning* (Rowley, Mass., 1972).
22. C. H. Williams, 'Ymagweddiadau tuag at y Gymraeg', *Swansea Geographer*, 14 (1976), pp. 55-64.
23. For a discussion of the effects of the socio-cultural environment on the attitudes of Welsh adolescents, see C. J. Thomas and C. H. Williams, 'A Behavioural Approach to the Study of Linguistic Decline and Nationalist Resurgence in Wales', *Cambria*, Part 1, 3, 2 (1976), pp. 102-24; Part 2, 4, 2 (1977), pp. 152-73.
24. C. H. Williams, 'An Ecological and Behavioural Analysis of Ethnolinguistic Change in Wales', in H. Giles and B. Saint-Jacques, (eds.), *Language and Ethnic Relations* (Oxford, 1979), pp. 27-55.
25. A. D. Smith, 'Toward a theory of ethnic separatism', *Ethnic and Racial Studies*, 2, 1 (1979), p. 26.
26. V. Van Dyke, 'Human Rights Without Distinction as to Language', *International Studies Quarterly*, 20, 1 (1976), pp. 3-37.
27. This does not imply that Plaid Cymru did not have its own economic philosophy. Saunders Lewis consistently argued, prior to this time, that the party should advocate a radical programme of social and economic reform—the regeneration of agriculture through co-operative farming and social credit banks, the reorganization of the coal industry and the nationalization of royalties, a revised currency and banking system, and a separate customs unit.

For details of this and the contribution of D. J. Davies, as an economic thinker and as a counterweight to the prevailing line see J. E. Daniel, *Welsh Nationalism: What it Stands for* (Cardiff, 1937); D. J. Davies, *The Economics of Welsh Self-Government* (Caernarfon, 1931); *idem.*, 'The Economic Case for Self-Government', *The Welsh Nationalist* (January, 1932), pp. 2-3; 'The Labour Government's Betrayal of the Miners', ibid. (February, 1932), p. 1; and S. Lewis, 'Some Economic Functions of a Welsh Government', ibid. (September, 1933), p. 1.

28. J. Trent, 'The Politics of Nationalist Movements: A Reconsideration', *Canadian Review of Studies in Nationalism*, 2, 1 (1974), p. 164.
29. The source of much of this economic small-scale nationalism in the Welsh context is the writing of Leopold Kohr, *The Breakdown of Nations* (Swansea, 1974), and *idem*, *Is Wales Viable*? (Llandybie, 1971); see also P. M. Rawkins, 'An Approach to the Political Sociology of the Welsh Nationalist Movement', *Political Studies*, 27, 3 (1979), pp. 440-57.
30. See A. D. Smith, op. cit., chapter 2 of this volume.
31. In the initial development period, most of its early branches were located in predominantly Welsh-speaking areas, whilst the number of branches grew from 52 in 1933 to 137 in 1944. Its membership rose from the original six founding members in 1925 to about 2,500 by 1945.

Plaid Genedlaethol Cymru 1925-45

Membership		*No. of branches at Summer School*	
1925	6	1933	52
1930	500	1934	64
1939	2,000	1935	67
1945	2,500	1936	72
		1937	94
		1938	111
		1944	137

However, a clear difference exists in the estimate of party support between paid-up members and the electorate. Precise figures for the former are in fact difficult to obtain because of Plaid Cymru's early practice of regarding individuals who paid one membership fee as near permanent members, regardless of whether or not they renewed their subscription. Also many branch secretaries did not return duplicate membership cards to the central office, estimates of active party membership must be treated with caution before the reorganization of the administration in the early 'fifties. Thus whilst the figures quoted above taken from the *Welsh Nation,* the *Welsh Nationalist* and from A. Butt Philip, op. cit. p. 17 cite only 2,500 paid up members in 1945, J. E. Jones in his volume, *Tros Gymru*, op. cit. claims that there were 6,050 members in 1945; see the table on page 308. Clearly much work remains to be done on checking the validity of early Plaid Cymru data.

32. *The Aberdare Leader*, 16 November, 1946.
33. Gwynfor Evans contested the seat at both the 1955 and 1959 elections, but his share of the vote did not vary significantly, being 22.1 per cent and 23.0 per cent respectively.
34. As Rudolph observes, anti-régime organizations challenge the political-constitutional principles and structures regulating the way decisions are made. Such organizations are likely to opt for a greater degree of regional autonomy motivated by considerations of economic and cultural development. Anti-community organizations go further and challenge the legitimacy of the multinational political community and pursue independence as 'true political separatists'; see below ch. 9, p. 274.
35. Philip suggests that in constituencies contested by Plaid both in 1955 and 1959 the average share of the poll rose from 11.0 per cent to 13.2 per cent; see op. cit., p. 78.
36. For a discussion of the development of the Welsh Language Society see C. H. Williams, 'Non-violence and the development of the Welsh Language Society', *Welsh History Review*, 8, 4 (1977), pp. 426-55.
37. Philip, op. cit., pp. 95-6.
38. *Annual Report of Plaid Cymru*, (Cardiff, 1965).
39. R. J. Johnston, 'Residential Area Characteristics: Research Methods for Identifying Urban Sub-Areas—Social Area Analysis and Factorial Ecology' in D. T. Herbert and R. J. Johnston (eds.), *Social Areas in Cities*, 1, (New York and London, 1976). See also S. M. Olsen, 'Regional Social Systems: Linking Quantitative Analysis and Field Work', in C. Smith (ed.), *Regional Analysis*, 2, (New York, 1976).
40. For details of the behavioural evaluation of the hypotheses suggested by the Principal Components Analysis see C. H. Williams, 'Language Decline and Nationalist Resurgence in Wales', unpublished Ph.D. thesis, University of Wales, (1978), chapters 10-13.
41. The religious data was compiled from denominational handbooks and the official records of the Church in Wales and the Catholic Directories. The data units were then matched as closely as possible to the Local Authority units used in the analysis. Some matching problems were encountered in the transformation procedure, but they were resolved by aggregating parish units upwards to the Local Authority boundaries. The need to include religious variables in this type of analysis is obvious, a response in part to this call from Busteed in 1975: 'There has been no enumeration of religious affiliation in Great Britain since 1851, yet it is undeniable that Protestant Nonconformity was a powerful element in Welsh politics in the late nineteenth and twentieth century serving to reinforce the anti-conservative and radical tendencies in the Welsh electorate and still surviving in some areas today'. M. Busteed, *Geography and*

Voting Behaviour (Oxford, 1975) p. 38; see also C. H. Williams, 'Religion in Wales', in H. Carter and H. Griffiths (eds.), *National Atlas of Wales* (Cardiff, 1981).

42. In the 1961 Principal Components Analysis a close social and spatial relationship between language, religion and radicalism was identified for the core region. However, not all the core area was described by the first leading component, the most striking area omitted was Anglesey. This county has always been prominent in Welsh affairs, so much so that historically it is referred to as *Môn mam Cymru*, (Môn, the mother of Wales), epitomizing the Welsh cultural, rural way of life. The 1961 evidence suggested that most of the county was marginal to the core region, in terms of the variables used in the P.C.A. Although the ability to speak Welsh is as high as that recorded elsewhere, ethnic identity has not been mobilized to the same extent, in that Anglsey continues to have a political structure quite distinct from that of the core, as traditionally defined. Its party allegiance is more typical of the U.K. norm, with a bi-polar contest between Labour and Conservative dominating both the 1959 and 1964 elections. (Labour's share of the vote rose from 47.0 per cent in 1959 to 48.2 per cent in 1964, whilst the Tory share remained steady at around 24.9 per cent, Plaid Cymru's share dropped considerably from 14.6 per cent in 1959 to only 6.4 per cent in 1964. The Liberals, meanwhile, appeared to have gained most from the Nationalist decline, their vote having climbed from 13.5 per cent to 20.4 per cent in 1964). Religious affiliation in Anglesey also showed a more even distribution than was true of the core, both in inter-denominational and inter-areal terms. Although Welsh Nonconformism was the leading religious system, it was not nearly as dominant as it was in the core, e.g. in Bala or Dolgellau, whilst both Anglican and Catholic adherence remained relatively strong. Consequently although the percentage Welsh-speaking was the second highest per county for 1961 at 75.5 per cent (after Merionethshire at 75.9 per cent), it would appear that Anglesey's cultural composition is more similar to the Welsh average than to the mobilized core region.
43. The familiar problems of an aged and sub-standard housing stock, depopulation, lack of balanced employment opportunities and an ageing population structure are most marked in this region. Two areas of acute need are identifiable, i.e. most of Radnorshire and Builth R.D. together with Machynlleth R.D. and northern Montgomeryshire. However, most of upland Wales is characterized by low quality housing, the only exception in Mid-Wales is Aberystwyth R.D. where suburbanization around Aberystwyth has served to imrpove the general facilities in the housing stock of this local authority.
44. Recent improvements in the region's transport network, notably the M.4 extension and the Merthyr-Cardiff trunk road, facilitate the creation of dormitory commuter settlements in the Rhondda and Cynon valleys.

45. This hypothesis received some support in the behavioural analysis carried out in the original research project, see C. H. Williams, op. cit., (1978), chapters 10-12.
46. The districts represented either side of the mean on Figure 6, are those areas which experienced a more even electoral contest in 1966 and 1970. Thus the 'safe' Labour seats of the Rhondda and Bedwellty, for example, give way to close fought or marginal Labour seats such as Anglesey, Conway and Barry. In the case of Barry and Conway, the intervention of a minority party candidate in a traditional bi-partisan seat reduced Labour support. However, the clearest example of minority intervention reducing once 'safe' seats to more balanced electoral contests is Anglesey. In 1966 Labour gained 55.0 per cent of the vote, the Conservatives 35.4 per cent. Plaid Cymru support at 9.4 per cent was relatively strong compared with its own showing in other parts of Wales. However, by 1970 increased Nationalist mobilization and a development of Plaid branches in the constituency resulted in its share of the vote climbing to 22.1 per cent. Both major parties suffered as a result of this resurgence with Labour's share of the vote dropping to 43.2 per cent and the Tory share down to only 28.5 per cent.
47. See C. H. Williams, 'Some Spatial Considerations in Welsh Language Planning', *Cambria*, 5, 2 (1978), pp. 173-81.
48. Internal dissention and deviations from the independence ideal have yet to be fully documented in the development of Plaid Cymru. The overwhelming impression gained from existing accounts of Welsh nationalism is one of a gradual, but inexorable, movement toward some form of autonomy; little attention having been paid to the spasmodic and chequered progress of the fairly well-knit political leadership in establishing its claims for Welsh sovereignty.
49. For a good summary of the administrative decentralisation debate and the impact of British regional policy in Wales see J. Osmond, *Creative Conflict: The Politics of Welsh Devolution* (Llandysul, 1977). Osmond's book ably contrasts the community politics emphasis of Plaid Cymru with the corporatist economic emphasis of the state-wide political parties operating within Wales.
50. For Gwynfor Evans's own interpretation of Welsh history and the seminal role he attributes to the Welsh national movement in modifying the course of current Welsh affairs see G. Evans, *Land of My Fathers* (Swansea, 1978); and *idem., Wales Can Win* (Llandybie, 1973).
51. I. McLean, 'The Politics of Nationalism and Devolution', *Political Studies*, 25, 3 (1977), pp. 425-30.
52. See C. H. Williams, 'An Ecological and Behavioural Analysis of Ethno-linguistic Change in Wales', in H. Giles and B. Saint-Jacques, (eds.), *Language and Ethnic Relations* (Oxford, 1979).
53. See J. Osmond, *Creative Conflict* (Llandysul, 1977), especially chapters 4 and 5; see also D. MacIver, 'The Paradox of Scottish Nationalism' in this volume, ch. 5.

54. See C. H. Williams, 'Language Decline and Nationalist Resurgence in Wales', op. cit., ch. 8, for details of Plaid Cymru's performance at Local Government elections.
55. A. R. Jones and G. Thomas, (ed.), *Presenting Saunders Lewis* (Cardiff, 1973).
56. C. H. Williams, 'Cynllunio ar gyfer yr iaith', *Barn*, nos. 179, 180, (1978), pp. 2-5.
57. For an account of the tensions which the language issue can engender see C. H. Williams, 'Non-violence and the Development of the Welsh Language Society', *Welsh History Review*, 8, 4 (1977), pp. 426-55.
58. The variation in the size of each constituency's electorate introduces a bias into the national voting pattern. Thus the larger the seat the greater the number of votes needed to win it, and so parties with strengths in smaller constituencies can gain more seats for a given number of votes than can parties which are strongest in the larger constituencies. At the October 1974 election in Wales, the number of votes per constituency ranged from 26,728 (Merioneth, Plaid Cymru) to 76,106 (Wrexham, Labour). Johnston has calculated that of the seventeen seats with less than the average number of votes (55,783), ten were won by Labour.
59. R. J. Johnston, 'The Compatibility of Spatial Structure and Electoral Reform: Observations on the Electoral Geography of Wales', *Cambria*, 4, 2 (1977), p. 142.
60. See C. H. Williams, 'Language Decline and Nationalist Resurgence in Wales' op. cit., chapters 10-13 for behavioural measures of the degree to which the general public associate Welsh national identification with support for Plaid Cymru. See also D. F. Balsom, 'The Nature and Distribution of Support for Plaid Cymru', *Studies in Public Policy*, 36, (1979).
61. P. J. Madgwick and D. Balsom, 'Changes in Party Competition in Elections: The Welsh Case in the British Context', *Parliamentary Affairs*, 28, (1974/5); see also P. J. Madgwick, 'Devolution in Wales', A.P.S.A. paper, (Washington, 1977).
62. B. Khleif, 'Ethnic Awakening in the First World: the case of Wales', in G. Williams, (ed.), *Social and Cultural Change in Contemporary Wales*, (London, 1978), pp. 102-19.
63. E. M. Burgess, 'The Resurgence of Ethnicity: Myth or Reality?', *Ethnic and Racial Studies*, 1, 3 (1978), pp. 265-85.
64. M. Hechter, *Internal Colonialism: the Celtic Fringe in British National Development, 1536-1966* (London, 1975); M. Hechter and M. Levi, 'The Comparative Analysis of Ethnoregional Movements', *Ethnic and Racial Studies*, 2, 3. (1979), pp. 260-74. See also the discussion by Smith and MacIver in this volume, chapters 2 and 5 respectively.
65. M. Hechter, op. cit., (1975), p. 30.
66. Ibid., p. 265.
67. A. W. Orridge, 'Structural Preconditions and Triggering Factors in

the Development of European Sub-state Nationalism', P.S.A. paper, (Sheffield, 1979).

68. Ibid., pp. 16-18.
69. I. Wallerstein, *The Capitalist World-Economy* (Cambridge, 1980). In a broader context the argument in the text would allow us to accept the cases of Norway and Finland, little differentiated from their metropolises by developmental differences and also cases such as Southern Italy and North East England, with uneven development but no nationalism. Yet as Orridge reminds us even this would be unsatisfactory as varieties of nationalism have occured in regions with little development whatsoever, as in the Balkan and Latin American cases.
70. Spain's Basque and Catalan regions, together with the Flemish region of Belgium counter this assertion; see Medhurst's and Rudolph's contributions to this volume below, chapters 8 and 9.
71. In Wales this has recently taken the form of demanding specific group rights as well as recognizing traditional individual rights in unitary states; for an examination of such claims see C. H. Williams, 'Language Planning and Minority Group Rights', *Cambria,* 9 (1982).
72. The best account in this genre is T. Nairn, *The Break-Up of Britain: Crisis and Neo-Nationalism* (London, 1977); see also the valuable discussion in T. Sandlund, 'Social Classes, Ethnic Groups and Capitalist Development—an outline of a theory', *Svenska Litteratursällskapet i Finland*, 24 (1976), Abo Academy, Finland.
73. W. N. Sloan, 'Ethnicity or Imperialism?', *Comparative Studies in Society and History*, 21 (1979), pp. 113-25.

CHAPTER 7

The Quebec Independence Movement

Richard Hamilton and Maurice Pinard

The Background: History and Demography

Canada's national question—whether one country or two—has its origins in the fateful year 1760, the year of The Conquest. At that point, Great Britain had a collection of thriving colonies in the New World. France had a struggling colony, one with a limited economic base in the fur trade, a colony that, relative to those of the British, was very much underpopulated. Europe was locked in a massive conflict, the worst since the Thirty Years War. At its root was a struggle between Frederick the Great and Maria Theresa, the Prussian king having stolen Silesia from the Austrian Empress. France had entered the fray on the side of Austria while Britain, together with its Hannoverian satellite state, had joined on the side of Prussia. With French troops occupied on the European continent and the British navy effectively preventing any re-supplying, the troubled colony was, to say the least, very seriously exposed. And on one September day, after a twenty minute battle, General Montcalm's forces were defeated. In the following year, in 1760, the vast territory of New France came into British hands.

In the two centuries following the conquest, British policy alternated, on one hand showing strong assimilationist ambitions, on the other making necessary practical concessions to secure French-Canadian loyalties. The key sector of the economy, the fur trade, was taken over by 'the British' and a number of English and Scottish merchants soon appeared on the scene and quickly dominated other areas of the urban economy. In the aftermath of the American Revolution, some thousands of Loyalists settled in Quebec, most of them in the Eastern Townships, in the farmlands to the south and east of Montreal. Throughout the nineteenth century, a steady stream of settlers arrived from the British Isles. At first these were English and Scots, but soon there was also a significant Irish immigration.

Most of this immigration consisted of poor farmers and working-class populations, but with them also came British entrepreneurs and investors.[1]

The twentieth century brought much investment to Quebec from 'English Canada' and recent decades have seen a considerable amount of American investment. The consequence, clearly, is that much of the industry and commerce of Quebec was, and still is, the property of 'the English.' For French Canadians, employment in these firms has typically been in the blue-collar ranks and, with infrequent exceptions, promotion to top ranks was out of the question.[2] *Le boss* (not *le patron*) spoke English. The twentieth century also saw the appearance of a 'third force' on the Quebec scene, this consisting of the many 'new immigrant' groups, Italians, Jews, Germans, Greeks, some Poles and some Ukrainians, most of whom, initially at least, were found in working-class and lower-middle-class occupations.

In the two centuries since the conquest, the French population increased from less than one hundred thousand to well over six million. For most of those intervening years Quebec has had one of the highest birth rates in the history of the world. The population explosion has been referred to colloquially as the 'revenge of the cradle' since it, in some measure at least, helped to 'undo' the conquest. The high birth rate compensated for the predominantly English immigration both to Quebec and elsewhere in Canada. The considerably increased numbers certainly provided a 'base' for defence of the French language, culture and institutions and for protection of the special emphases found in the French-Canadian development of Catholicism.

The farm sector of the Quebec economy, however, was not sufficient to provide for this population. A considerable number of those in the new generations were forced from the countryside and villages into the ethnically-mixed cities, particularly into Montreal, which, until recently, was the largest metropolitan area of Canada. Many were forced to leave Quebec entirely, some moving to Ontario and some moving into New England. In both of these settings, there was considerable incentive and/or pressure to assimilate.[3]

These losses, this erosion of the base for French culture and institutions has always been a source of concern to Quebec's intellectuals, to the clergy and later, in ever increasing measure, to the province's secular leaders. It is not surprising that the problem of *survivance* came to receive a very high priority on their scale of values. Nor is it surprising that all groups in the French-speaking population came to have a beleaguered feeling, one expressed in another colloquial phrase: '. . . we are only an island of French in a sea of English.'

It is useful to insert some numbers at this point. The 1971 Canadian census reports the population of Quebec to be just over six million persons. Asked about their ethnic or cultural background—on the male side—nearly four out of five (actually 79.0 per cent) said French. The 'other fifth' divides almost equally between 'English' and 'other ethnic groups.' That is a bit deceptive since the former category, 10.6 per cent of the total (some 640,000 persons) refers to those coming from the British Isles and thus includes English, Scots, Welsh, Irish (both Catholics and Protestants), and some who came to Quebec by way of the United States. The 'others' include 170,000 Italians, 116,000 Jews, 54,000 Germans, 43,000 Greeks. The native Indian population, 33,000 of them, form one half of one per cent of the total.[4]

The ethnic English, it will be noted, constitute only a very small part of the total population, some fraction of the 10.6 per cent. The term 'the English,' however, is often used to refer to 'all others,' that is, to all non-French populations. Most of these 'others' have seen the chances for social mobility to be better within the 'English' community than within the French. One important consequence is that they have preferred to see their children educated in English. This was the overwhelming choice of the so-called New Canadians. It was also the choice of some well-off French-Canadians.

Until recently, French-Canadians concerned with *survivance* viewed the situation as one posing a continuing serious problem. The processes of urbanization and secularization, with the ever-present threat of assimilation to the larger North American culture, certainly accentuated those concerns. In recent years, a development has occurred that led them to see the problem as having reached crisis proportions. Within a realitively brief span, Quebec's birth rate changed from one of the world's highest to one of the world's lowest. The rate is now below that of all the other Canadian provinces. Given the continued in-flow of New Canadians and their preferred link-up with the English cultural community, it appeared that the French percentage, that 79.0 figure, would suffer a steady erosion. For an outsider, that might not seem to pose a serious problem, the difference between 79 per cent and say a 75 or even a 70 per cent majority appearing to be a matter of no great moment.

There is one specification, however, that makes all the difference. The non-French populations are disproportionately concentrated in the Montreal metropolitan area. Within this area, which contains 45.5 per cent of Quebec's population, the French vs. Others proportion is roughly five to three. It is with respect to the metropolis that the demographers offered a key prediction: if the current trends continued unaltered, they argued, the metropolis would lose its French majority within a couple of decades. And if that happened, if the heart of the 'nation' were lost, the assimilation presumably would proceed at an even faster pace. The rest of the province, small town and rural Quebec, obviously could provide only a very limited and inadequate base for defense of people and culture.

An immediate imperative then was to reverse those trends. Survival, it seemed, depended on immediate action to alter those tendencies since by the 1980s or 1990s it would be too late. This 'fact,' in short, gave considerable urgency to the nationalist concerns that had long been present within Quebec society.[5]

Another consideration moving nationalists was the diminished place of Quebec within Canada. The province was becoming a smaller part of the Canadian whole with a corresponding decline in representation in the House of Commons. When the Canadian federation was established, in 1867, Quebec had 36 per cent of the deputies. In 1979, the province's share had fallen to 27 per cent. And, following the population projections, it was anticipated that by the year 2000 the share would be down to only 23 per cent. The possibility of defending Quebec's special interests within confederation would be continuously eroded, this supplying another telling argument for national independence.

The Background: Parties and Politics

In this limited space it is impossible to give an adequate picture of the political history of the province over the two centuries since the conquest. There were periods of nationalist uprising, these usually stimulated by assimiliationist pressures emanating from London or from elsewhere in Canada. In the first century after the conquest, government at all levels was dominated by 'the English' and, as elsewhere, much of the political struggle was concerned with wider access, with achieving some measure of responsible government. By the turn of the century, those reforms had been achieved in all settings and, except for English-speaking enclaves, virtually all governments in Quebec, provincial and local, were headed and run by French-Canadians.

Until recent decades, the dominant tendency of Quebec governments, regardless of party, was one favouring low-cost laissez-faire policies. This direction of affairs, however, was frequently embellished with some limited public works efforts and these invariably, so it seemed, were linked to special favour and subsequent scandal. Apart from economic matters, the predominant tendency is perhaps described as one of clerical (and cultural) conservatism.

This combination of economic and clerical conservatism broke down in the late fifties. Maurice Duplessis, the authoritarian leader of the *Union Nationale*, died in 1959 and, shortly thereafter, his immediate successor also died. A rejuvenated Liberal Party under Jean Lesage successfully campaigned on a programme that might best be described as one of economic and social modernization. The new régime brought substantial government funding for the planning and building of a modern economic infrastructure. Educational and welfare institutions were reformed with substantial investment being made in both areas. The transformation, the contrast between old and new, was so dazzling that it has been referred to as the Quiet Revolution (*la révolution tranquille*).[6]

That modernization created a large number of new jobs, in the schools and universities, in government, in social welfare agencies, and in some cultural enterprises (in radio, television and in related 'fine' arts). This amounted to the creation of a new intelligentsia. Many of these occupations, it will be noted, are concerned with the dissemination of culture and, potentially at least, with its defense. From the substantially enlarged ranks of this intelligensia came the cadres of the independence movement.[7]

Some of the leaders came from the established parties, the most notable case being that of René Lévesque, a popular and charismatic member of the Lesage government. As Minister of Natural Resources, Lévesque had pushed the policy of nationalizing the light and power companies, this as a step in the direction of 'recapturing' control of the Quebec economy. The demand to be *maîtres chez nous* (masters in our own house), originally put forward early in this century by nationalist historian Lionel Groulx, had been adopted by Lesage and the Liberal Party. It was this demand that Lévesque sought to implement.[8]

A regrouping of political forces occurred in the mid-sixties. Two small pro-independence parties, the Rassemblement pour l'indépendance nationale (RIN) and the Ralliement national (RN), appeared on the scene and first ran in the 1966 provincial election. Controversy over the pace and nationalist directions within the Liberal Party led to Lévesque's defection in 1967. At that time he formed an 'independentist' group called the Mouvement Souveraineté-Association. A year later, Lévesque created the Parti Québécois, bringing his followers together with the Ralliement national. The RIN dissolved and urged its members to join the new organization as individuals.[9]

The Parti Québécois ran its first province-wide campaign in 1970 and took 23 per cent of the total. In 1973, they fought their second campaign and gained 30 per cent of the vote. A sharp polarization of the electorate occurred at this time with a substantial majority of all the *other* voters (that is, those who had previously supported one of the three other major parties) now turning to the federalist (pro-Canada) Liberals. The latter won with 55 per cent of the votes, a substantial jump from the 45 per cent gained in the 1970 election.

The Liberals called the next election in November 1976 at a time of high unemployment and high inflation. A series of troublesome strikes had occurred in the public sector. There had been a number of scandals in the Liberal government, now under Robert Bourassa, that had commanded the headlines for some months. The Liberals had also undertaken a number of policy moves, most importantly, one limiting the free choice of schools, that caused an angry reaction among their own supporters, among 'the English' and the New Canadians who, ordinarily, provided the Liberals with heavy majorities.

The Parti Québécois, meanwhile, had separated the issues, arguing that they were now offering a 'good' (actually, *vrai*) government to replace the badly sullied Liberals. The question of independence, they said, would be decided at a later time and only after a public expression of opinion in a provice-wide referendum. With the issues thus divided, many dissatisfied voters felt 'free' to vote for the Parti Québécois. With 41 per cent of the vote (the Liberals getting only 34 per cent of the vote this time), the Parti Québécois took power, having gained 71 of the 110 seats in the provincial legislature (which, incidentally, is called the National Assembly.)[10]

Attitudes towards Independence

It is understandable that at least some Parti Québécois activitsts, despite the pre-election policy statements, choose to count this 41 per cent as a vote for independence. If that were the case, since few non-French support the party, it would mean that close to a majority of the French population favoured independence. And, given the evident trend in the vote from 1970 to 1976, it would clearly be only a question of time before that majority arrives. Moreover, given the age pattern among the party's supporters, younger cohorts leaning very heavily towards the Parti Québécois, an argument about the inevitability of independence has developed, the logic of which seems inescapable.[11]

Public opinion poll data however reveals a disparity between the vote for the party and the support for independence. At the time of the 1976 election, the one public study asking about this issue found 18 per cent in favour of independence, 58 per cent opposed, and 24 per cent undecided. Among the decided populations, it will be noted, the sentiment ran three to one *against* independence. Even if one took only the francophone voters, the picture would not be substantially changed, given the size of the French-speaking majority. The equivalent figures were 20 in favour, 55 opposed, and 25 undecided (Table 1).[12]

Questions on independence have been contained in public opinion polls going as far back as 1962. It is possible, therefore, to give some sense of the development of independence sentiment over some eighteen years, that is, beginning early in the period of the Quiet Revolution and coming up to the present. It should be noted that this 'pure' independence option is *not* the specific policy of the Parti Québécois. Their option, sovereignty-association, will be discussed below. The independence question, nevertheless, is useful to indicate the fundamental or core support for independence. It also provides us with the best evidence on the trend during this period.

From 1962 to 1973, support for independence increased at the rate of approximately one per cent per year. The percentage favouring independence went from eight to seventeen in that time span (Table 1). But then, from 1973 through to the end of 1979, this development stopped and pro-independence sentiment stablized with just under one fifth of the Quebec population making that choice.[13] In the first months of 1980, prior to the referendum of May, a significant rise in independence sentiment was indicated, two studies giving 28 per cent figures, the highest levels ever achieved. Three later studies, also before the referendum, showed some fall-off from that high level, independence sentiment returning close to the previous 'normal' level.

The lowest level of opposition to the independence option occurred in 1976, just prior to the election. It is important to note that the decline in opposition at that time was not associated

Table 1 Trend of Opinions in Quebec relative to Independence, 1962-80

			In favour %	*Opposed* %	*Undecided* %	*N**
				All Adult Quebec Citizens		
1962	(Opin.)	(Social Research Group)	8	73	19	(998)
1965	(Opin.)	(SRG)	7	79	14	(6910)
1968A	(Opin.)	(Gallup)	11	71	18	(202)
1968B	(Opin.)	(Meisel)	10	72	18	(746)
1969	(Opin.)	(Gelfand, Derry and Assoc.)	11	75	15	(367)
1970A	(Opin.)	(Regenstreif)	14	76	10	(820)
1970B	(Opin.)	(Pinard)	11	74	16	(1974)
1972	(Opin.)	(Hamilton-Pinard)	10	68	22	(778)
1973	(Opin.)	(Hamilton-Pinard)	17	64	19	(1006)
1974	(Opin.)	(Clarke *et. al.*)	15	74	11	(349)
1976B	(Opin.)	(Hamilton-Pinard/Nov.)	18	58	24	(1095)
1976C	(Vote)	(Hamilton-Pinard/Nov.)	12	66	22	(1042)
1977A to D**			19	66	15	(1750)*
1977E and F			19	71	10	(1100)*
1977G to J			18	70	12	(3500)*
1978B	(Opin.)	(INCI/Radio Canada/May)	14	79	7	(972)
1978C	(Opin.)	(Gallup/August)	12	74	14	(300)*
1978D	(Opin.)	(IQOP/Dim.-Mat./Sept.)	17	73	10	(721)
1979B	(Vote)	(Gallup/Jan.)	19	64	17	(300)*
1979C	(Opin.)	(Cent. Sond./R. Can./Feb.)	19	76	5	(1199)
1979D	(Opin.)	(IQOP/Dim.-Mat./March)	16	72	12	(773)
1979E	(Opin.)	(Gallup/June)	18	70	12	(561)
1979F	(Vote)	(CROP/MAIQ/June)	19	73	8	(995)
1979H	(Opin.)	(CROP/R. Can./Nov.)	19	72	9	(928)
1980A	(Opin.)	(CROP/R.Can./Feb.)	22	73	5	(906)
1980B	(Opin.)	(IQOP/Dim.-Mat./March)	28	64	8	(783)
1980C	(Opin.)	(CROP/R. Can./March-April)	28	64	8	(877)
1980E	(Opin.)	(IQOP/Dim.-Mat./April)	23	63	14	(761)

			In favour %	*Opposed* %	*Undecided* %	*N**
1980G	(Opin.)	(CROP/R. Can./April)	20	71	9	(856)
1980I	(Vote)	(Pinard-Hamilton/May)	23	61	17	(1020)
			Adult French Canadians Alone***			
1962			8	71	20	(880)
1963			13	43	23****	(987)
1965			8	76	16	(5488)
1967			7	87*****	6	(502)
1968A			13	65	22	(165)
1968B			11	68	21	(624)
1969			13	70	17	(294)
1970A			16	73	11	(696)
1970B			13	70	17	(1513)
1972			11	65	24	(660)
1973			19	60	21	(860)
1974			17	70	13	(277)
1976A			23	63	13	(725)
1976B			20	55	25	(954)
1976C			13	65	22	(755)
1977B			19	61	20	(600)
1977F			23	68	9	(700)
1977G			18	64	18	(616)
1978D			20	70	10	(617)
1979C			22	72	5	(942)
1979D			18	70	13	(672)
1979F			23	68	9	(801)
1979H			23	68	9	(791)
1980A			26	?	?	(805)
1980B			35	56	9	(?)
1980C			32	60	8	(759)
1980E			29	59	12	(587)

	In favour %	*Opposed* %	*Undecided* %	*N**
1980G	25	65	10	(726)
1980I	27	54	19	(863)

* Prior to 1980, whenever indicated in the sources, the 'no answer' category was eliminated. The N's for the 1965 study are weighted. In a few cases indicated by an * (e.g., some 1977 polls, 1978C, 1979B), the N's are approximate due to the lack of exact information.

** In 1977, following the election of the P.Q. in November 1976, there was no less than 10 polls made public in Quebec on the independence and related issues. In the first panel of the table, rather than present all of them or a sample of them, we present the average of the proportions for each category for the polls of January to April (4 polls), May to August (2) and September to December (4). In the second part (French Canadians only), we have simply reproduced the results of the 1977 polls for which the data were available for that group separately.

*** Ethnicity is variously defined by self-identification, mother tongue, language at home, etc. Our experience is that either one of these measures in Quebec yield the same results.

**** The total in this row is 79 per cent; the other (21 per cent) said they were not aware of separatist activities.

***** In that study, separation was one among other less radical options; 87 per cent is the total for the other options (see details Table 2, column 2).

with an equivalent increase in pro-independence sentiment but rather with a rise in the level of indecision. The most important fluctuations in Table 1, particularly in the 1970s, appear to involve shifts from opposition to indecision and back again. The most important trend in the period from 1976 to 1979 was an increase in the opposition to independence, this being correlated with a decline of indecision. In 1980, during the campaign itself, some larger fluctuations appeared. There is a strong suggestion that some converted from opposition to a pro-independence position. The latter studies, however, indicate a 'fall-back' to indecision. All of this may simply reflect some people's choice of the YES option in the referendum rather than a 'true' increase in independence sentiment.

Given the widespread currency of the 'inevitability' thesis, it is useful to examine these results in more detail. There is a general belief that independence sentiment is stable and committed. By contrast, it is felt that federalist sentiment is unstable and, with relative ease, could be shifted over to the independence column. There are some indications in this data suggesting the opposite case, that is, one of weakness or vulnerability of independence sentiment. The 1976B and 1976C studies involved the same respondents, this being a panel study that interviewed people before and after the November election. In the weeks immediately after the election, in an immediate nervous reaction apparently, one-third of the pro-independence respondents 'defected.' That was, to be sure, a very short term result since only a few weeks later pro-independence sentiment was back to its 'normal' level.

That 'normal' level, that 1973-77 plateau, also, appears to have suffered some erosion in 1978. All three of the 1978 studies in the public record showed independence sentiment to be below that previous 'high.' Two of these studies showed considerable falloff from that previous level. At the same time there was a considerable decline in the percentage of undecideds. It is the opposition to independence, obviously, that showed the corresponding gain. It was then back to the level of the 1960s. Only in the course of the referendum campaign itself was some instability in the opposition to independence indicated. Two studies then, as just noted, reached a high of 28 per cent, this being correlated with a decline in the percentage opposed rather than of the undecideds.

Another source of erosion is 'hidden' or implicit within the figures contained in Table 1. At all points in this recent history, there has been a fairly strong inverse relationship between age and support for independence. This fact provides the basis for the inevitability argument.[14] Each year, presumably, a new cohort of young pro-independence voters enters the electorate. And each year, the 'ultimate facts' of human demography work to remove tens of thousands of older persons, persons who, on the whole, lean heavily towards the federalist position. Were these the only processes operating, the obvious result would be a substantial net addition of pro-independence support each year. But this conclusion runs up against an equally hard fact, one that provides a clear and unambiguous challenge to the inevitability argument. The evidence in Table 1 does not show that pattern at all; apart from the brief 1980 fluctuation, the pattern is one of relative stability in the support for independence from 1973 to date. One might also find difficulty with the unexpectedly slow growth of independence sentiment in the 1962-1972 decade.

There is no mystery about this slow or absent growth. The key assumption in the inevitability argument, as noted, is that independence sentiment is permanent or at least is highly committed; once learned, the allegiance is never shed. But some studies, those that cared to ask the question, have discovered the relatively large numbers, approximately one third of those who have ever favoured independence later fell away from the faith. By age eighteen or twenty, many young French-Canadians either have learned or soon adopt the pro-independence position. The link with education, as will be seen, is very strong which suggests an obvious flow of influence. Once removed from the school and university milieu, however, a new set of influences is felt, so it would appear, and many of them shift away, either to indecision or else to the federalist choice.

One might also note that the period of growth of the independence movement involved years when large cohorts were coming of age. But Quebec's largest cohort, that born in 1959, is already part of the electorate. It is followed by thirteen successively smaller cohorts, this being one obvious implication of the falling birth rate mentioned above. That downward trend was reversed in 1973 but the cohorts born in recent years are still relatively small, about one-third below that of the 1959 peak. Simultaneously, the older and larger cohorts, those born in the fifties, have left (or will soon be leaving) the educational institutions to enter the labour force where, presumably, those different influences will make themselves felt.

Thus far we have indicated the dimensions of 'basic' independence sentiment within Quebec. This evidence suggests that if a straightforward independence question were used in a referendum at present, the proposal would be defeated by a margin of at least three to one.[15] The last line of Table 1 does not quite reach this three to one level—but those in the 'don't know' or 'non-response' categories in Quebec have generally been rather strongly opposed to the Parti Québécois and to its principal option.

Attitudes towards Sovereignty-association

The Parti Québécois programme actually calls for political independence while maintaining an economic association with the rest of Canada. This plan is referred to as sovereignty-association.[16]

The polls have not probed this question to the same extent as in the case of the independence question. The first effort in this area was undertaken in 1970 but then there was a long hiatus until 1977 when, in a period of suddenly heightened interest, five studies posed relevant questions. As compared to the independence series, there exists an additional problem in that the question wordings vary significantly and this, clearly, makes it difficult to establish trends. Fortunately, the principal alternatives, together with their implications, may be described with relative ease.

Responses vary by the degree of certainty indicated about the economic association, some speaking of it as a hypothetical possibility, some suggesting it to be a 'sure thing.' The most frequently expressed objection to the independence option involves a fear of the economic effects.[17] Sovereignty-association questions that assume the existence of an economic union with Canada, accordingly, tend to get high levels of support; those that are at all hypothetical or that suggest the linkup is open to some question, tend to get lower support.

The various questions used have yielded the results shown in Table 2. At no point prior to 1979, it will be seen, was there a plurality in favour of the sovereignty-association option.[18] The support for that possibility between 1970 and 1978 ranged from 25 to 42 per cent, with most results falling between 30 and 40 per cent. The opposition generally ran at 50 per cent or more although in three instances the opposition fell below 50 per cent, in one of these it ran at only 44 per cent. The indecision has varied between 10 and 20 per cent although again there are some 'outlyers,' one at 23 per cent and one at four per cent.

In 1979 and 1980, four studies turned up modest pluralities for sovereignty-association and two others showed a fifty-fifty

Table 2 Trend of Opinion in Quebec relative to Sovereignty-association, 1970 and 1977-80

			In favour %	*Opposed* %	*Undecided* + NA %	*N*
				All Adult Quebec Citizens		
1970A	(Opin.)	(Regenstreif)	35	53	12	(820)*
1970B	(Opin.)	(Pinard)	28	49	23	(1982)
1977B	(Vote)	(SORECOM/Feb.)	32	52	16	(742)
1977F	(Opin.)	(CROP/Aug.)	40	46	14	(823)
1977F	(Vote)	(CROP/Aug.)	38	44	18	(823)
1977G	(Vote)	(Hamilton-Pinard/Oct.)	26	56	19	(729)
1977H	(Opin.)	(Cent. Sond./Oct.)	40	50	10	(1458)
1977J	(Vote)	(Gallup/Dec.)	42	55	4	(1000)
1978A	(Vote)	(IQOP/Feb.)	25	58	17	(714)
1978B	(Opin.)	(INCI/May)	39	50	11	(972)
1978B	(Vote)	(INCI/May)	33	53	14	(972)
1978D	(Opin.)	(IQOP/Sept.)	35	48	17	(721)
1978E	(Vote)	(CROP/Oct.)	31	53	16	(856)
1979A	(Opin.)	(CROP/Dec.-Jan.)	33	60	7	(947)
1979A	(Vote)	(CROP/Dec.-Jan.)	31	54	14	(947)
1979B	(Vote)	(Gallup/Jan.)	46	39	15	(300)
1979C	(Opin.)	(Cent. Sond./Feb.)	35	46	21	(1199)
1979C	(Vote)	(Cent. Sond./Feb.)	37	36	27	(1133)**
1979D	(Opin.)	(IQOP/March)	30	40	30	(782)
1979F	(Opin.)	(CROP/June)	41	44	16	(1004)
1979F	(Vote)	(CROP/June)	41	41	18	(1004)
1979G	(Vote)	(CROP/Sept.)	25	56	19	(574)
1979H	(Opin.)	(CROP/Nov.)	31	50	19	(928)
1979H	(Vote)	(CROP/Nov.)	23	39	38	(928)
1979I	(Vote)	(IQOP/Dec.)	20	46	34	(803)***
1980A	(Opin.)	(CROP/Feb.)	42	49	9	(906)
1980B	(Opin.)	(IQOP/March)	46	44	10	(783)
1980C	(Opin.)	(CROP/March-April)	43	46	11	(877)
1980E	(Opin.)	(IQOP/April)	44	39	17	(761)
1980G	(Opin.)	(CROP/April)	42	46	12	(856)
1980H	(Opin.)	(IQOP/May)	39	39	22	(756)
1980I	(Vote)	(Pinard-Hamilton/May)	[illegible]	49	20	(1020)

		In favour %	*Opposed* %	*Undecided* + NA %	*N*
			Adult French Canadians Alone****		
1970B	(Opin.)	33	43	24	(1511)
1977B	(Vote)	38	46	16	(600)
1977F	(Opin.)	45	40	15	(700)
1977F	(Vote)	44	37	19	(700)
1977G	(Vote)	29	51	20	(617)
1978A	(Vote)	28	55	17	(593)
1978D	(Opin.)	39	45	17	(617)
1978E	(Vote)	35	47	18	(740)*
1979C	(Opin.)	41	38	21	(942)
1979C	(Vote)**	42	30	28	(890)*
1979D	(Opin.)	32	36	32	(679)
1979F	(Opin.)	45	39	16	(806)
1979F	(Vote)	49	33	18	(806)
1979H	(Opin.)	36	43	21	(791)
1979H	(Vote)	28	34	38	(791)
1979I	(Vote)	24	44	32	(?)
1980A	(Opin.)	48	?	?	(805)
1980B	(Opin.)	54	35	11	(?)
1980C	(Opin.)	49	39	12	(759)
1980E	(Opin.)	52	31	17	(609)
1980G	(Opin.)	51	37	12	(726)
1980H	(Opin.)	46	29	25	(589)
1980I	(Vote)	38	41	22	(863)

* Note that many polls (e.g. 1977F) have asked both how favourable people were to sovereignty-association (Opinion) and how they would vote on the issue in a referendum (Vote). Some N's (with *) are estimated.

** A group of 5 per cent of the respondents who had not heard about the referendum were not asked this question.

*** Question differs from others more than usual ('Si le référendum sur le souveraineté-association avait lieu demain voteriez-vous oui ou non à la question que serait posée?').

**** Limited to those polls for which the results were available to the author.

split among the decideds. The remaining results still showed plurality opposition. There is a considerable range in the percentages choosing the pro and con options and in the proportion of undecideds. This change is probably, in part at least, due to differences in formulation of the questions. The picture for the 'pro' forces obviously had improved somewhat, especially early in 1980, the polls at that time suggesting a very close contest. The actual situation was not as favourable as first appears, however, since the undecideds, as we will see, came disproportionately into the 'no' camp.

The actual wording of the referendum question was to be formulated by the majority party in the National Assembly, that is, by the Parti Québécois. It seemed likely, of course, that they would choose a wording favourable to their preference, the best of the lot prior to the 1979-80 opinion change being the question used in the 1977F study. That question treated the economic association as an accomplished fact.[19]

The economic association with 'the rest of Canada' was necessarily a very tentative or hypothetical matter. The referendum would precede any negotiation; it was the prerequisite condition for the negotiations. Many Canadian leaders, beginning with Prime Minister Trudeau, indicated their likely refusal of any negotiation. The Parti Québécois leaders in turn had to argue the plausibility of the link; Ontario and the rest of Canada, they said, needed the economic tie to Quebec. Others argued just the opposite, saying it was Quebec that needed the tie to Canada. Some argued that the rest of Canada would be better off economically without Quebec. There was no way, of course, for the Parti Québécois leaders to prove definitely that the association would be assured so as to allay the fears of economic isolation.

It is useful to take up the question of the stability of these responses. Some studies have asked an appropriate specifying question. Respondents who would vote for sovereignty-association were asked if they would still do so if the economic association were in question, that is, if there were doubts as to the possibility of its achievement. Approximately half of those initially favourable to the option broke away and, in this circumstance, changed their 'vote.'

Those who favour independence regardless of the chances of association, we have called the 'unconditional sovereignists'. And those whose positions hinge on the 'fact' (or strong likelihood) of economic union, we have termed the 'conditional sovereignists'. With the 'undecideds' redistributed, the results from the relevant studies are shown below. The unconditional sovereignists are roughly equal in strength to those favouring independence (in answer to the previously-discussed series). The conditional sovereignists, it will be noted, appear to have diminished somewhat in the course of 1977 and, correspondingly, those opposed to the option increased slightly.

Opinions on Sovereignty-association

	Favourable even without Association %	*Favourable only if Association* %	*Total favourable* %	*Not in favour* %
1970B	19	18	37	63
1977B	16	22	38	62
1977G	18	13	31	68

Another way of approaching the question of the stability or instability of opinion on this issue involves the use of a question of intensity. French-Canadian respondents were asked to indicate the degree of commitment they felt for their position (for or against) on sovereignty-association. Forty-eight per cent said they were 'very strongly' committed and another 38 per cent said they held their position 'somewhat strongly,' that making a total of 86 per cent. Only twelve per cent felt 'not too strongly' committed or were 'not at all' committed.[20]

The pro-independence forces dismissed these early public opinion polls with a claim that the referendum campaign had not yet begun. And many of those in the federalist camp, being well schooled in the 'verities' of mass society theorizing, were sure that 'subterranean' impulses would be tapped by shrewd and/or manipulative use of the mass media. These data on commitment however, suggested that only a small proportion of the electorate was in any way 'open' to new argument. Many of those were conditional sovereignists who, as noted, were worried about the possible economic impacts of independence. There was some reason, therefore, to think that they, together with most of the 'undecideds,' would choose the federalist option when faced with a simple yes-no choice. The argument of the campaign-not-yet-begun seemed a doubtful one since, for all practical purposes, the campaign had been conducted for more than a decade and had been at the center of public discussion, in one way or another, all of that time.

A 'Mandate' Question

Another referendum option that must be considered involved a more open-ended question, this asking for a 'mandate to negotiate' sovereignty-association rather than asking specific approval or disapproval of its substance. A number of questions of this sort had been asked in polls and these provided the Parti Québécois with its best showing, yielding pluralities in favour of the question. One of these, for example, asked:

> If, in this referendum, the Quebec government were to ask you instead for a *mandate to negotiate* sovereignty-association for Quebec with the rest of Canada, would you, yes or no, give it this mandate?

Forty-four per cent said yes, 39 per cent said no and 17 per cent expressed no opinion or refused to answer.[21]

In mid-October 1978, at the re-opening of the National Assembly, Premier Lévesque made his first public statement with respect to the options to be posed in the referendum. This statement, not too surprisingly in view of these opinion poll results, declared, first of all, that sovereignty and association were indissoluble and, secondly, that the government would be asking for a mandate. The word independence was missing from his address. Instead, emphasis was laid on the word 'sovereignty', it being noted that this was joined by a hyphen to the word 'association', the lesson being "not one without the other'.

In February 1979, in a position paper, *D'égal à égal*, the Parti Québécois started using freely the terms 'mandate' and 'negotiation'. Finally, in November 1979, the Parti Quéḃcois government published its White Paper on sovereignty-association that requested a 'mandate' to 'make this new agreement a reality through negotiation.'[22] As we shall see shortly, the official referendum questioned adopted in March 1980 simply asked for a 'mandate to negotiate' sovereignty-association between Quebec and Canada.

The Parti Québécois Coalition

As we noted earlier, support for the Parti Québécois cannot be taken as equivalent to support for independence. The party's electoral success in recent years, as may be seen from the following data, has been based on its ability to reach beyond the relatively narrow core of *indépendantistes* to attract voters moved by other considerations.[23]

	*For Separation or Independence** %	*Vote for Independentist Parties* %		*Differences* %
1965-66	8	9	(R.I.N. & R.N.)**	+1
1970	16	23	(P.Q.)	+7
1973	21	30	(P.Q.)	+9
1976	24	41	(P.Q.)	+17
Increases	+16	+32		

* Percentage recalculated so as to redistribute 'don't knows', undecided, etc.
** Refers to the two parties mentioned above in the text, the Rassemblement pour l'indépendance nationale (R.I.N.) and the Ralliement national (R.N.).

Two of the most decisive characteristics of those supporters are that they are young and well-educated (we are speaking here, of course, only of the French-Canadian population). The patterns with respect to sovereignty-association may be seen in Table 3. A third factor, socio-economic status, also plays a role although the relationsip here is more complicated.

Table 3 Percent Favouring Sovereignty-association by Age and Education: French-Canadians

		Age	
Education:	*18-34* %	*35-54* %	*55 or more* %
To 7 years	26	18	16
N =	(23)	(71)	(73)
8-11 years	34	17	21
N =	(100)	(63)	(42)
12 or more years	44	34	25
N =	(140)	(76)	(24)

Source: Hamilton-Pinard Study, October 1977. The figures are based on the totals, including the undecideds.

Middle-class populations in general are more favourable to both independence and sovereignty-association than are working-class populations and the latter, in most studies, have been more favourably disposed to those options than the farm populations.

One middle class group that stands out from all the others are those we may refer to as the intelligentsia. This consists of persons in the following occupations: teachers and professors, all scientists (biologists, chemists, social scientists, etc.), actors, writers, journalists, etc. All of these groups are contained within the census category of 'professionals and kindred' occupations. Most of these occupations are ones that involve the production of and/or dissemination of 'culture'. Given the fairly recent expansion of investment in this sector, an expansion that began only with the Quiet Revolution, it should come as no surprise that most persons in this category are young and, given the kinds of work involved, that they are also very well-educated. The contrasts between this intelligentsia and the French-Canadian population generally are very striking as the following figures from a 1977 poll indicate:[24]

Favour:	*Intelligentsia* %	*All French Canadians* %
The Parti Québécois	82	53
Sovereignty-association	50	29
Unconditional sovereignists	21	12
Independence	29	18

It is quite possible that these figures understate the extent of Parti-Québécois and pro-independence *influence* within French-Canadian intellectual circles. Those figures give only the personal opinions of the respondents. If the *péquisites* and *indépendantistes* were more active and more vocal in expression of their views, the others possibly being intimidated by the odds against them, the frequency of expression of such sentiments in everyday discussion might be greater than even these figures suggest.

It would be a mistake to consider an intelligentsia as just another seven per cent of the population, as if their influence, like their votes, would count for no more than those of any other equivalent-sized group. An intelligentsia is a unique segment in any population in their regular activity involves communication with large numbers of people. They transmit some kind of cultural content on a regular basis, either daily (as in a classroom or in a newspaper) or weekly (as in a regular television programme or magazine) or monthly, in all cases to some larger audience. Where a diversity of views exists among the members of that intelligentsia, their impacts could cancel each other out; any didactic or hortatory attempt by one group of intellectuals could be countered, to some degree at least, by another. But where a heavy uni-directional tendency exists, or appears to exist, the weight of their opinion, potentially at least may be considerable. Given their training, their verbal abilities, their command of 'the facts,' and their organizational expertise, they would certainly be among the most influential groups in the society.

We are not in a position to say precisely how these general comments apply in the Quebec case. The intelligentsia is unique in providing the highest support for the Parti Québécois, for sovereignty-association, and for independence of any group in the society. At the same time, it is clear that some diversity exists within the broad category since half of them do not support sovereignty-association (being either opposed or undecided) and seven-tenths do not support outright independence. Those working in the natural sciences and in mathematics, moreover, would not ordinarily be communicating a supportive lesson in their classrooms. Teachers of business administration, a large and growing field, are also included within our definition of the intelligentsia and they, it is said, are generally opposed to Parti Québécois initiatives.

It is nevertheless evident that a solid core of support for the party and for its key initiatives exists within this segment of the population. Together with some other groups of activists, most importantly, with those from the trade union movement, they have formed the cadres that have brought the Parti Québécois to the point where it stands at present. It is important to note, however, that their potential for influence runs up against some very strongly felt opposition sentiments within the larger population, some of which are firmly rooted in immediate interests.

Some Determinants of Support

What are the factors leading people to support Quebec independence? Among the principal considerations put forward by supporters of the movement are the following: There is the concern with the demographic facts. Those supposedly 'hard' and ineluctable realities make clear the urgency of the situation. Many of the other grievances, to be discussed below, have been 'constants' in the Quebec situation; this factor, however, is one requiring immediate action. Then too, it is said that the federal government has steadily encroached on provincial powers since World War II. This continuing process also, so it is said, requires an immediate and dramatic change with only political independence being sufficient to stop the erosion.

There are also a large number of more permanent grievances. Many French-Canadians, as indicated, have been worried about the survival of their language and culture. In 1970, more than four in ten French-Canadians (44 per cent) said one should worry 'a lot' about the survival of the French language and an additional quarter (27 per cent) said one should worry 'somewhat'.

Moreover, French-Canadians have traditionally occupied lower ranks in the Quebec and Canadian socio-economic hierarchies, and this is widely perceived by them: 62 per cent reported in the same study that English-Canadians are generally the wealthier, with only 2 per cent mentioning French-Canadians. Not only is this perceived, but it is also not seen as acceptable: 61 per cent of those who saw a difference said that it 'should be reduced,' with only 28 per cent seeing it as 'acceptable.' Close to three quarters (74 per cent) perceived English-Canadians as dominating Quebec business and finance sector and about six in ten of them stated this to be 'abnormal.' Similarly, a widespread sense of discrimination prevails. A majority (52 per cent) feel that at equal competence English-Canadians have a better chance of obtaining a job or of gaining a promotion than French-Canadians.

To these economic grievances must be added a set of status and power deprivations. The same study indicated that a large proportion of French-Canadians (44 per cent) feel they are treated as inferior by English-Canadians. Many (35 per cent) feel that French-Canadian representation in the federal government is less than it should be.[25]

Although such feelings are widespread within the French Canadian population, only some 'translate' those grievances into a preference for the independence option. The difference between the generality of the population and the more committed Parti Québécois supporters appears to stem from different estimates of the chances of improvement coming with independence. As we have mentioned, the poll data show widespread fear about the likelihood of economic deterioration. The possibilities are judged more positively, however, with respect to the self-development of the French people and the conditions of their language and culture. For instance, some 44 per cent of French-Canadians expect improvement in the situation of French language and culture to come with independence. Among the French-Canadians favouring outright independence, 86 per cent expect improvement. Even some of these *indépendantistes,* however, recognize that the economic conditions would be worse with independence (10 per cent).[26] Unlike others, they express a willingness to pay those costs.

A third condition affecting the choice of independence

involves the segmented character of Quebec society as currently constituted. French-Canadians, it is said, live in a separate society; they live in separate communities with a near-complete, separate and distinct set of institutions including means of communication, schools, religious institutions, and also, to a considerable extent, separate workplaces. Linked to the latter differentiation, one also finds separate trade unions and professional associations.[27]

This institutional separation provides another context out of which comes support for independence. A large part of the French-Canadian population comes to feel loyal to *their* society, and especially towards the government of Quebec. In the last-cited study, it was found that more than half, 58 per cent, identify first with the Quebec government while only 24 per cent felt their first loyalty was to the government of Canada. (The remainder identified equally with both (16 per cent) or else were undecided). Once again, however, there is a gap between the proportion of those making such identifications with Quebec and those indicating an unambiguous preference for independence.

The principal consideration standing in the way of a simple translation of ethnic grievances and ethnic loyalties into support for independence, clearly, is the economic factor. Specifically it is the feeling that there would be heavy costs to pay if Quebec were to separate. Among the more active supporters of the Parti Québécois, the sentiments range from a 'most favourable scenerio' foreseeing either little change or a recognition of some modest losses, the latter being justified in terms of the social and cultural gains. Among the general population, however, the possibility of independence is seen with much greater trepidation and less of a willingness to 'pay the price'. Among all French-Canadians, 46 per cent expect economic conditions to deteriorate with independence, while only 18 per cent expect improvements. Among those opposed to independence, the proportion expecting deterioration reaches 67 per cent, with only 4 per cent expecting improvement.[28] The responses given to open-ended questions range from moderate fears such as: '*Je ne suis pas certain que ça aiderait l'économie du Québec*', '*Personne ne m'a encore convaincue que ce serait mieux (sur le plan économique)*', to the extreme fears indicated by the following answers: '. . . *pour quelques années, ce serait la débacle et la misère, les capitaux sortiraient du Québec*', '*(Ce serait) la famine, la misère noire*', '*On va être plus dans la misère qu'on (ne) l'est (maintenant)*.'[29] Related to these statements one finds a recognition of the interdependence of contemporary economies, many respondents offering one or another variation on the theme that 'one cannot go it alone.'

Parti Québécois leaders most emphatically agree with the latter point, indicating that their option, sovereignty-association, is designed expressly to avoid the option of 'going it alone'. Up to the present, many of those who feel ethnic grievances appear to have concluded that any experimentation with the relationship is too risky; they are not willing to pay the price, or more specifically, are not willing to take the chance.

The differing expectations of the pro-independence group and the much larger group who also share a sense of ethnic grievances requires explanation. One possible explanation for this difference would involve the social pressures or reinforcements found within the immediate millieu. The intelligentsia would be more familiar with analyses that defend the plausibility of, or argue the viability of the economic association. Even if they had not read such materials themselves, others within their circles would have read such materials and could pass the lessons on informally. In most other settings within the society, in the other segments of the middle class ranks, among the blue collar workers, and among farmers, those lessons would appear with considerably less frequency.

It is also possible that the experiences of the various segments of the Quebec society have been different, that is to say, that the immediate felt circumstances may have been different. The intelligentsia, for instance, may well have acquired a greater knowledge of, and developed a greater sensitivity to, their group's grievances. They may be particularly sensitive to the denial of an equal ethnic status, as well as entertaining greater hopes of redress to follow from independence.

Moreover, they may have experienced more favourable economic circumstances. Where they are located in new middle class positions, they would have relatively stable and relatively well-paying jobs. Many of the jobs, most especially those located in the public sector, are clearly seen to be the result of recent 'nationalist' efforts. The new investment in this sector 'created jobs' and political independence would create many more. Some of the nationalist legislation, moreover, transfers jobs from one group to another. The law that shifts immigrant children from English-language to French-language schools will, in most cases, entail a change in the persons teaching those children. The requirement of a 'working knowledge' of French in order to practice a wide range of professions (regardless of the language of the clientele) has a similar impact. These changes would mean that many persons among the intelligentsia have already found the independence movement to be one providing real material benefits. So for them, it would be relatively easy to make a rather positive assessment about the long term effects.

The experience of many other groups in the society may have been quite different. Many workers, for instance, may not be as affected by status depriviations. Among them, status concerns may not be primary ones. Material needs, and the means to satisfy them—such as a good job, a steady income—are generally much more pressing. These in turn are perceived to require interdependent economies within an integrated Canada. Moreover, since the Parti Québécois came to power, there has been some flight of capital from the province (and, presumably, a failure of capital to come in). This has been reported in the press, on radio and over television with at least some regularity.[30] The implications of that too would lead to doubts about further moves towards independence. These developments, it will be noted, were taking place at a time when there was a *de facto* 'economic union' with 'the rest of Canada.'

The Parti Québécois found itself in a difficult position. Having chosen a democratic-consultative route towards independence, they discovered that the sharply-formulated (or 'hard') questions, in almost all of the pre-referendum soundings of opinion, yielded unfavourable results. 'Success' seemed to be possible only at the price of watering down or edging away from their basic preference, that is, through use of a 'soft' question. But the latter option led to disaffection and internal rebellion within the party.

Another possibility, temporizing, would avoid an early defeat but it would have meant going against a formal commitment to hold a referendum. It would also have had the disadvantage of continued uncertainty which would lead to a worsening of the economic situation. And that, in turn, would have confirmed the general fears about the economic consequences of independence, thus worsening their chances in the 'ultimate' referendum. Given the problem with a straightforward question, it seemed likely that *the* question would be an equivocal one. A positive result in that case would justify some kind of negotiation. At the same time, however, it would have provided the Parti Québécois with a serious problem in justifying a 'large agenda', that is, one calling for political independence. If the federal government rejected the aspirations of the negotiators, arguing the lack of a clear mandate, that would, party spokesmen indicated, have led to a second 'consultation,' that is, to a second-round referendum struggle, this one focused on the question of sovereignty alone.

The Quebec referendum was finally held on May 20th, 1980. The question used was decidedly 'soft' in character, it being made even more acceptable by the promise of a second referendum before any change would be affected.[31] Only 40.4 per cent chose the YES option and, obviously, a clear majority, 59.6 per cent chose the NO. This question, in short, yielded a result much less favourable to the Parti Québécois's option than the polls would have led one to expect. Many voters appear to have given a 'hard' answer even to this 'soft' question.[32]

Subsequent to this defeat, the Parti Québécois participated in a new round of constitutional negotiations during the summer and fall of 1980 within the framework of federalism, the discussions being pursued jointly with the federal government and those of the nine other provinces. A provincial election was called in April 1981 at a point when the referendum defeat and subsequent public opinion polls suggested a clear loss for the Parti Québécois. Once again, however, the party 'isolated' the independence question, announcing there would be no new referendum during the forthcoming legislative period. With 'the issue' thus removed from the discussion, voter preferences shifted and the Parti Québécois won 49 per cent of the vote. This was the best they had ever achieved, a result that gave them a commanding majority in the National Assembly.

Notes

1. The best of the general histories is that of Mason Wade, *The French Canadians, 1760-1967*, two volumes, (Toronto, 1968). For a briefer overview, see Kenneth McNaught, *The Pelican History of Canada* (London, 1969). A useful account of more recent events, up to the mid-sixties, is that of Edward M. Corbett, *Quebec Confronts Canada* (Baltimore, 1967). An important collection of relevant essays by a leading historian is that of Ramsay Cook, *Canada and the French-Canadian Question* (Toronto, 1966); *idem., The Maple Leaf Forever: Essays on Nationalism and Politics in Canada* (Toronto, 1971), especially chapters 6-8. For another, more recent account, see Kenneth McRoberts and Dale Postgate, *Quebec: Social Change and Political Crisis*, Revised Edition, (Toronto, 1980).
2. See Everett C. Hughes' community study, *French Canada in Transition* (Chicago, 1943), and, for more recent evidence, Raymond N. Morris and C. Michael Lanphier, *Three Scales of Inequality: Perspective on French-English Relations* (Don Mills, Ontario, 1977).
3. For a portrait of the basic strain, of the imbalance between rural

land and rural population, see Horace Miner, *St. Denis: A French-Canadian Parish* (Chicago, 1939). For accounts of French-Canadians in the American milieu, see Kenneth Underwood, *Protestant and Catholic: Religious and Social Interaction in an Industrial Community.* (Boston, 1957), p. 207 ff., 189-99, and Harold J. Abramson, *Ethnic Diversity in Catholic America* (New York, 1973, pp. 52-66, 98-3, 133-6, 158-67, and *passim*. To prevent the loss of population to Ontario and the United States, the Quebec clergy encouraged investment in the province. This little-known aspect of the history is covered in William F. Ryan, *The Clergy and Economic Growth in Quebec: 1896-1914* (Quebec, 1966).

4. Statistics Canada, 1971 Census of Canada. *Population: Ethnic Groups*, I, 3, Publication No. 92-723, (Ottawa, 1973). Within Quebec, the French-speaking, English-speaking, and 'other'-speaking populations are referred to respectively as francophones, anglophones, and allophones.
5. Possibly the earliest statement of this problem is that of Jacques Henripin, 'Evolution de la composition ethnique et linguistique de la population canadienne,' In V. W. Bladen, (ed.), *Canadian Population and Northern Colonization* (Toronto, 1962). For a more recent statement by Henripin see his 'Quebec and the Demographic Dilemma of French Canadian Society,' pp. 155-66 of Dale C. Thomson, (ed.), *Quebec Society and Politics: Views from the Inside* (Toronto, 1973). Some recent work has argued, with evidence, that the cause for alarm no longer exists; diminished in-migration, a disproportionate out-migration of 'the English' and an increased 'choice' of French-language education have changed the situation.

   On this, as on most other points covered in this paper, there is very intense dispute. We cannot hope to cover the many contributions on the subject in these brief footnotes.
6. For the Duplessis era, see Herbert F. Quinn, *The Union Nationale: A Study in Quebec Nationalism* (Toronto, 1963), and Conrad Black, *Duplessis* (Toronto, 1977). For the Lesage period and the Quiet Revolution, see Richard Jones, *Community in Crisis: French-Canadian Nationalism in Perspective* (Toronto, 1972), and Corbett, op. cit.
7. The best studies of the independence movement's militants are those of Réjean Pelletier, *Les militants du R.I.N.* (Ottawa, 1974), and François-Pierre Gingras, 'Contribution à l'étude de l'engagement indépendantiste au Québec,' (Ph.D. thesis, Paris: Université René Descartes, 1971). For a more recent analysis of the role of intellectuals in the movement see Maurice Pinard and Richard Hamilton, 'The 1980 Quebec Referendum: Strengths and Weaknesses of a Party of Intellectuals,' in Harold D. Clarke and Allan Kornberg (eds.), *Political Support in Canada: The Crisis Years* (Durham, N.C., forthcoming). For an excellent overall analysis of the current crisis, see Raymond Breton and Daiva Stasiulis, 'Linguistic Boundaries and the Cohesion of Canada', in R. Breton, *et al Cultural Boundaries and the Cohesion of Canada* (Montreal, 1980), pp. 137-328.

8. For a discussion and investigation of this episode, see Maurice Pinard, 'La rationalité de l'électorat: le case de 1962,' pp. 179-95 of Vincent Lemieux (ed.), *Quatre élections Provinciales au Québec: 1956-1966* (Québec, 1969).
9. On the Parti Québécois, see Věra Murray, *Le Parti Québécois: de la Fondation à la Prise du Pouvoir* (Montréal, 1976).
10. We have traced this electoral development in three articles: 'The Bases of Parti Québécois Support in Recent Quebec Elections,' *Canadian Journal of Political Science*, 9,1 (1976), pp. 3-26; 'The Independence Issue and the Polarization of the Electorate: The 1973 Quebec Election,' *Canadian Journal of Political Science,* 10,2 (1977) pp. 215-59; and, 'The Parti Québécois Comes to Power: An Analysis of the 1976 Quebec Election,' *Canadian Journal of Political Science*, 11,4 (1978), pp. 739-75. References to other relevant literature will be found in these articles. But see in particular Vincent Lemieux, Marcel Gilbert et André Blais, *Une Élection de Réalignement: L'élection Générale du 29 Avril 1970 au Québec* (Montréal, 1970), and Daniel Latouche, Guy Lord et Jean-Guy Vaillancourt (eds.), *Le Processus électoral au Québec: Les Élections Provinciales de 1970 et 1973* (Montréal, 1976).
11. Hamilton and Pinard, op. cit., (1976), p. 11. Sixty-nine per cent (N = 26) of French-Canadian 18-20 year olds chose the Parti Québécois in our 1973 study as against only 11 per cent (N = 28) of those 65 or more.
12. See also the discussion in Pinard and Hamilton, op. cit., (1978), pp. 742 ff.
13. There were some differences in the question wordings over this period; for poll sources and questions asked, see Pinard and Hamilton, op. cit., (1977), notes 57 and 58, plus Table 8, and Raymond Breton and D. Stasiulis, op. cit., (1980), Appendix 3.A.1.
14. In our study from October 1977, 35 per cent of the French-Canadians in the 18-20 age group favoured independence as against 13 per cent in the 65 and over group. For a more detailed discussion of the inevitability argument, see Richard Hamilton, 'Is Independence Inevitable?' *Montreal Star*, 8 June, 1977, or, for a French version, 'L'Indépendance du Québec: est-elle inévitable?' *Le Devoir*, same date.
15. These questions are put, obviously, at a given point in time with people being asked about their sentiment at the moment or else how they would choose 'tomorrow.' As a guide to prediction, however, one ought to keep in mind the implicit *ceteris paribus* assumption. It is by no means certain that all other conditions would be equal at that future point when the individual choices would be made.
16. Many recent polls have indicated that this concept is very poorly understood by the general population. A study done for Radio-Canada by INCI in May 1978 discovered that 30 per cent of Quebec's citizens expected to continue sending members to the Parliament in Ottawa under this arrangement. Thirty-six per cent

reported they would not be sending deputies while a third said they did not know. Just a few weeks before the May 1980 referendum on this issue, a poll we carried revealed little decline in the level of confusion; for instance, 38 per cent thought that under sovereignty-association, Quebec would remain a province of Canada, while only 46 per cent knew that this would not be the case, the rest (15 per cent) saying they did not know. This poor understanding should be kept in mind in the interpretation of the poll results to be discussed in the following paragraphs.

17. See the discussion below. Also Maurice Pinard, 'Self-Determination in Quebec: Loyalties, Incentives, and Constitutional Options among French-Speaking Quebecers' in W. Phillips Davison and Leon Gordenker (eds.), *Resolving Nationality Conflicts* (New York, 1980, pp. 140-76).

18. Prior to 1979, there was one study (1977F) that showed a plurality among the French-speaking population. The questions used assumed the existence of the economic association. For poll sources and questions asked, see Breton and Stasiulis, op. cit., (1980), Appendices 3.A.1 and 3.A.2.

19. The question reads: 'The solution presently favoured by the Parti Québécois Government is that of sovereignty-association, which is to say that Quebec would become a politically independent country with economic alliance with Canada. If a referendum were to be held today on this question, would you vote for or against sovereignty-association.' The same *ceteris paribus* assumption (discussed in note 15 above) should be kept in mind here. Still another possibility involves a mandate to negotiate the option with the government in Ottawa. This will be discussed below.

20. This analysis is based on studies done by the authors. A more detailed presentation is made in Maurice Pinard, op. cit., (1980), pp. 163-4.

21. This result comes from a CROP study published in *La Presse* (Montreal), 18 November 1978, p. A5. Another question in the report asked the same respondents if they would vote for sovereignty-association. In response to this enquiry about sovereignty-association, 31 per cent were in favour, 53 per cent opposed, and 16 per cent without opinion. For trend data on the mandate-to-negotiate questions, see Maurice Pinard, op. cit., (1980), pp. 164-6.

22. In subsequent explanation it was indicated that a vote for the 'mandate' would be taken as a demand to *realize* sovereignty-association, not just to discuss it. The statement of linkage, the no sovereignty without association argument, triggered some dissension within the party, some arguing that it amounted to 'selling out' the aim of independence. One local leader resigned over the question. Following Lévesque's original statement (in the Assemblée nationale on 10 October, 1978), there was a further letter of explanation (*La Presse*, 23 November, 1978), and the subsequent position paper, *D'égal à égal*.

23. These data are taken from our article, Pinard and Hamilton, op. cit., (1978), p. 743.
24. These data are taken from a study conducted by the authors in October 1977. As indicated, the relationship with 'socio-economic status' (in this case, occupation) is a complicated one. Within the middle class (non-manuals), the support for sovereignty-association is high among the professionals and semiprofessionals (37 per cent) and also among the clerical and sales employees (38 per cent). Among the managers and administrators, the level is relatively low (26 per cent), which is about the same level found among blue-collar workers (27 per cent). Among farmers, support runs at 10 per cent. Within the professionals category, as indicated in the text, there is an important division, with the 'intelligentsia' being especially high (50 per cent), see Pinard and Hamilton 'The 1980 Quebec Referendum . . .' (forthcoming). Many authors have stressed the central role of the intelligentsia in nationalist movements; see, for instance, Ernest Gellner, *Thought and Challenge* (London, 1964), chp. 7, pp. 147-78. and A. D. Smith's paper in this volume as well as 'Toward a Theory of Ethnic Separatism.' *Ethnic and Racial Studies*, 2 (1979), pp. 21-37.
25. The data of the last few paragraphs are taken from a study conducted by Maurice Pinard in 1970.
26. These data are from a study conducted by SORECOM in February 1977. Many of the early leaders and militants expressed such fears; see François-Pierre Gingras, op. cit., pp. 204-56.
27. On the degree of linguistic segmentation in Canadian society, see K. McRae, 'Censociationalism and the Canadian Political System' in Kenneth McRae (ed.), *Consociational Democracy: Political Accommodation in Segmental Societies* (Toronto, 1974), pp. 238-61.
28. From SORECOM study, February 1977.
29. 'I am not sure that it would help Quebec's economy.' 'No one has yet convinced me that it would be better (economically.' '. . . for a few years, it would be chaos and misery, capital would get out of Quebec.' '(It would be) famine, the worst misery.' 'We would be more destitute than we are now.' Data from Pinard's study, 1970. For further analysis along the lines of the last few paragraphs, see Pinard, op. cit., (1980), esp. pp. 167-72.
30. There is a disparity in the reporting of such matters with English-language media typically giving these capital movements heavy coverage and French-language media touching them more lightly. Even without the systematic media attention, however, many French-Canadians would 'get the message'. Blue-collar workers, especially those in construction, experience the results of the investment moves very directly in the course of their lives. Our investigation show that people blame the Parti Québécois for these economic difficulties, not Ottawa, not the business leaders.
31. The question as finally adopted by the Quebec National Assembly on March 20, 1980, reads as follows: 'The Government of Quebec has made public its proposal to negotiate a new agreement with the

rest of Canada, based on the equality of nations; this agreement would enable Quebec to acquire the exclusive power to make its laws, levy its taxes and establish relations abroad—in other words, sovereignty—and at the same time, to maintain with Canada an economic association including a common currency; no change in political status resulting from these negotiations will be effected without approval by the people through another referendum; on these terms, do you give the government of Quebec the mandate to negotiate the proposed agreement between Quebec and Canada? Yes. No.'

32. An important symbolic question arose in the aftermath of the referendum—how the francophones had voted? For Pinard's estimates, showing a slight majority *against* the mandate, see 'Les francophones et le référendum,' *Le Devoir* 25 juillet 1980, p. 9. For further discussion of the bases of support and opposition see Pinard and Hamilton 'The 1980 Quebec Referendum . . .' (forthcoming).

CHAPTER 8

Basques and Basque Nationalism

Ken Medhurst

Introduction

Within Western Europe the Basque Region of Spain has, in recent years, ranked alongside Ulster as a major centre of politically inspired violence. Basque separatist urban guerillas, belongoing to ETA (Euskadi Ta Askatasuna-Basque Homeland and Freedom) have presented the Spanish State with, possibly, its biggest single dilemma. During Franco's last years, ETA activists were at the centre of crises that affected the whole course of Spanish political development. In 1970, for example, the trial (at Burgos) by court-martial, of sixteen ETA members temporarily focussed world attention on the dictatorship's handling of Basque dissent and precipitated nation-wide political mobilization on a scale unknown since the régime's foundation.[1] Similarly, in December 1973, ETA adherents claimed responsibility for assassinating Franco's first Prime Minister, Admiral Carrero Blanco, and so perhaps decisively upset Franco's plans for perpetuating authoritarian rule.[2] It is, therefore, of more than passing interest to attempt some evaluation of the origins, development and character of Basque nationalism. Equally, it is appropriate to evaluate the responses made to this issue by Franco's successors. Finally, it is hoped, in the course of such an analysis, to see if the phenomenon of Basque nationalism can be readily accommodated by some of the more influential theories of nationalism.

The Basques are concentrated in the four northern Spanish Provinces of Alava, Navarra, Guipúzcoa and Vizcaya and, in smaller numbers, in three south-western départements of France.[3] They form an ethnically distinct group whose association with its present 'homeland' goes back well beyond Roman times. Their geographically remote position has guarded them against assimilation by successive waves of conquerors. Equally, they have preserved an ancient language which is unrelated to any other European tongue. Economically, their region has traditionally relied much upon a distinctive peasant agriculture.

Notably within Guipúzcoa and Vizcaya there has been a stable and relatively egalitarian pattern of social organization based upon largely self-sufficient and isolated homesteads. In such areas, there developed a class of small independent farmers whose independence, in social and political matters, had no real equivalents elsewhere in Spain. After the Counter Reformation it was also a society in which the Roman Catholic Church occupied an especially strategic position. The local clergy lived in unusually close association with the rural population and frequently acted as community leaders.

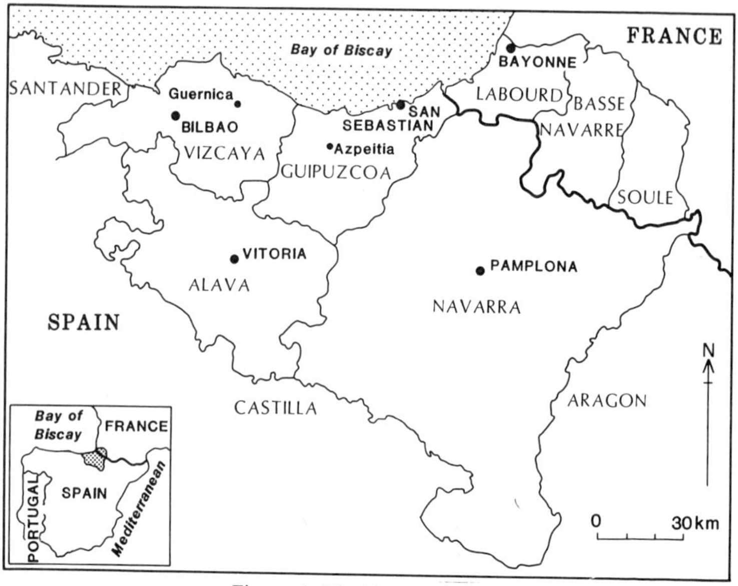

Figure 1 The Basque Country

Such largely introverted rural communities coexisted with fishing communities and a merchant class engaged largely in maritime trade. The latter were concentrated in such urban centres or ports as Bilbao. The tension between these centres and the surrounding rural society was a perennial feature of the region's politics.[4]

Politically, each of the Basque provinces had enjoyed its own separate and very long established relationship with the Kingdom of Castile. There was no equivalent of the single historic pre-existing Catalan political community. Rather, the four provinces had separate *fueros* (or charters) assuring each of them extensive autonomy. They had their own financial, legal and administrative structures and were exempted from the obligation to supply troops to the royal army. They could even conduct their own relations with foreign powers. The Provincial Councils, and municipal councils which underpinned them, were centres of unusually vigorous civic life that indicated and expressed a strong local commitment to the *fueros*.[5]

The link Castile forged with the Spanish Basque Provinces was part of a wider process whereby Castillian monarchs, through conquest and dynastic marriages, established their hegemony over neighbouring territories and so made their kingdom the 'heartland' of the Spanish state.[6] It was a process that, as in the Basque Region, sometimes left intact local institutions and loyalties. The Basque Provinces constituted only one, albeit a special, example of a more generalized phenomenon. It was a phenomenon pointing to the survival of potentially significant centrifugal forces within Spain and to an imperfectly accomplished process of national integration.[7]

Centralizing pressures acquired new momentum during the nineteenth century. In the wake of Napoleon's invasion of Spain a small 'Liberal' élite sought to impose a rationalized, uniform and highly centralized form of state authority, modelled on the French post-Revolutionary model.

In the Basque Region such trends provoked particularly strong reactions—reactions that were a major factor underlying Spain's nineteenth century Carlist Wars. These conflicts were partly dynastic matters involving rival claims to the Spanish throne. As such Carlism attracted one portion of Spain's aristocracy. It was only amongst the Basques, however, that the Carlists acquired an extensive following and so became a dynamic political force. Indeed, the Carlist Wars can, in large measure, be characterized as Basque 'Civil Wars' between local urban based 'Liberals' and neighbouring rural communities. The former saw existing administrative arrangements as obstacles to sound administration and, in particular, to the pursuit of economic interests within a wider Spanish market. The latter reacted strongly in defence of their traditional institutions and communal interests. Thus, large portions of the Basque peasantry rallied in support of the *fueros* and in opposition to urbanizing and centralizing forces at work in their midst. Equally, they were rallied by local clergy in support of Catholicism which was perceived as being under threat from anti-clerical liberal forces, allied with the Spanish State. It was this strand within Carlism which, in particular, gave it an intransigent and even fanatical dimension.[8]

In 1873 a final military defeat effectively destroyed Carlism as a relatively widespread popular movement. Its leadership was removed and remaining aristocratic sympathizers turned their attention away from the defence of Basque *fueros* to the quest for a Spanish theocratic state. Only in Navarra and, to some extent, in Alava did such Carlists retain significant portions of their established mass base. These Provinces are less isolated from the Castillian 'heartland', than the other Basque Provinces, and were less characterized by the type of peasant society that elsewhere had given rise to deeply rooted communal identities and strong support for local *fueros*.

In the aftermath of defeat these institutions were largely abolished. The one significant vestige, allowed to remain, was an arrangement whereby each of the Basque Provinces retained the right to negotiate with the State over their total tax liabilities whilst themselves determining the local distribution of this burden. Otherwise, centralizing forces seemed to triumph at the expense of local community interests. Thus, for example, the Basque language was eliminated from the educational system and restrictions were placed on its public use. An ancient tongue which was already experiencing serious problems in surviving and adjusting to the demands of socio-economic change was consequently placed further on the defensive. By contrast with Catalan it did not flourish as a modern literary language or as an effective means of mass communication. Rather, it became largely confined to some of the scattered rural communities from which Carlism had attracted its adherents.

Traditional Carlism was in no sense a nationalist movement. It was preoccupied with provincial particularism and was not committed to the concept of a single Basque people or nation with its own legitimate cultural or political demands. Indeed, Basque nationalism, when it did first arise was not the product of the Carlists' traditional hard core peasant supporters. They, for long, saw the restoration of the *fueros* as their goal. Carlism, however, can perhaps be characterized as a 'pre-nationalist' movement. By mobilizing large numbers of Basques in common opposition to what was seen as an externally inspired threat and by focusing attention on shared historical experiences it did open the way to the subsequent concept of a single Basque political community.

The Emergence of Modern Nationalism[9]

Significantly enough Basque Nationalism's universally acknowledged founder, Sabino Arana, and his chief collaborators, came from Carlist families. His transition to nationalism came within little more than twenty years of Carlist defeat. The general outlines of his ideology were sketched by 1894, and he laid the foundations of his Basque Nationalist Party—el Partido Nacionalista Vasco (PNV) in the same year. His ideology revealed Carlist affinities by referring back to the 'fueros' and by demanding the restoration of old provincial rights to the components of a new federal Basque Republic. Equally, his concern to defend the essentially Catholic nature of Basque society against alien intrusions indicates Carlist antecedents. On the other hand, Arana's thinking did in at least two respects represent a major new departure. Firstly, he talked of a historical Basque nation which should not merely seek political autonomy but should wholly separate itself from Spain. Secondly, he introduced a novel and frankly racist element by presuming Basque superiority over Spaniards and the need to guard against debilitating contacts with Spanish society.

Arana studied in Barcelona and his espousal of nationalism owed much to the example of Catalan contemporaries.[10] To that extent Basque nationalism was imitative. His thinking, however, differed much in style and content from that of his Catalan mentors. Thus Catalan nationalism was associated with a linguistic and literary revival and had an important cultural dimension whilst Arana and his followers stressed ethnicity. Equally, most Catalan nationalists saw their interests lying within a decentralized and revitalized Spanish State whilst the PNV's founders made a commitment to total separation that their successors have not wholly or explicitly renounced. Clearly, therefore, Basque nationalism's emergence and development cannot be adequately explained simply as an imitative phenomenon.

A more comprehensive explanation requires a closer examination of the particular environment from which Basque nationalism sprang and the dilemmas of those groups most closely associated with the movement's spread.

It is significant that the period between the defeat of Carlism and the emergence of nationalism was a period of major socioeconomic change within the Basque Region. It was particularly during this time that the area experienced a dramatic and extensive industrialization process that turned it (along with Catalonia) into one of Spain's two richest and most economically advanced regions. Whereas Catalan industrialization involved the emergence of medium-sized businesses producing such consumer goods as textiles, Basque industrial growth was based on large-scale heavy manufacturing and a local iron and steel industry. Likewise, Catalan industry grew up under the auspices of a local bourgeoisie whose interest lay in the relaxation of central controls whilst the leading Basque entrepreneurs were linked to nation-wide financial or banking concerns which dominated the entire Spanish financial system. They therefore had a much closer relationship with the Spanish State and little or no stake in the regional cause. For a while, a portion of this upper class business élite did lend some support to the PNV but it was for essentially limited and tactical purposes.[11] Moreover, by the time of Primo de Rivera's military dictatorship (1923-9) they had severed their nationalist links and confirmed their alliance with those conservative Castilian and other non-Basque elites who controlled the Spanish State. Thus industrialization, though it entailed some marked development in general regional prosperity, was seen principally to benefit groups whose ultimate loyalties or interests lay beyond the area.

The same process of industrialization also entailed the emergence of a substantial working class.[12] One section of this was recruited from the Basque rural hinterland but the larger part was formed by migrants from beyond the Basque area. These migrants frequently tended to live in segregated communities with low grade facilities. Moreover, they came with their own distinctive political values or expectations. Thus, the region's expanded urban labour force came to be largely organized under the auspices of the Spanish Socialist Party (the PSOE) and its affiliated trade union confederation (the UGT). Indeed, the Basque-based working class tended to make much of the running within the Spanish, nation-wide, Socialist movement. It was a movement that did not identify with distinctively Basque aspirations and sought to resolve working class problems within the framework of a centralized unitary state. Moreover, the Spanish left's anti-clericalism involved suspicion of and conflict with segments of the indigenous Basque Catholic population. Some native born workers were organized under the aegis of confessional unions, associated with the PNV, but they were a minority within the working class whose members generally tended to perceive such Catholic unions as instruments of business interests.

Basque nationalism may be interpreted as a reaction against such developments on the part of those groups within Basque society who perceived themselves as being most vulnerable to or threatened by the processes of change. Like Carlism it can be construed as a defensive reaction against traditional local interests and values. It is a reaction, however, against potentially much more disruptive forces and one expressed within the framework of an apparently more relevant ideology.[13]

Anthony Smith argues that the problems of identity and political purposes apparently underlying the emergence of nationalist movements are initially and most acutely experienced by members of the educated and professional middle classes or intelligentsia. In the Basque case this theory certainly bears scrutiny. Arana, and his co-founders of the PNV, can be fairly regarded as bourgeois and intellectuals caught up in crises of personal and group identity. The dominant position of the region's financial élite, on the one hand, and the rise of an organized working class on the other, trapped them in a situation that threatened their social group with powerlessness and a loss of status. By the same token, they were faced with the possible destruction of traditional frames of reference or values. Compensation and an alternative frame of reference therefore seems to have been sought in their quest for an independent Basque State. Their stress on the preservation of a Basque racial identity and traditional Catholicism is compatible with such a view. So are the attacks they made upon the disruptive effects of large scale industrial enterprise and class warfare—phenomena that were, significantly enough, seen as alien intrusions or imports into Basque society.

Similar considerations may also help to explain the spread of nationalism amongst sections of the Basque peasantry and of the (largely) rural clergy. Both groups had reason to react against the processes of industrialization—processes that seemed likely to destroy traditional Basque culture. In the case of the peasantry, however, nationalist protest also had a material base. Increasingly their traditional pattern of agriculture gave way to commercialized operations which would bring prosperity but could also render rural communities highly vulnerable to external economic forces. In particular, there was a tendency for local producers to become dependent on large-scale or monopolistic distributors. The insecurity thus engendered within rural communities found, in nationalism, an apparently appropriate political expression.[14]

Material factors similarly help to explain the recruitment, to the nationalist cause, of significant groups of medium or small-scale businessmen and of local professional elements. To some extent industrial growth benefitted such segments of Basque society. Many smaller business and professional opportunities emerged in the wake of big business. On the other hand, those concerned were frequently dependent upon the economically dominant groups and vulnerable to their pressures. They too had grievances that could be politicized within a nationalist context.[15]

The diverse nature of nationalist support helps to explain differences of emphasis that developed within the movement. Thus Arana's original insistence on a dramatic break with Spain was, in time, challenged by proponents of a gradualist approach who were willing, in the medium term at least, to settle for autonomy within the Spanish State as a step on the road to ultimate independence. The more intransigent tended to regard this latter position as a dangerous compromise which might lead to the abandonment of independence as a final goal. Equally, there were those who rejected any form of tactical alliance with Spanish political parties.

The Second Republic and the Civil War[16]

By the time of the Second Republic's foundation (1931), leadership of the movement had largely passed into the hands of 'moderates' who were prepared to settle for less than the maximum nationalist demands. The second generation of party leaders was inclined to adopt a somewhat gradualist and pragmatic line. They did not explicitly abandon Arana's goals but they were, in practice, constrained to set their sights on the more limited objective of a 'Statute of Autonomy', similar to that which the Republic, at the outset, conceded to Catalonia. Such leaders themselves tended to be cautious and conservative but they were also affected by electoral considerations. Thus, the smaller-scale local business interests associated with the PNV, tended to be particularly concerned with their economic grievances and were reluctant to identify with more far-reaching political aims. Equally, the party was vulnerable to the competition of nationwide Spanish parties. Fluctuating electoral fortunes certainly pointed to shifts of local opinion on the part of those only conditionally attached to the nationalist cause.

Relationships with Spanish or non-nationalist political parties presented the PNV with particularly serious dilemmas. On the one hand, its socially conservative and Catholic orientation made it an object of suspicion to the Socialist and Republican parties which had prime responsibility for establishing the Republic. Basque leaders, unlike their Catalan counterparts, were therefore excluded from the consultations which paved the way for the new régime's creation and they were also obliged to delay any consideration of their demands. On the other hand, Spanish conservatives, whose values were in many respects similar to those of the PNV, remained strongly attached to a form of Spanish nationalism that left no room for regional autonomy.

This situation explains why autonomy only came to be conceded, in 1936, after the outbreak of the Spanish Civil War. Earlier plans of a similar kind were aborted by the advent, in 1933, of a government dependent upon right wing anti-regionalist support. The outbreak of war eventually brought matters to a head not least by compelling the PNV to resolve doubts about its position *vis-à-vis* other Spanish political groupings. The difficulty was resolved by commitment to the forces of the Spanish left who, in return, finally acceded to nationalist demands by conceding a Statute that provided for substantial local autonomy.

Leadership of the regional government was in nationalist hands but Socialists, Communists and left wing Republicans also participated. Conflicts between these groups necessarily complicated its task. Equally, there was tension between the central Republican government, which gave priorty to the overall war effort, and the Basque authorities who were concerned to consolidate their newly won position. The latter, for example, had to take account of a dissident nationalist minority that argued for non-participation in what they regarded as a war amongst 'foreigners'. They also had to face opposition from two of the Provinces, Navarra and Alava, to which the nationalists had traditionally laid claim. These two areas had, at the outbreak of war, fallen under Carlist control and so left the Autonomous Basque Republic with a rich but limited territorial base formed only by Guipuzcoa and Vizcaya.

The Franco Régime

These problems contributed to a relatively rapid military defeat at the hands of the Spanish 'Nationalist' forces led by General Franco. This inevitably meant the end to local autonomy and the assertion of authoritarian political controls. Navarra and Alava were rewarded with the right to retain their own somewhat distinctive systems of provincial administration but otherwise all vestiges of the old 'fueros' were finally liquidated. Likewise, harsh repressive measures were instituted with a view not only to eliminating political dissent but also to destroying the basis of the distinctive Basque cultural identity. In other words the effort was made (as it was in Catalonia) definitely to reassert the hegemony of the Spanish State and to eradicate the local culture. Thus, a single monopolistic and centrally controlled 'Movement' replaced all pre-existing political parties.

Equally, independent trade unions were outlawed and gave way to government controlled structures. Opposition political and union leaders were executed, jailed or forced into exile. Also, (and the Basque Region was unique in this respect) measures were taken against members of the local clergy who had espoused the nationalist cause. Franco's forces, who sought to legitimize themselves by referring to their 'Crusade' against anti-Christian forces, regarded such clerical dissenters with peculiar abhorrence. Thus sixteen priests were executed and others jailed or sent into 'internal exile'. Likewise, the Spanish Church and State cooperated and so ensured that senior ecclesiastical appointments, in the Basque Country, were confined to non-Basques.[17]

Such efforts to break the link between Catholicism and the local culture were accompanied by a more direct assault upon the Basque identity. This included a ban on the use of the local language in ecclesiastical or any other public settings. Basque language books, journals, newspapers, speeches, sermons, street signs, and even tombstones, were outlawed. Similarly, casual street conversations in Basque could entail police harassment and summary fines. Above all, formal education, in the language, was forbidden and the education system largely placed in non-Basque hands. On top of this was a ban on traditional folkloric and cultural activities—a ban that affected many Basques who had never spoken the local language.

The initially limited opposition to this repression was led from outside Spain by members of the exiled regional government. Within the Basque Country itself, resistance tended to be confined to such symbolic gestures as flying the Basque flag. More substantively, the PNV contributed to Pyrannean-based guerilla operations. Even their activities, however, could be little more than irritants. On the other hand, the exiled Basque government, during the Second World War, established close relationships with the Western Allied Powers whose victory seemed likely, at the time, to precipitate Franco's downfall.

Ultimately, these expectations were disappointed. Allied pressure on Spain stopped well short of military intervention and Franco seized the opportunity to rally his supporters and outmanoeuvre opponents. Moreover, the 'Cold War' led the United States government to re-assess its view of Franco's government. By 1953 defence agreements had been concluded between Spain and the USA which brought his dictatorship fresh accessions of material and moral support. Such developments, in Spain as a whole, as well as in the Basque Country, effectively destroyed any hopes of speedy political change. Equally, domestic opposition was, for the time being, left isolated and in disarray. For example, 'the Cold War' meant the withdrawal of Communist representatives from the exiled Basque government and the exacerbation of already serious divisions within the opposition camp. In 1947 the PNV took the lead in promoting a widespread strike in the Basque Region. At its peak, it mobilized over 100,000 people and attracted cooperation from Socialists and other groups. This, however, proved to be the PNV's last major initiative and one without obvious long term significance. Indeed, even at the time, there were some doubts about the extent to which the party was in control of events.

The Creation of ETA and the Revival of Basque Nationalism

The PNV's difficulties point to the underlying weakness of its position in a dramatically changed political environment. It had developed as a moderately conservative Christian Democratic Party without the organization or experience needed to thrive in an underground situation. Its exiled leaders therefore increasingly tended to loose contact with Spanish political realities and its adherents, within Spain, appeared to loose effectiveness or relevance. In the Basque Region the running seemed to be made by sections of the local working class under Communist or socialist rather than Nationalist auspices.

This situation created frustration amongst the PNV's own adherents—especially amongst its youthful student members. In 1952 a group of the latter therefore broke away to form their own organization.

Initially this was merely a collection of discussion groups. Out of it, however, came ETA, which was founded in the late 1950s as a result of a merger between the breakaway group and a fresh wave of PNV student dissidents.[18]

This development gave Basque Nationalism a new lease of life and a fresh dimension. Initially ETA seemed innocuous and the Spanish police left it largely unmolested. In the early 1960s, however, a series of spectacular urban guerilla operations transformed the situation. These presented Franco's régime with an unprecedented challenge to which it responded with severe repression of immediate post-Civil War proportions. This repression came to affect large sections of Basque society and helped to precipitate major political crises throughout Spain.

ETA's confrontation with the Spanish State followed a 'classic' pattern of upward spiralling levels of violence. Violent opposition provoked repressive counter-measures which, in the long run, tended to intensify and broaden the base of opposition. Such a pattern was largely in conformity with the political analysis and intentions of ETA theorists. They include those who wished to provoke repression as a way of alienating Basque opinion and so attracting sympathy for their own cause.

The régime's response certainly fell into line with ETA's expectations. The widespread incidence of arbitrary arrest, torture and summary trials before special (and sometimes military) courts all served to heighten tensions and build up local hostility towards the State.[19] Likewise, the large numbers of state police and para-military personnel poured into the Basque Region, from outside, created the widespread sense of a country under occupation. Frequent small scale confrontations between such security forces and the local population had the cumulative effect of radically politicizing significant sections of previously apolitical or moderate Basque opinion. Equally, they tended to raise levels of national consciousness. Thus, the State's drive to destroy ETA succeeded chiefly in presenting the organization with reserves of support or, in many more cases, general sympathy amongst sectors of Basque society who traditionally would have repudiated its aims and methods. Not least, the extension of repression beyond the region's major urban centres and into surrounding towns or rural communities served to broaden the social base of opposition so as to include larger sections of the area's middle and lower middle classes. The practice of shutting shops and small businesses as signs of protest during political crises, was one indicator of this. Thus, when Franco died, the population of the Basque region was more radicalized than any other Spanish regional grouping. Equally, it was more mistrustful of the central government's intentions.

Before looking at the impact of this situation on more recent Spanish political developments it is necessary to ask three sets of questions about the growth of Basque opposition during Franco's last years. First, what was the exact nature of ETA? Secondly, what special factors underlie its development? Thirdly, to what extent can changes in Basque political attitudes be simply attributed to ETA?

ETA itself has, from the beginning, been a more complex phenomenon than hitherto suggested.[20] It has frequently been the subject of domestic disputes, ideological conflicts and schisms. In this respect, it is perhaps like other conspiratorial or sectarian groups obliged to operate underground and functioning in a relatively closed mental universe within which matters of ideological interpretation and rectitude acquire special significance.

Generally speaking, its internal conflicts have evolved around two separate if related sets of issues, concerning both ends and means. In the first place there have been disputes between separatists, for whom the achieving of Basque independence is the main aim, and those who tend to stress that the Basque cause should be seen as part of a wider struggle conducted ultimately in the interests of the entire Spanish working class. Whilst the former have sought total independence, the latter have been more inclined to see Basque independence as a necessary stage in the creation of a federal Spanish Socialist State. Exponents of both tendencies have, to varying degrees, been inspired by Marxist patterns of thought though it is adherents of the latter persuasion who can perhaps be regarded as the more orthodox or rigorous Marxists. Indeed, at one stage, one breakaway group seceded from ETA in order to establish a distinct Marxist-Leninist Party. For them the main aim was the destruction of Spanish capitalism and the central State institutions which, in their view, upheld the interests of the Spanish ruling classes. Their initial nationalist commitment or pursuit of 'national liberation' was not so much an end in itself as a means of raising local political consciousness and, more especially, of mobilizing local working class support. By the same token, they sprang from a wing of ETA that aimed to mobilize all relevant sections of Basque society, whether or not they were of local origin. Adversaries of such tendencies, within ETA, have, by contrast, tended to a romantic nationalist viewpoint which gives priority to the achieving of Basque independence and the establishment of a distinct Basque socialist polity. Equally, they have tended to emphasize ethnicity rather than class as the salient source of division.

In the second place there have been perennial debates, within ETA, over the appropriate methods of struggle. Thus some (generally more inclined to the 'romantic nationalist' position) have stressed the crucial role of violence, and the correspondingly pre-eminent role of a militant élite, in undermining the morale or credibility of the Spanish authorities. Others (frequently associated with a more 'orthodox' Marxian nationalism) have been inclined to see violence or urban guerilla activity as just one part of a more comprehensive strategy aimed at the mobilization, organization and retention of mass support. Some of this disposition, even during Franco's life-time, went so far as wholly to repudiate sporadic or individual acts of violence as an appropriate weapon. Generally, however, disputes concerned the nature and extent of violence rather than its suitability or legitimacy. Thus different fractions within ETA, have generally sustained a 'military front' alongside other specialized 'fronts' or agencies, covering the varied types of struggle embraced by the organization. Such a 'military front' involved usually well-trained and sometimes full-time activists whose support and shelter came from the wider organization. Likewise, the organization, at large, was constructed on a cell system, reminiscent of the Communist Party, designed to maximize security whilst engaged in armed or other forms of clandestine activity. This cell system sometimes facilitated the breakaway of armed groups, whom the official leaders could not control. On the other hand, it also guarded against police infiltration.

The aims, methods and ideological preoccupations of ETA have to be seen against the background of the context from which it emerged and in which it developed. As already observed, it initially emerged out of frustration with the PNV's inability to grapple with the special problems of underground resistance to dictatorial rule. This alone, however, is not sufficient to explain the new direction taken by the nationalist movement. The development of Basque nationalism, after ETA's emergence, and popular responses to the nationalist movement, during the same period, can only be adequately evaluated in the light of more general developments within the Basque Region and Spain at large.

Such developments can be grouped under three main headings which, in practice, are inter-related but which, for analytical purposes, can be treated separately. These headings separately refer to the socio-economic, cultural and religious dimensions of the issue.

The period during which ETA emerged and acquired significance coincided with a period of rapid Spanish economic development which had special consequences for the already substantially industrialized Basque Region. Thus Spain's already relatively dynamic centres of economic activity, such as the industrialized portions of the Basque Country, benefitted disproportionately from this new growth. The region's industrial base expanded and so ensured that its average income levels would continue to be amongst Spain's highest.[21] In the process, the existing Basque financial élite, still closely allied with nation-wide business interests and with the Spanish State reinforced its already dominant position in the area's economic life. Simultaneously, the region was subjected to further waves of immigration on the part of workers, from other parts of Spain, who were attracted to the Basque areas by its freshly burgeoning employment opportunities. Equally, there was further disruption of the Basque countryside as the area's own rural dwellers got caught up in the same population shifts.

Such rapid and dramatic changes drew attention to and aggravated precisely those dilemmas or tensions which, at the outset, had underlain the emergence of Basque nationalism. On the one hand there was a growth in the power and salience of large-scale business activity which might present fresh opportunities to the area's middle class or professional groups but which could also appear as a threat to their interests and to the values of the community with which they identified. Economic growth could benefit medium and small-scale local enterprises but it could equally reinforce vulnerability to or dependence upon large companies and financial institutions that the local economic élite continued to dominate. Similarly, it appears as if in the new and more modern economic sectors, senior managerial and administrative posts tended to go to non-Basques. This perhaps gave to the local middle classes a source of grievance not previously experienced.[22]

On the other hand, the rapid influx of largely working class immigrants caused further anxiety to those most concerned with the maintenance of a distinctive Basque identity. Sections of the Basque community, already feeling themselves under attack from the State came to feel themselves additionally beseiged by large numbers of unassimilated newcomers. As before, the problem seemed compounded because the expanded working class was largely organized under left wing Spanish auspices. During the 1950s and 1960s, as working class dissent renewed throughout Spain, workers from the Basque area were frequently in the vanguard of illegal strike movements, but these were largely directed by Communist and Socialist activists. The economic and, subsequently, political protests of the region's workers presented Franco's régime with major dilemmas but they could also give rise to ambivalent attitudes amongst frustrated nationalists and those for whom extensive upheavals entailed crises of communal and even personal identity.

As with Arana's generation, such crises were apparently most acutely felt amongst youthful members of the region's educated middle classes—the group which supplied ETA with its founders and chief source of recruits.[23] In grappling with their dilemmas, they repudiated the PNV's essentially conservative values in favour of new approaches that seemed to have more relevance in the context of an authoritarian polity and a society experiencing a rapid capitalist process of industrialization.

The need simultaneously to grapple with the twin problems of political repression and economic upheaval perhaps explains the Marxist component in the thinking of ETA adherents. In particular they were influenced by the Cuban revolution, Maoist concepts of people's warfare and by the Algerian independence struggle. (At a later date some were similarly attracted by the Uruguayan Tuparmaros and the Palestinian 'Black September' movement.)

The relevance of such models could be reasonably disputed. Nevertheless, the Spanish State's response to ETA's early activities did give some plausibility to the idea that the Basque region was a colonized territory in need of liberation. Equally, the often indiscriminate character of official repression helped to create popular identification with the Basque nationalist cause and sympathy for ETA on a scale that could not otherwise have been expected. On the one hand groups, with long term conflicts of interest, were drawn into common support for local opposition movements. On the other hand ETA attracted the sneeking regard of many who would have generally repudiated both its aims and its methods. This was true, for example, of traditional PNV supporters, of many working class activists and of local Catholic spokesmen.

The evoking of such widespread sympathy may have created the impression that popular mobilization, in the Basque Region, was directly and almost exclusively due to ETA. The organization's prestige and, for a while, heroic stature gave credibility to such a view. The resulting efforts, of other groups, to appropriate the ETA label had the same effect. In reality, however, ETA's endeavours should be seen as one, albeit important feature, of a more widespread radicalization process. This process was rooted in longer term socio-economic developments, in the Basque Country, developments that lay behind the organization's initial emergence. ETA's contribution was to provoke the state into retaliating against large sections of Basque society in a way that served to raise levels of popular political consciousness and to reinforce a distinctive local political identity. Its intervention helped to catalyse or accelerate a radicalization process that, to a considerable extent, remained beyond its own control.

This was true, not least, in the realm of working class politics.[24] ETA militants did seek to gain a foothold in factories and working class communities. Their challenges to the Franco régime also awakened much sympathy in such quarters. Likewise, at times of crisis, such as the Burgos trial, there was extensive working class mobilization in opposition to the régime's repressive policies. On such occasions, protest strikes spread well beyond the Basque Region but received particularly strong support from the local working class. Such mobilization, however, did not, for the most part, occur under ETA's own auspices. Rather it was a question of other and often non-nationalist working class movements participating in resistance to official onslaughts upon the local community. In practice, it was frequently difficult to disentangle nationalist from other and more specifically working class forms of resistance. In the post-Franco era, a working class expression of nationalism did emerge and it undoubtedly had its roots in the crisis which ETA did so much to precipitate. ETA itself, however, did not acquire an extensive working class base.[25]

Similar developments characterized the cultural domain. There also, ETA tended to claim credit for processes which had more complex origins.[26] Thus by the mid-1950s, the post-Civil War cultural repression had, to a limited extent, given way to a certain re-assertion of Basque culture. In part this was facilitated by changes in official policy. On the one hand Franco's régime, by the mid-1950s, felt sufficiently secure to offer modest concessions in this realm. On the other hand, it had become apparent that attempts to eradicate local cultures would, at best, be very long term matters. Consequently, the use of the Basque language was less strenuously resisted. Spanish retained its monopoly in official dealings but fewer barriers were placed in the way of its unofficial usage. Indeed, the 1960s saw the spread of a system of voluntary part-time schools, or 'Ikastolas', dedicated to the dissemination of the local language and culture. Popular support for these institutions was both cause and effect of a situation in which the local tongue made a limited, yet significant, come-back. Surveys made it plain that Basque remained much more of a minority affair than was the case with Catalan.[27] Nevertheless, in areas where Basque had traditionally shown its greatest staying power there were indications of quite substantial revival.

Though officially tolerated, the 'Ikastola' movement was the object of considerable official suspicion and periodic police harassment. In part this was due to the not entirely unfounded fear that cultural movements could be politicized and converted into additional centres of local political dissent. Certainly, in the situation that developed within the area, organized support for the local culture, almost by definition, represented an act of protest with some political content. Equally, nationalists, including members of ETA, gave encouragement to 'Ikastolas'. However, it would be mistaken to view this relatively broadly based cultural movement as simply part of a carefully orchestrated political strategy. ETA activities, by drawing attention to the Basque issue and raising general levels of local political consciousness, probably did contribute to the success of the 'Ikastolas'. But the organization could not claim to be an ultimately determining force behind the cultural revival. That revival was, in significant part, a popular response to post-Civil War repression and to the political repression of the 1960s and 1970s. Cultural revival was one significant expression of the heightened sense of communal solidarity and identity that repression did so much to produce.

The cultural revival probably owed as much to the support of local Roman Catholic clergy as it did to explicitly political movements.[28] To that extent the Basque Church simply remained attached to its traditional role within the local community. On the other hand, the Church's recent contribution must also be seen against the background of changes in its political attitudes and, not least, in the response, of some of its adherents, to Basque nationalism.

Church-State relationships in Franco's Spain were never wholly free from strain and, particularly during the 1960s and 1970s, such strains became increasingly evident.[29] From the outset, the Basque clergy had a special 'vanguard' role in the voicing of ecclesiastical dissent. Their distinctive historical position *vis-à-vis* the dictatorship pushed them in that direction. Initially (as already noted) such dissent coexisted with generally conservative values. Subsequently, however, significant segments of the Basque clergy emerged as pioneers in a radicalization process that, to varying degree, was to affect the entire Spanish Church. This process was partly due to changes in the international Catholic community associated with the Second Vatican Council. But the process was also due to the more specifically Spanish experience of disruptive economic change within the context of an authoritarian political system—an experience that had especially dramatic consequences for the Basque Region. In Spain at large, the result was a questioning of established economic inequalities and of traditional political alliances. In the particular circumstances of the Basque Country, the result was a reassertion and, for some, a re-interpretation of traditional links between Catholicism and Nationalism.

These upheavals necessarily entailed some fragmentation of

Catholic opinion. One minority group, within the Basque clergy (which initially included the episcopate) retained its traditional conservative and pro-régime position. Others, probably representing a majority of the local clergy, adopted more liberal theological positions and inclined politically to Christian Democratic or Socialist loyalties. A third group espoused a radical stance *vis-à-vis* their own ecclesiastical superiors and the political domain. Amongst the two latter groups there was, to varying degrees, considerable support for the nationalist cause. The 'radicals' included some who gave support to ETA and, in a few cases, ETA activists.

Pressure from some radicalized clergy played some part in pushing local Church leaders into conflict with the State. Of perhaps greater importance, however, was the State's own indiscriminate repression which led substantial portions of the Spanish episcopate at large, including local bishops, to protest publicly against official practices. Indeed, the very end of the Franco era witnessed an unprecedentedly grave crisis in Church-State relationships which had its origins in (unsuccessful) official efforts to banish the Bishop of Bilbao following his attacks upon official policy within the Basque Region. The degree of episcopal opposition pointed to the part played by the Basque issue in aggravating Church-State tensions. The crisis similarly confirmed that, despite internal divisions and mounting difficulties, the Church remained a significant articulator of communal grievances. ETA's founders reacted against the traditional forms of clericalism and testified to secularizing tendencies amongst post-Civil War generations of Basques—tendencies that the Spanish hierarchy's alliance with Franco's dictatorship probably encourged. Nevertheless, Catholicism was revealed as a still significant factor in Basque society with a continuing political role.

The Post-Franco Era[30]

The Basque problem constituted one of the thorniest legacies inherited by Franco's political heirs. Years of repression had so deeply marked whole generations of Basque citizens that latent conflicts within the area frequently yielded to a shared distrust of State authority.[31] This was true, for example, of tensions between the indigenous community and working class immigrants. Thus, on the one hand, traditionally high levels of local political awareness were further increased whilst, on the other hand, widespread refusal to participate in State referendums or elections indicated that such awareness frequently entailed repudiation of established institutions.[32]

Franco's death meant, if anything, heightened tension for it aroused expectations that his immediate successors were unwilling to meet. It was the subsequent appointment of a government led by Sr. Suarez that proved the major turning point for he was committed to the dismantling of authoritarianism and its replacement by liberal-democratic procedures.

The Basque issue remained a major obstacle to this strategy's successful implementation. Thus a still high local abstention rate in the referendum held to legitimize the transition indicated continuing mistrust and opposition to reform from within the old order.[33] Equally, groups associated with that order, notably within the military and security forces, continued to resist nationalist demands. They remained in combat with ETA adherents and still favoured traditional responses.

Ultimately, in 1977, general elections were held for a parliament charged with drafting a new Spanish Constitution and in March 1979 further elections chose the first legislature to operate under these fresh auspices. These two elections (which in the Basque Region produced very similar results) both tended to underline the distinctive nature of Basque opinion.[34]

At first glance, it might seem as if the restoration of competitive politics had facilitated a marked diminution of centre-periphery conflict. Thus, in 1977, a call from ETA's allies to boycott the election had only a limited impact. Similarly, in both 1977 and 1979, non-nationalist parties had apparently significant successes in the Basque Region. In 1977, for example, Suarez's recently formed centre-right and pro-government party (the UCD) won seven of the area's seats in the lower house of parliament and their chief Spanish opponents, the Socialist Party, won eight seats. Nationalists won only a minority of the available places—eight going to the traditionally moderate PNV and just one to new left wing nationalist groups.

Other developments, however, indicate that, on closer inspection, the Basque Region was less well integrated into the new Spanish political system than the above figures suggested. First, doubts about electoral participation, in 1977, were only removed at the last minute as a consequence of discreet but significant government concessions to popular demands for the amnestying of imprisoned nationalist activists.[35] Secondly, though this campaign was perhaps the last time ETA found itself at the centre of a widely supported popular movement, its legacy was nonetheless considerable. Thus local left wing Marxist inspired and revolutionary groups gained almost 10 per cent of the 1977 Basque vote (a far larger percentage than that acquired by the non-Communist revolutionary left in the other Spanish regions).[36] Clearly, significant middle and working class elements, in the Region, had been politicized under the auspices of groups linked to or significantly influenced by ETA adherents. Thirdly, it was apparent that such groups were, to some extent, the victims of an electoral system designed to discriminate in favour of centre or centre-right parties. The distorting effects of this system undoubtedly penalized left wing nationalists whilst exaggerating the extent of support for non nationalists. In 1977, for example, the UCD won 28.6 per cent of Basque parliamentary seats on the basis of just 16.4 per cent of the local vote.[37]

The 1979 elections confirmed the extent to which new left wing groups had established themselves within the nationalist movement. Of the ten Basque parliamentary seats which went to nationalists seven were secured by the PNV, one by the relatively moderate left wing 'Euskadiko Ezquerra and three by a freshly formed union of Marxist influenced groups—Herri Batasuna (United People).[38] The latter's complex composition and its sometimes populist postures raise questions about its long term coherence but its advent nonetheless underlines the novel extent to which working class, and other forms of radical dissent, now takes a nationalist form.[39]

The Basque electorate's distinctive nature is finally confirmed by examining the local support given to parties, of all types, committed to some local autonomy. Thus in 1977 over 75 per cent of the Basque electorate supported parties committed to regional self government (35.9 per cent supporting avowedly nationalist parties and 40.2 per cent backing Spanish left wing or centre parties favouring devolution).[40]

The strength of Basque feeling explains the Spanish government's willingness to make substantial concessions to local interests. Thus, after the 1979 elections a period of delicate negotiation resulted in an agreement between State and Basque representatives. It provided, in principle, for the devolution of unprecedently large powers, ranging from local policing to economic planning, to a regional government responsible to an elected regional parliament. The Spanish authorities, thereby clearly hoped to provide a durable solution to the Basque problem that would satisfy most citizens of the area and so isolate the minority committed to independence.[41]

The first regional parliamentary elections occurred in March 1980. The results pointed to many still unresolved difficulties.

Above all, there was a further advance for local parties at the expense of nationwide Spanish groupings. The PNV won 25 of the 60 available seats on the basis of 30 per cent more votes than it received in 1979. Herri Batasuna came second with 11 seats and a two per cent increase in support. Another left wing nationalist group, Euzkadido Ezkerra, increased its vote by 12 per cent to win six seats. By contrast, the local socialists lost 27 per cent of their 1979 vote in exchange for only nine seats and the UCD lost over 50 per cent of its support and took a mere six seats.[42]

The result of the election is a regional goverment principally dependent on the PNV. The party's relative moderation on the national issue and on socio-economic matters could provide the basis for fruitful co-operation with the Spanish government in the practical task of redefining centre-periphery relationships. Its job is complicated, however, by an inability to speak for all nationalists and the constant possibility of being outflanked by more intransigent and radical competitors. Equally, continuing ETA violence, albeit on the part of a sharply divided and now much more isolated organization, is a reminder of the dangers attached to compromising with the Spanish State.[43] Serious miscalculations could re-activate latent sympathies for militant activists.

Economic problems add to such difficulties. Recent nationalist advances may, in significant measure, be seen as a protest against the effects of recession and the long term decline of such traditional industrial activities as ship building. On the other hand, continuing violence and general uncertainty stands in the way of any coherent programme for economic recovery. Thus, there is something of a vicious circle which only considerable sensitivity and restraint on the part of both the Spanish and Basque authorities can hope to break.

In theory, complete independence offers an alternative escape from the dilemma. Several factors, however, point to its practical impossibility. First, the French State can be expected to co-operate with Spain in resisting such a development. It has no interest in encouraging its own regional minorities. Secondly, the possibility of independence could precipitate so far merely latent conflicts between indigenous Basques and portions of the working class immigrant community. Finally, the possibility of secession seems likely to provoke military intervention. Thus, the real choice seems to lie between the *status quo* and the re-assertion of traditional forms of Spanish State hegemony. Clearly, therefore, an inability to make existing arrangements work would have serious implications for the entire Spanish polity.[44]

Conclusion

This analysis indicates that Basque nationalism is a relatively complex phenomenon whose origins and development cannot readily be explained by mono-causal theories of nationalism.[45] For example, it cannot easily be attributed to colonial patterns of economic exploitation. Economic frustrations have underlain some of the movement's popular appeal and in recent years, particularly, it has been possible to point to some state neglect of the area's public services.[46] The region's general experience, however, has been of relatively advanced or privileged economic development.

This apparently bolsters theories stressing uneven economic development. Again, the latter has a bearing but is insufficient by itself, to explain the original nature of the movement's support and the precise content of its ideology. These may be best explained by references to the defensive reactions of traditionally significant groups in Basque Society whose status, interests and values seemed, as a consequence of industrialization, to be threatened. It was perhaps their heightened awareness of belonging to an ethnically distinct yet culturally beleaguered minority that gave their nationalism its characteristically intransigent quality.

Questions of group identity similarly help to explain Basque nationalism's dynamic character. The emergence of a left wing and more securalized nationalism has been partly due to industrialization but has also grown in response to communal experience of repression. Indeed, repression had the effect of intensifying communal solidarity in face of internal divisions, notably between native Basques and working class immigrants, that further industrialization might otherwise have accentuated. An adequte account of the movement must, therefore, examine the interactions of ethnicity, industrialization and repression. Equally, it is current perceptions and handling of these issues that are likely to condition its further evolution.

Notes

1. On this crisis cf. G. Halemi, *Le Procès de Burgos* (Paris, 1971) and K. Salaberri, *El Proceso de Euzkadi en Burgos* (Paris, 1971). The official Spanish view, at the time, was presented in F. de Arteaga, *E.T.A. y el Proceso de Burgos* (Madrid, 1971).

2. On the subject of Carrero Blanco's assassination of Julen Agirre, *Operación Ogre-Cómo y por qúe ejecutamos a Carrero Blanco* (Hendaya and Paris, 1974).
3. As will be noted Alava and Navarra have experienced a different modern historical development from Guipúzacoa and Vizcaya. Alava and Navarra have become more effectively integrated into the Spanish state than their neighbours and their social structure has developed along somewhat different lines. Support for Basque Nationalism and for the traditional Basque culture has been greater in Guipúzcoa and Vizcaya. Equally, Basque language speakers are more numerous in these provinces. At present the autonomous Basque Region is constituted by these latter two Provinces. In principle, and subject to approval in a local referendum, the option has been kept open for Navarra to become part of 'Euskadi'. Implementation of this remains, at the time of writing, a source of division between the central and regional authorities. Equally, Basque nationalists are divided between those 'moderates' who would only wish to integrate other areas into 'Euskadi' with the consent of those concerned and more intransigent elements who feel the search for such consent is not necessary.

   As for the French Basques, they do not form a part of this essay which, for reasons of space, must focus on their Spanish counterparts. Moreover, the nationalist movement has not developed the same sort of support in France as it has in the Spanish Basque Region. On the other hand, Basque Nationalists frequently have, as a long term objective, the total re-unification of what they see as their historic 'homeland', to include both French and Spanish Basques.
4. On the general historical development of the Basque Country, and its developing social structure, cf. Ortzi, *Historia de Euskadi, El Nacionalismo Vasco y E.T.A.* (Paris, 1975), especially pp. 1-63. On the contemporary class structure of the area, cf. Luis C-Nuñez, *Clases Sociales en Euskadi* (San Sebastian, 1977). A good anthropological study of the Basque people is J. Caro Baroja, *Los Vascos* (Madrid, 1971).
5. On the *fueros*, cf. Ortzi, op. cit., pp. 33-63.
6. Cf. J. Linz's contribution to the volume, S. N. Eisenstadt and S. Rokkan (eds.), *Building States and Nations* (London, 1973).
7. The distinguished Spanish historian Salvador de Madariaga emphasizes this point in his book, *Memorias de un Federalista* (Buenos Aires, 1967).
8. On the subject of Carlism, cf. M. Blinkhorn, *Carlism and Crisis in Spain 1931-1939* (Cambridge, 1976). This focuses on the modern period but has useful background material. Cf. also Ortzi, op. cit., pp. 66-106.
9. On the general subject of Basque nationalism, cf. Ortzi, op. cit. S. Payne, *Nacionalismo Vasco* (Barcelona, 1974); M. Garcia Venero, *Historia del Nacionalismo Vasco (1793-1936)* (Madrid, 1965); Antonio

Elorza, *Ideologías* del Nacionalismo Vasco, 1876-1937 (San Sebastian, 1977), and M. Heiberg, 'External and Internal Nationalism: The Case of the Spanish Basques', in Raymond L. Hall (ed.), *Ethnic Autonomy—Comparative Dynamics* (Oxford, 1979).

10. On these two movements, cf. S. Payne, 'Catalan and Basque Nationalism', *Journal of Contemporary History*, 1, 1 (1971). Also K. Medhurst, *The Basques and Catalans. A Report for the Minority Rights Group* (London, 1977).
11. For the links between 'big business' and Basque Nationalism, cf. J. Harrison, 'Big Business and the Rise of Basque Nationalism', *European Studies Review*, 7 (1977).
12. On the subject of the Basque Region's working class, cf. J. P. Fusi, *Pólitica Obrera en el Pais Vasco* (Madrid, 1975).
13. For an argument along such lines, cf. Milton M. de Silva, 'Modernization and Ethnic Conflict: The Case of the Basques', *Comparative Politics*, 7, 2 (1975).
14. Cf. Ortzi, op. cit., especially pp. 144-50.
15. Ibid.
16. Cf. Ortzi, op. cit., pp. 173-256.
17. On post-war repression, cf. K. Medhurst, op. cit., and Ortzi, op. cit., pp. 256-80.
18. Cf. ibid., pp. 276ff. for the development and nature of ETA.
19. On repression in the Basque Region in the last years of Franco's regime, cf. Batasuna—*La Répression au Pays Basque* (Paris, 1970). *Report of an Amnesty International Mission to Spain* (London, 1975). Cf. also Ortzi, op. cit., and Luis C-Nuñez, *La Sociedad Vasca Actual* (San Sebastian, 1977), pp. 119-35.
20. Cf. Ortzi, op. cit., and J. P. Moqui, *La Révolte des Basques* (Paris, 1976).
21. Cf. *Informe Sociológico Sobre la Situación Social de España 1970* (Madrid, 1970), p. 359.
22. Cf. Ortzi, op. cit., pp. 281-9.
23. Cf. J. P. Moqui, op. cit.
24. Cf. Luis C-Nuñez, *Classes Sociales en Euskadi,* op. cit., pp. 185-201.
25. In discussing working class politics in the Basque Region, mention needs to be made of significant developments in the traditionally conservative Carlist stronghold of Navarra. In the latter part of the Franco era, this Province for the first time became caught up in the same industrialization process that had earlier affected other parts of the Basque Country. Equally, its newly formed working class emerged as a significant opposition force. One substantial and unexpected response to this development was a radicalization of the official Carlist movement. Basque Nationalism, however, did not develop the appeal it had long since had in its traditional stronghold of Vizcaya and Guipúzcoa. The latter, in particular, provided the nationalist cause with its strongest base.
26. Cf. Ortzi, op. cit., pp. 289-91 and 349-50. Also, K. Medhurst, op. cit.

27. Cf., for example, *Informe Sociológico*, op. cit., pp. 1261-8. It should, in fairness, be stated that sympathizers of the nationalist cause feel this survey sometimes underestimates the vitality of the Basque language.
28. On Basque Catholicism, cf. Luis C-Nuñez, *La Sociedad Vasca Actual*, op. cit., pp. 55-91. Ortzi, op. cit., pp. 338-40 and K. Medhurst, op. cit.
29. On the general subject of Church-State relations, cf. N. Cooper, *Catholicism and the Franco Regime*, (London, 1975), and Juan J. Ruiz Rico, *El Papel Pólitico de la Iglesia Católica en Espana* (Madrid, 1977).
30. On the state of Basque opinion toward the end of the Franco era, cf. S. del Campo *et al.*, *La Cuestion Regional Española* (Madrid, 1977), pp. 210-32.
31. On the effects of repression, cf. Luis C-Nuñez, *La Sociedad Vasca Actual* (San Sebastian, 1977), ch. 6.
32. On levels of participation and its significance, cf. L. C-Nuñez, op. cit., pp. 41-54.
33. Ibid.
34. Ibid., pp. 187-98, for the 1977 election as it affected the Basque Region.
35. On the subject of the amnesty, cf. José Maria Portell, *Euzkadi: Amnestia Arrancada* (Barcelona, 1977).
36. Political parties in the Basque Country, including recently emergent left wing groups, are examined in, Alberto Pérez Calvo, *Los Partidos Politicos en el Pais Vasco* (Madrid, 1977). It should briefly be noted that nationalist groups, to the left of the PNV, had existed before the Civil War but they were not as significant nor as radical as recent left wing nationalists.
37. Cf. Luis C-Nuñez, op. cit., p. 190.
38. Cf. *The Economist*, 10 March 1979, p. 57.
39. On the subject of Herri Batasuna, the author had the opportunity to consult an, as yet, unpublished article by J. Hollyman. The observations, on this movement, are, however, entirely my own.
40. Cf. Luis C-Nuñez, op. cit., pp. 195-8.
41. The course of the negotiations leading to the 'Statute of Autonomy' can be followed, very briefly, in the *Economist* from March to October 1979.
42. For the results of the regional elections of March 1980, cf. *The Economist*, 15 March 1980. It should be noted that these elections were characterized by an abstention rate of about 41 per cent. Abstentions seem mainly to have involved supporters of Spanish parties. This is a further indicator of the pressures on those seeking to impelement the new arrangements.
43. ETA now appears to be principally divided between a fraction which places exclusive reliance upon armed activities and those seeking to combine armed struggle with political agitation. Some of those now involved seem to be caught up in their own 'sub-culture'

of violence and to have lost touch with many erstwhile allies. Some of their activities have certainly seemed poorly judged political exercises liable to alienate potential supporters. On the other hand, rivalry between the two tendencies may have the effect of stimulating additional violence as neither tendency wishes to be outflanked.

44. The various options were outlined in K. Medhurst, 'The Prospects of Federalism: The Regional Problem after Franco', *Government and Opposition* (Spring 1976). Issues raised in considering such options are discussed in J. Linz, 'Early State Building and Late Peripheral Nationalisms Against the State', op. cit. R. Dahl, *Polyarchy* (London, 1971). Cf. also the work of A. Lijphart on Consociational Democracy, notably, *Democracy in Plural Societies* (New Haven, Conn., 1977) and A. Lijphart, *The Politics of Accommodation: Pluralism and Democracy in the Netherlands*, (Berkley, 1968).
45. The types of theory alluded to are covered in the contribution made to this volume by Anthony Smith.
46. On this point, cf. Luis C-Nuñez, *La Sociedad Vasca Actual,* op. cit., pp. 15-40.

CHAPTER 9

Belgium: Controlling Separatist Tendencies in a Multinational State

Joseph R. Rudolph Jr.

In the idealized model of a political system, political stability and the system's survival are achieved by the constitutional and informal decision-making mechanisms responding with appropriate outputs to the demands placed upon them. These policies, in turn, have a feedback effect upon the environment, sometimes building additional support for the system and sometimes generating a new set of demands. This lineal paradigm of a political system in which the

→environment → demands → decision-making → outputs → feedback ←

has become a cornerstone of post-war political analysis. The curious can find an elaboration of it in virtually any textbook on political analysis written during the last two decades, although the work of its architect, David Easton, remains the logical starting point.[1]

The model can be readily applied to politics in Belgium, a constitutional monarchy with a parliamentary system of government in which the operative decision-making process was dominated until recently by the leaders of the country's three principle parties: the Social Christian Party, the Belgian Socialist Party, and the Liberal Party. To state the matter tersely, by responding to changing environmental circumstances and by being willing to re-evaluate both governmental outputs and the structure of the political system in the context of these changes, these élites were historically able to cope with the demands placed on the system. Indeed, so effectively did they function that despite the multinational nature of Belgium's political environment and serious grievances on the part of one national community dating almost from the country's birth, ethno-regional demands in Belgium seldom involved calls for political separatism.

In this chapter we shall probe some of the facets of politics in contemporary Belgium, focusing on the means and costs of accommodating ethno-regional demands in this country, and specifically seeking answers to three questions:

1. Why did significant ethno-regional movements not develop until recently in Belgium?
2. What factors account for their sudden emergence at the heart of contemporary Belgian politics?
3. What specific factors have prevented these movements from taking a separatist direction?

I. Belgium: A Multinational State

Let us begin our inquiry at the obvious point of departure: the multilingual-multinational character of the political environment. As the adjoining map indicates, the Belgian state which achieved independence from Dutch rule in the 1930s is divided by a 'linguistic frontier'—a line which has run east-west across northern Europe from Calais to Aachen since at least the early Middle Ages. North of the line in Belgium, in the four provinces of Flanders, the overwhelming majority of the people have spoken a local variety of Dutch known as Flemish since the mid-sixteenth century, when the Dutch revolt against Spanish rule to the north drew the Dutch-speaking élite of Flanders to the Netherlands and the language of Flanders began to stagnate into a series of local dialects and peasant idioms. South of the line, the population at Belgium's independence spoke either French or Walloon, a collective term for other Romance languages in the area closely related to French.[2]

Contemporary Belgium is still composed of these two linguistically differentiated groups, now divided by a linguistic frontier hardened into law. There is one major exception to this frontier, however. During the nineteenth century, Brussels developed into an increasingly French-speaking enclave north of the line, and today's *flamand* in officially bilingual but in practice 80 per cent French-speaking Brussels often feels 'a foreigner in his own country.'[3] There is also a third linguistic community in Belgium today: approximately 60,000 German-speaking Belgians living in a section of eastern Belgium which was acquired from Germany via the Treaty of Versailles. How many *national communities* inhabit Belgium is another question. If we use Rupert Emer-

Figure 1 Language Regions in Belgium

son's definition of a nation as 'the largest community which, when the chips are down, effectively commands men's [paramount] loyalty,'[4] it is probably correct to say that those who speak Flemish as their mother tongue constitute a distinct national as well as linguistic group. The same may be said of the German-speaking community. Unfortunately, matters are considerably more complicated with respect to French-speaking Belgium, where linguistic, territorial, and ethnic groupings less perfectly coincide.

Whereas the members of the Flemish community generally share a common ethnic origin and live almost exclusively north of the linguistic frontier, and whereas Belgium's German-speaking people are concentrated in the eastern canton of a Walloon province, the country's *francophones* are geographically divided and often ethnically dissimilar as well. French-speaking Belgium basically entails two areas: the four provinces of Wallonia and, across the linguistic frontier, the predominantly French-speaking city of Brussels. Furthermore, although contemporary Walloon *francophones* have generally descended from a common ethnic stock, the French-speaking *bruxellois* are composed of both Walloon-descended Belgians who have moved to the capital and the descendents of the ethnically Flemish people of northern Belgium who lived or settled in the Brussels area but at some point selected French as their mother tongue because of its advantage over Flemish as, traditionally, the language of upward mobility in the Belgian state. Thus, when we speak of past or present Flemish movements, we are speaking of nationalist movements generally based on a common language, ethnicity, and territorality, but when we speak of a *francophone* movement the operative criterion is essentially language. It is difficult to say whether there is a single nation of French-speaking Belgians with two regional components, or two national groups (Walloons and *Bruxellois*) linked by a common language and more recently by their common interest in protecting traditional *francophone* privileges in postwar Belgium.

The number of national groups in the country is not an unimportant subject, but fortunately for our inquiry this particular Gordian knot can be bypassed. Our concern is not with multinationalism *per se*, but the political movements resulting from a multinational environment and their interaction with one another in the political process. In Belgium, these movements have tended to be regionally based, and it is upon the country's postwar, regionalized ethno-linguistic movements (ethno-regional movements for short) that we will concentrate, including those ethno-regional organizations representing the two regions of *francophone* Belgium, the *Rassemblement Wallon* (RW) and the *Front démocratique des francophones bruxellois* (FDF). Here, however, we are getting somewhat ahead of ourselves in our study, so let us return to the fundamentals of our inquiry and an examination of the emergence of ethno-regional demands in the Belgian state.

II. Consociational Politics: Managing the Ethno-linguistic Cleavage in Belgium

As Aristide Zolberg has observed, Belgium's linguistic cleavage emerged as a politically sailent factor only in this century.[5] During much of the nineteenth-century language problems did not trouble the political process for the simple reason that the masses could not vote and the leadership of both northern and southern Belgium was French-speaking. Indeed, as a result of the territory's rule by Austria in the eighteenth century, when French replaced Latin as the language of secondary education and public affairs, its twenty years of rule by France after 1795, and the widely assumed superiority of the French culture at the time of the country's birth, Belgium's founding fathers were not only French speaking but thoroughly assimilationist in orientation. The state they fashioned reflected their outlook. Although the first official census (1846) revealed that less than 1.13 per cent of Flanders and one-third of Brussels spoke French, French became the country's only official language.[6] Flemish and Walloons alike were administered in French, received their secondary education in French, commanded in French in the army, and tried in French when brought before the courts. The Constitution did recognise a right to linguistic expression, but the Flemish language lacked any official status and, like Walloon, survived only as a tolerated vernacular of local life, the language of the lower classes.[7] The only 'linguistic problem' troubling the early rulers was how to make French the language of these 'ignorant' people.

Even the gradual enfranchisement and political mobilization of the masses, which began in the latter third of the nineteenth century, did not produce inter-communal strife. As the people were enfranchised, they were normally recruited into one of Belgium's socio-economic 'spiritual families' (Catholic, Liberal, or Socialist). Each of these 'had its own party, its labor-union federation, its auxiliary organizations . . . and press.[8] More importantly, each 'family' was organized on a system-wide basis, and the political parties which emerged from these families and collectively dominated Belgian politics for the next century were each composed of two linguistic wings. The parties therefore shared a vested interest in managing the ethno-linguistic cleavage dividing their country. It also divided them.

Two other factors were also of considerable importance in the pre-World War I containment of Belgium's linguistic cleavage. As Flemish nationalists began to emerge in small numbers (after 1840), their demands tended to focus on the realization of cultural equality for Flemish in an officially French-speaking state and, later, on the creation of an officially bilingual Flanders in which official affairs could be transacted in Flemish as well as French. Neither demand threatened the *francophone*'s way of life in Brussels or Wallonia or challenged his hold on the state. Consequently, they placed a relatively light load on the system. Still later, when turn-of-the-century Flemish nationalists began to make more aggressive demands—such as converting Flanders into an officially monolingual, Flemish-speaking region—cross-communal issues and cleavages tended to neutralize the abrasiveness of many of these demands. Indeed, of the three principal divisions in Belgian society (religious, economic, and linguistic), the linguistic cleavage has historically been of the least political consequence, the religious cleavage between the Catholics and secularists the most important.[9] While religious issues involving church-state relations (rooted in the country's origins) and questions concerning economic class (unleashed by the industrial revolution) dominated the public agenda, the potentially more disruptive linguistic issues tended to remain in the background.

There were other factors which also contributed to the infrequent appearance of divisive linguistic issues in Belgian politics before the Second World War. Most middle class Flemish joined the system-wide parties and supported the latter's leadership on most issues. Some were even willing to become bilingual and to melt into the *francophone* population, especially those living near Brussels and along the linguistic frontier. Flemish nationalists thus found it difficult to recruit the support of the Flemish middle class. Still, it was the *francophone* nature of the country's early élites, the fact that early Flemish demands could be accommodated without disrupting the balance of power inside the state, and the system-wide nature of the political parties and the cross-communal nature of the religious and economic cleavages they institutionalized which constituted the principal reasons why the state's multinational-multilingual character was not more troublesome before the postwar era. These factors also provided the framework within which Belgium developed that form of 'government by élite cartel designed to turn a democracy with a fragmented political culture into a stable democracy' which Lijphart has described as 'consociational democracy.'[10]

Fixing the precise date when linguistic demands became politically decisive is not easy. As we shall shortly see, there was an evolutionary-escalating quality to the demands of the Flemish nationalists, especially after 1870 when France's defeat in the Franco-German war dealt a severe blow to the prestige of the French language and culture at the same moment that social injustices in Flanders were becoming more visible and the enfranchisement of the Flemish masses was making Belgium's systemwide parties more sensitive to those injustices. External events also played a role in those sporadic moments when Flemish-*francophone* differences did influence Belgian politics; in particular during the early interwar years, when the charge of Flemish wartime collaboration with the Germans was used to discredit Flemish nationalism. In general, however, ethno-linguistic particularism remained manageable in Belgium during this period, as in most of Western Europe.[11] Indeed, as late as the immediate post-World War II period Belgium's consociational system was functioning well enough to control the Royal Question of whether Belgium should continue to be a monarchy (given the King's pre-war advocacy of a policy of strict neutrality, over Cabinet advice to the contrary). In a national referendum Leopold III won the right to return only because the majority in Flanders favouring his return was large enough to offset the majorities voting against it in Wallonia and Brussels. Yet the traditional parties were able to prevent an ethno-regional confrontation from taking place.[12]

In the long term, however, postwar changes in the environment of Belgian politics combined with a sharp increase in the visibility of a variety of (ethno-regionally sensitive) trends long in progress to make it impossible for Belgium's traditional leaders to control the country's ethno-linguistic cleavage. The Second World War itself had exacerbated communal tensions. Collaboration with the enemy occurred in northern and southern Belgium, but it was more conspicuous in the north and Walloon Belgians emerged from the war with the feeling that the country's *francophones* had once again been betrayed by the Flemish during wartime. Of even greater importance in politicizing the ethno-linguistic cleavage were demographic and economic changes affecting the relative importance of Flanders and French-speaking Belgium in the country. The 1947 census revealed that Flanders possessed an absolute majority of the state's population (51.3 per cent) while Wallonia's share had declined to only about one-third.[13] The bad news was just beginning for Wallonia, for while its metallurgy-centered economy—once the centerpiece of the Belgian economy—continued to slide throughout the postwar period, Flanders enjoyed a postwar economic boom.[14] In time, this steady shift of economic power from the south to Belgium's more populous north produced a strong sense of Flemish self-awareness and a corollary sense of frustration and resentment that Flemish-speaking Belgians were still not being accorded positions in the national government, bureaucracy, and military commensurate to Flanders' demographic and economic status in the Belgian state.[15]

It is likely that these changes alone would have eventually led to ethno-regional conflict between the Flemish north and Walloon south in the country's political process. What accelerated this development was a sudden, postwar decline in the importance of the cross-communal issues which had long helped to check communal-based rivalries. As late as the mid-1950s the ethno-linguistic cleavage was still of tertiary importance, and Belgium's consociational approach to problems still focused on the more important economic and religious issues dividing the country. Then, in 1958 Belgium's decision-makers disturbed that hierarchical ordering of cleavages upon which managing the linguistic division in the country depended. The occasion was the negotiation of the *pacte scolaire*, a political truce in which the principal parties agreed to table for twelve years the politically sensitive school issue. Insofar as the religious issue had come to centre on the issue of public versus church-controlled schools, the *pacte* depoliticized one of Belgium's two great cross-communal cleavages.[16] Three years later, in the Great Strike of winter 1960-1, the economic cleavage was regionalized when a reaction against the Government's post-Congo austerity programme turned into a general political protest much more widely supported in the Walloon south than elsewhere.

With the depoliticization of the religious issue and the regionalization of economic issues, the stage was set for the emergence of ethno-regional politics in Belgium. A strong expression of ethno-regionalism developed almost immediately in Flanders, where the *Volksunie*, a Flemish nationalist party born in the 1950s to replace a handful of smaller pro-Flemish parties, acquired a claim on nearly one-fifth of the Flemish electorate by the late 1960s. The *Volksunie's* mobilization of the Flemish community and success in achieving several of its goals, in turn, contributed to the development of defensive ethno-regionalism in *francophone* Belgium and the emergence of vigorous ethnonational parties in Wallonia (the RW) and Brussels (the FDF). The development of these latter organizations was perhaps inevitable. The articulation of ethno-regional sentiment could not be performed by the traditional parties; the resolution of ethno-regional demands could not be settled solely within them. Postwar Flemish demands that the linguistic frontier be frozen, that Brussels be confined to its existing territory, and that the disproportionate number of *francophones* in high positions be replaced by Flemish-speaking Belgians had a zero-sum edge not found in prior Flemish demands. They thus tended to place stress on the linguistic wings of the traditional parties rather than lend themselves to accommodation by these parties. Furthermore, by the late 1950s there were large numbers of highly educated, middle class professionals in both the Flemish and *francophone* communities who found themselves frozen out of the decision-making process monopolized by the traditional parties, and resented that situation. Politically ambitious and skillful, these men and women were eager to supply the leadership of new political parties committed to ethno-regional goals.

III. Representing the Ethno-linguistic Communities: the Ethno-regional Parties and the Belgian Political Process

By the mid-1960s there thus existed a growing sense of ethno-regional sentiment and newly born ethno-regional parties (as well as a variety of cultural associations) in each of Belgium's major regions: the RW in Wallonia, the FDF in Brussels and its French-speaking suburbs, and the *Volksunie* in Flanders and the Flemish-speaking areas of the province housing Brussels (e.g., Brabant). In the following decade, these parties enjoyed considerable electoral success and success in influencing the political process, and their achievements undoubtedly inspired the creation of the Party of German-speaking Belgians (the *Partei Deutschsprachiger Belgier*, or PDB) in 1971.[17]

Before we examine the specific effects which these parties have had on Belgian politics, let us give some attention to their similarities as ethno-regional organizations, especially in the area of composition. Although the RW and *Volksunie* developed as mass organizations with grass-roots networks while the FDF has remained a cadre party directed by its officials in Brussels, all three of these parties enjoyed considerable success during their peak period of growth in recruiting members from across Belgium's traditional spiritual families. As a consequence, their

Table 1 Party Strength in Brabant, Wallonia and Flanders, measured in Percent of the Vote in Belgium's 1965-78 Parliamentary Elections[a]

REGION: Party	1965	1968	1971	1974	1977	1978	CHANGE 1965-74[c]	CHANGE 1965-78
BRABANT[b]								
Catholic (PSC, CVP*)	27.1	29.2	24.5	27.6	30.9	30.2	0.5	3.1
Socialist (PSB, BSP*)	26.8	22.8	22.3	21.3	19.3	18.5	– 5.5	– 8.3
Liberal (PLP, PVV**)	30.0	25.6	18.3	10.4	14.8	14.6	–19.6	–16.4
FDF-RW	6.9	13.0	24.1	27.8[d]	21.3	21.2	20.9	14.3
Volksunie	4.3[c]	6.7	8.2	8.8	9.2	5.8	4.5	1.5
Communists	3.5	2.2	2.4	3.2	2.3	2.7	– 1.3	– 0.8
WALLONIA								
Catholic (PSC)	24.8	21.4	19.3	22.8	25.9	27.0	– 2.0	2.2
Socialists (PSB)	35.8	35.0	35.1	37.4	39.5	37.6	1.6	1.8
Liberals (PLP = PRLW)	23.0	26.2	17.7	15.1	18.9	17.2[e]	– 7.9	– 5.8
RW	3.2	9.8	19.6	17.6	10.6	8.6	14.4	5.4
Communists	9.8	7.1	6.0	5.9	5.6	4.7	– 3.9	– 5.1
FLANDERS								
Catholic (CVP)	44.7	39.5	38.4	40.3	44.2	44.3	– 4.4	– 0.4
Socialists (BSP)	25.2	26.2	24.7	22.6	23.0	21.3	– 2.6	– 3.9
Liberal (PVV)	15.5	15.2	15.5	16.7	14.0	16.9	– 1.2	1.4
Volksunie	12.5	17.5	19.4	17.0	16.3	11.6	4.5[c]	– 0.9[c]
Communists	1.2	1.4	1.6	1.6	1.2	1.8	0.4	0.6

* Initials for French-speaking wing listed first.

** In 1977 & 1978 elections, PRLW also contested seats in Brabant province.

a. Sources. *Le Soir*, 2 April 1968 (for 1965 & 1968 returns), 12 March 1974 (for 1971 & 1974 returns), 19 April 1977 (for 1977 returns), and 19 December 1978 (for 1978 returns).

b. In Brabant Province, composed of the election districts of bilingual Brussels, French-speaking Nivelle, and Flemish speaking Louvain, both linguistic wings of the system-wide parties (now split into essentially separate parties) contest elections, and sometimes the regional wings as well; for example, *Rode Leeuven*, the Flemish Socialists in Brussels, and the PLP-*bruxellois*, the French-speaking Liberal Party in Brussels. Except where otherwise noted, their votes are included in the appropriate spiritual family's party.

c. In actuality, the *Volksunie* made its electoral breakthrough in 1961, when it gained 6.0 per cent of the Flemish vote, versus 3.4 per cent in 1958; the FDF and RW ran in 1965 for the first time. Nevertheless, the 1965-74 represents a logical basis for comparing the performance of these parties. It was their common phase of growth and consolidation, before the leaders of these parties began to join the Government.

d. The PLP-*bruxellois* contested the 1974 general election in an alliance with the FDF, offering a common list of candidates.

e. This figure includes the *Parti Liberal Wallon* vote in 1978; discounting the vote of this splinter party, the PRLW polled 16.6 per cent of Wallonia's 1978 vote.

development constituted a reversal of the traditional pattern of Belgian party politics, from a system in which each of Belgium's vertically organized, spiritual families had its own party composed of two linguistic wings to one in which each ethno-regional community had its own, horizontally organized, party composed of elements from all three families. Their development also considerably reduced the traditional parties' share of the Belgian vote, from over 95 per cent in 1958 to under 75 per cent in 1974, eventually forcing the old cartel to acknowledge the electoral realignment taking place in Belgium by inviting the ethno-regional parties first into the informal intra-élite negotiations out of which policy has traditionally emerged in Belgium, and then into the Cabinet.[18]

On the other hand, the similarity of contemporary Belgium's ethno-regional parties can be overstated. In particular, because each of Belgium's major ethno-linguistic regions finds itself in a different social, economic, and political situation in the Belgian state, the ethno-regional spokesmen for Flemish and French-speaking Belgium have raised somewhat different demands on behalf of their supporters. For comparative purposes, let us return briefly to Easton's concept of the political system. Although all ethnonational organizations are likely to embrace similar nationalist rhetoric, their actual objectives may be grouped along a continuum encompassing four quite different types of political goals. (See Table 2) There are those ethno-regional groups primarily concerned with political decisions and with increasing their region's share of governmental *outputs* (for example, increased economic assistance). Other organizations are primarily concerned with who makes decisions; that is, the nature of existing political *authority* (for example, the low representation of members of the ethno-regional community among the decision-makers). Closely related, a third type of movement may focus on changing the nature of the régime, the political-constitutional principles and structures regulating the way decisions are made. Typically, ethno-regional organizations of this variety will opt for a federal-like system in which their region has autonomous control over those economic and cultural decisions effecting it. (This is the dimension of economic and cultural separatists.) Finally, ethnonational organizations may sincerely challenge the legitimacy of the multinational *political community* in which they find themselves and champion independence and/or irredentist goals.[19] These are the true political separatists and their demands are scarcely susceptible to accommodation. At the other extreme, those movements fundamentally concerned with governmental outputs are the most easily satisfied, at least in the short term. The middle zone, authority- and régime-oriented movements are also susceptible to accommodation in theory; however, in practice their price may be higher than a government will be willing to pay since accommodation will imply sharing decision-making authority with them and undertaking institutional reforms in devolutionary directions.

Table 2 Charting Ethno-regional Objectives

Anti-community	Anti-régime	Anti-authority	Output-oriented

LOW —— Susceptibility to Accommodation —— HIGH

Readers desiring to use this scheme to compare the various nationalist movements treated elsewhere in this volume are cautioned that the model has its limitations. Not only must similar nationalist rhetoric be cast aside to determine a group's immediate objectives, but because of the broadly aggregative nature of most ethno-regional organizations, individual movements are likely to embrace spokesmen for all four positions and a movement's operational goals may shift over time with changes in leadership. Furthermore, organizations may be encouraged by their initial success in achieving goals to escalate their demands qualitatively. Certainly all movements seem to be pulled in the same direction along the continuum to the point of demanding at least some form of institutional autonomy in order to protect and promote their people's way of life, and groups may generally travel from right-to-left along the continuum, feeding on past achievements and escalating their demands until political separatism is the only goal left for them to raise. Yet the reverse is also a possibility. Groups which are basically pursuing middle zone objectives may frequently adopt the rhetoric of organizations to their left on the scale in order to have bargaining room. In any event, whatever its defects this organizational schema does have its merits, for it offers a convenient basis for differentiating among and analysing ethno-regional movements and associations. Applied to Belgian groups, it suggests two preliminary observations: that the ethno-regional organizations in contemporary Belgium have generally been middle zone structures, seeking more than a new set of political outputs but less than an end to the existing, system-wide political community of the Belgian state; and that within this framework the individual ethnoregional movements have differed—often considerably—in their specific goals and orientations.

Flemish Belgium. Given the second class cultural and political status of the Flemish in the Belgian state at its inception, Flemish movements emerged shortly after statehood. However, the earliest Flemish associations were preoccupied with such cultural objectives as promoting Flemish literature, and it was not until 1861 that a Flemish organization emerged whose goals were essentially political. From then until World War I, Flemish nationalist associations pressed output-oriented goals aimed at developing Flanders and Brussels into officially bilingual areas. As we have already noted, these goals did not threaten the *francophones'* hold on the state, and the traditional parties tended to be sympathetic to them. Accordingly, Flemish nationalist organizations functioned predominantly as interest groups working through the existing parties. Moreover, their incremental progress was considerable. They achieved the right to use Flemish in the courts, administration, and secondary schools of Flanders during the 1874-83 decade, in the Belgian Parliament in 1888, and in the army in 1913. In 1896 Flemish acquired legal parity within Belgium at the national level, although in practice parity was to await more than another half century. It was not until 1930 that the Government was willing to create a unilingual Flemish university to educate a Flemish élite in Flemish.[20]

During the interwar years two principal changes occurred in the Flemish movement: Flemish demands, though still motivated by the second class status of the Flemish culture and the Flemish people in the Belgian state, changed from output-oriented to régime challenging goals, and the primary spokesmen for Flemish nationalism became Flemish nationalist parties. As the nationalists achieved their objective of making Flanders bilingual, they began to demand a restructuring of the state so that language, ethnicity, and political form would in part coincide.[21] The proposal: match the unilingual, *francophone* region of Wallonia with a unilingual Flemish region by changing northern Belgium into an officially monolingual, Flemish-speaking zone. Insofar as the plan, if fully implemented, would have led to a drastic reduction of *francophone* influence in the north, it was not greeted enthusiastically by the (French-speaking wings of the) traditional parties. Still, concessions were forthcoming, including the 1932 laws requiring education in Flemish north of the linguistic frontier and recognizing Flanders as a monolingual region in a bilingual state. Bilingual Brussels was excluded from these laws, however, and the frontier was subject to adjustment after each census by a linguistic headcount, so it was possible for the frontier to move northward as Flemish living along it bowed to the greater status of French and encouraged their children to learn French as their primary language.

The unwillingness of the traditional parties to go beyond the concessions to Flemish nationalism embraced in the 1932 laws opened an opportunity for a Flemish nationalist party to become a serious force in interwar Flemish politics. The opportunity was not missed. As Flemish nationalists recovered the credibility they lost during the war, when they collaborated with the occupiers in order to gain a Flemish univeristy and even created a provisional government for Flanders, a Flemish nationalist party emerged as Flanders' third largest vote-getter. In 1939, it won 15 per cent of the Flemish vote in the general election—over 40 per cent in some rural districts.[22] However, Flemish collaboration with the enemy in the Second World War and the fascist nature of the interwar nationalist party so discredited Flemish nationalism that postwar Flemish nationalists found very little electoral support in the immediate postwar period.

It was against this background that the *Volksunie* emerged in the 1950s to press an expanded, régime-oriented programme calling for the social, economic, and political autonomy of Flemish Belgium. The heart of the party's manifesto was a demand for cultural separatism embraced in the concept of 'federalism of two', in which each of Belgium's major linguistic groups would have a free hand to promote its own culture. Calls for political separatism were precluded, as in the past, by the status of Flemish Belgium, although that status had altered drastically since the days of the early nationalists. Then Flanders was too poor to have made an independent Flanders plausible and merger with the Netherlands was blocked by the latter's distain for Flemish as the tongue of the uneducated as well as by Protestant Holland's distain for the devoutly Catholic nature of northern Belgium. In the postwar period, however, the fact that Flanders contained a majority of the Belgian population meant that it could protect and promote its own interests in the Belgian state as long as it received parliamentary representation proportional to its share of the population and could summons the necessary self-esteem to use that political power to advance its social, economic, and political interests. Indeed, to the *Volksunie* the principal threat to the postwar Flemish culture was not an overbearing, French-speaking Government, but internal to the Flemish community: 'the social and psychological complex' of the Flemish people who for so long had been conditioned to the inferiority of their culture,[23] and the resultant threat that those living along the linguistic frontier or commuting to Brussels would abandon their language, thereby reducing the numerical strength of Flemish-speaking Belgium in the state. There was thus an edge of saving the Flemish from themselves behind the *Volksunie's* program. The cutting edge of the party's immediate demands, however, was aimed at *francophone* Belgium; for example, the *Volksunie's* demand that Brussels be frozen to its existing communes rather than be allowed to expand into the Flemish countryside as its commuting *francophones* became a majority in its suburbs, the party's demand that all policy making in cultural affairs be ultimately decentralized along linguistic lines to enable Belgium's Flemish to require the use of Flemish in private as well as public affairs in Flemish-speaking areas (thus removing any need for the Flemish to opt out of their own culture), and its demand that the channels of decision-making at the centre be opened to unilingual Flemish in general and Flemish nationalists (blocked by the monopoly of the traditional parties over political decision-making) in particular!

Francophone Belgium. Although early Flemish nationalist activity begat counter-activity almost immediately in Wallonia, significant *francophone* organizations are a product of postwar Belgium. *Francophone* dominance of the state during the nineteenth century and the central government throughout the first half of the twentieth century made both separatism and ethno-regional demands unnecessary and very nearly unthinkable. It was not until the early 1960s, when the declining political and economic influence of French-speaking Belgium in the state became apparent that politically important nationalist organizations emerged among *francophones* in Brussels and Wallonia.

The first ethno-regional party in *francophone* Belgium emerged in Wallonia in 1961, three years before the formation of the *Rassemblement Wallon.* The immediate cause of the former's birth was the negative reaction to the Government's post-Congo austerity programme by Walloons in the country's already austere postwar south. But other matters also worried the Walloons, especially *minorisation,* the continued decline of Wallonia's population and voice in Belgian affairs at a time when Flanders possessed a numerical majority in the country. By the mid-1960s, the RW was thus offering a somewhat variated programme. Insofar as separatism had to be excluded (a poor Wallonia could not survive as independent, and absorption by heavily centralized France was not appealing), the best alternative seed to be to press for guaranteed parity between French- and Flemish-speaking Belgium in the decision-making process at the centre and a devolution of decision-making authority in economic affairs to the regions, duly combined with a guaranteed share of national revenue to make that authority meaningful. Given the economic plight of Wallonia, economic concerns played almost as great a role in the RW's output- and régime-oriented demands as cultural concerns played in those of the *Volksunie*.

The federalist schemes proposed by Walloons did not attract much initial support in Brussels. Regionalism meant a reduction of the centre's influence and Brussels saw itself as Belgium's centre. Had it not been for the *Volksunie's* success in pressuring the system-wide parties into accepting several Flemish demands aimed at Brussels itself, the marriage of convenience which occurred in 1965 between the FDF and the RW would have surely been delayed. But during 1961-1963, Belgium's language laws were again revised to satisfy Flemish demands. The language frontier was frozen permanently in place. Bilingual Brussels received special status to the extent that limited bilingual facilities were permitted in six commuter suburbs, but these facilities did not include bilingual secondary schools. Moreover, the father's right to select his children's language of instruction was ended. Education was to be in the tongue of the father in Brussels and elsewhere in the regional language, including in Brussels' commuter suburbs located in Flanders. Intended to defuse Flemish nationalism, the laws stimulated the development of *francophone* nationalism in the capital.[24] The FDF emerged immediately, demanding the father's right to choose his child's language of education, the city of Brussels' right to reach its natural limits of growth, and the right of the region's Flemish to assimilate to the French culture if they wished to do so. The broader protection of *francophone* political prerogatives, however, soon led the FDF to join with the RW in demanding a régime change to a 'federalism of three' in which autonomy could be devolved regionally to Flanders, Wallonia, and Brussels, and in which Brussels could be master of its own house (and its *francophone* majority master of Brussels).[25]

German-speaking Belgium. The development and activity of the ethnonational party in German-speaking Belgium is more interesting as an example of 'piggy back' politics than as a serious development in Belgian affairs. Belgium's German-speaking community constitutes only a small, peripheral minority and under normal circumstances would have had little impact on the political process despite its own, very real concern over the slow erosion of its culture and the Frenchification of its people. Yet, as we have seen, circumstances have been rapidly changing in Belgium, and the pursuit of communal interests by the FDF, RW, and *Volksunie* provided German-speaking Belgians with an opportunity to press their demands which they seized. Viewed from this perspective, the PDB's political fortunes have provided a rough barometer of how seriously the German community desires to cling to its culture. In general, the party's showing has been good and other parties in the area have adopted its essentially output-oriented demands, which centre on protecting the German culture in the area and achieving a fair deal for those German-speaking Belgians who, annexed by Hitler in 1940 and forced to fight in the German army during the war, were subjected to some repression at its conclusion. Most significantly, some of the PDB's demands have been favourably acted upon by the Belgian political process. For example, in the early 1970s a Cultural Council for German-speaking Belgians was created in addition to those created for the country's French- and Dutch-speaking communities.[26]

IV. Ethno-regional Politics in Belgium: 1968-1980

In February 1968, under pressure from Flemish nationalists, the Flemish wing of the governing Social Christian Party refused to support the Cabinet's policy of neutrality on the question of whether the University of Louvain, located in Flanders, should continue to have a French-speaking section. The issue eventually caused the fall of the Government, forced new elections, and blocked the formation of a new Government for months, until it was finally agreed that the offending section would be moved across the linguistic frontier to a new campus in Wallonia or to bilingual Brussels. A rallying point for *francophone* Belgium, the Louvain affair ushered in an era of ethno-regional politics during which ethno-regional issues virtually monopolized Belgium's public agenda. During this period, the FDF, RW, and *Volksunie* have played a major role in influencing political events and were themselves influenced by these events.

The Parties. It was the ethno-regional organizations of Flemish- and French-speaking Belgium which articulated formal goals on

Table 3 Comparing Ethno-regionalists in Belgium

Community	Primary Spokesmen	Orientation	Principal Goals*
Flemish	Volksunie	Primary: Régime change	Maximum decentralization of decision making in culture affairs to linguistic community
		Secondary: Authority change	Increased Flemish (and Volksunie) participation in decision-making at centre
Francophone	RW in Wallonia FDF in Brussels	Primary: Régime change	Federal devolution of decision-making to regions; FDF emphasis on cultural matters; RW on economics
		Secondary: Authority change	Participation in central cartel
German-speaking	PDB	Output-oriented	Protection and promotion of German culture; official texts in German; etc.

behalf of the country's ethno-regional communities and mobilized the regional electorates sufficiently to make the neglect of these demands costly to the traditional parties. In the process, the ethno-regionalists expanded their programme to include a long list of output-oriented objectives susceptible to interim treatment within the existing system, but the core of their demands revolved around a reorganization of the régime along federalist lines.

The ethno-regional parties also effectuated an erosion in the strength of the traditional parties, not merely by reducing their support in the electorate but by placing pressure on them which eventually led to a decline in their cohesiveness. Because each traditional party did contain two linguistic wings, these parties were vulnerable to an ethno-regionalist attack. Often their candidates had to choose between protecting their electoral flanks by adopting the campaign rhetoric and proposals of the nationalists, or adhering to a neutral, system-wide platform at the cost of political defeat. Survival being a political imperative found everywhere, the choice was predictable but the consequences were dear. Since 1968 each of the traditional parties has seen their two linguistic wings (or, in the case of the Liberals, three regional wings) separate to become essentially *de facto* parties in their own right, negotiating the formation of new political alignments with one another in the same manner that the separate system-wide parties once did.

More broadly, the ethno-regional parties have also significantly effected the system's outputs. An action-interaction relationship developed in Belgium after 1968 between these organizations and the political process in which the parties articulated latent ethno-regional feelings into specific demands and created broad regional coalitions which enabled them to extract concessions from the political process.[27]

During the same period, the ethno-regional parties also changed—from outside challengers in 1968 to system participatory parties by 1978. The RW's entry into the Government in 1974, and the *Volksunie's* and FDF's in 1977, represented the realization of their shared (authority-oriented) goal of gaining admission to the country's existing political cartel. The costs of participation, however, have been unexpectedly high. When challenging the system and articulating demands, the parties did not have to concern themselves with striking political compromises. Nor did they have to worry about expediting the daily activities of government in such a way as to not displease one group of supporters while perhaps pleasing another batch of followers. Once a part of the Government, the situation became different. Individually they were forced into political compromises with the spokesmen for the other regional communities. In supporting Cabinets, they had to identify themselves with the positions of at least one of the traditional parties. The result has been some serious political slippage, most acutely felt thus far by the RW (in the 1977 parliamentary election) and the *Volksunie* (in the December 1978 parliamentary balloting).

In 1976 a schism developed in the RW between its ministers in the Government, who preferred to concentrate on the party's federalist goals while otherwise supporting the policies of the governing coalition, and the party's more militant officials, who desired to give the RW a more specific, ideological dimension by broadening the party's programme in a leftward direction. This split came into the open following the party's poor showing in the October 1976 local elections, which its members in the Cabinet blamed on the RW's turn to the left.[28] Shortly thereafter, these same Cabinet ministers resigned from the party to join with the Walloon Liberal Party in forming a new Walloon federalist party (the *Parti des Reforms et de la liberté de Wallonie,* or PRLW), and in the 1977 general elections the RW suffered a serious decline throughout Walloon Belgium.[29] (See Table 1)

The price of participation in the Government has also been costly for the *Volksunie,* whose supporters began to make their displeasure known to the party's members in the Government shortly after the latter's endorsement of a 1978 plan worked out at Egmont Palace in order to defuse ethno-linguistic issues in the country by means of a series of compromises to be enacted over the subsequent six years. One member of Parliament quit the party almost immediately,[30] Flemish cultural associations picketed it, many of its constituent organizations censored its leaders, and it became an overnight target of the Flemish press ('We don't want their heads,' wrote one editorialist, 'they were already lost at Egmont.')[31] Potentially more ominous, the party's support noticeably declined in public opinion polls following its endorsement of the Egmont Accord. In two surveys reported in March 1978, for example, only 12 per cent of the voters in Flanders said they would support the party if elections were held immediately, in contrast to the 16.3 per cent who voted for the *Volksunie* in the previous year's elections.[32] In the December 1978 parliamentary elections in Belgium, these polls proved to be all too accurate—the party drawing 171,296 fewer votes than it had the previous year and seeing its share of the vote drop by nearly a third in both Flanders and Brussels and its number of seats in the Belgian Chamber of Deputies plunge from 20 to 14.

The State. Even more important than the changes in Belgium's ethno-regional parties have been the changes in the nature of the Belgian state since 1968. It has been the subject of a thorough and still on-going reorganization, based on the goal of accommodating through constitutional reform ethno-regional sentiment which lesser concessions have been unable to placate.

In theory there are several devices available to governments for managing ethnic conflict. In his study of *Conflict Regulation in Dividend Societies,*[33] Erik Nordlinger identifies six of these: inclusion of rival communities in the same coalition; adherence to the principle of proportionality; a mutual veto power in the hands of the rival communities; the purposeful depoliticization of sensitive issue; compromises on divisive issues; and concessions to communal demands. Since the early 1960's, Belgian leaders have utilized all of these techniques. The 1961-1963 language laws were intended to settle communal demands by freezing the linguistic frontier, making Flemish the exclusive language of education and public affairs in the north, and according Brussels a special status. To understate the matter, the effort did not succeed. Next came the *dédoublement* phase of accommodation of the mid-1960s, when political leaders tried to contain ethno-linguistic sentiment by creating separate administrative facilities in sensitive areas for the country's two linguistic communities. During the same period, the principle of parity governed the creation of Cabinets (composed of equal numbers of Flemish- and French-speaking ministers) and the principle of communal proportionality controlled such matters as the composition of the civil service.

Near the end of the sixties accommodation efforts shifted in focus from the linguistic communities to the regional groups, largely as the result of the two ethno-regional movements of *francophone* Belgium projecting oft-differing sets of demands—the RW stressing the need for economic assistance/autonomy for Wallonia, the FDF focusing on the political right of Brussels' *francophone* majority to control its own affairs. The creation of advisory regional economic councils for Brabant, Flanders, and Wallonia in mid-1970 signalled this shift.[34] The major change in emphasis, however, was from lesser devices to a reform of the regime as the means of placating communalism in the Belgian state. Thus far, this constitutional revisionism has involved two phases. (See Table 4) During the first phase, which began with the election of a parliament/constituent assembly in 1968,[35] the ethno-regional parties participated in the deliberations leading to constitutional revisions, but political leadership remained in the hands of the traditional parties and reform stopped far short of the federalized state endorsed by the ethno-regionalists. The revised Constitution did provide a basis for regionalizing power in the state (especially in Article 107-*quatre*, which provided for the creation of autonomous regional assemblies); however, at least as much attention was given at the time to creating cross-regional decision-making arrangements to minimize the importance of the regions. The Cultural Councils for Dutch- and French-speaking Belgium were thus created *inside* the central parliament out of its Dutch- and French-speaking members. Also created was an elaborate warning bell system giving a majority in one community a veto over the other in specified, sensitive areas. Even the advisory regional assemblies created in 1974 were 'for the moment' composed of members of the Belgian Parliament. They were also so unimportant that their dissolution three years later provoked scarcely any reaction.[36]

Table 4 Constitutional Revision in Contemporary Belgium

I. The Regionalization Phase

December 1970—Revision of Belgium's 1830/31 Constitution provides a basis for a regionalization of power in Belgium. The Revised Constitution creates or promises to create separate institutions for 4 linguistic regions (including Brussels), 3 cultural communities (including German-speaking Belgium), and three political and administrative regions.

21 July 1971—Separate Cultural Councils for Dutch- and French-speaking Belgium are constituted inside the Belgian Parliament.

26 July 1971—The creation of an elected council for the agglomeration of Brussels is authorized, membership to be governed by the principle of parity between the two linguistic communities in the Brussels area.

10 July 1973—The creation of a Cultural Council for German-speaking Belgium is authorized.

July/August 1974—Advisory regional assemblies are created for Belgium's three principal regions as interim measures until autonomous assemblies can be constituted under Article 107-*quatre* of the Constitution.

II. The Federalization Phase

24 May 1977—The *Pacte communautaire* is concluded by six parties representing 80 per cent of the seats in the Parliament. The ratifiers of the accord agree to further constitutional reform in order to resolve ethno-regional disputes in the Belgian state.

January/February 1978—Announcement of the *Accord d'Egmont*, a detailed blueprint for constitutional revisions to take place over a four year period.

28 February 1978—Paliament votes 153-to-32 to study the proposals contained in the Egmont Accord.

December 1978-April 1979—Disagreements within the governing coalition over how to implement the Egmont agreement precipitates the fall of the Government and necessitates new elections in December 1978. A new Government is not finally installed until April 1979, when agreement is reached among its members that implementation of the Egmont Accord should be in three stages. Only the FDF of the ethno-regional parties remains in the Government.

January 1980—a new crisis in the Government over the issues of federalization. Members of the PM's own Flemish Catholic party refuse to support the Government's effort to move to the second (regional assembly) state of institutional reform unless assured that the final Belgium will not be based on three equal regions in which a fully integrated Brabant province, dominated by a *francophone* majority, will be one. Before the turmoil ends the Government agrees to extend the transitional stage to 1984 as the new target date for completing the federalization process and to treat the issue of Brussels' final status only at that time. Upset that the Flemish 'are dictating the terms of constitutional reform,' the FDF withdraws from the Government.

April/May 1980—another crisis in the Cabinet provoked by the Flemish Catholic party's members in Parliament, and their hard line stance on the issue of Flemish rights in Brussels. This time the PM resigns and a new Cabinet is formed in May, composed entirely of the wings of all three of Belgium's traditional parties and committed to completing the reform process by 1982 (the Walloon Socialists' price for joining) and the establishment of Assemblies for Wallonia and Flemish Belgium immediately.

5 August 1980—The bill on devolving power to autonomous regional assemblies to be established in Flanders and Wallonia is passed by the Belgian Parliament by a vote of 156-19 (5 abstentions). The assemblies are to be accountable to regional executives composed of members of the Belgian Parliament (at least for the moment), and to have responsibility initially for items representing about 10 per cent of the public budget.

The steps towards additional constitutional reform which followed Belgium's 1977 elections differed from the 1970-4 developments affecting the Constitution both in their mode of formulation and in their intended results. Hence, although 'government by elite cartel' remained the *modus vivendi* of Belgian politics and the key personalities in post-election negotiations remained party leaders, the cartel's composition altered considerably. The Liberals were absent from those discussions leading to the Egmont Accord, which became the country's blueprint for further constitutional reform. In the place of the Liberals were the spokesmen for Belgium's 'fourth family,' the ethnoregional parties.[37] Moreover, because further progress towards successful constitutional reform depended on the willingness of the FDF and the *Volksunie* to undertake compromises, the Egmont discussions were often led by these parties. And the Egmont accord reflected their presence in the decisive revision of the Belgian regime in a federalistic direction which it embraced. Under the terms of this accord, the central government is to retain substantial authority, but an expanded list of cultural items are to be regulated only by the Cultural Councils constituted inside the Parliament and still other matters of communal concern are to lie within the competency of autonomous, directly elected regional assemblies for Wallonia, Flanders, and Brussels. In short, for cultural affairs the *Volksunie*'s 'federalism of two' was to be the rule (although the assemblies will be inside the national parliament); for another long list of items the 'federalism of three' regions endorsed by the FDF and the RW was to be the *modus operandi* of Belgian politics under the terms of the Egmont Accord.[38]

The principal trade-off between the FDF and the *Volksunie* in this Accord involved Brussels. Under the plan, Brussels' limits were to be frozen and its Flemish citizens entitled to the same benefits in cultural matters as Dutch-speaking Belgians in Flanders. In return, *francophones* in those six commuter suburbs already entitled to some bilingual facilities were to be permitted the same rights where they live as Flemish inside the city, and *francophones* in another seven peripheral communes were to have access to Brussels' (bilingual) judicial, fiscal, and administrative facilities. They were also to be able to vote in Brussels (rather than 'waste' their vote in heavily Flemish communes) and, for the next twenty years, educate their children in French schools.

Even Belgium's German-speaking community was not ignored at Egmont Palace. The territory in which it lives is to be amalgamated into a single sub-region with its own executive, and the Cultural Council representing German-speaking Belgians, whose powers have been advisory to date, is to have its power elevated to equal that of the other Cultural Councils (that is, to be able to pass decrees with the force of law). Its competency is also to be expanded to equal the other Councils'.[39]

It is too easy to get caught among the trees of the Egmont Accord and thereby miss the forest, especially since the accord has subsequently been the subject of numerous Cabinet-level disagreements, re-agreements, dilutions, and reconstitutions. [Even the deadline for its implementation has been an important political football, the original 1982 target date having been first extended to 1984 (to appease Flemish Catholics) and then reset for 1982 (to retain the support of the Walloon Socialists). See Table 4] Nevertheless, the important point remains the same: that as the Egmont Pact and its successors are implemented, the régime will change in an essentially federal direction, and the consequences of this development for the Belgian political process and the country's political communities will be far from slight. Transitional steps already undertaken, for example, will enable the Flemish to establish, for the first time in three centuries, their own Parliament.[40]

Ethno-regional Sentiment. On the other hand, even the thorough and prompt implementation of the Egmont Pact is not likely to quell ethno-regional sentiment in the Belgian state. Given the salience ethno-regional issues have achieved in Belgian politics and the mobilized nature of the country's large ethno-linguistic communities, not to mention the fact that these communities physically as well as politically collide in the country's capital, perhaps the best that the country's system-wide leaders can hope is that the significance of ethnonational issues will ebb and flow on the public agenda over time. And even this expectation may border on wishful thinking. Thus, although there was some decline of ethno-regional sentiment within the Belgian population following—and in part because of—the signing of the Egmont agreement,[41] by the end of the same year (1978) a disagreement within the Government over key provisions in the Accord forced Belgium to hold new parliamentary elections. Similarly, the implementation of those provisions in the Accord pertaining to Brussels has kept subsequent Belgian Cabinets in turmoil and—at this writing—has had to be continually postponed by a Government concerned with undertaking other parts of the Egmont agreement and with addressing the other very real problems facing the country (including an unemployment rate of 7.5 per cent by 1980).

It may be argued, as Zolberg has done, that the fires of linguistic and communal conflict have persistently been fanned by the political class rather than the masses, that constitutional reform has been primarily a response by the cartel to threats to its status, and that even the ethno-regionalist leadership has been as concerned with using communal issues to gain entry to the cartel as with articulating mass sentiment.[42] Some of the developments cited above would seem to support this interpretation, and public opinion polls are admittedly inconclusive in the area. However, opinion surveys are notorious for not reflecting the intensity of feelings, and the argument might be turned. Thus, to cite a 1978 poll taken at the peak of the goodwill surrounding the Egmont Accord and at a time when Belgium was otherwise facing serious, system-wide economic problems, the fact that 20-25 per cent of the respondents in Brussels and Flanders chose to rank language as the most serious or second most serious issue besetting the Belgian state may well testify to a deep-rooted and persistent concern among Belgium's rank-and-file voters with those ethno-linguistic demands which the *Volksunie* and FDF leaders have articulated (for whatever objectives) and which the leaders of the traditional parties have tried to accommodate lest ethno-linguistic issues erupt in less trying times to affect adversely their fortunes as well as Belgian politics.

V. Afterthoughts and Conclusions

Does a study of politics in Belgium belong in a study of separatism in the developed world? Certainly, as we have seen, a variety of factors have historically precluded demands for political separatism in Belgium. In the post-war years these factors have included the willingness of political leaders to try to accommodate ethno-regional demands, the desire of ethno-regional spokesmen to join the country's decision-making cartel, the unattractiveness of integration into neighbouring states, and—for the Flemish—the possibility of controlling the central government. Yet another reason might be equally relevant: the sophistication of voters who, not driven to desparation by a Government insensitive to their concerns, are well aware of the costs of separatism and find them excessive. In any event, calls for complete separatism have been rare in Belgium, and its ethno-regional organizations have been uniformly characterized by a willingness to work within the system to change the régime.

Nevertheless (to answer the question posed above) I believe that, despite the absence of movements in Belgium challenging the country's existence, a study of Belgian politics not only has a place in an examination of separatism in Europe, but that Belgium's recent experience with ethno-regionalism raises some important questions concerning the nature of ethno-regional parties and politics in democratic societies. To take the former argument first, it should be noted that although political separatism has been shunned as a goal by political activists, a separatist mentality, in which the ethno-regional communities have sought maximum control over political affairs short of secession, has been very much present. As a result (and another reason why ethnonational politics are unlikely to die out in Belgium in the foreseeable future) almost all issues on the Belgian political agenda have been caught up in ethno-linguistic or ethno-regional politics, including the purchase of military equipment,[43] the composition of coalition governments,[44] the construction of ports,[45] and the language used among police.[46] As one commentator has observed, 'once an object is defined as valuable by one side, its opposite becomes valuable for the other.'[47] Small wonder that ethno-regional politics remain alive and well in the Belgian state today despite the (grudging) willingness of the established parties to undertake constitutional reform, and that ethno-regional politics can be expected to remain a part of Belgian politics in the future, with ethno-regional parties championing a changing set of output-, authority, and régime-oriented goals on behalf of the altering needs and situations of the communities they represent. Viewed from this perspective, even a federalized Belgium will not so much settle ethno-regional issues as provide a new setting for the continuing process of considering them.

The creation of a regionalized or federalized state as a response to ethno-regional pressure does raise some intriguing questions concerning the institutionalization of ethno-regionalism. To be sure, instances of uniqueness such as the size and number of linguistic groups in Belgium may make analogies between Belgium and other states misleading; however, the drift towards accommodation and the development of ethnic substates being a general feature of contemporary European politics,[48] Belgium's experience in this area should be of interest elsewhere.

The most obvious set of inquiries concerns the ethno-regional parties. Can their spokesmen actually make the jump from articulators of system-challenging demands to participants in the political process without damaging their organizations? This is not the place for an extensive reply, but certainly the recent experience of the RW and the *Volksunie* does not augur well for the possibility. During the past decade and a half, they have essentially passed through three stages. During the first, the organizational and growth phase, the broadly aggregative nature of the ethno-regional issues they articulated was their primary political asset. It enabled them to become umbrella parties containing elements from all of Belgium's traditional 'spiritual families.' During the second phase, however, when attention shifted to consolidating support and expanding their programmes, and especially during the (third) phase of participating in the decision-making process, the diversity of their support and often the diverse orientations of their leaders became sources of vulnerability. As the RW discovered after joining the Government, in undertaking the day-to-day activities of government, a party may antagonise some of its followers (or, alternately, ideological purists among the party's officials). Similarly, when system-wide parties have themselves adopted some of the demands of the ethno-regionalists, system-participatory ethno-regional organizations may begin to look like 'all the other parties.' In either event the likely result is a defection of some followers, as befell the *Volksunie* as well as the RW in Belgium's 1978 general elections, when there was a solid movement of voters from the *Volksunie* to the Flemish Catholics and from the RW to the *francophone* Socialists.[49]

Continued participation in the Government in a democracy also involves a willingness to compromise, another iron law of politics. Yet compromising once uncompromisable demands can also be hazardous, as the decline in the *Volksunie's* support suggests. On the other hand, if ethno-regional parties cannot engage in the give-and-take on policy matters expected of them when inside the Government, there are also serious implications for a consociational decision-making process. The utility of consociationalism as a means of managing divisive issues and potentially disruptive cleavages depends on the leaders' ability to secure the consent of their constituents to the political bargains they strike. Unless this ability exists, not only will the parties lose support but policies will lack legitimacy.

The experience of Belgium's ethno-regional parties in seeking to make the transition from system-challenging to system-participatory institutions leads to the other obvious set of questions—those involving the relationship between institutional adjustments and the accommodation of ethno-regional cleavages in multinational polities. Walker Connor may be correct in theorizing that ethno-regional sentiment feeds on both 'adversity and denial'—on a rejection of ethnonational demands and on concessions to them. Both can become rallying points for the ethno-regional community.[50] The same thesis may apply to ethno-regional parties as the vehicles for the articulation of those demands; that is, during their growth stage.[51] Nevertheless, it may be that the institutionalization of ethno-regional cleavages and the co-optation of ethno-regional leaders *can* contain ethno-regional sentiment on a short and middle term basis. Not, however, as normally envisioned!

In theory, accommodation is supposed to neutralize ethno-regionalism by sating the appetites of the masses, thereby taking the issues away from the ethno-regionalists. In practice, the accommodation process may work the other way. By the stress it places on suddenly system-participatory ethno-regional organizations, either at the centre or in regional assemblies, institutionalization may neutralize ethno-regional parties as effective agents for articulating demands on behalf of still present ethno-regional sentiment. In the long therm, of course, if ethno-regional sentiment is not itself neutralized, new 'uncompromising' spokesmen for it are likely to emerge.

Other, related questions could also be posed under the rubric of 'accommodating ethno-regional sentiment.' What, for example, happens to this sentiment 'beyond accommodation'? Does it decline in absolute importance, relative importance, or only seem to decline in saliency because of the disarray inside the regionalist camp and/or the successful co-optation of ethno-regional leaders? What becomes of movements which were able to collaborate in challenging the system? Will a tri-regional Belgium, if established, lead to rivalry between Brussels and Wallonia for resources, further eroding the former FDF-RW alliance and substituting a new if softer ethno-regional rivalry in Belgium for the *francophone*-Flemish one?[52] And what about the political process? How well do governments function, in general, when their energy is being diverted towards engineering constitutional reform in order to accommodate ethno-regional sentiment? How quickly can a government return to normality after such activity?

These are not the questions with which we began our study, and they require their own investigation. They are inevitably raised, however, by Belgium's recent efforts to institutionally satisfy ethno-regionalism. And, in a continent where an increasing number of states are undertaking similar activities, the answers to these questions, too, should be of interest not only to students of politics, but also to the political practitioners in other multinational states.

Notes

1. See David Easton, 'An Approach to the Analysis of Political Systems', *World Politics*, IX (1957), pp. 383-400.
2. Aristide R. Zolberg, 'Transformation of Linguistic Ideologies: the Belgian Case', pp. 445-72 esp. 446-7 in *Multilingual Political Systems: Problems and Solutions*, Jean-Guy Savard and Richard Vigneault, (eds.), (Québec, 1975). It was not until 1974 that the language of Flanders became officially designated as Dutch (*Nederlandsch*) rather than Flemish (*Vlaamsch*) in all schools and all official documents, by order of a Cultural Council for Dutch-speaking Belgium created in 1971. *The New York Times*, 3 February 1974, p. 14.
3. Ant. Van Overschelde, 'La capital belge vue par un Flamand', *Le Monde Diplomatique*, February 1978, p. 20.

4. Rupert Emerson, *From Empire to Nation* (Boston, 1960), pp. 95-6.
5. Zolberg, op. cit., pp. 445-6.
6. The official figures recorded only 22,134 French-speaking people out of a total population of 1,959,672 in Flanders in 1846. Cited in Patricia Carson, *The Fair Face of Flanders* (Ghent, 1969), p. 229.
7. See Zolberg, op. cit., pp. 449-50, and Pierre De Voss, 'Les origines d'un Nationalisme: Opprimée comme l'Irlande . . .', *Le Monde*, 20-21 February 1977, p. 5.
8. Martin O. Heisler, 'Institutionalizing Societal Cleavages in a Cooptive Polity: the Growing Importance of the Output Side in Belgium', *Politics in Europe: Structures and Processes in Some Post-Industrial Democracies* (New York, 1974), pp. 178-200 in M. O. Heisler (ed.), esp. 195.
9. See James A. Dunn, Jr., 'Consociational Democracy and Language Conflict: A Comparison of the Belgian and Swiss Experience', *Comparative Political Studies*, V (1972), pp. 3-40, esp. 25-6; and Derek W. Urwin, 'Social Cleavages and Political Parties in Belgium: The Problem of Institutionalization', *Political Studies*, XVIII (1970), pp. 320-40.
10. Arend Lijphart, 'Consociational Democracy', *World Politics*, XXI (1969), pp. 207-25 esp. 216.
11. Milton J. Esman, 'Perspectives on Ethnic Conflict in Industrial Societies', in M. J. Esman, (ed.), *Ethnic Conflict in the Developed World*, (Ithaca, 1977), pp. 371-390 esp. 387.
12. In response to opinion rallied by the traditional parties against his resumption of the throne, Leopold III almost immediately abdicated in favor of his son—a solution generally acceptable to the three regions. For a discussion of the Royal Question in the context of World War II's impact on communal differences, see Zolberg, 'Splitting the Difference: Federalization without Federalism', pp. 103-42 in Esman, *op. cit.*, esp. 111-12.
13. Between the majority living in Flanders at the time of Belgium's first census, and the Flemish-speaking peoples of Brussels, it may be supposed that Flemish-speaking Belgium has constituted a majority in the country since statehood. Politically, however, this advantage was blunted by (a) the willingness of Flemish to become *francophones* and (b) a representation system which lagged behind population changes, underrepresenting Flanders, whose population has steadily increased, and over-representing Wallonia, whose per cent of Belgium's population had steadily declined.
14. For an interesting, recent work on Wallonia's post-war decline and Flanders' post-war prosperity, see Michel Quevit, *Les Causes du Déclin Wallon* (Brussels, 1978). Among other theses, Quevit argues that one source of Flemish prosperity was a *de facto* alliance between Flemish industrialists and the Catholic Party's Flemish wing, which reduced the saliency of the class issue in Flanders (and substituted for it the north/south ethno-linguistic cleavage in Belgium).
15. Heisler, op. cit., *Politics in Europe*, p. 199.

16. Val Lorwin, 'Belgium: Religion, Class and Language in National Politics', Robert Dahl, (ed.), *Political Opposition in Western Democracies* (New Haven, 1966), pp. 147-87 esp. 170.
17. In addition to the *Volksunie*, FDF, and RW, and the much smaller PDB, there are also a few very small ethnonational parties in Belgium. The most celebrated is the *Retour à Liège* party, which regularly wins over 50 per cent of the vote in a small *francophone* canton which is part of an essentially Flemish-speaking area transferred from the Walloon province of Liège to Flanders in the early 1960s. The votes involved are small, however: 1,174 in the 1977 general elections. By way of comparison, in 1971 the RW and FDF each drew about 300,000 votes and the *Volksunie* over 550,000 (in a total vote of about 5 million). Even the PDB obtained 7,734 votes in 1977. *Le Soir* (Brussels), 12 March 1974 and 19 April 1977.
18. Zolberg, op. cit., (1977), pp. 117, 139. For a discussion of the initial reaction of the traditional parties to the ethno-regional challenge, see also pp. 117-19.
19. I am extremely grateful to John K. Wildgen for suggesting this classification system in his most helpful critique of an earlier article.
20. A comprehensive list of legislation pertaining to the legal equality of Flemish and French in Belgian is included in Robert Senelle, 'The Revision of the Constitution, 1967-70', *Memo From Belgium* (Brussels, Government Printers), Nos. 144-6 (1972), pp. 166-8. For a discussion of early Flemish nationalism, see Hans Kohn, 'Nationalism in the Low Countries', *Review of Politics*, XIX (1957), pp. 155-85.
21. Zolberg, op. cit., (1975), pp. 446, 451f, and op. cit., (1977), pp. 109-10. Quasi-federal proposals could be found among Flemish and Walloon militants on the eve of World War I, but they attracted little public attention.
22. Flemish wartime collaboration has been exaggerated after both wars. Even during the First World War only two of the Flemish deputies in the Belgian Parliament supported the creation of a provisional government in Flanders, and the Germans had difficulty findng enough cooperative, Flemish-speaking professors to open the University of Ghent as a unilingual institution.
23. Citing Urwin, op. cit., pp. 339-40. For a comprehensive discussion of the origins and initial success of the *Volksunie*, see 'La Volksunie (I-II)', *Courrier Hebdomadaire du Centre de recherche et d'information socio-politique* (*CH du CRISP*), Nos. 336 and 345 (1966).
24. Zolberg, op. cit., (1977), pp. 120f.
25. The FDF and RW have persistently operated as allies, not two wings of the same party. In elections, each offers an individual manifesto, as well as a common manifesto based on *francophone* Belgium's 'shared interests.' See 'Le FDF-RW (I)', *CH du CRIPS*, 516 (1971) on the development and early history of this alliance.

26. For additional details on Belgium's German-speaking community and the PDB, see 'La poussée du parti communautaire continue dans les cantons de l'Est', *Le Soir*, 24-25 March 1974, p. 2, and 'History's 62,000 Casualties', *The Times*, 28 September 1974. Since 1971 the PDB's vote has averaged 20-30 per cent in the most heavily German-speaking districts of Liège Province. Its vote has fluctuated widely, however, depending upon its ability to attract and retain candidates from among the known politicians in the area.
27. For a more extensive discussion of the impact of ethno-regional parties on Belgian politics, see Jospeh R. Rudolph, Jr., 'Ethnonational Parties and Political Change: The Belgian and British Experience', *Polity*, IX (1977), pp. 401-26.
28. In the October communal elections, the RW polled only about one-third its vote in the 1974 general elections. See William Fraeys, 'Les Elections communales du 10 Octobre 1976', *Res Publica*, XVIII (1976), pp. 427-44. Other reasons why an ethno-regional organization might lose public support when in the Cabinet are suggested in the text, *infra*.
29. The RW's public distintegration can be followed in *Le Soir* between October and December 1976. See especially the coverage of October 21, 22, & 27, November 10, 21 & 22, and December 6. Concerning the RW's search for a role as 'a party of the opposition with a foot in the Government' (its FDF ally) following the 1977 general elections, see *La Libre Belgique*, 12-13 March 1977. The formation of the PRLW and its election manifesto in 1977 are concisely discussed in *Le Soir*, 30 March 1977.
30. *Le Soir*, 2 June 1977, p. 2.
31. Ibid., 12-13 February 1978, and *La Libre Belgique*, 14 September 1977. The quotation is from the latter, citing an editorial in *Het Volk*.
32. The findings of the survey conducted by the *Institut Inter-universitaire de Sondage d'Opinion publique* are reported in *Le Soir*, 21 March 1978, p. 2; those of the *Institut de Conseil en sondage l'opinion publique* are reported in the same source, two days later. Both surveys reported that the FDF's support had declined only marginally, perhaps because that party's cadre nature and frequent consultations between party officials and members in the Government have spared it criticism by constituent units or disgruntled party officials.
33. Cambridge, Massachusetts, Center for International Affairs Occasional Papers in International Affairs No. 29 (1972).
34. See 'Les Conseils economiques regionaux: CER (I)', *CH du CRISP*, 584 (1972).
35. For constitutional reform to take place in Belgium, the out-going parliament must pass a resolution before its dissolution declaring that the parliament to be elected will function as a constituent assembly. Because the legislature dissolved in 1977 failed to take

this step, the new assembly elected that spring could not complete all those changes in régime agreed to in the Egmont Accord. Some will require further revision of the Constitution.

36. Concerning the process of revising Belgium's 1830-1 Constitution, see Maurice Boeynaems, 'Les années 1970 et 1971 sur le plan communautaire et linguistique', *Res Publica*, XV (1973), pp. 881-914, Senelle, op. cit., and Jan Gootaers, 'La Revision constitutionnelle de décembre 1970', *CH du CRISP*, Nos. 555-6 (1972). With respect to the reformed document, including the Cultural Councils authorized by it, see especially Senelle, 'The Belgian Constitution: Commentary', *Memo Fom Belgium,* 166 (1974), and James A. Dunn, Jr., 'The Revision of the Constitution in Belgium: A Study in the Institutionalization of Ethnic Conflict', *Western Political Quarterly,* XXVII (1974), pp. 143-64.
37. The 'fourth family' designation springs from no less an authority than the Belgian Prime Minister at the time of the Egmont Accord, Leo Tindemans. See, for example, *Le Soir*, 8 December 1977.
38. Only a scant summary of the Egmont Accord is offered here. Other federalist features included a plan to convert the second chamber of the Belgian Parliament into a Senate of Regions and a plan to dissolve the provinces in favour of twenty-five under-regions. The predominantly Flemish- and French-speaking areas of Brabant province outside of Brussels (e.g., the *arrondissements* of Louvain and Nivelles respectively) are to be integrated into the regions of Flemish-speaking Belgium and Wallonia, leaving only the *arrondissement* of Brussels to constitute the country's third region.
39. The 37-page *pacte communautaire* preceding the Egmont Accord, which was signed by 'six' Belgian parties (the FDF, the *Volksunie*, the Flemish Catholic Party, the French Catholic Party, the Walloon Socialists, and the Flemish Socialists) and constituted an agreement to seek agreement on aspects of constitutional reform, is summarized in *Le Soir*, 24 May 1977. The *Pacte d'Egmont* was presented by the parties negotiating it in two 'lectures'. The first of these was reported in *Le Soir*, 18 January 1978; the second in the same source, 23 February 1978. The proposed changes involving the German-speaking community are summarized in *Le Soir*, 3 March 1978, p. 5.
40. M. Schlitz, cited in *Le Soir*, 3 March 1978, p. 2.
41. In one 1978 poll taken shortly after the announcement of the Egmont Accord and concerned with identifying the relative importance of four issues in Belgium (linguistics, economics, finance, and employment), linguistic issues were ranked third or fourth by a two-thirds majority in each region. See *Le Soir*, 1 March 1978 and 2 March 1978.
42. Zolberg, op. cit., (1977), pp. 104-5.
43. See *Le Monde*, 6 February 1978 for a discussion of the debate on the purchase of replacement missiles for the country's NATO units. An earlier debate on military aircraft nearly caused the fall of the

Government in 1975 when RW members of the Cabinet demanded that the Government pursue the French connection and buy French rather than American fighters. See *The New York Times* 10, 13 June 1975.

44. For a discussion of the refusal of four Walloon Catholics to take the oath of office required of Cabinet members because Flemish Catholics received more important portfolios in the Cabinet, see *The Times*, 4 June 1977, p. 4.
45. *Le Soir*, 1 December 1977. A decision to construct a port in Flanders provoked immediate demands by the RW, Walloon cultural associations, and the Walloon Regional Economic Council that Wallonia receive 'compensatory' investment should the Government actually construct this port.
46. *Le Soir*, 30 December 1977.
47. Zolberg, loc cit., (1977), p. 104.
48. See this author's 'Ethnic Sub-States and the Emergent Politics of Tri-level Interaction in Western Europe', *Western Political Quarterly*, XXX (1977), pp. 537-57, esp. pp. 541-8.
49. The FDF has been less seriously affected by these trends, but it too has lost some support to the *francophone* Socialists. These voting trends, which were already somewhat apparent in Belgium's 1977 general election, mark a reversal of those trends which characterized the rise of the ethno-regional parties in the 1960s.
50. Walker Connor, 'The Politics of Ethnonationalism', *Journal of International Affairs*, XXVI (1973), pp. 1-21 esp. 21.
51. Rudolph, op. cit., (1977), p. 423.
52. See especially the discussion of this possibility in *La Libre Belgique* 5 January 1978, p. 1.

CHAPTER 10

Conclusion
Ethnic Identity and the Modern State

D. N. MacIver

The problem of national separatism arises from the discrepancy between the ideal of the ethnically homogeneous nation state and the widespread reality of polyethnic states in the modern world. Few states are in fact ethnically homogeneous and many face the problem of disaffected ethnic minorities in their territories. Québécois in Canada, Basques and Catalans in Spain, Bretons and Corsicans in France, Flemings in Belgium, Scots and Welsh in the United Kingdom, Macedonians and the Serbo-Croat rivalry in Yugoslavia, Kurds in Iraq and Iran, Ukrainians and the Muslim minorities in the Soviet Union, Ibos in Nigeria, Eritreans in Ethiopia, Baganda in Uganda, Nagas in India, Kayas in Burma, Tamils in Sri Lanka, Tibetans and the non-Han minorities in China are some of the better known and more salient examples. In the mid-twentieth century, in the wake of decolonization ethnic minorities have proliferated all around the world with the spread of the Western state system. Most of these minorities are little heard of outside their own states, while many are quiescent, weak or silenced by oppressive governments. On the other hand, while some are militantly separatist, effective secession movements are very rare and Bangladesh is in fact the only completely successful secession since the Second World War.

While ethnic minorities within states are thus a ubiquitous phenomenon, they are not a new element in the history of the state. Historically most European states have been ethnically heterogeneous and national minorities have been a major cause of political instability, repression and international conflict. The rise of ethnic nationalism was one of the principal factors in the disintegration of the old empires of Central Europe and the Middle East. The political geography of modern Europe has been determined to a very large extent by the ethnic composition and distribution of the population. Attempts have been made to overcome the inevitable problems of minorities and multi-ethnic populations by annexation, secession, boundary changes, population transfers, internal domination, assimilation and various forms of socio-cultural pluralism. Despite a long experience of polyethnicity, however, political and international law traditions, both of which give recognition to the rights of minorities and a number of ingenious constitutional arrangements for the harmonious organization of multi-ethnic societies, there are, even in Europe, very few wholly successful examples of polyethnic states. The nub of the problem has always been to persuade ethnic minorities to abandon their desire for special treatment, political autonomy or even independence. In our own time, the political resurgence of ethnic minorities may yet present a threat to the integrity of existing 'nation' states.

A nation state is a political community with three major properties or capabilities of integration. These are first, that it is able to exercise a monopoly of political authority and legitimate force within its territory; second, that it has a government which is a decision-making centre able to determine or significantly influence the allocation of resources in the society; and third, that it operates as a focus for political identification, loyalty and support amongst the population. These capabilities may be described as coercive, instrumental and identive. When all these capabilities are functioning satisfactorily, they are normally assumed to be mutually reinforcing. The existence of disaffected or separatist groups indicates at least some failure of integration. The resurgence of minority nationalisms in advanced western societies has thus renewed interest in the complex problems of maintaining the state in polyethnic societies. Moreover, by exposing shortcomings in the identive and instrumental capabilities of such states, it raises two general issues relevant to the persistence of the state. In particular it suggests first, that the extent and effectiveness of political integration in advanced societies has possibly been overestimated and second, that the traditional centralist state may not be fully capable of making an effective or adequate response to the challenge of ethno-territorial disaffection and national separatism.

National separatism is a political process and like other political processes may be understood in terms of the factors and conditions which initiate it and subsequently determine its course and development. These may be identified as the social and environmental conditions and the integrative capabilities of the sub-unit in relation to the political system as a whole. Social factors include the condition of the state before the beginning of the secessionist movement, the ethnic composition and distribution of the population, the strength, mode and agencies of resistance to secession, the economic relationship of the sub-unit to the larger system and the extent to which the sub-unit could itself be objectively regarded as a separate community and finally the exact nature of the separatist movement and the extent of its support. While ethnic, cultural and linguistic homogeneity are no longer believed to be essential to maintaining a stable political community, they may be more important for a successful secession. On the other hand, if internal cleavages, for example on religion, are very deep, a secession movement may not be wholly successful.

Environmental conditions include the territorial definition and size of the separatist sub-unit and its location in relation to the territory of the existing state. The quality of the physical and natural environment is also important, in particular whether it has experienced any significant recent change which would affect the propensity to separation as, for example, the discovery of North Sea Oil was supposed to have influenced the demand for political autonomy in Scotland. Environmental factors also include other states which may encourage or support the secessionist movement. If favourable social and environmental conditions are present in strength, there is a greater chance of a separatist movement developing and gaining support.

Integrative factors are assets which the seceding unit may develop or deploy in order to effect a successful separation. These assets may be described as coercive, instrumental and identive. Coercive assets are primarily an autonomous structure for maintaining authority, control and security in the form of a legal administration, courts, police and military forces. Instrumental assets are economic, technological, administrative and human resources and the ability to utilize them effectively. Identive assets are values, symbols, traditions, religious and cultural institutions which endow the seceding unit with legitimacy, social cohesion and political coherence. The crucial part of the process of secession is the internalization of these assets, especially the identive assets, within the sub-unit, i.e. their transfer from the existing socio-political system to the sub-unit. The internalization of integrative assets not only strengthens the integrative factors themselves but may add to the strength of social and environmental factors as well. Moreover, it places additional stress on the existing system which may make secession more probable and more practical. This would suggest that some containment responses to ethno-territorial disaffection, especially the expansion of political autonomy in the form of home rule or devolution, may be counterproductive because the enhanced opportunity they provide for the internalization of integrative assets may actually increase the possibility of secession.

The failure of integration, especially of identive and instrumental capabilities, and the internalization of integrative assets in sub-units presents a potentially serious threat to the persistence of the state in advanced western societies. Doubts on this point may be dispelled or at least reduced by consideration of the case of Norway. In 1905 Norway seceded from Sweden after a non-violent Norwegian uprising following several decades in which the Swedish-Norwegian state had experienced progressive disintegration due mainly to the internalization of integrative, particularly identive assets within the Norwegian sub-unit. Even when Norway was transferred to Sweden, after four hundred years of union with Denmark, a Norwegian nationalism was emerging based on a rapidly reviving Norwegian identity and the creation of Norwegian tradition from the legacy of a proud if distant heritage. The establishment of a home rule constitution for Norway made it possible to internalize coercive, instrumental and identive assets in the Norwegian sub-unit, which weakened the legitimacy of Swedish rule and reduced the integrative capability of the union. Latterly the separation of Norway was accelerated by the increase in instrumental and identive assets notably economic resources, political institutions and national consciousness. In the end the union became an obstacle to the further development of the Norwegian political community and the final separation was almost a formality.

Similar, though of course not the same observations may be made of the Irish case. Since a full study of the Irish case is included in the text, however, it is not necessary to discuss it at any length here. It may be noted, nevertheless, that it was largely the rapid internalization of identive assets and the strengthening of anti-union social and integrative factors after 1916 that was responsible for the shift in support from home rule to complete separation of Ireland from the British state.

Although none of the states considered in the present volume are faced with imminent political disintegration, fundamental conflict over the nature of the régimes, including the very basis of government as well as its composition structure and purpose may be found in Belgium, Spain and Northern Ireland. Even when states do not face this advanced crisis of legitimacy, their governments, in a wide range of political systems and constitutional arrangements, frequently do face a more managerial problem of credibility deriving from their failure to satisfy expectations which they have themselves raised. The general complaint of ethnic and national minorities has been that the state, if not actually hostile to their aspirations and malign in its handling of their interests, is at least ineffective, unresponsive, remote and indifferent to their special concerns. What ethno-territorial communities then seek is greater control over their own affairs in the belief that they can then apply their own resources more efficiently in pursuit of their own interests.

Governments are thus faced with competing demands for the expansion of local autonomy and participation on the one hand and for the maintainence or raising of the standards of general welfare and material prosperity on the other. These require different applications of government power and resources. One demands differential treatment and differential outputs, while the other demands the even-handed exercise of power to produce uniform outputs. Governments come under pressure from all sections and interests to pursue both kinds of objectives. This places governments under increasingly severe political and institutional stress to the point where their capability to meet their accumulating and incompatible responsibilities is itself brought into question.

Governments have responded to these challenges in a variety of ways but a general pattern can possibly be discerned. Governments have sought to define their purposes more openly while adapting their structures and making concessions to politically irresistible demands. They have sought to improve the efficiency and effectiveness of their operations through increased consultation and wider participation in decision making. To a large extent they have met the pressure on government structures with various combinations of territorial and functional deconcentration and devolution.

Much of the discontent expressed by minority national groups, while presented in the rhetoric of nationalism as a demand for greater political autonomy is really generated by the unsatisfactory performance of regional economies and the failure of regional policies for which central governments are held and wish to remain responsible. Reform has thus usually been presented as the expansion of local or regional autonomy and a contribution to more democratic and more effective government. While they undoubtedly enhance regional influence, however, most reforms have in fact been an attempt to accommodate the needs of central administration to ethno-regional political demands while still maintaining the balance in favour of the former.

In trying to deal with minority nationalist demands in this way, however, there is another problem. From the point of view of effective government the argument for enhancing provincial or regional autonomy is that it produces more effective government than would be possible under continued central control. The logic of centralism, however, is that economic growth, increased wealth and improved material standards require resources and coordinating powers which only central authority can deploy. Moreover, if there is a large and continuous demand for the products of central government then there must be a limit to decentralization and devolution of power. From the perspective of political integration, on the other hand, there is no such operational optimum limit to the expansion of autonomy. If the demand for autonomy reflects the failure of integration, the rise of strong ethno-regional identities and the internalization of integrative assets within the region at the expense of the centre, then the reaction to central authority is likely to be undiminished hostility and demands for further autonomy.

It is not simply that there is a difference of view between central authorities and ethno-territorial groups about the efficiency and effectiveness of government. Central governments do seek to make their operations efficient and to provide their services efficiently. Moreover they seek the cooperation, assistance and active participation of their client groups and electorates in achieving this. Territorial ethnic groups demand effective government, not only in respect of their own special needs and aspirations, but also in maintaining standards of welfare, prosperity and development equivalent to those of the larger society. To this end they seek privileged access, preferential outputs and special decision making arrangements sometimes including autonomous legislative powers. The dilemma facing central authority is then that conceding special treatment and autonomous powers to ethnic minority groups may mean yielding some of the powers which central authorities themselves believe to be necessary to the uniform provision of effective government. On the other hand, withholding such concessions is likely to fuel the anti-centralist sentiment which undermines the legitimacy of central authority and weakens its capability. Thus while the benefits of centralism are eagerly sought some of its concomitant effects are vigorously resented. In such circumstances it may only be possible to resolve the dilemma by the moderation of ethno-territorial demands or by the break-up of the existing state.

The break-up of the state is not a necessary object of ethnic nationalist groups and is not always in their interest. The moderation or dissipation of group demands, however, does not itself enable the state to escape the dilemma in which minority ethnic nationalism places it. Much depends on the reasons for such moderation and its effect on the internal politics of the group. As in Quebec the leaders of a movement committed to secession may find that support given for objects short of secession may not be forthcoming for outright separation. This apparent moderation of group demands however does not allow the state to ignore the secession threat as its potential for renewal remains. On the other hand, accommodation between the state and nationalist groups, involving the admission of nationalist leaders to a share of power, may be regarded by the movement at large as a betrayal leading to a further intensification of its demands under a new and less compromising leadership.

One remaining problem which faces potentially all governments in polyethnic societies is the immanent possibility of political extremism on the part of certain ethnic élites. Most ethno-territorial secession movements receive only intermittently strong support from the mass of the population. Particularly in times of economic uncertainty and adversity, the ultimate dependence on the central authority and resources of the state sharply curtails ethno-nationalist aspirations and support for secession. Then the more romantic and tough-minded members of the movement, their own enthusiasm and commitment undiminished, may resort to more extreme tactics including terrorism and assassination as is the case with ETA in the Basque provinces of Spain. In these circumstances ethnic communities are frequently capable of fairly high levels of mutually supportive collective action. Even secret soldier societies and para-military nationalist groups can provide the necessary means of political organization around which whole communities can be effectively mobilized for resistance or separation. So long as such groups can retain even the passive support of the ethnic community there is always the potential for clandestine warfare and political violence. As has been amply demonstrated in Northern Ireland, this may be the most intractable problem for the state in a polyethnic society.

Given the complexity and scale of modern government and the individual's alienation from it, the politicization of ethnic minority groups may be no more than the assertion of a human desire for more intimate units of identification. The expression of ethnic identity may then be simply a defence against the all-embracing and overwhelming presence of the impersonal and technocratic state in a modern mass society. As we have seen, however, the low coincidence between state and ethnic boundaries results in conflicting demands which threaten the integrity of states. There are approximately 156 states in the world, only about a dozen of which may be described as mono-ethnic, but several hundred ethnic groups. States are increasingly expected to provide security, order, justice, economic development and social progress for their heterogeneous societies at a time when ethno-national interests are more widespread and often more virulent than ever before. Many ethnic demands, however, except on the part of small numbers of extremists, are not necessarily for political independence, which many regard as impracticable and undesirable, but for recognition together with administrative and economic support to preserve their cultural identity. If this is the case the problem facing the state is more tractable and solutions which could preserve the integrity of the state more likely to be found.

The available solutions include various forms of regional government and devolution, federalism and consociationalism. Regional devolution is the solution most widely canvassed in the United Kingdom. One objection to such a form of territorial decentralization is that it is unlikely to provide the effective control of economic and social policy which many ethno-territorial groups demand and the territorial government may not be able to establish a sufficiently credible independence from the centre to maintain an adequate level of support. Moreover, it may be difficult to design a stable arrangement which will not result in demands for increased powers and accelerate the movement to secession.

In this sense federalism possibly offers more hope. The theory of federalism is that sovereignty is vested in the people who delegate powers to federal and provincial governments. There is thus no notion of the centre, centralization or decentralization, but rather of non-centralism. Federalism may thus facilitate political integration in polyethnic societies through such a process of shared rule. It thus offers the possibility of maintaining the integrity of the state while satisfying both the interests of the existing state and ethno-territorial aspirations. Many states hence embraced this solution to the problems of polyethnicity including those as diverse as Canada, India, Austria and Yugoslavia. Whether federalism can offer an adequate framework for maintaining polyethnic political communities is, of course, problematic. In Canada and, to a lesser extent, in Yugoslavia it is under considerable strain. It would appear, however, to offer a better chance than unitary systems which are more likely to facilitate the dominance of majority ethnic groups. Then 'one man, one vote' ceases in and by itself to be a completely satisfactory principle of just rule with inevitable and possibly unsustainable stress on the political system.

An alternative possibility is to maintain voluntarily segregated communities using established cultural institutions and élites for the conduct of inter-communal activities, politics and government. Where there are religious, cultural, linguistic or ethnic divisions on the basis of which political communities form, the political system may be structured on the basis of these groups in a consociational arrangement as has been the case in the Netherlands and Belgium. Consociational arrangements have tended to develop gradually and almost informally before becoming institutionalized. Their institutionalization, sometimes formal and legal, brings them close to federalism. This is the case in Switzerland where highly complex ethnic, linguistic and religious divisions are accommodated in a system which has elements of both consociationalism and federalism. The most notable point about federalism and consociationalism is that they offer a greater opportunity for the effective diffusion of power in polyethnic societies than many existing arrangements. The significance of this cannot be underestimated, since the political survival of ethnic, as opposed to state and imperial nationalism in western societies, is likely to remain a major feature of social change posing a recurring threat to the stability and integrity of states. The persistence of minority nationalisms through decades, if not centuries, of repression, indifference and neglect, is itself perhaps, sufficient comment on their stamina and vigour.

Contributors

D. G. Boyce. Senior lecturer in the Department of Political Theory and Government, University College of Swansea. He has published widely on Irish history and politics and is the author of *Englishmen and Irish Troubles: British Public Opinion and the Making of Irish Policy 1918-1922* (London, 1972) and joint editor of *Newspaper History: From the Seventeenth Century to the Present Day* (London, 1978). At present he is completing a book on nationalism in Ireland.

Richard Hamilton. Department of Sociology, McGill University. An acknowledged authority on elections in Quebec, Professor Hamilton has co-authored with Professor Pinard a series of important articles analysing the rise of the Parti Québécois, which have appeared in the *Canadian Journal of Political Science.*

Donald N. MacIver. Lecturer in the Department of Politics and International Relations, North Staffordshire Polytechnic. He was educated at the University of Aberdeen and the London School of Economics and Political Science. Prior to his present appointment he was an assistant professor in the Department of Politics at the University of Manitoba. His twin research interests are contemporary Scottish politics and the Lloyd George Liberal Government.

Kenneth N. Medhurst. Professor of Politics, University of Sterling. He was educated at the University of Edinburgh and the University of Manchester where he was successively lecturer, senior lecturer and reader in the Department of Government. He has also been a visiting professor at Colombian State's Escuela Superior de Administracion Publica, the University of Javeriana (Bogota) and a lecturer in the Centre of Latin American Studies, University of Liverpool. His primary research interests are Comparative West European Politics, the Politics of Development and the empirical and philosophical dimensions of the relationship between Politics and Religion. He is the author of *Government in Spain* (Oxford, 1976), *The Basques and Catalans* (London, 1977) and editor of *Allende's Chile* (London, 1972).

Andrew W. Orridge. Lecturer in the Department of Political Science, the University of Birmingham. He was educated at the Universities of Keele and Manchester. His main research interests are in the field of nationalism with particular reference to Europe; he has recently completed a major study in the field of race relations in the United Kingdom. He has published widely on macro-social theories of autonomist nationalism.

Maurice Pinard. Professor of Sociology, McGill University. He has published extensively in the field of Political Sociology with particular reference to minority parties in Quebec. Prior to his present appointment Professor Pinard was at The John Hopkins University where he was awarded both Canada Council Fellowships and a Hopkins Woodrow Wilson Fellowship. His major contribution to the theory of Political Sociology is his volume *The Rise of a Third Party: A Study in Crisis Politics* (Montreal & London, 1975).

Joseph R. Rudolph, Jr. Associate Professor and Chairman of the Department of Political Science, the University of Tulsa. He was educated at the University of Virginia. The author of several articles on nationalism and a text on European Politics, Dr Rudolph is a former Fulbright scholar to Belgium. Much of the research and preparation for his chapter was accomplished in 1977-8 whilst he was on sabbatical leave.

Anthony D. Smith. Lecturer in the Department of Sociology, the London School of Economics and Political Science. He was educated at Wadham College, Oxford, reading Classics as an Open Scholar. He then read Politics at the College d'Europe in Bruges, before going on to do a Master's and doctorate at the L.S.E. He taught at the Polytechnic of the South Bank, and the Universities of York and Reading before returning to the L.S.E. His publications include *Theories of Nationalism* (London, 1971); *The Concept of Social Change* (London, 1973); *Nationalism,* A Trend Report and Bibliography, *Current Sociology,* 21, 1973; *Social Change* (London, 1976); *Nationalist Movements* (Ed., London, 1976); *Nationalism in the Twentieth Century* (Oxford, 1979) and *The Ethnic Revival* (Cambridge, 1981).

Colin H. Williams. Senior lecturer in the Department of Geography and Sociology, North Staffordshire Polytechnic. Educated at the University of Wales, Swansea, and at the University of Western Ontario as an English Speaking Union Scholar, Dr Williams has been a visiting research fellow at McGill University and Dartmouth College. His main research interests are language planning, nationalism and minority group rights. He has published several articles and chapters on these issues as they relate to Wales, Quebec and Western Europe. He is the founding editor of *Discussion Papers in Geolinguistics*.

Index